GUSTAV MAHLER
The Symphonies

Constantin Floros

GUSTAV MAHLER
The Symphonies

Translated from the German by

Vernon Wicker

Reinhard G. Pauly, General Editor

AMADEUS PRESS
Portland, Oregon

784.2
FLO

Frontispiece illustration by Emil Orlik (1902).

Original edition, *Gustav Mahler III: Die Symphonien,*
copyright © 1985 by Breitkopf & Härtel, Wiesbaden
All rights reserved.

English-language translation copyright © 1993 by Amadeus Press
(an imprint of Timber Press, Inc.)

ISBN 0-931340-62-4
Printed in Singapore

AMADEUS PRESS, INC.
9999 S.W. Wilshire, Suite 124
Portland, Oregon 97225

Library of Congress Cataloging-in-Publication Data

Floros, Constantin.
   [Gustav Mahler. 3, Symphonien. English]
   Gustav Mahler : the symphonies / Constantin Floros ; translated
from the German by Vernon Wicker ; Reinhard G. Pauly, general
editor.
      p.   cm.
   Includes bibliographical references and index.
   ISBN 0-931340-62-4
   1. Mahler, Gustav, 1860-1911. Symphonies. I. Pauly, Reinhard G.
II. Title.
ML410.M23F5513   1993
784.2'184'092--dc20   92-21193
                                      CIP
                                      MN

Contents

Part Three: The Late Symphonies

Acknowledgments

This book provides a comprehensive review of Mahler's symphonies from various aspects: source studies, genesis, biography, world view, compositional technique, semantics, historic reception, and esthetics. The source studies would not have been possible without the help of numerous institutions and persons. The author expresses a cordial word of thanks to the International Gustav Mahler Society, the Society of the Friends of Music in Vienna, the Vienna City Library, the Pierpont Morgan Library in New York, the New York Public Library, the Stanford University Memorial Library of Music, the Willem Mengelberg Foundation in Amsterdam, the Jewish National and University Library in Jerusalem, the Bavarian State Library; Robert O. Lehman (New York); Dr. Herta Blaukopf, Emmy Hauswirth, Dr. Otto Biba, Peter Riethus (Vienna); and Karl Dieter Wagner (Hamburg), who kindly made available galley proofs of the 2nd edition of *Erinnerungen an Gustav Mahler* (Remembrances of Gustav Mahler) by Natalie Bauer-Lechner, published in fall 1984 by his publishing house. I also feel greatly obliged to *Hofrat* Dr. Günter Brosche and to the most helpful personnel of the Music Collection of the Austrian National Library in Vienna.

This project, which I have worked on for many years, was completed in spring 1984. My special thanks go to Dr. Gerd Sievers (Wiesbaden), who with untiring interest, critical thinking, and utmost thoroughness read the manuscript.

Introduction to the English Edition

The nineteenth century viewed the artist as a kind of prophet who predicted and anticipated future developments. His contemporaries, it was thought, did not understand him because he was ahead of his time. The great works of Beethoven, Berlioz, Liszt, Bruckner, and Wagner achieved general acceptance only after their composer had died. Richard Wagner inveighed against fashion, the taste of the day that inhibited the growth of new, original art.

As early as 1910, the Leipzig conductor Georg Göhler stated that Mahler was not a "true" contemporary, not a man of his time, because his music made no concessions to the taste, the fashions of the day. As a composer, Göhler added, Mahler offered nothing to his world but would offer that much more to the future—his time was yet to come.

Mahler believed in the significance of his own music, but he doubted that he would live to see "his time." In a letter written in 1904 he asked: "Must we always die before the public allows us to live?"

As a composer, Mahler all his life stood in the shadow of his far more famous friend and rival, Richard Strauss. While Strauss' tone poems and his operas *Elektra* and *Salome* were widely acclaimed at home, Mahler received recognition as a conductor but remained controversial as a composer. To be sure, a few far-sighted critics realized that this was bound to change. As Ernst Otto Nodnagel put it, Strauss reigned at the time, but the future belonged to Mahler.

Nodnagel proved to be right. Today, at least in German-speaking countries, Mahler's symphonies are achieving greater popularity than the symphonic poems of his formerly more famous friend. According to German statistics, Mahler ranks high in public favor: below Mozart, Beethoven, and Brahms, but above Haydn, Dvořák, and Tchaikovsky. A remarkable Mahler renaissance began around 1960 and has lasted to this day.

This astounding popularity has a number of reasons, including some practical ones. After 1961, due to copyright laws, Mahler's music became more easily (thus, more cheaply) available to concert managers, the record-

11

ing industry, and the media in general. Record manufacturers were quick to realize that Mahler's music was particularly effective in stereophonic sound. Luchino Visconti's film *Death in Venice* (1971) contributed to the Mahler renaissance, with the character of Gustav Aschenbach displaying traits of Gustav Mahler. The sound track featured the Adagietto movement of Mahler's Fifth; for many viewers it represented the essence of Mahler's music. This may be one of the reasons why the Fifth has achieved such great popularity. It seems to be favored especially by young conductors.

Our likes and dislikes in music as in other arts govern our attitudes to works of the past. Throughout the nineteenth century Beethoven remained a leading figure. His energetic music served well to express the heroic ideals of his own and succeeding generations. Thus in 1918 Hugo Riemann could tell of soldiers who, in the trenches, were analyzing Beethoven piano sonatas. Until World War I, Wagner's lofty music dramas with their passionate, ecstatic music enthralled all Europe. Today, heroic ideals are less in vogue. Many people identify with Gustav Mahler, finding in his deeply moving music an answer to their search for beauty, for life's meaning, for a better world. Interestingly enough, the emerging Mahler renaissance coincided with renewed interest in *Jugendstil,* in the Vienna *Sezession,* and in the paintings of Gustav Klimt.

Thomas Mann pointed out that Schopenhauer's philosophy was not only "a matter of the head, but of the whole man: heart body, and soul." The same can be said of Mahler; his music is a mirror of and addresses itself to the whole human being. In the summer of 1904 Mahler wrote to his friend, the somewhat younger Bruno Walter:

> There is no doubt that our music involves everything human, including the intellect. As in all art, one must choose the appropriate medium of expression. When we make music we do not paint or tell stories. Music represents the whole human being—feeling, thinking, breathing, suffering (GMB[2] 239f).

Indeed, Mahler's music not only provides esthetic pleasure but also proclaims a message.

In 1946, five years before his death, Schoenberg wrote an essay "Criteria for the Evaluation of Music" in which he stated:

> My personal feeling is that music conveys a prophetic message, revealing a higher form of life towards which mankind evolves. And it is because of this message that music appeals to men of all races and cultures.[1]

Such a view may help explain the tremendous impression Mahler's music could make on people in Japan, where I spent some time in 1987. During a visit to the town of Tsuyama, near Osaka, I attended a performance of Mahler's Second Symphony, in a large stadium, with an audience of five thousand. At the end there was an incredible outburst of applause—the music's message had been received. No doubt few of the attending Japanese knew any German, or had been told of Mahler's specific intentions, yet somehow they comprehended that in this symphony Mahler had given expression to some existential questions that had moved him profoundly.

Countless listeners all over the world have responded similarly to Mahler's music. It speaks to them because it appeals powerfully to a wide range of emotions. It is calm and passionate, traditional and innovative, full of humor and pathos, irony and the sublime. Bruno Walter sought an explanation for this in the radical, extreme facets of Mahler's personality, in his tendency to push toward the limit. Pathos, Walter believed, has to be contrasted with humor, and passion affects us only when it stems from a soul that has regained tranquility. Mahler's music encompasses a universe represented through virtually all kinds of musical expression and characterization.

Soon after his death, Mahler became the spiritual leader, the artistic ideal for those few inspired musicians who recognized his stature. In his *Theory of Harmony,* published in 1911, Schoenberg referred to him as a "martyr" and a "saint." For Anton Webern and Alban Berg, Mahler, next to Schoenberg, was the most influential figure. In their letters they speak of him with awe and veneration. His influence on the so-called second Viennese school was considerable, especially on Berg's music. During his lifetime Mahler had acquired some enthusiastic followers in Holland; their number grew after his death. Willem Mengelberg and Bruno Walter became the chief advocates of his symphonic œuvre.

During the 1960s, men and women from many walks of life began to identify with Mahler, among them students who, toward the end of the decade, demonstrated against the educational and cultural establishment. The world in general continues to be fascinated by the varied stages, the ups and downs of Mahler's career that resemble events in a novel: his arduous career as a conductor, his years as director of the Vienna Court Opera, the tragic events of 1907, and the last years in North America and Europe. Mahler became the paradigm of the composer who failed to win recognition during his lifetime.

Today we are concerned with the exploitation and destruction of nature, of our environment. Mahler seems to have anticipated that our relation to nature might become problematic. He loved nature, and he said of his early symphonies that the sound of his music always expressed nature. His Third Symphony includes two movements with the poetic titles "What the Flowers in the Meadow Tell Me" and "What the Animals in the Forest Tell Me."

We continue to think of Mahler as an artist who represents steadfast adherence, without compromise, to highest standards. His music attracts many who see in it an antidote to trends of superficiality that have invaded much of our culture, including the world of music. The spirit of his music, its expressive power, and especially its humanity—these may serve as guideposts in an age in which men and women seek new ways to give direction to their lives.

Translated by Reinhard G. Pauly

Introduction

> We modern people need such a large apparatus to
> express *our* thoughts whether great or small.
>
> GMB² 108

Content in Mahler's Symphonies

In February 1893, Gustav Mahler was busy in Hamburg with the revision of his First Symphony. On 7 February he wrote a long letter to Gisela Tolnay-Witt, who had asked him "whether it is necessary to employ such a large apparatus as the orchestra to express a great thought" (GMB² 106). In very broad strokes, Mahler sketched the development of occidental music since Bach, established why chamber music was no longer satisfying to him, and elucidated the increasing enlargement of the orchestral apparatus more or less as a necessity: "The more music develops, the more complicated the apparatus becomes to express the composer's ideas."

Mahler went on to make several extremely important statements regarding the concept of "content" in the more recent symphonic writing since Beethoven:

> Hand in hand with the imitation of musical tones came the *tendency to adopt newer elements of feeling*; the composers began to include areas of increased complexity and depth from their emotional lives in the realm of their creative work, until the *new era* of music began with Beethoven. From then on, not just the *basic mood* (e.g., sheer joyfulness or sadness), but also the transition from one mood to another—conflicts, nature and its impact, humor, and poetic ideas—were the objects of musical creation (GMB² 107).

These sentences contain not only an interpretation of Beethoven's symphonic writing but also the artistic program of Mahler's symphonic writing, which thrives on "poetic ideas." Corresponding to his principles, Mahler provided

15

the movements of his early symphonies with poetic titles, explained his intentions in numerous letters, and even wrote detailed programs.

In October 1900, Mahler disassociated himself from the current direction of illustrative program music as Richard Strauss (his great antipode)
practiced it.[1] Nonetheless he associated after this with the "inner" programs
of the newer music since Beethoven. In a letter to Max Kalbeck, he wrote:

> And so once again: Down with every program! After all, one has to bring
> along ears and a heart and, last but not least, be willing to give oneself to
> the rhapsodist. A remnant of mystery always remains—even for the
> creator![2] (GMB[2] 254).

(Several years later, interestingly enough, Romain Rolland expressed support for preserving the "mystery" of music. In a letter to his friend Richard
Strauss, he recommended that Strauss keep silent about the programs of his
works.[3])

In spite of a categorical refusal to interpret his symphonies programmatically (AME 368), Mahler offered important hermeneutical directions in
conversations with his wife, friends, and confidants. Yet more significant is
that in Mahler's numerous manuscript sources (sketches, portions of manuscripts, drafts of full scores, clean copies, and proof sheets), notes, cues, and
entries with hermeneutical meaning are frequently found.[4] They impressively
document that his entire symphonic writing must not under any circumstances be classified as *absolute music,* but must be perceived as music that
expresses things personal, biographical, literary, and philosophical. Charac-
teristically, Mahler wrote to his friend Bruno Walter in summer 1904 "that
our music involves in some way the 'purely human' (and everything that goes
with this, therefore also the 'intellectual') cannot be denied" (GMB[2] 293).

Mahler's conflicting relationship to program music (on the one hand an
unshakable faith in the "inner" programs, on the other a hesitation to make
the programs known) had and still has implications on the esthetics of reception. Since he had been branded as the absolute musician in many places, his
works were received mostly without regard to his early programs. His
symphonic writing is commonly accepted as pure music. Some scholars insist
with all sincerity that the authentic programs of Mahler are incidental to the
reception of his work. One may ask, however, whether the message Mahler
addressed to humanity was understood correctly.

In his Munich declaration Mahler articulated the naive belief that a composer, even without commentary, would automatically be able to thrust onto
his listeners the emotions that engulfed him during composition. In this
matter Mahler deceived himself because the programmatic and ideological
foundations of his symphonic creations do not lend themselves to pure per-
ception by the emotions without the assistance of the mind. His contemporaries had indeed noticed that his symphonies sought to express extra
musical meaning and repeatedly called for explanatory programs.[5] But
Mahler consistently refused all interpretation, and in doing so he himself
barred the way to a deeper understanding of his works.

The meaning of Mahler's music is the place where research must begin today. Studies of formal esthetics and of compositional techniques used in his symphonies are not lacking. There is, however, a lack of research relating structural aspects to semantic formulations, research directed not only to compositional techniques but also to style, expression, and idiom. This research should consider every hermeneutic hint of Mahler (even the slightest) and strive to decipher his symbolic language while seeking to comprehend what is new in his music.[6]

The Division of Mahler's Compositions into Time Periods

For many composers assigning their works to time periods cannot always be for precise biographical or stylistic reasons. The symphonic work of Gustav Mahler, however, can clearly be divided into certain periods.

In a very informative letter that was most likely written in June 1910, Bruno Walter wrote that he discerned two periods in Mahler's works:

> In your songs, the first period contains settings of poems from *Des Knaben Wunderhorn* and the second period contains poems by Rückert. In the symphonies (which were created in the same time periods as the songs), the first period encompasses your First through Fourth and the second period encompasses your Fifth through Eighth. In the first four symphonies, the music is in praise of eternal things and is partly expressed by words and is partly concealed but transformed into pure music. The Fifth, Sixth, and Seventh are not influenced by any kind of concealed text, but are shaped purely by music. In the Eighth, everything gained is combined into something new, the music about the final mysteries being supported by words.[7]

When Walter wrote this letter, he knew neither *Das Lied von der Erde* ("The Song of the Earth") nor the Ninth, though he would later premiere both of these works.

Mahler himself discerned three periods in his work, as his friend Alfredo Casella reports.[8] Accordingly, the first four symphonies, several of which are symphonic cantatas, belong to the first period. The three middle instrumental symphonies (the Fifth, Sixth, and Seventh), as well as the Eighth (another symphonic cantata), belong to the second period. With the Ninth Symphony, Mahler felt that a new style was beginning. Paul Stefan rightfully draws to our attention that the "Ninth" Symphony, meaning *Das Lied von der Erde,* and the work known as the Ninth reveal a new Mahler.[9]

In fact, biographical as well as stylistic and idiomatic evidence support Mahler's divisions into three time periods: the First through the Fourth (1887–1900), the Fifth through the Eighth (1901–1906), and *Das Lied von der Erde* through the Tenth (1907–1910). To touch only on the biographical reasons here: the meeting with Alma Schindler in November 1901 made a deep impression on Mahler, and the tragic happenings of summer 1907—the death of Mahler's older daughter and the diagnosis of his heart trouble—left even deeper marks. Both events profoundly changed Mahler's attitude toward life and his emotional state, which indirectly influenced the expression and idiom of his late works.

The Early Symphonies

Fundamentals of "Tetralogy"

> You will see: I will not live to see the victory of my
> cause! Everything I write is too strange and new for
> the listeners, who cannot find a bridge to me.
>
> BL² 50

In a conversation with his friend the Viennese violinist Natalie Bauer-Lechner, Mahler once stated that there was a close connection between the Fourth and the first three symphonies, and that those three even found their completion in the Fourth. "The content and structure of the four are combined to create a definite unified *tetralogy*" (BL² 164). One can comprehend what Mahler means by this only if one works through the characteristics of the early symphonies and closely examines their programmatic assumptions.

Regarding the outward characteristics of the first four symphonies, many deviations from the usual immediately stand out: the number and order of movements, the arrangement of the sections and their conception as symphonic cantatas, the borrowing from song-compositions, and the setting of poems from *Des Knaben Wunderhorn*. Let us recall that the First originally had five movements, the Second has five, the Third has six, and the Fourth has only four. Another innovation is that the Second, Third, and Fourth close with slow movements, and the Second and Third represent the symphonic cantata type, which includes choirs and vocal soloists. The Fourth, however, finishes with an orchestra. Furthermore, in all four symphonies Mahler borrowed from his own song compositions, inasmuch as he drew upon the instrumental substance of pre-existent songs and worked them through symphonically or included an orchestral song. Also to be noted are the thematic connections between the Finale of the Fourth and the fifth movement of the Third—*Was mir die Engel erzählen* ("What the Angels Tell Me")—connections that Mahler himself found to be unusual and "strange" (BL² 164).

The concept of "tetralogy," of course, focuses more on the ideological connection between the four works. These are so close that they allow one

21

symphony to appear as a continuation of another. Mahler believed that the Second tied directly onto the First (GMB[2] 150) and that the Third, which soared "above that world of battle and distress" found in the first two, could emerge only "as their result" (BL[2] 35). These statements are better understood if one recognizes that Mahler saw his symphonic writing as an expression of his world view, and made the personal, philosophical, and religious questions that concerned him the subjects of his early symphonies.[1] To give examples, the fundamental philosophical thought of the autobiographically conceived First is the idea of transcendence—overcoming misery and suffering. The eschatological question of death and dying is the subject of the Second Symphony. The idea of a hierarchy of being, the formation of the world, the position of humankind within it, and Mahler's personal profession of *eternal love,* form the cosmological subject of the Third. The four movements of the Fourth may finally be denoted as symphonic meditations on *life after death.* All of this shows that those who have spoken of the *metaphysical music* of Mahler and who have called him a *symphonizing philosopher* are not all wrong!

If one seeks further evidence of the remarkable relationship between the first four symphonies, one would have to consider the sound and the idiomatic aspects of the music. The characteristic sound of Mahler is already unmistakable in the First Symphony.[2] Idiomatically, the four symphonies constitute—in spite of their differences—a unified world of expression due in no small part to the common vocal component. The inclusion and assimilation of vocal models, Mahler's "lied melodic style," prove to be a style-forming factor of the first rank, and Paul Bekker surely touched upon a truth when he spoke about an ideal synthesis of symphony and song in Mahler's early works.[3]

In regard to "sound," Mahler was fully aware of the originality of his music and attributed the difficulty audiences experienced in understanding his works largely to this factor. He considered the components, beginning with *Das klagende Lied,* to be so "Mahlerian," so sharp and completely distinct in their own way, "that there is no longer a connection [with tradition]" (BL[2] 50). He especially felt that his first two symphonies departed so much "from anything familiar," that finding any point of reference was virtually impossible.[4]

Mahler's early symphonies are founded upon the principle of a rather well-established esthetic that he described in a conversation with Bauer-Lechner on 12 July 1897 (BL[2] 95). In this conversation, he basically revealed himself to be a follower of the old doctrine of mimesis—the representation of reality in works of art using details derived from ordinary life. He further believed that various artistic styles depend on the artist's attitude toward nature:

> The artist—like everyone else—draws all material and form from the surrounding world, though in a different and more extensive sense. Whether one's relationship with nature is happy and harmonious, painful and

miserable, or hostile and defiant, or whether one considers nature from a lofty standpoint with humor and irony, these attitudes provide the basis for an artistic style that is beautiful and sublime, sentimental, tragic, or humorous and ironic.

The more one gets acquainted with the style, expression, and idiom of the early symphonies, the more one recognizes that all four styles identified by Mahler—beautiful and sublime, sentimental, tragic, and humorous and ironic—are represented. For example, the humorous and ironic style, or the grotesque, for which Mahler had a particular passion, includes *Todten-marsch in Callots Manier* ("Death March in Callot's Manner") in the First, the symphonic version of *Fischpredigt* ("The Fish Sermon") in the Scherzo of the Second, *Was mir die Thiere im Walde erzählen* ("What the Animals in the Forest Tell Me") in the third movement of the Third, and *Das himm-lische Leben* ("The Heavenly Life") in the Finale of the Fourth.

The First Symphony

> What kind of a world is this that casts forth such
> sounds and shapes as a reflection. Something like the
> death march followed by the outbreak of a storm
> seem to me like a burning accusation of the creator.
>
> GMB² 372

> But by no means do I suggest the First; that one is
> very difficult to understand.   GMB² 313

Origin

In the composition of his early symphonies, Mahler borrowed relatively often
from his own works and from other composers. The First Symphony presents
an extreme case in this regard. One would exaggerate only a little by calling
it a work based upon pre-existing material. The basis for the main movement
and the middle section of the slow movement is the music of two songs from
the cycle *Lieder eines fahrenden Gesellen* (*Songs of a Wayfarer*), which
Mahler composed in 1884.[1] The "Blumine movement"—originally the
second movement of the Symphony—is derived from the music that accompanies *Der Trompeter von Säkkingen* ("The Trumpeter from Säkkingen"),
which was written "within two days" during June 1884.[2] Motifs from the
song *Hans und Grete* of 1880 are found in the Scherzo. Mahler based
Todtenmarsch in Callots Manier on the melody from the student round
Bruder Martin ("Brother Martin, Are You Sleeping?") and for the Finale he
borrowed several motifs from Liszt's *Dante Symphony* (1856) and Wagner's
Parsifal (1882). If one bears all this in mind, one has a better understanding
of what Mahler meant when he told Natalie Bauer-Lechner that

> composing is like playing with building blocks, where new buildings are
> created again and again, using the same blocks. Indeed, these blocks have
> been there, ready to be used, since childhood, the only time that is
> designed for gathering (BL² 138).

From August 1886 to May 1888, Mahler worked as second conductor at the Leipzig City Theater. His work there stood under a cloud because of his rivalry with Arthur Nikisch, who had the position of first conductor. Nonetheless, in Leipzig Mahler was able to achieve success: His arrangement and completion of Carl Maria von Weber's opera *Die drei Pintos* (*The Three Pintos*), which premiered 20 January 1888, received high recognition.

It is certain that Mahler started to work on his First Symphony after this premiere, though there are conflicting statements regarding the chronology of the work. According to Natalie Bauer-Lechner, he composed the whole symphony in spring 1888, "within six weeks, while continuously conducting and rehearsing" (BL[2] 175); however, according to Guido Adler[3] and Fritz Löhr[4], the beginnings of this work extend back to the year 1884 in Kassel. Meanwhile several documents confirm the statements of Bauer-Lechner, and in March 1888, Mahler informed his friend Fritz Löhr of the completion of his work. "It became so overpowering—as it flowed out of me like a mountain river!" he wrote with great enthusiasm, adding that "for six weeks I had nothing but my desk in front of me!" (GMB[2] 70). Much later, in a letter to Annie Mincieux, Mahler indicated having composed the First in the year 1888 (GMUB 123). Incidentally, several interesting remarks by the well-known Strauss biographer Max Steinitzer corroborate the information of Bauer-Lechner.[5] Steinitzer, who socialized frequently with Mahler during the 1887–1888 season in Leipzig, tells that Mahler entered a period of "almost feverish composing" after arranging *Die drei Pintos* and that Steinitzer was not quite convinced of the artistic success of the First Symphony, in view of Mahler's age, until he saw sketches of it, which caused him to change his mind.

After all this we can surely assume that the First was for the most part composed during the time between 20 January and the end of March 1888. The remarks by Guido Adler and Fritz Löhr refer most likely to the date Mahler began composing *Lieder eines fahrenden Gesellen* and the music to *Der Trompeter von Säkkingen*.

The First Performance and the Various Versions

It was only natural that Mahler was concerned about performing the Symphony immediately following the completion. He rejected the suggestion of Steinitzer to have the first performance of the work within the context of an entertainment concert. Even after his departure from the Stadttheater in Leipzig on 17 May 1888, he did not abandon the hope of performing the Symphony there. In a letter sent from the town of Iglau, he asked Steinitzer for his advice in the matter (GMB[2] 72), but the work did not premiere until eighteen months later. Mahler, who took the position of Artistic Director of the Royal Hungarian Opera in fall 1888, conducted the Symphony in Budapest in a Philharmonic concert on Wednesday, 20 November 1889. In the program the work was designated as *Symphoniai költemény két részben*

("A Symphonic Poem in Two Sections").[6] The performance was a fiasco. According to a report by Fritz Löhr, the Pest circle close to Mahler was deeply moved, but

> a considerable part of the audience, in its usual heartless way, had no understanding of anything formally new, particularly the dynamic vehemence of the tragic expression that was raging here; they were uncomfortably startled out of their thoughtless habit (GMB[2] 416).

The review by August Beer in the *Pester Lloyd* was more precise:

> The reception of the Symphony was as divergent as the two halves of the work. Our concert audience, which was back today in full number, listened with alert interest to the first section, and Mahler, who also conducted, received warm applause after every movement. After the Death March the mood changed, and after the Finale there was slight but nevertheless audible opposition.[7]

Many years later, Mahler himself expressed the following to Natalie Bauer-Lechner in regard to the premiere:

> In Pest, where I performed it for the first time, my friends bashfully avoided me afterward; nobody dared talk to me about the performance and my work, and I went around like a sick person or an outcast. You can therefore imagine what the critiques looked like under such circumstances (BL[2] 176).

It is no doubt due to the failure of the Budapest premiere that Mahler locked his manuscript in a drawer for three years. It was not until 1893 that he revised it in Hamburg, where he was working at the time. The (Hamburg) autograph, kept in the Osborn Collection at the Yale University Library, shows the following revision dates: for the "Blumine" movement, 16 August 1893; for the Scherzo, 27 January 1893; and for the Finale, 19 January 1893. Since the autograph of the Budapest premiere has still not surfaced, a comparison of the Hamburg version with the Budapest original is not possible. Nevertheless one can say that the Hamburg revision concerns the instrumentation and that it must have been drastic. "As a whole, everything has become more slender and transparent," Mahler wrote to Richard Strauss on 15 May 1894, adding that the instrumentation of the introduction in the strings had "completely changed."[8] From the notes of Bauer-Lechner we learn that the strings did not originally play their long pedal point as a harmonic. Mahler stated:

> In Pest, when I heard the A in all registers, it sounded to me like far too much sound for the shimmering and glimmering of the air I had in mind. Then it struck me to give all string players harmonics (the violinists the highest and the basses, who also have harmonics, the lowest): Now I had what I wanted (BL[2] 176).

In this revision, the First was played on Friday, 27 October 1893 in Hamburg during a concert in which some Mahler songs were also performed by Clementine Schuch-Prosska and *Kammersänger* Paul Bulss. This performance was a success. Ferdinand Pfohl, Mahler's friend who had been music critic of the respected *Hamburger Nachrichten* since 1892, wrote an appreciative review.[9]

Encouraged by the good reception of the work in Hamburg, Mahler anticipated further performances. He turned to Richard Strauss, who was conductor at the Saxon Court in Weimar and who in that position enthusiastically supported program music and the modern new German school.[10] Strauss included the work in the program of the Music Festival, and thus the First was performed in Weimar on 3 June 1894 under Mahler's direction. The reception by the audience was divided. As Mahler wrote to his friend Arnold Berliner, "My symphony was received with furious opposition by some and with wholehearted approval by others. The opinions clashed in an amusing way, in the streets and in the salons!" (GMB[2] 112).

On the side of the "furious opposition," it would be safe to count Ernst Otto Nodnagel, a critic and composer from Königsberg who later became an enthusiastic Mahler fan.[11] As he himself wrote, he had subjected the Symphony to "an emphatically negative discussion" in reviews for the *Berliner Tageblatt* and the *Magazin für Litteratur* and "condemned" it because it appeared under the guise of program music. Nodnagel considered the printed program, which indirectly referred to Jean Paul's *Titan* and *Siebenkäs,* as "in itself confused and unintelligible." He could not recognize any relation between the program and the music, and he rejected the "Blumine" movement as "trivial."

Mahler must have taken Nodnagel's objections to heart because at the next performance, which he conducted on 16 March 1896 in Berlin (GMB[2] 147), he did without the program, introducing the work simply as "Symphony in D Major" and dropping the "Blumine" movement—to the great satisfaction of Nodnagel, who gladly stated that the work now found "lively approval, even from part of the hostile press." But even this performance did not bring the great success Mahler dreamed of. Although Bauer-Lechner, who was present, spoke of a "rather warm and affirmative" reception by the audience, she added that Mahler was painfully aware of "the cold effect on the listener" and stated "most sadly" over and over: "No, they have not understood it!" (BL[2] 47).

Further performances were not able to change much about this situation. Over and over Mahler wondered about the lack of understanding met by the First. On the occasion of a performance in Lwow in 1903, for example, he reported to his wife,

Following this, I played my First with the orchestra, which behaved splendidly and was obviously well prepared. Several times I had chills running down my back. Confound it, where do the people have their ears and hearts that they don't get this! (AME 285).

Similarly he wrote in August 1906 to Josef Reitler, who was trying to push for a performance of a Mahler symphony in Paris: "But by no means do I suggest the First; that one is very difficult to understand. The Sixth or Fifth would be preferable" (GMB[2] 313). And he wrote to Bruno Walter in December 1909 from New York: "Day before yesterday I presented my First! Apparently without any particular response whereas I was actually quite content with this early work" (GMB[2] 372).

The score of the First was initially published in 1899 by Weinberger Verlag in Vienna. This first edition greatly differs from the Hamburg version in its instrumentation. Mahler decided to reinforce the orchestral apparatus in this printed edition and to re-orchestrate many sections as well.

The Program

The question regarding the programmatic aspects of Mahler's symphonic writing already appears with the First Symphony and confronts us with a number of problems that require thorough attention. Those willing to undertake a detailed study will certainly not be disappointed by the result.

At the Budapest premiere Mahler had classified the First as "A Symphonic Poem in Two Parts" but did not provide a programmatic explanation. The five movements are simply called

First Section
    1. Introduction and Allegro comodo
    2. Andante
    3. Scherzo
Second Section
    4. A la pompes funèbres; *attacca*
    5. Molto appassionato

This stands in contrast to the Hamburg concert notes, which provide the following extensive program:[12]

"Titan," a Tone Poem in Symphonic Form (Manuscript)

Part 1: *Aus den Tagen der Jugend, Blumen-, Frucht- und Dornstücke*
    ("From the Days of Youth," Music of Flowers, Fruit, and Thorn)
  I. *Frühling und kein Ende* ("Spring and No End") (Introduction and Allegro comodo). The introduction pictures the awakening of nature from a long winter's sleep.
  II. "Blumine" (Andante)
  III. *Mit vollen Segeln* ("Under Full Sail") (Scherzo)

Part 2: "Commedia humana"
IV. *Gestrandet!* ("Stranded!") (*Todtenmarsch in Callots Manier*). The
    following may serve as an explanation for this movement: The
    author received an overt suggestion for it from *Des Jägers Leichen-
    begängnis (The Hunter's Funeral Procession*), a parodistic picture
    that is well-known to all Austrian children and is taken from an old
    book of children's fairy tales. The animals of the forest escort the
    coffin of a deceased hunter to the gravesite. Rabbits carrying a
    banner follow a band of Bohemian musicians accompanied by
    music-making cats, toads, crows, and so on; stags, does, foxes, and
    other four-legged and feathered animals of the forest follow the
    procession in amusing poses. At that point the piece in some ways
    expresses an ironic, humorous mood and in other ways expresses an
    eerie, brooding mood, followed immediately by
V. *Dall' Inferno* (Allegro furioso)—as the sudden outburst of despair
    from a deeply wounded heart.

Mahler had this program published for the Weimar performance, but with
some changes: the subtitle of the first part was corrected to read *Aus den
Tagen der Jugend, Blumen-, Frucht- und Dornenstücke* ("From the Days of
Youth", Music of Flowers, Fruit, and Thorns); the introductory explanation
was revised to describe "the awakening of nature in the forest in the earliest
morning"; the titles of the second and fourth movements were changed to
Blumine-Capitel (Andante) and *Des Jägers Leichenbegängnis, ein Todtenmarsch in Callots Manier,* respectively; the fifth movement was given the
more complete title *Dall' Inferno al Paradiso.*

The Weimar program caused much resentment. After Nodnagel declared
it to be confused and unintelligible, Mahler hastened to retract it, an action
that seemed to be a denial. On 20 March 1896, four days after the performance in Berlin, he assured Max Marschalk that he had "thought up" the
program titles and explanations after the fact:

> The reason for omitting them this time is not only that I consider them to
> be less than comprehensive—indeed, I do not even believe them to be
> accurate characterizations—but I have seen how the audience is misled
> by them (GMB[2] 147).

Mahler's withdrawal of the program was not without consequences. His earliest interpreters did not hesitate to declare that the program was not binding.
As Richard Specht said,

> There is an extensive program to the First that is so extravagant, blurred,
> and alien to the character of the music that it seemed to come not from
> the composer but from one of the worst types of enthusiastic com-
> mentator.[13]

Paul Stefan assumed that the program probably was not in existence at the premiere in Budapest.[14] This assumption proves to be wrong after a more thorough investigation, as evidenced by the disclosure that the title page of the Hamburg autograph already contained a short version of the infamous program:

Symphony (Titan)
in 5 movements (2 sections)
by
Gustav Mahler

Part I: *Aus den Tagen der Jugend*
1. *Frühling und kein Ende*
2. "Blumine"
3. *Mit vollen Segeln*

Part II: *Commedia humana*
4. *Todtenmarsch in Callots Manier*
5. *Dall' Inferno al Paradiso*

Even more significant is the observation that the hermeneutic indications August Beer made in his review of the Budapest premiere probably refer to oral explanations given by Mahler. Beer said that a "true spring atmosphere" spread over the first movement, which he apostrophized as "a poetically perceived forest idyll." He described the second movement as a serenade in which one could easily recognize the lovers, "who in the secret of the night express their tender feelings" (later Mahler spoke of a "love episode"), and he felt the Scherzo resembled an "honest-to-goodness peasant dance."

Special attention should also be given to the semantic analysis of the Finale. The most important allegorical motifs of the movement symbolize the inferno and the paradiso, as detailed investigations have shown.[15] The title, *Dall' Inferno al Paradiso,* is not to be understood in a poetic way; instead, it quite accurately describes the underlying programmatic idea. From all this we may conclude that the program of the First was already fixed in its main characteristics when the music was created.

How does this program relate to Jean Paul and specifically to his great novel *Titan*? Considering how complex this question is, it comes as no surprise that opinions vary greatly. Alma Mahler (AME 140) and Bruno Walter attributed the title of the Symphony (*Titan*) to the passionate love Mahler had for Jean Paul. Bruno Walter reports: "We often talked about the great novel, especially the figure of Roquairol, whose influence is noticeable in the funeral march of the First and who was the subject of detailed discussion."[16] Josef B. Foerster also explains that in creating the work, Mahler relied on impressions he had received from Jean Paul, and out of gratitude he used the title of the book from which most of the suggestions had come.[17] Foerster speculated that Mahler first announced the program in Hamburg and Weimar, where he could assume the audience would be familiar with the works of Jean Paul.

All those favoring the idea of a connection between the Symphony and Jean Paul's novel refer to the fact that the programs published in Hamburg and Weimar contained literary references to Jean Paul. Thus the title *Blumen-, Frucht- und Dornenstücke* alludes to Jean Paul's *Siebenkäs,* and the title "Blumine" alludes to Jean Paul's *Herbstblumine*.[18] The literary historian Jost Hermand cites these reasons to defend the opinion that Mahler's *Titan* indeed seems to be based on the work of Jean Paul more than it might appear. Above all, Hermand suspected that the connections to Jean Paul were to be found in Mahler's inner "openness," which "is not adverse to a radical change to the grotesque," and in Mahler's frequent emphasis on the "contrasting nature" of the individual motifs.[19]

Ferdinand Pfohl, however, reports that in Hamburg during 1893 Mahler was "desperately" looking for a grand and bold title for his First Symphony and that one of his musically enthusiastic friends prompted him to use the title *Titan*.[20] The writings of Natalie Bauer-Lechner reveal that Mahler protested the association of his First with Jean Paul's *Titan*: "What he had in mind was simply a strong, heroic person, living and suffering, struggling with and succumbing to destiny, *for which the true, higher resolution is not given until the Second*" (BL[2] 173). In conversations with Bauer-Lechner, Mahler interpreted the first four movements of the Symphony to be, in certain ways, stations in the life of his hero. "In the first movement we are carried away by a Dionysian, jubilant mood that has not yet been broken or dulled by anything." In the Scherzo, "the young lad still roaming around the world is much stronger, rougher, and more fit for life." Mahler described the "Blumine" movement, which was later removed, as a "love episode," and he commented on the *Todtenmarsch*: "Now he (my hero) has found a hair in his soup, and his meal is spoiled." Finally, we can thank Alma Mahler for the important information that Mahler eliminated the title *Titan* because he was constantly asked to explain how "various situations from the novel were interpreted in the music" (AME 140). We can conclude from this that the allusions to Jean Paul in the program of the First have to be understood as mere analogies. The true nature of the program of the First will be explained in the following sections.

Frühling und kein Ende ("Spring and No End")

In a quoted letter to Gisela Tolnay-Witt, Mahler considered "nature and its effects upon us" to be among the objects "of musical representation" in symphonic music (GMB[2] 107). The "awakening of nature from a long winter's sleep" (as mentioned in the Hamburg program), and the description of its delightful effect on people, form the poetic idea in the First Symphony's first movement. An analysis of the movement reveals that Mahler succeeded in transferring this idea into music in an especially original way.

Hearing the introduction of the movement for the first time, one cannot suppress the feeling of surprise about the quasi-impressionistic, atmospheric character of the music. Especially obvious is the apparent heterogeneity of the musical figures: a theme of a fourth in the woodwinds and later in the violins and a "very mellow" horn melody alternating with a clarinet fanfare, with a trumpet fanfare "in the far distance," and with shrill clarinet cuckoo calls. The composition appears so unusual that to do it justice it has been referred to as being "collagelike" and "discontinuous."[21] What one has tried to explain formally is programmatically conditioned and motivated. As the constant change of tempo in the introduction discloses, the development of the music takes place on two levels: those sections in the first tempo *Langsam. Schleppend* (Slowly. Dragging) represent the slumber of nature, while the clarinet and trumpet fanfares, characterized as *più mosso,* along with the cuckoo-calls, are to be understood as awakening calls. Mahler's comment "Like a sound in nature" (found only in the printed score) refers solely to sections in *Tempo I.* The following outline will explain the organization:

Mm.	1–9	*Langsam. Schleppend* (Slowly. Dragging)	Theme of fourths
		Wie ein Naturlaut	(Nature Theme)
	9–15	Più mosso	Clarinet fanfare (Awakening call)
	16–21	Tempo I	Theme of fourths
	22–27	Più mosso	Trumpet fanfare (Awakening call)
	28–29	Tempo I	Theme of fourths
	30–31	Più mosso	Cuckoo calls
	32–35	Tempo I	Very mellow horn melody
	36–39	Più mosso	Trumpet fanfare
	40–43	Tempo I	Mellow horn melody
	44–46	Più mosso	Trumpet fanfare and cuckoo calls
	47–58	Tempo I	Chromatic bass motif and theme of fourths

Mahler borrowed the music of the sonata movement (*Immer sehr gemächlich)* following the introduction largely from the second of the *Lieder eines fahrenden Gesellen:* "Ging heut morgen über's Feld" ("Went this morning across the field"). The text of this song, its emotions and thoughts, express an affirmation of life and closeness of nature. "Wie mir doch die Welt gefällt!" ("I like this world so much!") is the underlying sentiment. The music is correspondingly bright, in places even exuberant. Mankind is in harmony with nature and with the world in general. Quite appropriately there are extended passages in a pastoral vein; they are characterized by slow harmonic rhythm, drone basses, sustained lines, and ostinatos. This movement provides an excellent example of Mahler's *Baßlosigkeit* [passages in which the bass is sustained for a long time].

Exposition

Mm. 62–74   Song theme
     75–108   Music of the Song's third verse
     109–135   Music of the Song's first verse
     136–162   Final group (taken from the Tirili motif)

Development

163–206   Part I: New form of the introduction (now with a gradual
          retard) without the use of clarinet and trumpet fanfares and
          including the Tirili motif; preparation of the cello theme
207–304   Part II
209–220   Fanfare theme of the horns
221–229   Cantabile cello theme (functioning as a secondary theme)
225–304   Renewed statement and development of the song motif in
          changing colors, including the cantabile cello theme
305–357   Part III: A foreshadowing of the inferno in anticipation of a
          section from the Finale (mm. 574–628)
352–357   "Breakthrough": Trumpet fanfares and woodwind and horn
          signals

358–442   Recapitulation

443–450   Coda

If one evaluates the exposition of the movement according to textbook
criteria, one has to call it irregular. It has neither a contrasting second nor (as
in the expositions of Bruckner's movements) a third theme. The song theme
and the music of the song's third and first verses are all followed by a short
closing group, which Mahler develops from a Tirili motif.[22] The (unusual)
resorting to the song model accounts for the structural abnormalities.

Of the three parts into which the development falls, the first (mm. 163–
206) presents a new version of the introduction. The mood of predawn
twilight that Mahler presents here does not include the energetic clarinet and
trumpet fanfares from the beginning; *piano* is the dynamic level throughout.
A pedal point of high strings on the high A harmonic, together with a pedal
point (beginning m. 180) in the basses and the tuba on low F, frame the
seemingly heterogeneous sounds that are heard one after the other: bird calls
(cuckoo calls and Tirili motif), sounds of nature, the theme of a fourth from
the beginning and the motifs of the stopped horns. In between, we hear fragments of a new cantabile cello theme, which will play an important role in the
second part of the development.

The first part of the development is remarkably static, as is the music of
the second part (mm. 207–304) which at first does not seem to move at all.
The horns present a fanfare in triple *piano,* evoking thoughts of Carl Maria
von Weber, of forests, and of hunting. Not until the cantabile melody of the

cellos (mm. 221ff.) is the actual development introduced, and the occasional use of this cantabile melody alters the phrases and motif of the *Lieder eines fahrenden Gesellen,* which appear now in a vacillating light. Since the exposition does not go beyond the realm of D major and A major, the development now opens up the circle of flat keys. The modulation proceeds as follows: D major (m. 221), A major (m. 229), D-flat major (m. 243), A-flat major (m. 258), C major (m. 276), F major (m. 279). The measure numbers show that the harmonic planes are broad.

The third part of the development (mm. 305–357) at first establishes a dark mood (in the foreground are the keys of F minor and D-flat major) that seems to be an extraneous element within the movement but, with minor deviations, anticipates a section from the Finale (mm. 574–628). The method of anticipating a whole section of the Finale in the first movement is rather unusual in nineteenth-century symphonic writing (it is unknown to Bruckner). Here it surely does not serve formal considerations, such as the need for unity, but rather a programmatic intention, as if to explain that the gloomy world of the inferno casts its shadow onto the main movement. Mahler's expression regarding the main movement's "Dionysiac mood of jubilation, not yet broken or darkened by anything" (BL[2] 173) does not take this section into account.

In measures 352–357, a rather staccato but strong intensification from *ppp* to *ff* leads to the climax of the development and of the entire movement. The awakening calls by the trumpets are joined by impressive signals in the horns and high woodwinds. This passage unites the dominant chord of D major with the tonic chord. However, the way Mahler proceeds from F minor to D major in no way corresponds to the strict rules of composition and instead evokes something violent and sudden. The term "breakthrough," coined by Paul Bekker, indeed suits the situation.[23] Following Bekker, Theodor W. Adorno spoke of a "cleavage" coming "from outside the music's own momentum."[24] Adorno considered such a breakthrough to be a basic form category of Mahler.

Mahler hated exact repetitions in the recapitulation, and repetition in general. He believed that every repetition was a "lie" and that a work of art, like life itself, always has to develop further (BL[2] 158). Bearing this in mind, one is not surprised that the recapitulation of the main movement, with its 85 measures (mm. 358–442), deviates considerably from the exposition (100 measures). Typically, it begins with the fanfare of the horns, now performed *fortissimo,* and only then does it turn to the new cantabile theme (mm. 364–367) and the song motifs. The recapitulation, like the exposition, is geared toward a climax. The metronome numbers indicated by Mahler himself in the printed score increase from $\sib = 84$ to $\quarter = 92$ and further to $\quarter = 112$. The movement ends with a short coda consisting of only 8 measures. In a conversation about this coda with Bauer-Lechner, Mahler said:

> The listener surely will not understand the end of this movement correctly; it [the movement] will fall into oblivion, although I could easily

have shaped it more effectively. My hero breaks out in laughter and runs away. Certainly no one will discover that theme, given at the close to the timpani (BL² 173).

To Bruno Walter he said that in his "boisterous" closing he had Beethoven in mind "how he broke into loud laughter and ran away."[25] Walter, who was prejudiced against any kind of programmatic interpretation of Mahler's works, felt that the laughing Beethoven actually had nothing to do with the experience, which, according to Mahler himself, gave rise to the First Symphony. Mahler's remarks, however, are not contradictory and in fact offer proof—along with the music—that in the conception of this coda, Mahler let himself be guided by his notion of musical humor. The short, abruptly articulated, staccato wind motifs, separated from one another by complete rests, truly appear to be witty and are reminiscent of Beethoven's humor. The "theme given at the close to the timpani" is, by the way, the main motif from the *Lieder eines fahrenden Gesellen,* reduced to the interval of a fourth. At the same time it points to the blows of the repeated interval of a fourth in the *Todtenmarsch*.

"Blumine"

The initial performances of the First Symphony in Budapest, Hamburg, and Weimar contained a serenade-like movement that Mahler called Andante or "Blumine," which was eliminated after the performance in Weimar. Since the Berlin premiere on 16 March 1896, the First has been played as a work of four movements. The first edition appeared in 1899 without the "Blumine" movement. It was not until 1968 that the movement was published by the Theodore Presser Company (Bryn Mawr, Pennsylvania); musicologists were able to identify the work as one of the seven pieces of incidental music that Mahler composed in June 1884 for a performance of the popular verse-epic *Der Trompeter von Säkkingen* by Joseph Victor von Scheffel at the Kassel Theater.[26] On 23 June 1884 the first production and the music of these seven "living pictures" met with vivid approval. They were also performed in Mannheim, Wiesbaden, and Karlsruhe.[27]

Mahler did not think much of his incidental music. He took to Leipzig only the serenade-like movement, which begins and ends with a cantilena for the trumpet. According to a report of Max Steinitzer, Mahler considered the piece to be "too sentimental," and was annoyed by it.[28] Steinitzer had to promise that he would destroy the piano reduction he had made.

What prompted Mahler in 1889 to insert into the First an older piece that in 1887 he had considered to be sentimental? He may have decided that a serenade-like movement would fit well into the atmosphere of the first part. And the "Blumine" movement had been conceived from the beginning as a serenade, particularly the serenade that the trumpeter Werner played "in the moonlit night to the castle across the Rhine where Margareta lives"

(Steinitzer). August Beer, the critic at the Budapest premiere, also perceived the Andante to be a serenade. He wrote:

> The following serenade is an intimate, impassioned trumpet melody that alternates with a melancholic song of the oboe. We easily recognize the lovers exchanging their tender feelings in the silence of the night. The two obbligato instruments are very sensitively accompanied by the string quartet.

In a conversation with Bauer-Lechner, Mahler characterized the "sentimentally impassioned" movement as a "love-episode" (BL² 173).

Mahler also stated to Bauer-Lechner that he had removed the Andante mainly "because of too strong a similarity of the keys in neighboring movements" (BL² 169), a statement that seems puzzling if one considers that in the Hamburg autograph the "Blumine" movement is in C major. We can almost be certain that Nodnagel's criticism contributed to Mahler's decision to take the movement out. It is also possible that he eliminated the movement so as not to violate the norm of the four-movement symphony, since after withdrawing the program and the piece he allowed the Symphony to be performed in Berlin as if it were "absolute music." One must finally consider that Mahler was probably disturbed by the flavor of salon-music that the piece contains. Whatever the reason, Mahler's decision is evidence of his sure sense of quality; the "Blumine" movement does not come up to the standard of the other movements.

Mit vollen Segeln ("Under Full Sail")

In the Hamburg autograph, this movement of the First Symphony (originally the third movement) is marked Scherzo. Kräftig bewegt! (Langsames Walzertempo) (Scherzo. Strongly moving! [Slow waltz tempo]). In the first edition Mahler did without the word Scherzo and contented himself by merely marking Kräftig bewegt—rightly so, because the movement is a mixture of ländler [a dance] and waltz. Four different dance types follow one another. The main movement combines a variation of the leisurely ländler (for which the shouts of "Hurrah!" at the beginning are characteristic) with the waltz; the trio, however, combines a slow ländler with a Valse.²⁹ Main movement and trio are not only different in character but also in tempo: for the main movement the markings ♩. = 66 are provided; for the trio, however, ♩. = 54. Although the main movement shares a number of rhythms and turns with the early lied Hans und Grete (1880), it is indeed a completely new composition.³⁰

It hardly needs mentioning that the movement is conceived as a dance scene. August Beer characterized it quite precisely when he wrote:

> The third movement takes us to the village pub. It has the title Scherzo but is an honest-to-goodness peasant dance. The piece is full of healthy

realism taken from everyday life, with purring, buzzing basses, shrieking violins, and squeaking clarinets, to which the peasants dance their "stomper." The trio is more refined, a slow waltz in the idealized style of Volkmann.

The movement shows peculiarities of technique and style several of which recur in later dance scenes by Mahler. The Mahler-like aspects of this prototypical movement are manifested above all in the preference for broad harmonic areas, ostinato rhythms and motifs, as well as in harmonic harshness and some very unrefined gestures. He also makes use of the device of parenthesis (insertion). For example, the ostinato rhythms $\frac{3}{4}$♩ ♩ | ♩ ♩ ♩ and $\frac{3}{4}$♪♪♪♪♪♪ | ♩. prove to be the primary rhythms of the outer sections. (The latter rhythm also plays an important part in the Scherzo of the Fourth Symphony.) The violins and violas persist (mm. 44–51) in the ostinato motif:

In the middle section of the main movement, broad harmonic areas develop: E major (mm. 44–51), D major (mm. 52–59), C-sharp major/C-sharp minor (mm. 60–107). In measures 47, 49, and 51 the tonic and the dominant clash; in measures 97–103 C-sharp major is coupled with F minor or B-flat minor in a bitonal manner. Mahler himself marked the passage at No. 8 "wild." Finally, in the middle of the trio (mm. 229–236) we find an insertion from the main movement: *Etwas frischer* (A little more brisk). Mahler later applied his unique "parenthetical" method even more cleverly in the trio of the third movement in the Seventh Symphony.

Todtenmarsch in Callots Manier ("Death March in Callot's Manner"): Mahler's "Heart-rending, Tragic Irony"

> For a few moments in eternity poetry has put on the mask of irony in order for her pain-grieved face not to be seen.
>
> Robert Schumann (1835)[31]

The chief characteristic of the slow movement of the First Symphony may be seen in its changes in mood from one extreme to the other. The movement that begins as an eerie death march, with ostinato timpani and tam-tam beats, soon becomes sentimental (No. 5), then turns trivial and merry (No. 6), and still later expresses an elegiac mood (mm. 63). Such changes from one mood to a contrasting one were part of the artistic program that Mahler described in his letter to Gisela Tolnay-Witt (GMB[2] 107). The ambivalence of moods in the *Todtenmarsch* was a novelty that put

Mahler's contemporaries to the test, even if one takes into consideration that the grotesque had been found in music ever since the Finale of Berlioz's *Symphonie fantastique.*

Mahler did not think it necessary to prepare the listeners of the Budapest premiere for the uniqueness of his funeral march. Yet marking the movement *A la pompes funèbres* was too vague. Surprisingly, August Beer more or less figured out Mahler's intentions or else, as is entirely possible, Mahler gave him some information before the performance. Beer wrote:

> The following funeral march snatches the listener suddenly out of the idyllic spring atmosphere that the author captured so well. In addition, the underlying parodistic tone of the first two movements strikes us as quite strange. The death march begins with the well-known song, reproduced faithfully note for note, "Brother Martin, Are You Sleeping," a humorous round sung in Germany by male choirs and young men in pubs in a jocular, chanting manner. The second section, which has a Hungarian flavor, unmistakably resembles in theme and harmony a number from Schubert's *Moments musicaux*; here, too, the parodistic tone is unmistakable in the ironic accents of the violins. Only in the trio, with its lovely, gentle, comforting cantilena, do we find the true character of a funeral rite.

After the premiere in Budapest, Mahler seems to have acknowledged the fact that the piece needed an explanation because he provided more extensive commentary for the Hamburg performance. At that time he admitted receiving inspiration for the piece through the parodistic painting *Des Jägers Leichenbegängnis* (most likely the woodcut by Moritz von Schwind[32]), and he explicitly pointed out the ambivalent character of the composition, which he wanted understood "as an expression of a sometimes ironic and happy and sometimes eerie and brooding mood." Ferdinand Pfohl reports, by the way, that the title of the movement *Todtenmarsch in Callots Manier* goes back to him.[33] He had felt the music was "strange, grotesque, and bizarre" and had pointed out to Mahler the *Fantasiestücke in Callots Manier* (*Fantastic Pieces in Callot's Manner*) by E. T. A. Hoffmann.

After the Weimar premiere, Mahler refused to provide programmatic commentary for the movement. He introduced it to the audience of the Berlin performance on 16 March with the laconic title *Alla marcia funèbre.*[34] That made everything even worse because no one expected a grotesque, absurd death march. It was to be expected that the movement would be misunderstood, and Mahler had to reconcile himself to that. But in 1901, when Ludwig Schiedermair[35] thought that the movement was flowing along happily and boisterously, Mahler lost his patience and wrote to Bernhard Schuster:

> What [Schiedermair] wrote about my First Symphony is just as mindless as the jokes of the Berlin critics. Just to give you an example: the third movement, which he finds to be so boisterous, is heart-rending, tragic irony and is to be understood as exposition and preparation for the

sudden outburst in the final movement of despair of a deeply wounded and broken heart.[36]

Mahler had expressed himself similarly a few years before in the well-known letter of 20 March 1896 to Max Marschalk (GMB[2] 147):

It is true that I received the external inspiration for the third movement from the well-known children's painting (*Des Jägers Leichenbegängis*). But at this point the scene in question is irrelevant. Only the mood matters, and out of it—abruptly, like lightning out of a dark cloud—leaps the fourth movement. It is simply the outcry of a deeply wounded heart preceded by that very eerie, ironic, and brooding sultriness of the death march. It is ironic in the sense of Aristotle's *eironeia*.

It is possible that the reference to Aristotle was intended consciously to distinguish Mahler's meaning from the Socratic concept of irony.[37]

The presence of tragic and trivial happiness is without doubt an important characteristic of the *Todtenmarsch*. It is also a strange phenomenon for which Mahler himself delivered a plausible, psychological explanation. In the course of a psychoanalytic conversation he had in Leyden with Sigmund Freud in August 1910, he suddenly said that he understood why his music at the most noble points, especially those inspired by the deepest emotions, never could attain the perfection strived for because some kind of vulgar melody would interfere and spoil everything. According to Freud,

Mahler's father treated his wife very badly, and when Mahler was still a small boy an especially embarrassing scene had taken place between them. It became unbearable for the little one, and he ran away from home. But just at that moment the well-known Viennese song *Ach du lieber Augustin* ["Oh, you dearest Augustin"] rang out from a hurdy-gurdy. Mahler thought that from this moment on, deep tragedy and superficial entertainment were tied together indissolubly in his soul and that one mood was inevitably tied to the other.[38]

In November 1900, Mahler made extremely informative remarks about the uniqueness of *Todtenmarsch* in a conversation with Bauer-Lechner:

On the surface one might imagine this scenario: A funeral procession passes by our hero, and the misery, the whole distress of the world, with its cutting contrasts and horrible irony, grasps him. The funeral march of "Brother Martin" one has to imagine as being played in a dull manner by a band of very bad musicians, as they usually follow such funeral processions. The roughness, gaiety, and banality of this world then appears in the sounds of some interfering Bohemian musicians, heard at the same time as the terribly painful lamentation of the hero. It has a shocking effect in its sharp irony and inconsiderate polyphony, especially when we see the procession returning from the funeral (after the beautiful middle section), and the funeral band starts to play the usual happy tune (which pierces here to the bone) (BL[2] 174).

Todtenmarsch in Callots Manier has been discussed innumerable times and has been variously analyzed.[39] Nevertheless, new insights can be gained, especially if one seeks to isolate the factors to which the uniqueness of the movement can be attributed. In this context, four factors deserve emphasis: the skill with which Mahler knew how to join heterogeneous elements without giving the impression of a break, the novelty of the instrumentation, the skillful creation of a climax, and the effective counterpoint. We will consider these four aspects in more detail.

In the first part of the *Todtenmarsch* the strange, gloomy canon (mm. 1–38) and the "happy tune" marked "with parody" (mm. 45–49) form an extremely strong contrast.[40] Mahler bridges this with the section in which the oboes perform a rocking melody in thirds and sixths and the trumpets perform an expressive, contracting melody (mm. 39–44). At the same time, the passages for two trumpets connects the music of this section with the music of the next, which is meant to be a parody. The section that is kept expressive and elegiac (mm. 63–70)—in Mahler's interpretation, "the terribly painful lament of the hero"—intervenes in a similar way between the varied repetition of the parody section (mm. 57–60) and the hint of the round's return (mm. 70–81).

When Natalie Bauer-Lechner once spoke of the "unbelievable aural impact" the *Todtenmarsch* had on her, Mahler pointed to the orchestration, saying that the instruments are "disguised and muffled," walking around like strange apparitions; everything should sound "dull and blunt, like shadows passing us." He added that "in the round, the new entrance always is distinct, in a surprising timbre, drawing attention to itself. To orchestrate this was no mean task—to write what affects you today in that odd and scary manner" (BL[2] 175). If one examines the entries of the round more closely, one finds that they are often introduced by unexpected tone colors: double-bass solo in a high register (m. 3); muted cellos (m. 11); bass tuba (m. 15); first bassoon and first clarinet (m. 17); muted violas (m. 19); first horn (m. 21); four flutes (m. 23); English horn, two clarinets, and bass clarinet (m. 25); violas and cellos an octave apart (m. 27); and four muted horns and harp (m. 29). Added to this are the entrances of the characteristic counterpoint in the first oboe (m. 19) and in the first oboe and E-flat clarinet (m. 29), an instrument for which Mahler had a special preference and which he does not use until this movement.[41] As the *Todtenmarsch* continues, there are numerous surprising timbre combinations. The combination of oboes and trumpets at No. 5, for instance, is especially striking. The trite sound effect at No. 6 results not only from the trivial motifs of the woodwinds and the quite primitive accompaniment of the strings playing *col legno*[42], but also from including Turkish cymbals and bass drum.[43]

As the basis for the lyric middle section of the movement, Mahler chose the last stanza from the last selection of *Lieder eines fahrenden Gesellen,* "Die zwei blauen Augen von meinem Schatz" ("The Two Blue Eyes of My Beloved"). This borrowing is musically fortunate and semantically appropriate. The song stanza tells about the tranquility and forgetfulness that the tired traveler found under the linden tree; likewise the rhythms at the end of the *Todtenmarsch* suggest that the resting place under the linden tree is a gravesite. This also makes it reasonable that the last part of the symphonic movement represents a varied and intensified recapitulation of the first. The canon melody enters in E-flat minor (No. 13) rather than in D minor as it did in the beginning, and it is not until No. 16 that it repeats in D minor. It is not impossible that Mahler observed in the "Dies irae" of Hector Berlioz's *Requiem* how effective such a transposition can be. Berlioz first presents the "Dies irae" melody in A minor; a little later (at "Quantus tremor est futurus") he transposes it to B-flat minor!

Speaking of this movement, Theodor W. Adorno noted that the "pointed" oboe melody is set against the round (No. 3) and considered it to be the first example of typical Mahler counterpoint.[44] The two-voice trumpet melody (mm. 124–131) that serves as counterpoint to the melody of the round (here in E-flat minor) is no less characteristic and is dealt with later in an extremely interesting manner. At No. 16 the trumpet melody returns (now in D minor) in contrapuntal interweaving with the round melody. The section marked *plötzlich viel schneller* (suddenly much faster) sounds like a Czardas and is also set for two voices in the high woodwinds, to be played *äußerst rhythmisch* (very rhythmically):

The contrast between the three melodies, arranged here in layers, is extreme. The passage is noteworthy not only for its technique but even more so for its implied meaning. In the first part of the movement, the gloomy canon alternated with the happy tune; now they are heard simultaneously to illustrate how the tragic and the trivial coexist in the world. The procedure reminds one of a passage in the Finale of Bruckner's Third Symphony, where a chorale and a polka are heard at the same time—a passage that Bruckner himself interpreted as a union of contrasts ("happiness and distress of the world").[45] Mahler knew Bruckner's symphony and may have been influenced by it, but the boldness of his arrangement surpasses Bruckner by far.

The close proximity of the tragic and the trite, and the awareness that the trivial world is indifferent to the misery of the individual are central themes, not only of the *Todtenmarsch in Callots Manier* but also of other Mahler compositions. This is how the drama of the *Hochzeitsstück* (from the third part of *Das klagende Lied*) develops out of the polarity of contrast between the pompous world of the castle and the inner drama.[46] And in the first of the *Lieder eines fahrenden Gesellen,* "Wenn mein Schatz Hochzeit macht" ("When My Beloved Has Her Wedding"), the constant change of mood coupled with a change of tempo describes a similar emotional state: the trivial music of woodwinds, timpani, triangle and harp illustrates the "happy" wedding music in a faster tempo, while the "sad" melody of the soloist, accompanied by strings at a slower tempo, in turn represents the lonely one.

Dall' Inferno al Paradiso

Richard Strauss heard Mahler's First Symphony in Weimar and probably received a strong impression from it. In a letter to Mahler, though, he expressed concern regarding a certain passage and asked the composer for clarification. Unfortunately this letter so far has not been found, but from Mahler's response it is obvious that Strauss's criticism referred to a passage in the Finale. On 19 July 1894, Mahler wrote to Strauss:

> I cannot agree with you about this matter. That you would want this passage to be the conclusion and summary of everything only shows me that I have completely failed to express myself clearly—and that, of course, would be bad enough. If it does not bore you, I will return to this matter in Bayreuth and explain to you what I think about it. Just one thing today: at that specific passage, a solution only *seems* to be offered (the whole thing being, in the true sense of the word, a fallacy) and before a true victory can be found after such a battle, the whole situation must be turned around. My intention was simply to represent a battle in which victory is always farthest away at the exact moment when the warrior believes himself to be closest to it. This is the character of every spiritual battle, since it is not so easy to become or to be a hero.[47]

This statement is crucial to a deeper understanding of the Finale, but its true meaning can be recognized only if Mahler's other comments are taken into account. On 16 March 1896 in a conversation with Bauer-Lechner, Mahler emphasized his opinion that the ultimate goal of art was to be "liberated from and to rise above sorrow," and he added,

> this [liberation] is not missing in my First, but it does not attain victory until the death of my struggling Titan who, as often as he lifts his head above the billows of life, is again and again dealt a blow by fate and sinks down anew (BL² 46).

In November 1900, Mahler expressed himself even more clearly, again in a conversation with Bauer-Lechner:

> The last movement, which follows the preceding one without a break, begins with a horrible outcry. Our hero is completely abandoned, engaged in a most dreadful battle with all the sorrow of this world. Time and again he—and the victorious motif with him—is dealt a blow by fate whenever he rises above it and seems to get hold of it, and only in death, when he has become victorious over himself, does he gain victory. Then the wonderful allusion to his youth rings out once again with the theme of the first movement. (Glorious Victory Chorale!) (BL² 174f.)

At the heart of Mahler's statements are the key words *battle, fate, death, victory, overcoming the self.* All these ideas may be derived from programmatic symphonic music. Yet one cannot dismiss them as being commonplace, since they express quite precise musical situations. The battle about which Mahler speaks is a conflict described dramatically through music, and the victorious motif he refers to (in which earthly concerns are overcome or risen above) can be clearly identified. Furthermore, the programmatic title of the movement, *Dall' Inferno al Paradiso,* is by no means arbitrary. A semantic analysis showed that Mahler symbolized inferno and paradiso with musical motifs borrowed from Liszt's *Dante Symphony* and Wagner's *Parsifal.* A more detailed investigation shows that not only the motivic, thematic, and mental concepts of the movement are based on a program, but also many aspects of layout and texture.

Exposition

Mm.		
	1–54	Introduction in F minor (*Stürmisch bewegt*) [Stormily moving]: Inferno
	55–142	First complex of themes in F minor (*Energisch*) [Energetic]: Inferno
	143–166	Sequences of swelling brass sounds (*Mit großer Wildheit*) [With great ferocity]: Inferno
	167–174	Transition
	175–237	Secondary section in D-flat major (*Sehr' gesangvoll*) [Very songlike]
	238–253	Epilogue in D-flat major (*Langsam*) [Slowly]: Recall of the slow introduction of the main section and inferno motif

Development

254–289 First part in G minor (As at the beginning)
290–316 First statement of the "victorious" motif in C major, *pianissimo*
317–369 Second part in C minor
370–427 Second entrance of the "victorious" motif (*Pesante*) (Modulation from C major to D major) and Chorale theme in D major (Paradiso)

428–457 Recall of motif of the main section (very slow); Mahler, "*wundervoller Anklang an die Jugend des Helden*" ["wonderful allusion to the hero's youth"]

Recapitulation

458–532 Secondary section with transition in F major
533–573 Main theme in F minor (*Tempo I*): the Inferno image now has been moved to the distance (*ppp*)
574–622 Intensification of material from the main section
623–695 *Höchste Kraft* (Utmost strength): breakthrough, third occurrence of the "victorious" motif and Chorale theme in D major (Paradiso)
696–731   Coda

If the standards of traditional sonata form are used as a basis for analyzing this movement, numerous deviations are found. Most obvious is that according to the traditional rules of composition, the beginning of a sonata movement should be in the same key (or in a related key) as the ending; Mahler's Finale begins in F minor and ends in D major. This key relationship expresses a programmatic intention: F minor is the key of the inferno, the contrasting D major characterizes the paradiso. The dynamics of the movement represent the repeated efforts to overcome the level of the inferno and to arrive in the sphere of the paradiso.

A comparison with Franz Liszt's *Dante Symphony* of 1856 (which consists of the movements "Inferno" and "Purgatorio," as well as a "Magnificat" that stands for the "Paradiso") suggests itself and is essential to recognizing Mahler's intentions. To be sure, Mahler's poetic and musical execution of the idea is quite different from Liszt's; at the same time, he borrowed some of Liszt's motivic symbols and probably assumed that these would be recognized as such.

Two of Mahler's most important inferno symbols stem from Liszt: the concise chromatic triplet motifs (hereafter referred to as inferno triplets),

Mm. 21–24

and a motif that emerges at the beginning of the development:

Mm. 254–261

Following the example of Liszt, whom he outdid greatly, Mahler created the frightening sequences of swelling brass (No. 12: *very wild*) that enter after the first complex of themes. From Liszt's world of musical symbols he also borrowed the aural symbol of the Cross, which was originally a Gregorian phrase that appears here in two versions: a minor version (with minor second and major third) and a major version (with major second and major third). In the world of the inferno, the symbol of the Cross always appears in the minor version.

Using the building blocks mentioned earlier and some additional elements, Mahler constructs the movement's introduction (mm. 1–54) in the following manner:

Mm. 1–5   Dissonance, interpreted by Mahler as *Aufschrei eines im Tiefsten verwundeten Herzens* (Outcry of a deeply wounded heart) (GMB² 147)
    6–8   The Cross symbol in the minor version
   8–18   Inferno triplets
 19–21   Anticipation of a motif from the main theme
 21–24   Inferno triplets
 25–32   Wail (cf. *Das klagende Lied,* No. 81)
 32–39   Inferno triplets
 39–54   Fourfold Cross motif in the minor version

The sphere of the paradiso is represented by a chorale in D major with a number of musical lines. Mahler gained the first line by modifying the nature theme of the main section.

Nature theme, first movement, mm. 18–21

Chorale theme (first line), Finale, mm. 388–391

The analysis of the movement clearly reveals that Mahler assigned a special role to the Cross symbol. Its task is to break through the world of the inferno and to lead to the sphere of the paradiso. Thus in the exposition of the movement and even in the first part of the development, the Cross symbol always appears in the minor version. It is first performed in the major version at the end of the first development section, measures 296–304 (No. 26), by the first trumpet in C major—and, you will note, *pianissimo*. At the same time, it is combined with a second motif to form a characteristic theme:

A closer look reveals (not surprisingly) that this theme is nothing but a rhythmic variation of the Grail theme from Wagner's *Parsifal,* which is shaped from Liszt's Cross symbol and the Dresden Amen. Evidently Mahler had this theme in mind when he talked to Natalie Bauer-Lechner about the "victorious" ("overcoming" and "rising above earthly concerns") motif.

According to Bernd Sponheuer, the first part of the development is not to be understood as a result of intensification, but rather as something "quite surprising, somewhat inorganic and sudden."[48] One does gain this impression if one looks at Mahler's music in purely formal–esthetic terms. The surprise effect of this passage and the very striking dynamic (*pianissimo*), however, are due to a programmatic intention: Mahler's remark to Strauss about victory always being farthest away from the warrior when he thinks it is closest, refers to this.

The "victorious" motif is heard a second time in measures 370–375. This time, however, it is played *pesante* and *fortissimo* and begins in C major and closes in D major, a special feature that is also programmatically motivated. The rather forced modulation symbolizes that now, with the move to D major, the sphere of the paradiso has been reached (at No. 35 the horns indeed perform the chorale). In the summer of 1893, Mahler rather unmistakably explained the passage in this spirit in a statement to Bauer-Lechner:

> Maybe this was even more obvious in my First Symphony, at a transition that gave me so much trouble. There the concern was to gain a triumphant, lasting victory, after the music, having expressed short rays of hope, would always fall back into deepest despair. After a long search, it became obvious to me that I had to modulate from one key to the next higher one—from C major to D major, the tonic of the piece. One could have accomplished this easily by using the half-step in between, moving up from C to C-sharp and then to D, but everyone would have known it to be the next step. Instead, my D chord, had to sound as if it had fallen

from heaven, as if it had come from another world. Thus I found the transition by way of a very free and bold modulation that for the longest time I did not want to use. And if there is anything great about the whole symphony, then it is this passage which, I am convinced, has no equal (BL^2 27).

The slow section (mm. 428–457) inserted between development and recapitulation is also programmatically motivated. Here Mahler flashes back to the main movement and brings back the most important motifs. We hear sounds reminiscent of the nature theme (the dynamic level never leaves the sphere of *piano* and *pianissimo*), including the awakening fanfares and the singing of the birds (quail call, cuckoo call, Tirili motif). We are also reminded of the chromatic bass-step motif and of the first motif of the main theme (mm. 453–454). In between we hear the inferno triplets (mm. 433–434) like shadowy images, and a reminiscence of the secondary theme of the Finale (mm. 443–447). This whole section, a good example of music with a far-away sound, has an unreal quality and was interpreted by Mahler as a remembrance of the hero's youth.

The form of the recapitulation is somewhat irregular. Mahler exchanges the two theme complexes (the secondary theme here precedes the main theme), and the varied main theme is now performed in triple *piano*. The eerie-sounding part obviously means that the inferno has now receded into the distance, and the "victorious" motif and the triumphant chorale follow the intensified section and the final breakthrough at No. 52.

Sketches for the first movement of the Second Symphony (*Todtenfeier*)
Austrian National Library, Music Collection, Mus. Hs. 4364 II, fol. 6v
First Publication
Programmatic cue word *Meeresstille*: an allusion to the Goethe poem of the same
name, specifically to the lines
Todesstille fürchterlich! / In der ungeheuren Weite/ Reget keine Welle sich
(Deathly silence! / In the dreadful vastness/ not a wave is moving)

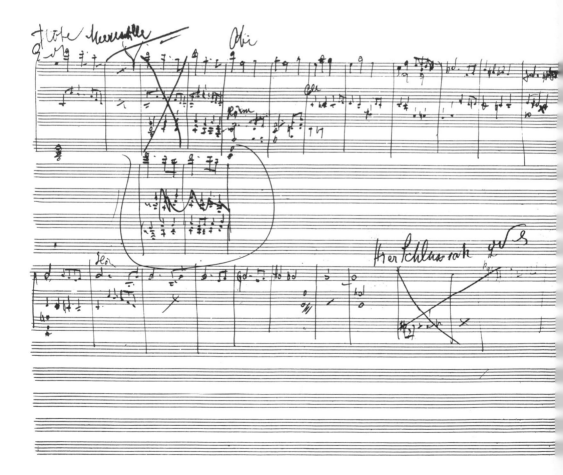

The Second Symphony

Everything sounds as if it is coming from another world.   GMB² 119

Origin

Mahler composed many of his symphonies in two-year cycles. According to a report by his wife, he had to plan his work in this way. "He always created a work within the two months of summer and drafted the short score. During the two summer months of the following year, he would complete the score and the orchestration" (AMML 34). He had adopted this practice when he began work on the Third Symphony; it did not apply to his work on the Second Symphony, which extended over a period of seven years, from 1888 to 1894. The Second is an exception in other ways as well. In the five-movement form in which we know it, the Symphony gives the impression of remarkable unity. The movements seem to fit wonderfully together in terms of both music and moods. Therefore, it is all the more surprising to learn that several movements were conceived independently of each other.

The beginnings of the Symphony most likely date back to January 1888. Natalie Bauer-Lechner, who is an invaluable source of information about Mahler's sensitivity and power of imagination, mentions that Mahler, while writing the "Death March" in the first movement of the Second Symphony, saw himself "dead, laid out in state, beneath wreaths and flowers" (BL² 50). The flowers he had received at the performance of *Die drei Pintos* were still in his room. Eventually his landlady, Mrs. Weber, took all the flowers away (BL² 50). Since the premiere of *Die drei Pintos* took place in Leipzig on 20 January 1888, Mahler must have worked on the first movement shortly thereafter. Work must have moved along quite well because on 8 August 1888 he had already completed the sketch of the full score of this movement (today in the collection of the Jewish National and University Library in Jerusalem).[1] He completed his final copy a month later in Prague, 10 September 1888.

The manuscript (previously in the collection of the Willem Mengelberg Foundation in Amsterdam) bears on the title page the heading *Todtenfeier* ("Funeral Rites"). Underneath is the crossed-out marking *Symphony in C Minor* and the subtitle "Movement I" (not crossed out). Whether Mahler added the word *Todtenfeier* later cannot be determined.

While in Leipzig (between 20 January and 17 May 1888) Mahler also sketched the two themes of the movement that would later become the Andante moderato of the Second. In the following years he regretted not having developed this sketch. He said to Natalie Bauer-Lechner:

> I always felt sorry (and with good reason, as I now can see) about those two little pieces of paper on which they [the themes of the Andante] were written when I was still in Leipzig and conducted the *Pintos* there (BL^2 25).

It is important to note that he did not originally intend to add the Andante to the first movement (BL^2 133).

After completing the *Todtenfeier,* Mahler evidently dismissed the idea of extending the movement into a symphony by composing further movements. In an October 1891 letter to Dr. Ludwig Strecker, head of the publishing house B. Schott's Söhne in Mainz, he called the *Todtenfeier* a "symphonic poem" (GMB^2 92).[2] At the time he also busied himself with composing the songs from *Des Knaben Wunderhorn*. Between 1888 and 1892, a number of songs for piano or orchestra were written for this collection.

In 1893 Mahler spent his summer vacation in Steinbach at the Attersee. Here he resumed work on the Symphony and on the *Wunderhorn* cycle, completing on 8 July the piano version of *Des Antonius von Padua Fischpredigt*. The score of *Urlicht* ("Primeval Light") was finished on 19 July, and the orchestra version of *Fischpredigt* was finished on the first of August. He completed the sketch of the full score of the Scherzo on 16 July and the Andante on 30 July.[3] These dates reveal an astonishing productivity. According to Bauer-Lechner, he completed the Andante in seven days (BL^2 25), and the Scherzo seems to have been completed in an equally short period. This is remarkable, even though Mahler based the main parts of the Scherzo on the music of *Fischpredigt*. One must not forget that the trio is completely new, and the thematic material of *Fischpredigt* is developed in several ways. Therefore Natalie Bauer-Lechner was rightfully surprised by the procedure that Mahler himself tried to explain with his theory of unconscious creativity (BL^2 27). Incidentally, the musical setting of *Urlicht* was originally conceived for voice and piano—we still do not know exactly when. Mahler did not initially intend to bring the song into the Symphony.[4]

In the winter of 1893–1894, Mahler revealed to his friend Josef B. Foerster that he had started a new symphony:[5]

> The first movement you know; it is my *Todtenfeier*. Three movements are already completed. The second is a slow movement, the third a very

lively scherzo. As soon as you come to visit me, you will get to hear those movements.

Mahler and Foerster agreed that after the powerful first movement it would be difficult to compose a finale of equal rank.

During the memorial service for Hans von Bülow on 29 March 1894 in Hamburg, Mahler made the final decision to conclude the Second with a choral finale. In the famous letter to Dr. Arthur Seidl of 17 February 1897, he described the exact circumstances:

> The way in which I received the inspiration for this work is very typical for the nature of artistic creativity. For a long time I had been pondering the idea of including a choir in the last movement. Only the fear that this might be considered an overt imitation of Beethoven made me hesitate again and again! When Bülow died, I attended his funeral. The mood I was in as I sat there thinking of the deceased was very much in the spirit of the work I had on my mind at that time. Then, from the organ loft, the choir sang Klopstock's chorale *Resurrection*! This hit me like lightning, and everything appeared clearly and distinctly before me! Every creative artist waits for that stoke of lightning; it is a kind of holy conception! (GMB[2] 200).

On the afternoon of that same day, Foerster found Mahler at work.[6] He revised *Todtenfeier*, enlarged the orchestral apparatus,[7] and made other changes and cuts. At the end of the first movement, the autograph of the complete Symphony bears the date "Sunday, 29 April 94—revised." In the following months, Mahler sketched the Finale. He reported the completion of the composition to his friends Fritz Löhr and Arnold Berliner on 29 June and in July 1894, respectively. On 10 July he wrote to Arnold Berliner from Steinbach:

> The fifth movement is grand and closes with a choral piece for which I wrote the lyrics. The sketch is completed down to the smallest detail, and I am now working out the full score. It is a bold piece of grand proportions. The final climax is colossal (GMB[2] 114).

In a letter to Richard Strauss on 19 July 1894 he states:

> In recent weeks I have completed the final movement of my Second Symphony. When you hear it you will understand why I had to do something other than correct my shed skin [meaning his First Symphony]. I have grown a new one—a better fit. In fact, my new work in relation to the one you know is like a man to a newborn baby.[8]

The Eschatological Question as Program

Gustav Mahler is one of those artists whose art and personality cannot be separated. His symphonic writing, paradoxical as this might seem, expresses his world view; it has a literary and philosophical background. His religious and philosophical thinking cannot be separated from his work. The Second Symphony, in particular, is a statement of Mahler's thoughts on the theme of death and resurrection. Those who want to understand the work more deeply must investigate its ideological presuppositions.

Mahler's thinking often centered around metaphysical and eschatological questions. All aspects of metaphysics—ontology, cosmology, religious problems, and existentialism—fascinated him. The meaning of existence and the paradox of death and dying preoccupied him to such an extent that one might speak of a metaphysical agony. In order to find solutions to metaphysical and eschatological problems, he engrossed himself in philosophy and the natural sciences.

The religious interpretation of death and the hereafter especially fascinated Mahler. Several reports testify how strongly he was haunted by thoughts concerning death.[9] As was earlier mentioned, when he composed the first movement of the Second, he saw himself "dead, laid out in state, beneath wreaths and flowers" (BL[2] 50), a vision that borders on the psychopathological. According to Ferdinand Pfohl, he always tortured himself with metaphysical riddles and found comfort in faith in the hereafter: "the hereafter was the alpha and omega of his life, his art."[10]

The program of the Second Symphony is transmitted in several versions that differ in wording and in detail but basically capture the same images, concepts, and thought patterns. A first version was recorded in January 1896 by Natalie Bauer-Lechner (BL[2] 39ff.). A second version is found in a letter from Mahler to Max Marschalk dated 26 March 1896 (GMB[2] 150). A third version was compiled by Mahler in 1901 "by request of someone in high position" (*in sehr hohem Auftrag*) for a performance in Dresden (AME 267–269). In the last two versions, the subject of the Second is formulated as an existential and eschatological question: "Why have you lived? Why have you suffered? Is all of this just a terrible joke?" (GMB[2] 150). Furthermore: "What is this life and this death? Is there a hereafter for us? Is all of this a wild dream, or has this life and this death a meaning?" (AME 267).

The history of the Symphony's origin documents that Mahler wrestled with these questions for many years. Thoughts about life after death—*Leben nach dem Tode* (Gustav Theodor Fechner)—and the Second Coming seem to have occupied him for a long time before he attended the funeral for Hans von Bülow in March 1894; Klopstock's chorale *Resurrection* fell on fertile ground. It is indeed characteristic that Mahler could not decide to base the choral finale of his symphony only on the three stanzas of the chorale he had heard in St. Michael's church.[11] Instead, he wrote six additional stanzas of his own that contain a personal, eschatological confession.

In a letter to Dr. Arthur Seidl, Mahler describes his experience with the

Finale of the Second by saying that he searched through "the whole of world literature, including the Bible, in order to find the redeeming word," and that he finally found himself forced to "express his feelings and thoughts in his own words" (GMB[2] 200). Actually, this claim is somewhat overdone because Mahler did find the "redeeming word" in the Bible. The verse that constitutes the central thought of the Second and is the culmination of the lyrics (No. 47) reads, "Die I will, so that I might live!" This idea is derived from First Corinthians 15:36: "You foolish man! What you sow does not come to life unless it dies." The fifteenth chapter of this first letter to the Corinthians in general forms the background of Mahler's lyrics.

One must concede, however, that this text combines Christian ideas with modern thought. Mahler's first stanza implies a subjective faith in the Second Coming and at the same time expresses the conviction that existence could not be meaningless (No. 39):

> *O glaube, mein Herz, es geht dir nichts verloren!*
> *Dein ist, ja dein, was du gesehnt,*
> *Was du geliebt, was du gestritten.*
> *O glaube: du wardst nicht umsonst geboren,*
> *Hast nicht umsonst gelebt, gelitten!*

> Oh believe, my heart, nothing will be lost for you!
> Yours, yes yours, is what you have longed for,
> What you have loved, what you have fought for.
> Oh believe, you were not born in vain,
> Nor have you lived or suffered in vain!

At the same time, it is typical that Mahler moves away from the strictly dogmatic view of Judgment Day. In the program for Dresden, the Day of Judgment for the world, which believers fear and which is part of the teachings of the church, appears only as a vision. In Mahler's own view of the Apocalypse there is no judgment: "There is no sinner, no righteous one, no one great—and no one small—there is no punishment and no reward! An almighty feeling of love illuminates us with blest knowledge and being" (AME 269).

The Second Symphony had a broad effect during Mahler's time. From the beginning it was considered his classic work. In considering the reasons for this, several things must be kept in mind: the purely artistic qualities of the work; the urgency of musical expression; its unique character as symphonic cantata, as oratorio and mystery of redemption; and finally, its spiritual content. In 1915, Gerhard Specht conjectured that it is precisely this spiritual content that accounts for the broad effect:

> The problems of the hereafter and immortality, for which this work provides such a redeeming and promising answer, are problems with which everyone has wrestled. What is expressed here in tones is the echo of all fear, all hope, and all doubt, which everyone carries about in the depths of his being and which is ever-present.[12]

Allegro maestoso: *Todtenfeier* ("Funeral Rites")

The autograph of the original version of the first movement bears the title "Todtenfeier." The heading seems appropriate for music that primarily has the quality of a funeral march or requiem. Nevertheless, the question remains: What does the title mean? And above all: What caused Mahler to choose this name?

In looking for an answer, one must consider that in 1887 the epic *Funeral Rites* (Dziady) by the great Polish poet Adam Mickiewicz was translated into German by Siegfried Lipiner and published by Breitkopf & Härtel in Leipzig. Lipiner was among Mahler's closest friends. Mahler was keenly interested in his work,[13] and so it is quite possible that Mahler, who was living in Leipzig in 1887, came to know the book immediately after it appeared. In any case, it is certain that Mahler appreciated Mickiewicz's *Funeral Rites*. In a letter to Bruno Walter dated December 1909, he quoted (from memory) a verse from the book: "You are not their father, you are their Czar!" (GMB[2] 372).

Was Mahler inspired by Mickiewicz's *Funeral Rites*? Is there possibly a connection between his *Todtenfeier* and Mickiewicz's epic? Mickiewicz's work consists of four independent parts, the second of which is the actual *Funeral Rites*. The name refers to an old Slavic custom honoring deceased ancestors in which the spirits of the deceased in purgatory are exorcised so that their souls will find rest. In the second part of the epos, Guslar (a priest and poet) summons the souls of the deceased who then speak about their former lives. On 26 March 1896, Mahler wrote to Max Marschalk about the first movement of the Second: "I have called the first movement *Todtenfeier*, and if you would like to know, I am interring the hero of my D Major Symphony, whose life I capture in a pure reflection from a higher vantage point" (GMB[2] 150). The Dresden program is similar: "We are standing at the coffin of a beloved person. His life, struggles, suffering, and ambition pass one last time by our spiritual eye" (AME 267). These references prove the existence of several parallels between the mood of the two works.

The first movement of the Second Symphony was rightly designated by Richard Specht, as one "of the master's freest symphonic movements."[14] Although many scholars have detected the structural plan of sonata form, opinions vary as to where the secondary section and the development begin.[15] The unusual length of the development is immediately obvious: At 212 measures, it is almost twice as long as the exposition (116 measures) or the recapitulation (117 measures).[16] But the movement shows many other peculiarities. The following outline is designed to give an idea of its structure and musical qualities:

Exposition

Mm. 1–42   First part with funeral march character in C minor
43–47   Transition
48–62   Secondary theme with lyric, pathetic character, beginning in E major and closing in E-flat minor
63–73   First theme (!)
74–96   Third complex of themes (Starting with a Cross symbol), beginning in A-flat major leading to G minor
97–116 Closing group in G minor: Funeral music over a bass ostinato with tam-tam

First Development

117–128 Introduction (connecting to the secondary theme), beginning in C major and leading to E major
129–146 Pastorale in E major (with a new motif in the English horn)
147–174 New section primarily in E minor, developing different motifs
175–207 Development of the third theme complex (at the beginning again the Cross symbol)
208–225 Variation of the secondary theme: Music from a distance (like chamber music)
226–243 March from a distance in B major
244–253 Return to the main motifs of the movement, beginning in a triple *forte* and fading away *bis zur Unhörbarkeit* [until no longer audible] (tam-tam)

Second Development

254–269 Restatement of m. 147ff., now in E-flat minor with sighing motifs (laments) of the English horn at the beginning
270–294 Anticipation of the Finale (mm. 289–313): Dies irae theme, main theme motifs, Cross symbol, Resurrection motif, Eternity motif, Dies irae motif, climax on a dissonance
295–328 Closing section with plunging motif (mm. 318–320) and again a catastrophic climax

Recapitulation

329–356 First part in C minor
357–361 Transition
362–391 Secondary theme and Pastorale in E major

Coda

392–438 Synthesis of closing group and portions of the first part, beginning with tam-tam: funeral march/funeral music[17]
439–445 Major-minor seal, followed by a plunging motif

The key relationships in the exposition reveal quite a bold plan for which parallels can be found only in Bruckner's symphonies:[18] the first part is in C minor, the secondary theme begins in E major and ends in E-flat minor, the third theme complex begins in A-flat major and leads to G minor, the closing group is in G minor. Mahler devised a four- or five-key plan and each section has a distinct character that contrasts strongly from one section to another. The first part, as Ernst Otto Nodnagel recognized, is a "complete, regular funeral march of 42 measures."[19] After the lyric, pathetic secondary theme that brightens up at the beginning, there follows, completely against the rules, another entry of the first theme. A mysterious, festive A-flat section then introduces the third theme complex, the material of which is associated with the main section. The final group, built upon a bass ostinato, represents funeral music with tam-tam. The A-flat major passage (mm. 74–78) is semantically important because it starts out with Liszt's "tonic symbol of the Cross," a plagally harmonized (I–IV–I^6) figure of the trumpet:[20]

The development consists of two sections of 137 and 75 measures. They are so different from one another that Richard Specht[21] was the first one to speak of two developments.[22] The sections both develop the material of the exposition by combining it in new ways and layers, yet they present something altogether new. They present many new elements and more importantly, they form new musical characteristics. Instructive in this regard, first of all, is the Pastorale in E major with sustained fifths in the bass (mm. 129–146), which opens up a completely new realm of expression. In the recapitulation, it is combined with the secondary theme (mm. 362–391). The section developed in measures 208–225 could with some justification be considered a variation of the secondary theme.[23] Mahler, however, gives it the distinctive quality of "music from a distance," for which he had a special love. Finally, there is no precedent in the exposition for the marchlike section in a bright B major (mm. 226–243).

Bearing in mind the form of these sections, one can better understand Mahler's critique of the classic development technique. He stated to Josef B. Foerster in Hamburg:

Mozart still wrote developments. He took his themes and mixed them masterfully. But we find nothing of that kind in Beethoven; he always had something specific to say. The fact that Mendelssohn and Schumann resumed writing developments is their own business. They surely missed the mark.[24]

   Mahler's dramatic approach to the development is not altogether without
a model. He could have studied Bruckner's technique of beginning the
development very quietly (mm. 117–128). Also from Bruckner he may have
learned to place the greatest climax of a movement at the end of the
development.
   Detailed sketches of the first movement of the Second Symphony have
been preserved. They allow deep insights into Mahler's compositional
process.[25] Most of the many cues are technical terms, such as Main theme,
Song, Final section, Middle section, Return, and Development.[26] We also
come across several other revealing remarks which disclose that Mahler by
no means always thought in musical categories. Thus he designated the
pedal-point passage (mm. 80–86) specifically as "dramatic."[27] Even more
interesting is the heading *Meeresstille* (calm of the sea), which appears in the
sketches at three places.[28] On folio 6v of the second fascicle it is found next
to the remark "E major flute" and refers to the following phrase (which corresponds to measures 370–377 of the final version):

   What is the meaning of the phrase *calm of the sea* in a composition that
the composer himself named *Todtenfeier*? It may be an allusion to Goethe's
Meeresstille poem (Mahler knew Goethe's works thoroughly). This assumption gains validity if one bears in mind that the key verses of Goethe's poem
read:

> *Todesstille fürchterlich!*
> *In der ungeheuren Weite*
> *Reget keine Welle sich.*
>
> Terrible silence of death!
> In the dreadful vastness
> Not a wave is moving.

Thus it is definitely possible that Mahler used the word *Meeresstille* as a
metaphor for *Todesstille* ("Silence of death") and wanted to express this idea
musically with the pastorale (mm. 129–146 and 370–391), which never
leaves the sphere of *piano* and *pianissimo*. An argument for this hypothesis
is also to be gained from the fact that in *Das himmlische Leben* he gave features of a pastorale to the *musica coelestis* of paradise.[29]
   Measures 270–294 of the development are of paramount relevance to the
interpretation of the movement. Its themes and motifs can be programmatically explained, since they reappear with minor differences in the Finale
(mm. 289–313). They prove that Mahler did not think of Judgment Day and
the Resurrection for the first time when conceiving the Finale in 1894; he had
already considered these topics in 1888 when he was composing *Todtenfeier*.

Mm. 270–277

Dies irae

Mm. 282–290

Cross motif   Resurrection motif

Eternity motif   Dies irae   Dies irae

Mahler seems to have derived the first line of his Resurrection Chorale of 1894 from two of the motifs mentioned. For comparison:

First movement, mm. 282–285

Finale, mm. 472–475

From all this we can establish with certainty that Mahler's composition contains numerous programmatic elements that justify its title. Highly dramatic sections including the funeral march, requiem, and lament alternate with pastoral, quiet, and seemingly unreal episodes. One gets the impression that in *Todtenfeier* Mahler wanted to express artistically all perceptions of death developed by mankind, including those that hint at the Final Judgment and Resurrection.

Andante moderato

To say that the first and second movements of the Second Symphony form an extraordinarily strong contrast to each other would not be an exaggeration. While the first movement is boldly conceived and of a basically dark character, the Andante moderato conveys an idyllic feeling in its main sections. Here and there it is pleasant and dancelike, and it remains within the usual bounds. The reactions of some of Mahler's contemporaries to these two movements are therefore understandable. When Hans von Bülow first heard *Todtenfeier* in winter 1891, he fell "into a nervous fright" and stated that *Tristan* was a Haydn symphony compared to this piece.[30] Claude Debussy, Paul Dukas, and Gabriel Pierné, on the other hand, felt that the Andante moderato was definitely too tame. When they heard the Second during April 1910 in Paris, they expressed their disapproval in the middle of the second movement by getting up and leaving, a gesture that hurt Mahler deeply (AME 213). In spite of this, the Andante moderato is anything but a completely conventional piece. Whoever listens carefully can perceive the typical Mahler sound, and an analysis reveals methods distinctive to Mahler.

The movement is divided into five sections that are joined according to the following scheme:

Mm.	1–38	Part A	Andante moderato. *Sehr gemächlich* (Very leisurely). *Grazioso* in A-flat major
	39–85	Part B	*Nicht eilen* (Not hurrying). Very leisurely in G-sharp minor
	86–132	Part A¹	Tempo I in A-flat major
	133–209	Part B¹	*Energisch bewegt* (Energetically moving) in G-sharp minor
	210–285	Part A²	Tempo I in A-flat major
	286–299	Coda	In A-flat major

The music of the first two sections is fully varied or developed in the three sections that follow, so Mahler could rightly speak of "variations." In a conversation with Bauer-Lechner, he pointed out Brahms's strict variation style, considering his own variations to be "ornamentations, paraphrases, and entwinements, rather than a subtle following—and working—through of the same cycle of notes" (BL² 153).

The five sections elicit interesting observations. The first section represents a kind of leisurely ländler, a dance that Mahler especially enjoyed. The second part is structured like a scherzo; the strings develop a staccato theme that is always played *più pianissimo*. Mahler borrowed it from the Scherzo of Beethoven's Ninth.[31] Quite ingeniously, the mysterious, scherzolike music of the strings forms a kind of sound carpet above which the woodwinds (beginning at No. 4) play songlike (*dolce, espressivo*) and legato melodic phrases. Even if the building blocks of this music were formed by Beethoven, and perhaps also by Schubert,[32] Mahler uses them to build something completely new for which there are no prototypes.

In the third section, the art with which Mahler creates the songlike countermelody of the cellos (*molto espressivo*) against the ländler-like melody of the violins is also remarkable. The cello melody seems to have been conceived completely independently from the primary melody; the term *double theme* may certainly be applied.

The music of the fourth section forms the climax of the movement. Mahler composed it in a dynamic and agogic manner, far removed from the idyllic mood of the beginning. The inner tension of the music is maintained even when the outward dynamic level occasionally moves from *fortissimo* to *pianissimo*. The ostinato beats of the timpani (m. 183ff.) create an eerie effect. It is no wonder that after this climax the ländler, performed *pizzicato* and *più pianissimo* by the strings at the beginning of the fifth section, seems practically shadowlike.

Mahler was fully aware of the extremely strong contrast between the first two movements of the Second (he called it a "discrepancy"), and therefore indicated a break "of at least five minutes" after the first movement. In a letter to Professor Julius Buths dated 25 March 1903, he described the Andante as an intermezzo and gave it a programmatic interpretation: it is the "echo of days gone by in the life of the one whom we carried to the grave in the first movement—days when the sun was still brightly shining for him." He explained that the movement was there by itself, interrupting "in a certain sense the severe, stern course of events," while the other movements were linked together "thematically and in regard to their mood" (GMB[2] 279).

As early as 1899, Mahler had expressed a similar viewpoint to Bauer-Lechner:

> One fault in the C minor Symphony is that the cheerful dance rhythms contrast the Andante too sharply (and inartistically) with the first movement. The reason for this is that I designed the two movements independently of each other, without any thought of connecting them. Otherwise I could at least have begun the Andante with the cello melody followed by the present beginning, but to revise it now is no longer possible (BL[2] 133).

Scherzo: *Die Welt wie im Hohlspiegel* ("The World as in a Concave Mirror")

Mahler based parts of the third movement of his Second Symphony on music from his *Wunderhorn* song *Des Antonius von Padua Fischpredigt* for two primary reasons. For the symphony he was working on, Mahler needed a scherzolike movement; the music of *Fischpredigt* seemed just right, bearing the character of a *perpetuum mobile*. In addition, *Fischpredigt,* which he understood to be a "satire on humanity" (BL[2] 28) and a parable of senselessness (St. Anthony preaches to the fish after he has found the church empty), had a deeper meaning that suited his intentions.[33]

The programmatic idea of the Second Symphony's Scherzo is the dreadful recognition that the meaning of existence cannot be understood and that life itself seems senseless. To explain the movement, Mahler used the parable of the hustle and bustle of life and the image of a dance that can be seen but not heard. In a conversation with Natalie Bauer-Lechner in January 1896 he stated:

> What is expressed in the Scherzo can only be illustrated like this: if you watch a dance from a distance through a window, without hearing the music, the gyrations of the couples seem strange and senseless because the key element, the rhythm, is lacking. That is how you have to imagine someone who is destitute and unlucky: To such a person the world appears as in a concave mirror, distorted and mad. The Scherzo ends with the terrible outcry of such a martyred soul (BL[2] 40).

On 26 March 1896, Mahler wrote to Max Marschalk:

> When you finally wake up from this melancholy dream and again have to face this confused life, then this endlessly moving, never resting, never-to-be-understood hustle and bustle of life may seem dreadful to you, like the surging of dancing figures in a bright and illuminated ballroom into which you look from the dark night outside—from so far away that you cannot hear the music that goes with it! *Senseless* is how life seems to you then, a cruel nightmare from which you might jump up with a cry of disgust![34] Such is the third movement! (GMB[2] 150).

The Dresden program states:

> The spirit of unbelief, of negation, has overpowered him [the one who later dies]. He looks at the flood of apparitions and, having lost the pure mind of a child, he altogether loses the solid hold that love alone can give; he despairs of himself and of God. The world and life become for him a weird apparition; disgust for everything present and future grips him with an iron fist and drives him to the outcry of despair (AME 268).

This program must have been in Mahler's mind when he conceived the movement because his Scherzo culminates in an instrumental outcry (m. 464ff.).

The structure of the composition's five sections follows this scheme: introduction (mm. 1–12), Part A (mm. 13–189), Part B (mm. 190–347), Part A¹ (mm. 348–440), Part B¹ (mm. 441–544), Part A² (mm. 545–581). For the A parts, Mahler used the substance of *Fischpredigt;* the B parts, however, are new. It is noteworthy that the parts become shorter and shorter: Part A is 189 or 177 measures, Part B is 158 measures, Part A¹ is 93 measures, Part B¹ is 94 measures, Part A² is 36 measures.

As to the emotions expressed in the movement, we can discern at least four: the humorous, the lyric, the sinister, and the solemn. Humor, found in *Fischpredigt* and the A parts, can be attributed to various style traits: the restless sixteenth-note movement; the especially "curly" melodic phrases, such as those of the clarinets in measures 52–60 and 91–97 (the performance markings in these places read "with humor"[35]); the abrasive major sevenths in the outer voices (e.g., mm. 22, 54–55); the Phrygian turns (e.g., mm. 30–31); the preference for parallel thirds; parallel triads (e.g., mm. 27–31); ornamentation (numerous grace notes); the staccato articulation (notice, for instance, the second bassoon in measures 103–120); unexpected turns, such as the chromatic plunging motifs with tam-tam (mm. 98–103 and 402–406), which provide startling accents; and so on. In all these instances, the humorous is combined with characteristic expression. Mahler described the situation very well when he talked about the "bittersweet" humor of *Fischpredigt* (BL² 28).

At the beginning of the B part, a new, "very massive" theme in C major is introduced, though it is performed *piano* by the cellos and double basses. Added to this, the first flute and the piccolo play a long, sustained, whistling sound (the C above the staff with its octave). The unique coloring of this passage is unforgettable. Coupled with a fanfarelike melody of the winds, this theme is also presented and developed in D major (No. 37) and in E major (No. 39). The only lyric passage of the movement follows in E major, with melodies of the first trumpet or the woodwinds ("very sustained and songlike," No. 47). Mahler referred to this as the "most beautiful passage" and remarked that it "appears only once in the surging surf of this piece and does not return" (BL² 149ff.). Several measures at the end of the B part (mm. 340–347) then open up a completely different realm of expression—the sinister. Here Mahler provides sharp dissonances in the brass, cymbal and timpani rolls, and a chromatically gliding figure.

That the sinister is firmly integrated into this Scherzo becomes especially evident in the second B part (No. 49). Although the passage begins noisily in C major, the music soon becomes turbulent. There are urging motifs in the woodwinds and signal calls in the horns and trumpets above threatening chromatic passages in the low instruments. A towering *fff* results in the shrieking dissonance of a B-flat minor chord above a pedal point on C. This outbreak is Mahler's frequently mentioned instrumental outcry. Then the suspense rapidly subsides. A harmonized, descending scale, diminuendo, leads to a thirdless C major chord. The following passage is solemn, and it does not leave the *pianissimo* level. The trumpets play two prominent motifs in measures 496–501 and 508–514; at the same time, the first violins present a descending melodic line (mm. 509–514) from which Mahler will gain an important theme in the Finale:

Both the shattering climax of the Scherzo and the series of motifs just mentioned point toward the Finale. The connection of the movements—their thematic material and their moods—cannot be overlooked.

After the substantial B^1 part, the following short A^2 part fulfills the function of an epilogue. The tam-tam beat at the end once again gives the movement a sinister accent.

Urlicht ("Primeval Light")

The fourth movement of the Second Symphony, a setting of the *Wunderhorn* text *Urlicht* for alto and orchestra, occupies a kind of key position within the dramaturgy of the work. It answers the questions raised in the Scherzo and leads into the Finale, which is a symphonic cantata. Mahler could not have found a more suitable text for this movement. The poem gives expression to the old longing for mystical union with God and represents, as Mahler explains, "the questioning and agonized searching of the soul for God and for its own eternal existence" (BL^2 40). The poem reads as follows (DKW 2, 10):

> *O Röschen rot,*
> *Der Mensch liegt in größter Not,*
> *Der Mensch liegt in größter Pein,*
> *Je lieber möcht' ich im Himmel sein.*
> *Da kam ich auf einen breiten Weg,*
> *Da kam ein Engelein und wollt mich abweisen,*
> *Ach nein, ich ließ mich nicht abweisen.*
> *Ich bin von Gott, ich will wieder zu Gott,*
> *Der liebe Gott wird mir ein Lichtchen geben,*
> *Wird leuchten mir bis in das ewig selig Leben.*

> Oh, little red rose,
> Mankind lies in great need,
> Mankind lies in great pain,
> Rather I would heaven claim.

Then I came upon a wide, broad way,
Where a little angel came and wanted to send me away,
Oh no, I did not let myself be sent away.
I am from God, I want to return to God.
The loving God will grant me a little light,
Will light my way to blissful life eternal and bright.

In his setting Mahler observed the structure of the poem in three verses, but he used the words "Oh, little red rose" as a motto, followed by a chorale of 11 measures. It is performed by nine wind players (one bassoon, one contrabassoon, four horns, and three trumpets) placed in the rear area of the orchestra space. Here is an outline of the structure:

Mm. 1–13 Motto and choralelike introduction (*Sehr feierlich, aber schlicht*) [very solemn, but plain]
     14–35 First stanza: Part A
     36–54 Second stanza: Part B (*Etwas bewegter*) [somewhat livelier]
     55–68 Third stanza: Part A' (*zart drängend, Molto riten., wieder langsam, wie zu Anfang*) [gently urging, molto riten., again slowly, as at the beginning]

Structurally the setting is distinguished by remarkable unity. The choralelike line that the wind players perform (mm. 3–7) returns in measures 27–30 (to the words "Rather would I heaven claim!") and in measures 63–65 (to the words "blissful life eternal and bright"). The A sections are based on the same motif and thematic substance without having the same structure. The melodic phrases exposed at the beginning of Part A change into more intense, urging motifs at the beginning of Part A'.

Mm. 14–20

Der Mensch liegt in   größ - ter   Noth! Der Mensch liegt in   größ - ter   Pein!

Mm. 54–58

Ich   bin— von Gott und will wie-der zu Gott! Der   lie - be Gott, der   lie - be Gott

The middle section (vision of the angel) distinguishes itself in every respect from the main sections, not only motivically and agogically (somewhat livelier), but also in its modulations and instrumentation. While the introduction and the main sections are basically in D-flat major (or C-sharp minor), the middle part enters in B-flat minor and leads to A major(!), A minor, and F-sharp minor. As to the instrumentation, the tone color of the angel scene is mainly established by the clarinets, Glockenspiel, harp, and solo violin, which stand out for the first time. Mahler told Natalie Bauer-Lechner that "the sound of the little bell" made him think "of the soul in heaven, where in 'the state of a chrysalis' it must begin again as a child" (BL[2] 168). Accordingly, the seven(!) tones of the Glockenspiel ring in eternity.

Finale: The Apocalyptic Vision

> The Apocalypse archetype is not closed to music.
>
> Ernst Bloch
> *Das Prinzip Hoffnung* (The principle "Hope")

Paul Bekker's extreme thesis[36] regarding Mahler's "Finale symphonies" surely does not do justice to all symphonic works of the master. It is, however, entirely appropriate in its assessment of the final movements of the Second, Sixth, and Eighth Symphonies. The Finale of the Second is one of the most powerful Mahler wrote. It is truly the goal to which the previous movements lead, resolving the stated symphonic problem and giving the whole—musically as well as semantically—a deeper meaning.

In a letter to Arthur Seidl, Mahler explained the inclusion of choir and soloists (one soprano and one alto soloist) with a reference to Beethoven's Ninth:

> Whenever I conceive a large musical form, I always arrive at the point where I have to turn to the *word* as a bearer of my musical ideas. Beethoven must have had a similar experience with his Ninth, only at that time the appropriate material was not yet at hand (GMB[2] 200).

The connection between the two works becomes evident if one remembers that Mahler, like Beethoven, begins his movement orchestrally and does not include the "word" until later. Moreover, he modeled the "fright fanfare" at the beginning after Beethoven's fanfare.[37] Inspiration Mahler received from Richard Wagner, Franz Liszt, and Hector Berlioz is equally important. One must not forget he used devices of stage music, such as the trumpets placed "at a great distance," and at the end of the century he generally hoped for and expected the renewal of symphonic art to be enriched by the modes of expression found in Wagner's music drama (GMB[2] 149).

The movement clearly divides into an introduction and three sections, which suggests comparison with the exposition, development, and recapitulation of sonata form. If one decides to operate within this framework, one must always bear in mind that the movement is constructed with remarkable freedom, as shown by the key relationships. The exposition (No. 3) begins in F minor, but the recapitulation (No. 29) is in F-sharp minor. Similarly the first line of the chorale (No. 31) is in G-flat major, whereas the Symphony itself ends in E-flat major. Decisive for proper analysis and interpretation of the movement is an understanding of the programmatic concept that determines the layout as well as all details of form. All in all, the Finale of the Second is a movement full of semantic implications that can be deciphered down to the smallest detail. Mahler based the vocal part of his symphony cantata on the same material he used in the instrumental portion; therefore all themes and motifs of the movement can be deciphered semantically by examining the text and by considering other clues. The following outline of the structure also takes into account the results of semantic analysis:

Mm.   1–42   Introduction

      1–25   "Fright fanfare" over a pedal-point C
   26–42   Eternity and Ascension theme in C major; Glockenspiel

   43–193   Exposition
Der Rufer in der Wüste
["The One Calling in the Wilderness"]
(= Announcement of Judgment Day)

   43–61   Horn calls and triplet motifs = first announcement by the Caller (*pianissimo*)
   62–77   First eschatological statement by the caller: Chorale: Dies irae followed by the Resurrection theme in F minor (*pianissimo*)
   78–96   Thematic material of the Caller in F minor = second announcement by the Caller (*pianissimo*)
  97–141   "Entreaty" = anticipation of the section *O glaube, mein Herz, o glaube* ("Oh believe, my heart, oh believe"): instrumental recitative and arioso in B-flat minor
142–161   Second eschatological statement by the Caller: Chorale: Dies irae followed by the Resurrection theme beginning in D-flat major and ending in C major
162–190   Thematic material of the Caller in C major/C minor; inclusion of the Ascension motif = third announcement by the Caller (now *fortissimo*)
191–193   Percussion crescendo: "The earth is shaking, the graves are opening up" (AME 268)
194–447   Development (Vision of the Last Judgment)
194–219   Fear and Dies irae motifs, often contrapuntally combined, in addition to shouting motifs
220–288   Allegro marziale using Dies irae, Resurrection, and Fear motifs: mm. 251–262 a chorale in the trumpets
289–309   Return to the first movement (mm. 270–290)
310–324   Collapse: Fright fanfare linked contrapuntally with tritonic variations of the Dies irae motif and inferno triplets

325–401 Repeated anticipation of the "Entreaty" in addition to "trumpets of the Apocalypse" (AME 269): instrumental recitative and arioso, large climax

402–417 Fright fanfare over a pedal point on C-sharp ~mm. 1–25

418–447 Eternity and Ascension theme in D-flat major ~ mm. 26–42; again seven tones of Glockenspiel

448–764   Varied Recapitulation
                  Der grosse Appell (The Great Roll-call)
                  (= Resurrection: The True Apocalypse)

448–471 Caller motif, bird calls, fanfares of the Apocalypse, beginning in F-sharp minor

472–493 First text stanza = First choral verse: four-line Resurrection Chorale in G-flat major

493–511 Intermezzo (Caller motifs, Ascension theme, Eternity theme) in G-flat major

512–536 Second stanza = Second choral verse: Variation of the four-line Resurrection Chorale in G-flat major

536–559 Intermezzo (Ascension theme and Eternity theme, Glockenspiel) in G-flat major

560–617 Third stanza: Alto and soprano solo = Entreaty in recitative-arioso style in B-flat minor ("Oh believe, my heart, oh believe")

618–639 Fourth stanza = Third choral verse: Different variation of Resurrection Chorale, beginning in B-flat minor, modulating to E-flat$_7$

640–672 Fifth and Sixth stanzas: Alto and soprano duet with mostly independent thematic material; melodic material from *Urlicht* (mm. 660–672)

672–711 Seventh stanza = Fourth choral verse: Imitative treatment of the Ascension theme; the Eternity theme in E-flat major (m. 696ff.)

712–732 Eighth stanza = Fifth choral verse: new variation of the Resurrection Chorale in E flat major

732–764 Postlude (Eternity theme, bells in triple rhythm): Transcendence

Of decisive importance for the structure of the movement (and not only for it) are two programmatic headings that are in the autograph and in the vocal score by Hermann Behn[38] but which Mahler left out in the published full score. They are *Der Rufer in der Wüste* (No. 3) and *Der grosse Appell* (No. 29). In comparing these titled parts, one notices that they correspond in many ways and that they both start with the same thematic material. They are related to each other in the same way as the exposition and the recapitulation.[39] The development—and there is no disagreement about this—begins at No. 14. The events in this movement are outlined below.

The Finale follows *Urlicht attacca* (without break) and "in the tempo of the Scherzo, wildly emerging." It begins with the shrill, dissonant sound of that movement (the B-flat minor chord over the pedal point on C), a sound Mahler also interpreted as "Death Cry" (BL[2] 40) and into which he now inserts a fanfare for trumpets and trombones "with raised bell"—the Fright Fanfare:

Mm. 5–18

As in the Scherzo, a descending scale leads to a quiet section in C major (*Sehr zurückhaltend* [Very hesitant], No. 2), in which the two solemn trumpet motifs from the Scherzo (mm. 497–501 and 509–513) are quoted and in which the horns present a distinctive theme:

Mm. 31–35

The two motifs which form this theme also appear independently and can clearly be identified as the Eternity and the Ascension motifs.[40] Also in this section the tones of the Glockenspiel ring in eternity, as they did in the angel scene in *Urlicht*.

After this introduction, the first part of the Finale (*Der Rufer in der Wüste*) begins with the call of horns, "as many as possible," placed "in the far distance." In the Dresden program Mahler explained this section as follows: "The voice of the Caller is resounding; the end of all living creatures has come; the Last Judgment is at hand, and all the terror of this day has erupted" (AME 268). The following comments express the vision of the last Judgment and the Resurrection. What were Mahler's literary sources?

The heading "The One Calling in the Wilderness" clearly refers to Isaiah 40:3–5:[41]

A voice cries in the wilderness: Prepare the way of the Lord, make straight in the desert a highway for our God. Every valley shall be lifted up, and every mountain and hill be made low; the uneven ground shall become level, and the glory of the Lord shall be revealed, and all flesh shall see it together, for the mouth of the Lord has spoken.[42]

Mahler nonetheless seems to have received—and so far this has escaped notice—the decisive inspiration for his Apocalyptic vision from a poem in *Des Knaben Wunderhorn* (his favorite collection of poems). The poem is entitled "Herald of the Final Judgment" and was written by a seventeenth-century Capuchin, Father Friedrich Procop.[43] The long poem begins with the proclamation of Judgment Day:

> *Da schrie und rief die tiefe Stimm*
> *Wohl bei dem Feuerthron mit Grimm:*
> *Der Jüngste Tag wird sich bald finden,*
> *Solches verkündge den Menschenkindern!*

> Then the deep voice shouted and called out
> There by the fiery throne in anger:
> The Judgment Day is soon to come,
> Tell this to all mankind!

It then tells of the events during the fifteen days before the final happening, describing the changes in creation (The earth turns red with blood, / There surely will be great hardship); refers to Isaiah (And the earth will become straight); describes the anguish, fear, and terror of the people (People cry most pitifully . . . thus they greatly fear Judgment Day); and prophesies the death and the resurrection of humanity, closing with the following verse:

> *Am funfzehnten Tag, das ist wahr,*
> *Da wird eine neue Welt gar schön und klar,*
> *Alsdann müssen alle Menschen auferstehen aus dem Grab;*
> *Wovon uns die Heilige Schrift klar Zeugnis gab;*
> *Der Engel mit dem großen Zorn*
> *Ruft allen Menschen durch das Horn!*

> On the fifteenth day, that is true,
> There is going to be a new world, beautiful and clear,
> Then all people must rise from the grave;
> To which the Holy Writ gave witness;
> The angel in great fury
> Calls all people with the horn!

A semantic musical analysis of the first section reveals an extremely poetic conception. The voice of the Caller is at first heard softly from a distance, then more loudly. The Caller's eschatological pronouncements refer to the Last Judgment and Resurrection. Between those proclamations frightened mankind make themselves heard and seek to regain their security. This content is musically interpreted in an extremely graphic way.

The first section of this first part (mm. 43–61 beginning in F minor and closing *pianissimo* with a C major chord without a third) opens with horn calls in triplet motifs that belong to the thematic material of the Caller. In measures 51–54, the trumpet motif from the Scherzo is played and answered by the horns. The sequence of chords in measures 55–57 (A-flat major—E major—D-flat major—A major—F major—D major—B-flat major—G-flat major—C major) provides very attractive timbres.

The general pause has the effect of a colon. A chorale in F minor for wind instruments follows (mm. 62–77); it is the Caller's first eschatological proclamation. The chorale melody for wind instruments (partly accompanied by the strings, pizzicato, in triplets) consists of the Dies irae theme and the Resurrection theme:[44]

Dies irae theme

Resurrection motif

The next section (mm. 78–96), very soft and in F minor, is likewise presented with Caller motifs. It corresponds to the first section but differs noticeably in details of form. In measures 82–84, the horns perform a fragment of the Ascension motif.

The following B-flat minor section (mm. 91–141) has quite a different appearance. It anticipates the thematic material of the entreaty to be heard much later: "Oh believe, my heart, oh believe" (No. 39). It amounts to an instrumental recitative and arioso, has an excited character, and is distinguished by sighing motifs. The section's timbre is strongly conditioned by the tone color of the English horn that dominates at the beginning. The music, *im Anfang sehr zurückgehalten* (at the beginning very restrained), becomes increasingly urgent but does not actually reach a climax. At the end, the suspense diminishes, *wieder zurückhaltend* (again restrained).

After another general pause the second eschatological statement of the Caller follows (mm. 142–161). The chorale is now fully harmonized and performed in low or mid-range. This time it begins *pianissimo* and ends (after a crescendo) *fortissimo*. Immediately afterward, the Caller's third proclamation follows (mm. 162–190); his motifs now are stated in new combinations, *fortissimo*. At the end of the section the dynamic level declines: m. 183 *ff*, m. 184 *f*, m. 185 *mf*, m. 186 *p*, m. 187 *pp*.

A famous crescendo for percussion (mm. 191–193) begins *ppp* and "very slowly and consistently increases to the greatest force," using small and large drums, two tam-tams, and timpani.[45] This crescendo leads into the development and was interpreted by Mahler to be an earthquake: "A trembling passes over the earth. Listen to the drum roll and your hair will stand on end" (BL[2] 40).

The development is conceived as a fearful vision of the Last Judgment. Clearly divided into seven sections, it provides drama, suspense, and intensity and does not lack in harsh features. The themes and motifs of the Exposition are now manipulated, combined with each other, contrapuntally entwined, and placed against each other. Following the program, the Dies irae motif, a Fear motif, and a Shouting motif take the lead (for the latter, a shrill motif of a minor ninth is employed). Mahler paints a musical image of fright, though here and there he does include the Resurrection motif. Dies irae and Resurrection themes often confront each other. In measures 245–250 the tam-tam and bells are heard successively as well as simultaneously, as if to symbolize the proximity of death and resurrection.

Mahler would not have been able to impart this much variety to the development had he not mastered the subtle art of motivic-thematic metamorphosis. Motifs are developed into phrases and themes, and appear in different forms, rhythmic designs, and variations. Thus character and expression are often totally changed. A few metamorphoses of the Dies irae motif illustrate this technique.

Original form
Mm. 270–271

Original form, expanded into a marchlike theme:

Mm. 220–223

Variations emphasizing intervals of a fourth:

Mm. 210–213

Mm. 214–217

Fl., Ob., Cl. *fff*

Tritone variants:

Mm. 227–280

Trb. *f*   Trpt. *ff*

The above examples demonstrate that one well may speak of "developing variations" in Mahler's music.

We will now examine the seven sections of the development. The first section (mm. 194–219), beginning in F minor, initially exposes the theme of the Fright Fanfare (first and second trumpets and low bass instruments); added to this, Shouting motifs are heard in the piccolos, oboes, and E-flat clarinets. Mahler's indication "the graves are opening up" (AME 268) refers to this mood of fright. In measures 210–218, the Dies irae motif (in a version containing a fourth) and the Fear motif are combined contrapuntally.

The second section (mm. 220–288), beginning in F major, is an Allegro marziale—a very affective death march: "the dead rise and walk in an endless procession" (AME 268). Here Mahler developed a 16-measure march-like theme from the four-note Dies irae motif. It is played alone and also coupled contrapuntally with the Resurrection theme and with choralelike lines of the horns and trumpets (mm. 248–262). In measures 267–288 the Dies irae motif appears again, coupled with the Fear and Shouting motifs, in most imaginatively altered rhythms and variations.

In the third section (mm. 189–309), Mahler uses (with a few modifications) the substance of measures 270–290 from the first movement.

The fourth section (mm. 310–324) offers a vision of collapse: a dissonant double-dominant chord (F—B-flat—D-flat—E—G) played *fff* and gradually losing intensity. At the same time, the music "plunges" from above into ever-lowering regions. Mahler's way of combining motifs is eloquent: the trombones proclaim the Fright Fanfare, the trumpets play tritone variations of the Dies irae motif, while the triplet runs in the woodwinds symbolize inferno.

In the fifth section (mm. 325–401) the substance of the entreaty "(Oh believe, my heart, oh believe") once again is anticipated. Compared with the corresponding section of the exposition (mm. 97–141), this new version seems like a broad realization of a sketch. The effect is much more intense, the climax much more long-winded and violent. The structure is also much more complicated. During the instrumental recitative and arioso, we hear cantabile phrases in the cellos and bassoons and later in the violins. "Musical sounds, barely audible, are transported by the wind." Trumpets, triangle, cymbals, and bass drum "placed as far away as possible" announce the Apocalypse, its sound coming closer and closer. In measure 380ff., the trumpets, contrabassoon, trombones, tuba, and double basses take over the motivic lead (the passage contains something eerily massive and urgent); in measures 395–399, the tritone (G-flat—C) occurs obtrusively several times, while sighlike figures and rising chromatic lines in the upper ranges lead to a climax.

At this point the trumpets play the Fright Fanfare "with raised bell" (sixth section, mm. 402–417). The dissonant sound that surrounds the fanfare is now transposed a half step up (C-sharp—F-sharp—B—D), and the trombones play the Dies irae motif three times (mm. 409–416) in the version containing a fourth.

The mysterious last section of the development (mm. 418–447) is dominated by the Ascension and Eternity themes; again the seven tones of the Glockenspiel ring in the beginning of eternity. Mahler explained the last sections of the development: "The call for mercy and grace is frightening—an outcry that fills us with growing terror. We lose all our senses, all consciousness vanishes from us at the approach of the Eternal Spirit" (AME 269).

The following recapitulation mostly uses the motifs and themes of the exposition. However, the Dies irae motif, the Fear motif, and the Shouting motifs do not return. Dominant are the Resurrection, Ascension, and Eternity motifs. Even if we did not have the text of this section, we could conclude from the motivic relations that in Mahler's imagination the true Apocalypse was nothing other than the message of the Second Coming.

"The Great Roll-call" (No. 29) enters with horn signals of the Caller in the wilderness. In measures 452–453, the bird of the night calls twice.[46] Then the trumpets, "placed in the far distance," announce the Apocalypse. Mahler's instruction that "the four trumpets must sound from opposite directions" has been praised as a prophetic anticipation of today's stereophonic sound. Hardly any attention, however, has been paid to the biblical reference of this passage. It is stated in Matthew 24:31 that at the Apocalypse the angel of the Lord will gather "His chosen from the four winds, from one end of heaven to the other." In the conception of this Finale, Mahler was guided by poetic and musical ideas. To these belong the singing of the nightingale heard from flute and piccolo—in Mahler's interpretation, "a last trembling echo of life on earth" (AME 269).

Of the eight strophes of the following cantata, the first two were written by Klopstock, and the other six were written by Mahler. They are indispensable for an understanding of the music and are therefore quoted here:

> *Auferstehn, ja auferstehn wirst du,*
> *Mein Staub, nach kurzer Ruh!*
> *Unsterblich Leben*
> *Wird, der dich rief, dir geben.*

Wieder aufzublühn, wirst du gesät!
Der Herr der Ernte geht
Und sammelt Garben
Uns ein, die starben.

O glaube, mein Herz, es geht dir nichts verloren!
Dein ist, ja dein, was du gesehnt,
Was du geliebt, was du gestritten.
O glaube: du wardst nicht umsonst geboren,
Hast nicht umsonst gelebt, gelitten.

Was entstanden ist, das muß vergehen,
Was vergangen, auferstehen!
Hör auf, zu beben!
Bereite dich, zu leben!

O Schmerz, du Alldurchdringer,
Dir bin ich entrungen!
O Tod, du Allbezwinger,
Nun bist du bezwungen!

Mit Flügeln, die ich mir errungen,
In heißem Liebesstreben
Werd' ich entschweben
Zum Licht, zu dem kein Aug' gedrungen.

Mit Flügeln, die ich mir errungen
Werde ich entschweben.
Sterben werd' ich, um zu leben!

Auferstehn, ja auferstehn wirst du,
Mein Herz, in einem Nu!
Was du geschlagen,
Zu Gott, zu Gott wird es dich tragen.

Arise, yes, you will arise,
Dust of my body, after a brief rest!
Immortal life
Will he, who called you, grant to you.

You are sown that you might bloom again!
The Lord of harvest goes
And gathers sheaves,
Gathers us, who died.

Oh, believe, my heart, nothing is lost for you!
Yours, yes, yours alone is what you longed for,
What you loved, and what you fought for.

Oh believe, you were not born in vain,

Nor have you lived or suffered in vain!

That which was created must perish,
What perished will arise!
No longer tremble!
Prepare to live!

Oh agony, you piercing pain,
From you I have escaped!
Oh death, all-conquering claim
Now you are defeated!

With wings that I have gained,
In seeking to perfect my love
Will I ascend
Into the light which no eye has ever reached.

With wings that I have gained
Will I ascend.
I will die to be alive!

Arise, you will arise,
My heart, within a moment!
What you have conquered,
To God, to God it will bear you up.

For the structure of the cantata, the Resurrection Chorale is of over-whelming importance. It consists of four lines and is sung by the choir four times but in four versions, each differing from the other (= first, second, fourth, and eighth stanza).[47] The other sections of the cantata function as interludes or "secondary subjects." The latter is true especially for the alto and soprano solo ("Oh believe, my heart, oh believe") and for the alto and soprano duet ("Oh agony, you piercing pain").

The disposition of timbres in the cantata suggest music gradually coming closer and closer from a far distance, an effect that Mahler was very fond of creating. The first two stanzas of the Resurrection Chorale (marked *Slowly, Misterioso* at the beginning) are to be performed *ppp*. The mystic effect of these two stanzas can partly be attributed to the dynamics. The third stanza ("Oh believe, my heart, oh believe") moves to *piano*. The breakthrough does not occur until the fourth stanza (= third stanza of the Resurrection Chorale), characterized by enormous dynamic contrasts. "That which was created must perish" is to be sung *pianissimo*; "What perished will arise!" is sung *forte*. An even harsher contrast is seen between "No longer tremble!" (*ppp*) and "Prepare to live!" (*ff, mf dim.* to *ppp*). This accentuation prepares the upswing of the fifth stanza (No. 44). The seventh stanza ("With wings that I have gained in seeking to perfect my love will I ascend") extends an arch from *ppp* to *ff* at "I will die to be alive!" In the very last stanza, Mahler adds the organ, and the choir enters *fff*.

The postlude (mm. 732–764) is dominated by the Eternity theme. Three bells ("low and different timbres, without definite pitch") ring out here in strict triple rhythm and collide, in a way, with the four-four meter:

Mm. 732–743

The number symbolism of the triple time is quite obvious.

Sketches for the second and first movements of the Third Symphony
Stanford University Memorial Library of Music
First Publication
Programmatic cue words *Pan schläft* (Pan is sleeping): hidden allusion to the poem
"Genesis" by Siegfried Lipiner, specifically to the lines *Es war, als wär' nur Eine*
grosse Wolke / das ganze All- / die Wolke lag und schlief (It was as if there was only
one large cloud / the whole universe / the cloud rested and slept)

Sketches for the first movement of the Third Symphony
Stanford University Memorial Library of Music
First Publication
Shown here is the beginning of the E-flat minor March (m. 539ff.)

Keyboard sketch of the second movement of the Third Symphony (to No. 3)
Stanford University Memorial Library of Music
First Publication

Third movement of the Third Symphony, No. 14
Autograph in possession of Robert O. Lehman (New York)
First Publication
Programmatic cue words *Der Postillon* ("The Stagecoach Driver"): an allusion to the
poem of the same name by Nikolaus Lenau

The Third Symphony

My symphony will be unlike anything the world has ever heard! All of nature speaks in it, telling deep secrets that one might guess only in a dream!

GMB[1] 163

But now it is the world, nature in its entirety, that awakens from unfathomable silence to ringing and resounding.

GMB[2] 180

Origin

Those looking for proof to support the opinion that several Mahler symphonies are programmatically conceived will find ample evidence in the case of the Third Symphony. One can refer to Mahler's often very detailed hermeneutic interpretations found in letters and conversations, as well as to the autograph.[1] Programmatic indications occur in the titles of all six movements and in other places throughout the work. Mahler, who in later years categorically resented commenting on the programmatic basis of his symphonic writing, was in 1895 and 1896 extraordinarily communicative about the Third. In letters to friends and acquaintances he frequently mentioned the movement titles, hinting that he wanted a reaction to those headings from those to whom he had written.

To discuss the origin of the Third, it is advisable to begin with the headings of the movements in the autograph. They reveal that Mahler at first envisioned a cosmogonic dream and the idea of a tiered arrangement of being:

> *Einleitung: Pan erwacht*
>   folgt sogleich
> *Der Sommer marschirt ein (Bacchuszug)*
> *Was mir die Blumen auf den Wiesen erzählen*
> *Was mir die Thiere im Walde erzählen*

Was mir der Mensch erzählt
Was mir die Engel erzählen
Was mir die Liebe erzählt

Motto: *Vater, sieh an die Wunden mein!*
       Kein Wesen laß verloren sein!

Introduction: Pan awakes
       followed immediately by
"Summer Marches In" ("Bacchus's Parade")
"What the Flowers in the Meadow Tell Me"
"What the Animals in the Woods Tell Me"
"What Mankind Tells Me"
"What the Angels Tell Me"
"What Love Tells Me"

Motto: Father, look upon my wounds!
         Let no creature be lost!

All available evidence indicates that the five movements of the second part were written during the summer of 1895, along with sketches for the first movement, which was not completed until the following summer. As uncomplicated as this may sound, the details of the Symphony's history are quite complex.

As far as is known, Mahler did not start work on the Third until the summer of 1895 in Steinbach. It is strange, however, that the two marchlike themes of the first movement in B-flat major appear in a sketch labeled "1893, Steinbach."[2] Although this heading is apparently not in Mahler's hand and therefore does not offer certain proof, it does support the thesis that Mahler sketched those two themes in 1893 while he was working on the middle movements of the Second Symphony.[3]

The program headings that Mahler mentioned to his close friend Natalie Bauer-Lechner (BL[2] 36) in the summer, most likely in June or July, and on 17 August 1895 to his friends Hermann Behn (GMUB 23ff.) and Arnold Berliner (GMB[2] 126) differ very little from the titles in the autograph. Thus the order of the movements was already decided at that time, though Mahler originally planned to close the Symphony with a seventh movement that was supposed to bear the title *Was mir das Kind erzählt* ("What the Child Tells Me") or *Das himmlische Leben* ("The Heavenly Life"). It is well known that *Das himmlesche Leben* is the title of a *Wunderhorn* song that Mahler had composed in 1892.

Two program sketches (unfortunately undated) that Paul Bekker and Alma Mahler transmit in two slightly different versions show, in fact, that the initial order of movements did differ essentially from that of the final version (AME 53). The older of the two versions reads as follows, according to Bekker:[4]

Das glückliche Leben
Ein Sommernachtstraum
(nicht nach Shakespeare. Anmerkungen eines Kritikers
[im Text durchgestrichen] Rezensenten):

I. *Was mir der Wald erzählt*
II. *Was mir die Dämmerung erzählt*
III. *Was mir die Liebe erzählt*
IV. *Was mir die Dämmerung erzählt*
V. *Was mir die Blumen auf der Wiese erzählen*
VI. *Was mir der Kuckuck erzählt*
VII. *Was mir das Kind erzählt*

The Happy Life
A Summer Night's Dream
(not according to Shakespeare. Remarks of a Critic
["Critic" crossed out in the text] Reviewer)

I. "What the Woods Tell Me"
II. "What the Twilight Tells Me"
III. "What Love Tells Me"
IV. "What the Twilight Tells Me"
V. "What the Flowers in the Meadow Tell Me"
VI. "What the Cuckoo Tells Me"
VII. "What the Child Tells Me"

The second draft, which comes closer to the later version reads as follows, according to Alma Mahler:

Ein Sommernachtstraum

1. *Der Sommer marschiert ein (Fanfare und lustiger Marsch) (Einleitung)*
   (Nur Bläser mit konzertierenden Contrabässen)
2. *Was mir der Wald erzählt (1. Satz)*
3. *Was mir die Liebe erzählt (Adagio)*
4. *Was mir die Dämmerung erzählt (Scherzo) (nur Streicher)*
5. *Was mir die Blumen auf der Wiese erzählen (Menuetto)*
6. *Was mir der Kuckuck erzählt (Scherzo)*
7. *Was mir das Kind erzählt*

A Summer Night's Dream

1. "Summer Marches In" (Fanfare and Merry March) (Introduction) (wind players and concertante double basses only)
2. "What the Woods Tell Me" (First Movement)
3. "What Love Tells Me" (Adagio)

4. "What the Twilight Tells Me" (Scherzo) (strings only)
5. "What the Flowers in the Meadow Tell Me" (Menuetto)
6. "What the Cuckoo Tells Me" (Scherzo)
7. "What the Child Tells Me"

From these drafts it is evident that the idea of a tiered arrangement of all creation was not consistently developed at the beginning. Although the overall plan included a flower piece and an animal piece, the further steps of the ladder, mankind and the angels, were missing. Mahler, therefore, had not yet planned to set the following to music: the "Midnight Song" from Friedrich Nietzsche's *Also sprach Zarathustra* (Thus Spake Zarathustra) and the *Wunderhorn* text *Es sungen drei Engel einen süßen Gesang* ("Three Angels Were Singing a Sweet Melody"). *Was mir der Kuckuck erzählt* is, however, an earlier version of *Was mir die Thiere im Walde erzählen*. Mahler used the substance of the 1892 *Wunderhorn* song *Ablösung im Sommer* ("Change in Summer," which begins with the verse "The cuckoo has fallen to death") as the basis for this movement.

The placement of the Adagio (*Was mir die Liebe erzählt*) is noteworthy. It is neither the last nor the next-to-last movement, as in the later versions; it is in third place, which is conventional. Not until later did Mahler decide to go against the norm and place the Adagio at the end.

Something else deserves emphasis: The second program draft leads one to conclude that the passage in the autograph labelled *Das Gesindel* ("The Rabble") (No. 44) was conceived and sketched first. This passage, marked *Marsch* (March) by Mahler in the score, is scored for cellos, double basses (or strings playing in unison), and winds. The markings in the draft may serve as a comparison: *Fanfare und lustiger Marsch* (Fanfare and happy march), *Einleitung* (Introduction), *Nur Bläser mit konzertierenden Contrabässen* (Only winds with concertante double basses). This thesis is also clearly supported by the sketch.

An attempt will be made to reconstruct Mahler's work in the summer of 1895 as accurately as possible. Right after Mahler arrived in Steinbach on 5 June[5] he composed *Blumenstück* ("The Flower Piece"), according to Bauer-Lechner's diary: "On the first afternoon, when he looked out the window of his little house, embedded in grass and flowers, it was sketched and completed in one go" (BL[2] 49). And Bauer-Lechner adds: " 'Whoever does not know the location,' Mahler said, 'would almost guess it; this is how unique it is, just the place to inspire such music.' "

The other movements of the second part probably were tackled immediately after *Blumenstück*. Mahler told Bauer-Lechner (most likely in June or July) that he was not embarrassed to include words and the human voice in his Third and that he would base the "vocal parts of the short movements" on two poems from *Des Knaben Wunderhorn* and "one magnificent poem" by Nietzsche (BL[2] 35). By this he meant, as already mentioned, the

Wunderhorn poems *Ablösung im Sommer* and *Es sungen drei Engel einen süßen Gesang,* as well as the "Midnight Song" from *Also sprach Zarathustra.*

Work must have progressed quickly because by 17 August Mahler reported to his friend Herman Behn in Hamburg: "All except No. 1 is completely finished in the full score" (GMUB 24), and on 29 August he wrote to Fritz Löhr: "No. 1 is not yet done and has to be kept for later" (GMB² 128).

Here we should briefly consider a problem raised by *Blumenstück.* A sketch from the estate of Bauer-Lechner (now at the Stanford University Memorial Library of Music) bears the heading *Was das Kind erzählt* (1895).⁶ This suggests that Mahler had originally conceived *Blumenstück* as a children's piece, an assumption that contradicts Bauer-Lechner's report that the composition was inspired by the landscape. At any rate, it is certain that even the earliest program drafts included a flower piece as well as a children's piece and that Mahler (in his letters from the summer of 1895) sometimes called his final movement *Das himmlische Leben* and sometimes *Was mir das Kind erzählt.*⁷ Two things deserve consideration in this context. For a long time, Mahler planned to base the first movement of the Third on melodic material from the song *Das himmlische Leben* composed in 1892. In a sketch now at the Austrian National Library, measures 225–238 are followed by melodic material from the song.⁸ Furthermore, Mahler abandoned his intention to end the Third with *Das himmlische Leben* in June 1896 at the latest. In a letter to Anna von Mildenburg, the title of the final movement reads *Was mir die Liebe erzählt* (GMB² 165).

Natalie Bauer-Lechner, who visited Mahler in Hamburg in April 1896, found him to have been busy, "recently completing the mostly finished part of his Third and preparing the final copy" (BL² 49). While she was there, he was working on *Blumenstück.* He could not begin the composition of the first movement until June 1896, when he was back in Steinbach. It was at this time that Mahler accidentally left the sketches to the first movement in his Hamburg apartment. In desperation he wrote by express mail to Hermann Behn, who was at the beach in Timmendorf, asking him to go to Hamburg, look for the sketches, and send them to him right away. Behn did him this favor, and Mahler could then begin work on the movement. On 21 June he thanked Behn for the trouble, and on 11 July he was able to announce to him "the completion of the composition. On this occasion he wrote Behn:

> You, dear Hermann, deserve much credit because without the sketches I could not have done anything. I am most grateful. To you those few sheets of music must have seemed quite unimportant, but in fact they contained (according to my way of sketching) all the seeds for the now fully grown tree. I hope that you will feel rewarded for all your trouble when you see the complete work (GMUB 29).

From Bauer-Lechner's diary we learn that the movement was not actually completed until 28 July: "He composed this first movement, which is longer than a whole symphony in less than six weeks. During the winter, in addition to all professional duties, he will have to work out all the details" (BL² 65).

While Mahler, as we have seen, already had definite ideas about the titles of the movements in the summer of 1895, he was uncertain for a long time about the work's overall title. He soon rejected the original heading, *The Happy Life*. After that he considered various titles: *A Summer Night's Dream, My Happy Science, The Happy Science, Dream of a Summer Morning,* and *A Summer Noontide Dream*. In the end he rejected all of them, obviously wanting to avoid confusion with the well-known works of both Shakespeare and Nietzsche.

Mahler's Cosmology and Its Sources

At the conception of his Third Symphony, Mahler allowed himself to be inspired by the idea of a tiered arrangement of creation (plant world, animal world, human world, and angel world) and also by the idea that love is the highest level from which one can contemplate the world. His understanding of love was eternal rather than earthly, as he expressly stated in a letter to Hermann Behn (GMUB 24). The title that he gave to the sixth movement (*Was mir die Liebe erzählt*) provides his work with a religious and moral accent.[9] Like Novalis, he understood love to be "the highest reality—the source of all being."[10] These thoughts soon were combined with the idea of summer's arrival—the subject of the first movement.

In his well-known letter to Fritz Löhr of 29 August 1895, Mahler explained his thinking:

> The performance time of my new symphony will probably be approximately 1½ hours; everything is in *large* symphonic form. The emphasis on my *personal* emotional life (that is, what things tell *me*) corresponds to the unique thought content. [Movements] II–V inclusively are meant to express the tiered arrangement of all creation, which I will express as follows:
>
> II. "W[hat] t[he] Flowers T[tell] M[e]
> III. "W. t. Animals T. M."
> IV. "W. t. Night T. M." (mankind)
> V. "W. t. Morning Bells T. M." (angels) the last two numbers with text and voice
> VI. "W. Love T. M." is a summary of my emotions toward all creatures, where deeply painful feelings cannot be avoided. But these eventually evolve into blissful confidence: the "joyful science." At the end is "T[he] H[eavenly] L[ife]" (VII), which, in fact, I finally titled,
>
> "What the Child Tells Me"

No. 1, "Summer Marches In," is meant to imply the humorous, subjective content. Summer is the victor in the midst of all that is growing and blooming, creeping and flying, imagined and longed for and, finally, sensed (angels—bells—the transcendental). Above everything hovers eternal love, like light rays converging in a lens. Do you understand now? (GMB[2] 127).

On 1 July 1896 Mahler wrote from Steinbach to his friend Anna von Mildenburg:

> But in the symphony, dear Annie, we are speaking of a different kind of love than you think. The motto for this movement (No. 7) reads:
>
> *"Vater, sieh an die Wunden mein!*
> *Kein Wesen laß verloren sein!"*
>
> ("Father, look upon my wounds!
> Let no creature be lost!")
>
> Do you understand now, my dear, what we are speaking of here? It is the zenith, the highest level from which the world can be viewed. I could also name the movement something like "What God Tells Me," in the sense that God can only be comprehended as "love." In this sense, my work is a musical poem, ascending step-by-step, encompassing all steps of evolution. It begins with lifeless nature and rises up to the love of God! (GMB[2] 166ff.).

In the summer of 1896, as this letter indicates, Mahler already harbored cosmogonic ideas about evolution and the beginning of life from inert matter. Thus in June 1896 he stated to Bauer-Lechner in regard to the introduction to the first movement:

> This almost ceases to be music, containing mostly sounds from nature. And it is eerie how from lifeless matter (I could just as well have named the movement "What the Mountains Tell Me") life gradually breaks forth, developing step-by-step into ever-higher forms of life: flowers, animals, human beings, up into the realm of spirits, to the angels (BL 56).

Regarding the heavy shadow of "lifeless nature, of still uncrystallized inorganic matter," a shadow that is cast on the end of the animal piece, Mahler felt that "here it rather means a relapse into the lower, animal-like forms of nature, before the huge jump into the spiritual realm, the mind of the highest creature on earth, the human" (BL[2] 56). He demonstrated the unity between the outer movements of the symphony with the following picture: "What was dull and rigid there has grown here to highest consciousness, from unarticulated sounds to highest articulation" (BL[2] 56).

Mahler emphasized the evolutionary aspect of his cosmology in a letter written on 18 November 1896 (after the completion of the Third) to Richard Batka:

No one will hear, of course, that nature encompasses everything that is eerie, great, and even lovely (this is precisely what I wanted to express using the whole work as a kind of evolutionistic development). It always seems strange to me that most people, when they talk about nature, can think only of flowers, little birds, forest fragrance, etc. No one mentions the god Dionysus or the great Pan. There, now you have a kind of program, that is, a sample of how I make music—always and everywhere only the sound of nature! This seems to be what Bülow once described to me so appropriately as "the symphonic problem." I do not recognize a different kind of program, at least not for my works. If I have now and then given them titles, I wanted to provide sign posts for the emotion, for the imagination. If words are needed to achieve this, then the human, articulated voice is there, which can then realize the boldest intentions, precisely in connection with the illuminating word! Here it is the world, nature as a whole, that is awakened out of unfathomable silence and sings and rings (GMB[2] 180).

Writings on evolution were so widespread during the nineteenth century that it should not be necessary to name philosophic literature from which Mahler could have gotten inspiration. Nevertheless, it seems remarkable that his opinions regarding the steps of development, beginning with lifeless nature and rising up to the love of God, come close to ideas expressed much earlier by Athanasius Kircher. In *Ars Magna Sciendi sive Combinatoria* published in 1669, Kircher presents an ontological table containing *Deus, Angelus, Coelum, Elementa, Homo, Animalia, Plantae, Mineralia, Materialia.*[11]

Mahler hardly would have heard of Athanasius Kircher. Arthur Schopenhauer's "stepwise succession of ideas" or "hierarchy of beings" (inorganic nature, plant and animal kingdom, mankind) in whom the "will" is objectified[12] may indeed have been known to him along with the teachings of Gustav Theodor Fechner.[13] The first volume of Fechner's *Zend-Avesta* contains two chapters with the headings "Regarding God and the World."[14] Fechner designates man as "the highest step on the earthly stair" and views God as the "highest being in relationship to the details of the world," regarding Him as "foundation, fulfillment, and completion of all existence" and explaining that God rises above everything.

As has been documented elsewhere,[15] in developing the program of the Third symphony, Mahler was greatly influenced by a poem by Siegfried Lipiner entitled "Genesis" which is conceived as a cosmogonic dream.[16] It presents a poetic vision of the creation of the world from a large, resting cloud that begins to speak. In a language rich with images, Lipiner tells how out of the cloud the firmament, the earth, suns, the plant kingdom, the animal kingdom, and mankind came into being.

A comparison of the poem with Mahler's program reveals clearly that the poem served as Mahler's literary model. He adopted many of its basic thoughts and images, as well as giving it additional meaning. While Lipiner speaks generally about love without precisely defining its character, Mahler understands "eternal love" as love in the religious and moral sense. And it is very typical that Mahler constructs a cosmological hierarchy that includes not only inorganic nature and the plant, animal, and human kingdoms, but also the kingdom of the spirits. In his view, the angels intercede between mankind and God, who is understood as love.

Mahler Versus Nietzsche

As mentioned earlier, Mahler at various times had planned to name the Third Symphony *The Happy Science* or *My Happy Science* and had discussed the idea with Josef B. Foerster (probably in 1895).[17] Foerster was not surprised, since he knew that Mahler was reading Nietzsche at the time. In a conversation with Natalie Bauer-Lechner in the summer of 1895, Mahler called Zarathustra's round "Oh, Human! Be on Guard!" (the poem he used as the basis for the fourth movement in the Third) "a magnificent poem" (BL[2] 35). His remarks about "the god Dionysus and the great Pan" in a letter to Richard Batka (GMB[2] 180) reflect impressions he received from Nietzsche's book *The Birth of Tragedy*.[18] And in a letter to Annie Mincieux from the beginning of November 1896 he said that the final movement of the Third was "the final step of differentiation: God! or if you like, the superhuman" (GMUB 127).

All of this might well cause one to wonder whether the spiritual substructure or superstructure of the Third is indebted to the philosophy of Friedrich Nietzsche. When Mahler first met Alma Schindler (1901), he was a decided opponent of Nietzsche's philosophy (AME 29). What he thought of Nietzsche at the time the Third was composed (1895, 1896) is not specifically known. Comparing Mahler's hermeneutic commentary regarding his Third with Nietzsche's *The Happy Science* and *Also sprach Zarathustra,* it is clear that the Symphony's programmatic concept is diametrically opposed to Nietzsche's philosophy. To clarify: Nietzsche's doctrine of the super-human derives consistently from the statement that God is "dead."[19] In *The Happy Science,* Nietzsche calls himself expressly "Godless and Antimetaphysical."[20] Mahler, however, believed strongly in metaphysics, the transcendental, and in the existence of God, whom he understood as love.[21]

Mahler understood the fifth movement of the Third, which is based on the *Wunderhorn* poem "Es sungen drei Engel einen süßen Gesang," to be a humoresque. The choice of text also suggests that his world view included the heavenly kingdom. He often considered changing the title of his song *Das himmlische Leben* to *Was mir das Kind erzählt* and he took naive, childlike faith seriously. On the contrary, Nietzsche laughed at this childlike faith. *Also sprach Zarathustra* includes the following sentences: "Surely, unless you become like children, you will never enter the kingdom of heaven. (Zarathustra points his hands upward.) But we do not want the kingdom of heaven. We have become men—thus we want the earthly kingdom."[22]

Finally, the Third Symphony proclaims the message of love to be understood as charity. Mahler had adapted Schopenhauer's idea that all love (*agape, caritas*) is compassion, as expressed by this statement: "It means, essentially, that we can never be completely happy as long as there are others who are unhappy" (AME 278). On the contrary, the concept of love was suspect for Nietzsche. In *The Happy Science,* Nietzsche insists—in contrast to Schopenhauer—that from sexual love one "had taken the concept of love as an opposite of egoism, whereas it may be precisely the most unabashed expression of egoism."[23]

It may therefore be concluded that the intellectual content of the Third Symphony is diametrically opposed to Nietzsche's philosophy, leading Mahler to toy from time to time with the idea of calling the work *My Happy Science.*

The Symphony as an Image of the World

According to a belief expressed by Dieter Schnebel, Mahler's music differs from that of his contemporaries in its "linguistic variety."[24] In his symphonies we find not only the highly developed language of classical music but also the dialects of folk music and, indeed, even the low or simply unschooled language of popular or light music. These qualities appear in the Third Symphony in a harsh, even provocative manner. Here one finds the jargon of military music and the more elevated language of funeral marches in the first movement; the classical music of the concert hall in the second movement; the music of the "lower class" and the music of times past in the third movement; the language of church music and related folk music in the fourth movement; the musical language of children in the fifth movement; and "a non-elitist language of music, including that which qualifies as 'high' and as 'low' in like manner" in the final movement. Following Schnebel, other scholars have also talked about the "idiomatic diversity" of the Third Symphony.[25]

Although there is some truth to these observations, something decisive is ignored: The idiomatic diversity of the Third as well as its entire compositional form is determined by the basic programmatic idea. Mahler planned to design a musical cosmology, and he had put this plan into action by the summer of 1895. The six movements of the Third resemble the six chapters of the highly poetic story of the creation he had in mind. The first movement, a structure of gigantic dimensions, is followed by five shorter movements that form the second part. All aspects of technique and expression are governed by the program: the inclusion of the voice in the fourth and fifth movements; the large orchestral apparatus; the varied, subtle orchestration; the incredible variety of characterization; the diversity of genre; the universality within the musical realm.

In this light, Mahler's much-quoted remarks to Bauer-Lechner in the summer of 1895 take on a new meaning:

Calling it [the Third] a Symphony is actually incorrect because in no way does it adhere to the usual form. But, in my opinion, creating a symphony means to construct a world with all manner of techniques available. The constantly new and changing content determines its own form (BL^2 35).

A year later, on 4 July 1896, he said to Bauer-Lechner that the movements of the second part were "as varied as the world itself," finding the redeeming solution in "love" (BL^2 61).

Pan erwacht: Der Sommer marschiert ein (Bacchuszug) ("Pan Awakens: Summer Marches In [Bacchus's Parade]")

Mahler seems to have had clear notions about program and about the second part of his Third from the beginning, but his plans for the first movement matured more slowly. They took on concrete form over time and were subject to quite a few modifications. From the dates marking the symphony's history, it can be seen that very early on Mahler connected the idea of summer marching in with the first movement. In the summer of 1895 he said to Natalie Bauer-Lechner: " 'Summer is Moving In' will become the prelude," and he explained the program as follows:

Of course, this does not happen without a battle against the opponent, winter, but he is overconfident and easily overthrown; summer, strong and superior, soon prevails. This movement, as an introduction, is definitely humorous, indeed, baroquelike (BL^2 35).

And in a similar sense he wrote to Fritz Löhr on 29 August:

No. 1, "Summer is Marching In," is meant to imply the humorous subjective content. Summer is the victor in the midst of all that is growing and blooming, creeping and flying, imagined and longed for and, finally, sensed (GMB^2 127).

As parallel or alternative train of thought, Mahler developed the concept of a Dionysian parade. In a letter to Bauer-Lechner of 3 September 1895, he marked the number of the first movement with a question mark and wrote "Parade of Dionysus" next to it (in smaller letters) and "or: Summer is Marching In" below it (BL^2 37). By June 1896, he had added the concept of the creation of life from "lifeless matter" (BL^2 56).

For now we will consider the structure of the movement, which is quite original. After an unusually long, slow introduction that is rich in thematic material, a movement in irregular sonata form follows. It is clearly divided into exposition, development, and recapitulation and consists primarily of marchlike material, but it also often returns to the thematic material of the introduction. The movement falls into numerous, self-contained sections,

each with distinct character. Almost all genres typical of Mahler are represented: the instrumental recitative and arioso, the chorale, the song without
words, the march, the funeral march, the music from far away.[26] The
following outline conveys an impression of the structure and character of the
movement. It should be kept in mind that the program headings set in caps
are found only in the autograph.

Introduction

Mm.   1–10   THE AWAKENING CALL: Intonation of the march theme
        11–26   *Misterioso* (anticipation of the introduction of the midnight
                 song)
        27–56   Funeral March (*Schwer und dumpf*) [heavy and dull]
       57–131   Recitative/Arioso (mm. 115–126 a sleep motif)
      132–147   PAN IS SLEEPING: Chorale (with songlike melody as
                 counterpoint)
      148–163   THE HERALD: Fanfare that dissolves into music from far
                 away
      164–224   Recitative/Arioso (at Nos. 13–16 funeral march rhythms as
                 accompaniment; mm. 214–224 a sleep motif)
      225–246   Music from far away (Chorale with songlike counter melody,
                 later fanfare *sich gänzlich verlierend* (completely vanishing)
                 ~Mm. 132–163

Exposition

      273–346   March music from a distance, coming closer and closer (with
                 songlike character at the beginning): Entrance of Summer
      347–368   Hymnlike, then intense climax: Anticipation of the Finale

Development

      369–449   Recitative/Arioso
      450–491   Music from far away
      492–529   Song without words in two stanzas, in G-flat major
      530–642   *March* (marked thus by Mahler in the score)
                 No. 44: *DAS GESINDEL* ("The Rabble")
                 No. 49: *DIE SCHLACHT BEGINNT* ("The Battle Begins")
                 No. 51: *DER SÜDSTURM* ("The South Storm")
                 naturalistic description of the storm

Recapitulation

      643–654   Statement of the march theme
      655–670   *Misterioso*
      671–736   Recitative/Arioso (with funeral march beginning)

737–856 March *aus weitester Ferne sich nähernd* (from very far away coming closer)
857–862 Intense climax: Anticipation of the Finale
863–875 Victory fanfare

To reconstruct the origin of this movement, we have to examine the sketches at Stanford University. They are dated "1895" and reveal that in the summer of 1895 Mahler sketched the marchlike music of the exposition and two further sections that were to become part of the development. He wrote out measures 247–321 of the exposition. A comparison with the final version reveals that except for the first and last measures, the principal melodic line (the bass being suggested only in a few places) already shows the final form. At the entrance of the actual exposition in measure 273, Mahler notes the word *Trommel* (drum). It is surprising that this entire marchlike section is written in E major rather than in F major, as in the final form.

On a different sheet, Mahler sketched measures 463–481, the passage that seems to come from "very far away" and features pedal points, seemingly bitonal effects, and mysterious trumpet and horn signals (mm. 468–472, 478–481). Mahler inserted the words *Pan is sleeping,* proving that in the conception of the movement he was guided by programmatic ideas. It may be a hidden allusion to Lipiner's poem, which begins with the following verse:[27]

> *Es war, als wär' nur eine große Wolke*
> *das ganze All—*
> *die Wolke lag und schlief*

> It was as if there was only one large cloud
> The whole universe—
> The cloud rested and slept.

On two other pages Mahler wrote measures 539–569, the extremely shrill E-flat minor march. The numerous indications for the instrumentation—piccolo, trumpet, bassoon, E-flat clarinet, double basses—provided for this draft, along with the remark "*Tuba und Posaunen roh dreinblasen!* (Tuba and trombones [should] play crudely!)" disclose that even in early drafts Mahler had precise ideas about the orchestral sound. The passage is set for winds and double basses or strings playing in unison, and in the autograph bears the title *Das Gesindel*. Bauer-Lechner recorded what Mahler meant:

> "Summer is Moving In" is to be the prelude. There, to attain the rough effect of arrival of my martial fellow, I immediately need a military band. It will really sound as if a band from the castle comes marching in, attracting the kind of rabble one would seldom see at other times (BL[2] 35).

Mahler drafted the introduction to the first movement in June 1896, as we also learn from Bauer-Lechner (BL[2] 56). The sketches preserved in the Austrian National Library most likely date from this time. They contain material mainly from the introduction in the form of a score sketch of measures 164–238. Alma Maria Mahler's claim that this is the "first sketch" can hardly be maintained.[28] Two places in these sketches also carry the heading "Pan is Sleeping."

Mahler's program headings in the autograph and his other hermeneutic explanations regarding the first movement do not merely provide general information; they can also be related to the music, allowing a reliable programmatic interpretation. The basic programmatic idea of the introduction is the awakening of Pan, the creation of life out of lifeless matter. Mahler said: "It is eerie, how out of lifeless matter (I could just as well have named the movement 'What the Mountains Tell Me') life gradually breaks forth" (BL[2] 56). One recognizes how authentic this statement is when hearing that Mahler, according to a letter of June 1896 to Anna von Mildenburg, in fact wanted to give the first movement (meaning the introduction) the title "What the Mountains Tell Me" (GMB[2] 165). The following explanations are no less descriptive (BL[2] 56):

> The introduction to this movement expresses once again the mood of brooding summer midday heat. No breeze is moving, all life is at a standstill, the sun-drenched air trembles and flickers. I can hear the sound in my mental ear, but how to find the real sounds? In between, a young man moans, struggling for salvation. Life is still chained in the abyss of lifeless, rigid nature (as in Hölderlin's "Rhein"), until it emerges victorious in the first movement, which follows the introduction *attacca*.

These explanations and Mahler's music are very closely related. The funeral march and the recitative-arioso sections that lend special character to the introduction symbolize lifeless nature, the lament of the chained life. The sleep motifs (mm. 115–126 and mm. 214–224), together with the choralelike parts, represent Pan's sleep. The section entitled "The Herald" and the march "from far away" (mm. 247–272) proclaim the arrival of summer and of life. The fact that the exposition and also the recapitulation do without the usual thematic dualism or pluralism is also programmatic. The march coming from the distance, beginning very softly and swelling little by little to *fortissimo*, depicts summer's arrival.[29]

The development is largely programmatic. Three sections definitely refer to images in Lipiner's poem, which also deals with the battle of colliding heavenly bodies, with battle cries, and with a thunderstorm. These pictures correspond with the cues in the autograph: "The Rabble" (No. 44), "The Battle Begins" (No. 49), and "The South Storm" (No. 51). The first passage shows extreme sharpness of expression, deliberate triviality and rudeness, and its instrumentation is shrill.[30] The performance indications—*roh* (rude), (m. 545) in the horns and trombones and *grell* (shrill) (m. 579) in the oboes—are original. The second section is distinguished by martial motifs and signals. The third section, however, is a realistic illustration of a storm, with timpani rolls, inclusion of the complete percussion section, and stormy sixteenth-figurations in the strings. In a conversation with Bauer-Lechner on 4 July 1896, Mahler explained the passage as follows:

> The first movement sweeps in, raging like the southern gale we are experiencing here these days and which—I am sure of this—brings with it fertility, coming from faraway, fruitful, hot countries, not like the gentle east wind we usually wish for. With a sweeping march tempo it roars, closer and closer, louder and louder, swelling like an avalanche, until all the loud, jubilant noise engulfs you. In between we hear mystic sounds, extraordinary, mysterious resting-points: *"O Mensch, gib acht!* [Oh, human, be on guard!]" (from "Night") (BL² 60).

Regarding the victory fanfare at the end (mm. 863–875) Mahler said: "I hope nothing will happen to me because these 16 measures, this gigantic salute to Pan by all that wild rabble—no one else could complete it" (BL² 65.) These remarks also reveal that he understood the first movement to represent not only the entry of summer but also the Bacchus Parade. Incidentally, it is typical for the strictness of the compositional form that this "gigantic salute" (based on the chord sequence G-flat₆—G—F) is by no means freely designed. Instead, it sums up, like an overview, the motifs and rhythms of the E-flat minor march from the development.

Was mir die Blumen auf der Wiese erzählen ("What the Flowers in the Meadow Tell Me")

The second movement of the Third Symphony shows a distinct five-part structure: a minuet-like main section alternates twice with a scherzolike trio. Gracefulness, refinement, and (in the scherzolike parts) agility are characteristics of the composition, which represents an original concept of variation form. In a program sketch Mahler stated that the main theme was characterized by "variations that become increasingly rich."[31] This statement can literally be applied to the whole movement. The first two parts are elaborately varied at each recurrence.

In this program sketch, Mahler produced a kind of thematic analysis of the movement. He lists four themes and points out the motif relationships between them. Applying these specifications to an analysis, the following form or scheme becomes apparent:

Mm.	1–49	Main section (Part A) in three-part song form, A major
	50–90	"Trio" (Part B)
	50–69	2nd theme in ⅜ meter, F-sharp minor
	70–78	3rd theme in ²/₄ meter, F-sharp minor

The scheme only hints at what becomes noticeable in a more detailed study of the music, namely, that the trio has three themes of different meter and character. It may also be observed that when the trio recurs, it is longer: Part B is 41 measures, Part B¹ is 73 measures. Those studying Mahler's variation technique should above all compare these two trio sections with each other. The third theme, originally nine measures long, is later developed into a small, three-part form of considerable size (34 measures). The theme now is in G-sharp minor, not in F-sharp minor as in the beginning. It is especially remarkable that in the last part of the second trio section (mm. 198–201), the third and fourth themes at times appear contrapuntally entwined.

Mahler based the minuet-like main section (Part A) on a seemingly simple form. It is true that the structure follows the scheme of a small three-part song form: A (19 measures) + B (14 measures) + A' (16 measures). The borders between sections B and A, however, are blurred, and at the beginning of the last section the theme is varied.

Mm. 1–4

Mm. 34–37

An early sketch from the collections at Stanford shows that the theme gave Mahler quite a bit of trouble:

In conversations with Bauer-Lechner about *Blumenstück,* Mahler explained that in his compositions he often used pictures as his point of departure, pictures that decisively determined the formal aspects of the music. Thus he stated in April 1896:

> It is the most carefree music I have ever written, as carefree as only flowers can be. It all sways and ripples like flowers on limber stems sway in the wind. Today I realized to my surprise that the basses have nothing but pizzicato, not *one* firm stroke, and that the low, heavy percussion is not used at all.[32] On the other hand, the violins, again with a solo violin, have the most lively, flowing, and charming figures.... That this innocent flowery cheerfulness does not last but suddenly becomes serious and weighty, you can well imagine. A heavy storm sweeps across the meadow and shakes the flowers and leaves. They groan and whimper, as if pleading for redemption to a higher realm (BL[2] 49).

Similarly he said on 1 July 1896:

> The picture of flowers in their resting position soon becomes useless for illustration of the music. Now I viewed them as tossed about by storm and thunder, then again cradled by mild breezes, transformed and caressed by the rays of the sun (BL[2] 58).

Was mir die Thiere im Walde erzählen ("What the Animals in the Forest Tell Me")

The *Wunderhorn* poem *Ablösung* ("Change") gives expression to a contrasting thought. The first verse relates the death of the cuckoo; in the second, the nightingale is proclaimed his successor. Mahler's setting of 1892, *Ablösung im Sommer,* took this antithesis into consideration. The first part of the song, with its bird-call motifs, parallel triads, and Phrygian turns, is in minor; the pleasant sixteenth-note movement of the bright second part is in major. The song ends in minor, and the postlude (nine measures) brings back motifs from the first verse.

Mahler used the instrumental substance of this song, which lasts only 67 measures, as the basis for the Third Symphony's third movement. It is a composition of enormous dimensions (590 measures). In doing so, he developed the song's motifs and composed several completely new sections.

The designation of the movement as "Scherzo" can most likely be attributed to Mahler himself, yet it is inappropriate, for the movement features a variety of moods and genres. The scherzando-like main part (written in $\frac{2}{4}$ meter) is followed by sections with a pastorale, scherzo, and also polk character, not to mention the two post horn episodes derived from a completely different musical sphere.

The attempt to explain the structure of the movement as a scherzo with two trios is also unfortunate. Upon closer examination, the arrangement shows rondolike features, and it is important to know that Mahler himself understood this movement as a rondo.[33] The following outline will clarify the rondolike structure:

Mm.   1–68   Part A in $\frac{2}{4}$ meter and in C minor/C major: *Scherzando* character
         69–120   Part B in $\frac{6}{8}$ meter and in C major: pastorale-like or scherzolike character
         121–210   Part A′
         211–228   Part B greatly shortened and modified
         229–255   Transition
         256–346   Part C: Post horn episode in F major
                   (Post horn *wie aus weiter Ferne*) [as from far away]
         347–373   Part D in $\frac{2}{4}$ meter, beginning in F minor and ending in C minor: *Mit geheimnisvoller Hast!* (With mysterious haste!)
         374–431   Part E, beginning in F major and ending in C minor: *Lustig, übermüthig* (Merry or boisterous) No. 22: polkalike character
         432–465   Part B′: *Grob!* (Crude!)
         466–484   Transition
         485–528   Part C′: Post horn episode in F major (Post horn *in weiter Entfernung*) [from a great distance]
         529–556   Crescendo from *ppp* to *fff* and diminuendo down to *pppp*. Development of the bird-call motif: *Der schwere Schatten der leblosen Natur* (the heavy shadow of lifeless nature) (BL² 56)
         557–590   Coda

Those who speak of a basic five-part structure probably go by the observation that Parts D and E are partly based on motifs from Part A. But one must not ignore that Mahler creates something completely new from these (and other) motifs and gives these parts a distinct character. Let us compare Part D with Part A. At the beginning of Part D (mm. 347–350) Mahler uses a four-measure phrase from Part A (mm. 5–8), but by means of a different key (F minor instead of C minor), rhythm, dynamic (*pp* instead of *f*), articulation (tremolo), and instrumentation completely changes the phrase's character:

Mm. 5–8

Mm. 347–350

The scherzando-like character of Part A here gives way to a mysterious character. The heading in the printed score reads *Mit geheimnisvoller Hast!*

Even more instructive is the way in which Mahler obtains the motifs of the polkalike section (Part E). The phrase in which the leading melody is performed by the first horn (mm. 370–373) is taken from the song, which is borrowed from Part A. At the beginning of Part E, this phrase appears (now as the lower voice) in a completely different form. Rhythm and articulation have remained the same, but the intervals have been radically modified. On this new basis, Mahler creates a polkalike melody:

Mm. 370–373

Mm. 374–377

According to the changing moods, the music also changes considerably, moving between the extremes of gentlest poetry and noisiest exuberance. The piece begins scherzando-like, a mood that increases throughout to *Lustigkeit* (merriment) at No. 19, *Übermut* (boisterousness) at No. 22, and even *Grobheit* (rudeness) at No. 23. The many bird calls and bird imitations are evidence that Mahler imagined animal sounds and the animalistic in general from the beginning.[34] On 2 July 1896 he remarked to Bauer-Lechner: "All the animals always seemed to be so different, characteristic and lively, so that there always was ample material for humor" (BL[2] 58). Further in the summer of 1899 he remarked:

> The Scherzo, the animal piece, is the most ludicrous and at the same time the most tragic. Only music can mystically lead us from one to the other in one breath. This piece really sounds as if all of nature were making faces and sticking out its tongue. But there is such a horrible, paniclike humor in it that one is overcome with horror rather than with laughter (BL[2] 136).

A special place is occupied by the two post horn episodes, of which the second is considerably shorter than the first. Sounding more like distant folk music, they contrast strongly with most of the other sections of the movement. Much has been written about the function, the folk songlike melodies, and the supposed sentimentality of the episodes. Monika Tibbe[35] successfully counters the accusation of supposed banality.[36] The episodes' meaning, on the other hand, has hardly been discussed. For the Berlin premiere of three movements of the Third under Felix Weingartner on 9 March 1897, Mahler supplied a brief program for this movement. In it, he states that the animal movement illustrates

> the quiet, undisturbed life of the forest before the appearance of man. Then the animals catch sight of the first human being and, although he walks calmly past them, the terrified [animals] sense that future trouble will come from him.[37]

Several interesting suggestions for the interpretation of the post horn passages were made by Ernst Decsey, who associated with Mahler in later years.[38] Decsey said that to understand the post horn passage correctly, one would have to think of Lenau's poem *Lieblich war die Maiennacht* ("Lovely Was the May Night"). In the music as in the poem, a lonely sound drifts through the woods. Mahler was supposedly very surprised by Decsey's comment, asked to see him, and exclaimed: "That's exactly what I had thought! The same poem and the same mood—how did you know this?" The thought that Mahler, who was so responsive to literature, was inspired by Lenau gains in probability if one recalls that Lenau's poem bears the title *Der Postillon* ("The Stagecoach Driver") and that in Mahler's autograph, *Der Postillon* is written at the beginning of the first post horn episode (No. 14).[39] Another poem by Lenau, *Das Posthorn,* is also related to the mood of Mahler's movement.[40]

Both post horn episodes greatly affect the course of the movement. The music reacts to the first episode *mit geheimnisvoller Hast*; the *pianissimo* passage, Nos. 17–19 (our Part D) emerges as a surprising variation on the movement's beginning. The second post horn episode is followed by an unusual dynamic arch that begins *ppp*, rises to *fff*, and finally diminishes to *ppppp* (Nos. 30–32). The climax occurs on an E-flat minor chord, which is foreign to the key. The motif material is entirely based on the bird-call motif that is heard in augmentation in measures 545–556. Mahler interpreted the passage as follows: "At the end of the 'Animals' movement we once again feel the heavy shadow of lifeless nature, of as yet uncrystallized, inorganic matter" (BL[2] 56).

Was mir der Mensch erzählt ("What Mankind Tells Me")

In June 1896 Mahler thought of most movements of the Third as humoresques, considering only the fourth and sixth movements to be "profoundly serious" (BL[2] 57). The remark becomes more understandable if one considers that while the other movements are descriptive, in these

Mahler speaks about himself. How close to his heart these two movements were is also revealed in a letter to the conductor Josef Krug-Waldsee in the summer of 1902 (at a time when he had distanced himself from Strauss's type of program music.) In regard to the titles of the Third that he had withdrawn, Mahler stated:

> They give you an idea of how I imagined the ever-increasing articulation of sentiment, from the dull, rigid, elementary state (of the powers in nature) all the way to the gentleness of the human heart, which in turn points and reaches higher (to God) (GMB[2] 274f.).

Nietzsche's "Midnight Song" (the subject of the fourth movement) concludes two chapters of *Also sprach Zarathustra*—"Das andere Tanzlied (The Other Dance Song)" in the third part and "Das trunkene Lied (The Drunken Song)" in the fourth part. In the latter chapter, the poem evolves little by little. The thoughts expressed in each individual section lead every time to the formulation of a new verse. Mahler found several things in "Midnight Song" that must have appealed to him: the midnight mood, the idea of eloquent midnight;[41] the awakening from a deep dream;[42] the dialectic of night and day, pain and pleasure, decay and eternal life; and finally Nietzsche's interpretation of eternity as a return.[43]

The evocative power of the poem is due to the wealth of images and words imbued with meaning and to its musicality. In eleven lines, the word *deep* occurs no less than eight times. Johann Siering spoke of a "circling, a spiraling-in of words."[44] Mahler's music increases this effect by means of further word repetitions. The words *O Mensch!* ("Oh, human!") and *Gib acht!* ("Be on guard!") are repeated at the beginning. Using another device, Mahler further repeats the apostrophe *O Mensch!* after the sixth line, thereby dividing his setting into two parts (81 and 66 measures) that are in many ways interrelated but are not identical. These correspondences can be seen in the "mystic" harmonies of the beginning,[45] in the sounds of nature, and also in the final section, the first part of which (mm. 57–81) is purely instrumental and the second (mm. 119–147) being vocal and instrumental.[46]

The style and expression of this song contrast strongly with all other movements of the Third.[47] Dynamics and timbre are exceptional. The dynamic level never departs from *piano* and *pianissimo,* and for long stretches the sound of a fifth in cellos and double basses provides the foundation (mm. 18–42, 46–56, 94–99), which is then relieved by tremolos of the divided violas. The harmony is sometimes characterized by major-minor shifts and at other times by a mixed major-minor mode.

The song is based on the concept of the mysterious music of nature that can be heard only in a dream. The unusually high, "long-echoing" sounds of the trombones alternating (mm. 20–23) with unusually low tones of the piccolos and with harmonics played by the harps, violins, and violas are all meant to be understood as sounds of nature. The passage offers us a very instructive example of Mahler's willful style of instrumentation which he described as follows:

If I want to achieve a soft, subdued tone, I do not let it be played by an instrument that can easily produce it; rather I give it to one that is able to produce it with only great effort, indeed, often with extreme exertion that exceeds its usual limits. That is why basses and bassoons often have to squeak for me in the highest register, and the flute blows way down low (BL[2] 175ff.).

The corresponding passage in the second part (mm. 96–99) is scored differently. Here Mahler combines the trombone with the flutes and has it alternate with the piccolo and muted trumpet and with harmonics.[48]

Mahler also wanted the call-like motifs to be understood as sounds of nature. They appear in five places, starting in the oboe, then in the English horn, then again in the oboe. In several of these places the autograph contains the heading *Der Vogel der Nacht* (The Bird of the Night).[49] If one considers that the first oboe call answers the question of the alto solo *Was spricht die tiefe Mitternacht?* ("What does the deep midnight say?"), it becomes understandable that the calls of the bird of the night represent midnight, speaking mysteriously and revealing the world's secrets.

Was mir die Engel erzählen ("What the Angels Tell Me")

The theme of the poem *Armer Kinder Bettlerlied* ("Poor Children's Beggar Song") from *Des Knaben Wunderhorn* is the story of Peter's guilt (transgression of the Ten Commandments) and his absolution through Jesus.[50] We do not know whether Mahler (in the summer of 1895) intended all along to incorporate the angels into the Third Symphony and came upon this poem in search of a suitable text or whether the poem inspired him to compose a kind of *musica angelica*. At any rate, he seems to have liked this poem very much because it speaks not only of the "sweet" singing of the angels but also of "heavenly joy that has no end." Apparently this text corresponded completely to his concept, which was that "humor should be called on to express only the highest thoughts that cannot be expressed any other way" (BL[2] 57).

Corresponding to the concept of a *music coelestis,* the timbre of the composition (except for the middle section) is distinctly bright. Mahler wrote the song for alto solo, boys' and women's voices, and included four tuned bells and a Glockenspiel.[51] All this (and also the instruction that the choirs of bells and boys should be placed "up above") is reminiscent of Wagner's *Parsifal,* a work for which Mahler felt deep admiration.[52] The prominent wind timbres are typical of Mahler's concept of sound. Violins and timpani rest altogether (and are therefore all the more effective in the Finale), while the low strings (violas, cellos, and double basses) are at first used sparingly.

Of the five stanzas of the poem, performance of the first two and the last two should be *lustig im Tempo und keck im Ausdruck* (merry in tempo and cocky in expression), corresponding with the sweet singing of the three angels and with heavenly joy. The hymnlike melody fits in well, as do the archaic-sounding harmonies that make frequent use of secondary chords. Only the middle part of the movement (mm. 35–81) is gloomy (due to the content of the third stanza of the poem), bordering on a funeral march at the end; Peter still laments the transgression of the Ten Commandments. No wonder Mahler uses tam-tams, which in his music often suggest death; here they symbolize horror as well as the fear of spiritual death. Mahler borrowed the substance of measures 39–63 from his song *Das himmlische Leben,* which he completed in 1892 (here mm. 57–74) and which he referred to in 1900 when he mentioned to Bauer-Lechner that "no less than five movements of the Third and Fourth had developed from this song."[53]

In the final section, Mahler put the poem's divisions aside and combined the last two stanzas. This was possible because both tell of the heavenly joy. More significant is a text change thus far unrecognized. Mahler changed the words of the third line in the fourth stanza from *Und bete zu Gott nur allezeit* ("And pray to God at all times") to *Liebe nur Gott in alle Zeit!* ("Love only God at all times!"). Following this verse the women's and boys' choirs sing a four-measure, choralelike movement a cappella (mm. 86–89). It is the only part of the entire song that is performed without instrumental accompaniment.

At the closing words *durch Jesum und Allen zur Seligkeit* ("through Jesus and for the blessedness of all") (mm. 100–107), the music takes on a choralelike character, and the entrance of the trombones underscores the solemnness of the moment. The song closes with the sound of fading bells.

Was mir die Liebe erzählt ("What Love Tells Me")

In the years 1895 and 1896, Mahler reflected much upon the Third, seeking to determine its special qualities. He therefore viewed it under different aspects. In the summer of 1895 he found that it "entirely disregarded" customary form (BL[2] 35), yet one year later he found in it the "same basic structure" as in the classic symphonies of Haydn, Mozart, and Beethoven:

"Adagio, Rondo, Minuet, Allegro, and within that the old structure, the known periods" (BL² 64). However, he also commented that "in my work the sequence of movements is different, and greater variety and complexity occur within the movements."

Regarding the final movement Mahler said that within it "everything has dissolved in peace and quiet": the "Ixion wheel" had finally been brought to a standstill.⁵⁴ He added that his Third, like his Second, would close "against all custom" with an Adagio, "a higher as opposed to a lower form" (BL² 68).

Analyzing the Adagio of the Third, one may find that Mahler gave clear indications for its proper understanding and interpretation in a letter of 29 August to Fritz Löhr. "*Was mir die Liebe erzählt* is a summary of my emotions about all creatures. Deeply painful interludes cannot be avoided, but these gradually turn into blessed confidence: 'the joyful science' " (GMB² 127).

The movement shows an unconventional four-part structure with qualities of a rondo or sonata. A main–theme complex in D major with hymnic character is contrasted by a minor complex that includes a chorale theme and a secondary theme.

Part I

Mm.	1–40	Main–theme complex in D major
	41–50	Chorale theme (with transitional function)
	51–62	Secondary theme in C-sharp minor (mm. 55–60, the chorale theme given to the horn)
	63–91	Transitional section, beginning with the primary motifs of the main theme and leading into reminiscences of the main movement

Part II

92–123	Main–theme complex in D major (varied)
124–131	Chorale theme (with transitional function)
132–148	Secondary theme beginning in C-sharp minor
149–197	Modulating development-like passage leading into a quotation from the "Midnight Song"—*Tief ist ihr Weh!* ("Deep is the lament!")

Part III

198–219	Main–theme complex in D major (shortened)
220–244	Reminiscences of the high points in the first movement
245–251	Transition

Part IV

252–299	Main–theme complex in D major (extended)

300–328	Coda

The main theme, recurring four times, suggests a rondo. It first appears as a small three-part song form according to the scheme A (8 measures) + B (12 measures) + A' (8 measures) + Coda (12 measures). At every recurrence the parts are placed differently or are varied, or both. In the second part of the movement the parts appear, for instance, in an inverted order: A' (8 measures) + B (8 measures) + B (8 measures) + A (16 measures).

According to the model of sonata form, a transitional passage (Chorale theme) and a contrasting secondary theme in C-sharp minor follow the main theme complex. These also return in the movement's second part, which contains a longer development-like passage. But the structure of the third part is unusual in that the Chorale and secondary themes do not recur. This apparently expresses the idea that the "painful interludes" gradually dissolve into "a blessed confidence."

The extremely excited passages into which the first three parts of the movement flow certainly express these "painful interludes," and it is significant that at all three places Mahler quotes from the first movement or from the "Midnight Song." The second of these three climaxes (mm. 174–197) quotes note for note the passage *Tief ist ihr Weh!* from the "Midnight Song."

Fourth movement, mm. 105–106

Finale, mm. 182–185

This far exceeds the intensity of the first (mm. 71–91). The third climax (mm. 220–244) sets even more dramatic accents than the second by means of sighlike turns and dissonances, such as the minor-ninth chord and the thirteenth chord (B—D-sharp—A—C—E—G).

A *pianissimo* passage in the first flute (mm. 245–249) announces the turning point. The trumpets (*zart hervortretend*—gently standing out) and occasionally the horns take over the hymnlike main theme, which up until now was almost exclusively entrusted to the strings. On 31 July 1896, Natalie Bauer-Lechner wrote in her diary that in the morning Mahler had changed the end of the Adagio because it was "not plain enough. It now dies away in broad chords and only in the one key: D major," he told me (BL[2] 66).

The Adagio of the Third is the first typical Mahler Adagio. The seeds it contains were later to bear fruit in several slow movements.

A page from the short score of the first movement of the Fourth Symphony
Stanford University Memorial Library of Music
First Publication
Measures 77–101 and 341–349

The Fourth Symphony

I am still living somewhat in the world of my Fourth.
It is basically different from my other symphonies.
But it must be that way; it would be impossible for
me to repeat myself, and just as life moves on, I
likewise explore new paths in every new work.

GMB² 248

And yet it is so necessary that you know it [the
Second Symphony] because my Fourth will be very
strange to you. It is all humorous, "naive," etc.; it
represents the part of my life that is still the hardest
for you to accept and which in the future only
extremely few will comprehend.   AME 276

Origin

In composing various movements of his first three symphonies, Mahler
borrowed from himself, developing the instrumental substance of his own earlier songs. He continued this practice in developing his Fourth but extended it
to the limit. *Das himmlische Leben,* an orchestra song composed in 1892,
functions not only as the Finale of the Symphony but also serves as the seed
from which the first three movements grow. Though Mahler certainly based
every one of the first three movements largely on independent thematic
material, he nonetheless quoted and paraphrased motifs and themes from the
orchestra song. These connections were so important to him that on 8
February 1911 he wrote to Georg Göhler, who was writing an introduction
to the Fourth and had asked Mahler for an honest critique of his essay:

> I am missing one thing: Did you overlook the thematic connections that
> figure so prominently in the work's design? Or did you just want to spare
> the audience some technical explanations? In any case, I ask that that
> aspect of my work be specially observed. Each of the three movements is
> connected thematically with the last one in a most intimate and meaning-
> ful way (GMB² 403).

Mahler believed in the "mystique of creating" (BL[2] 26); he once mentioned to Bauer-Lechner (BL[2] 161): "One does not compose; composing is a passive state."[1] To explain the strange borrowing from his own songs, he created an entire theory for himself. According to it, the particular songs contained "fertile seeds" that fulfilled their "design and development" in the symphonic process. *Das himmlische Leben* astonished him the most because, as he stated, no less than five movements in the Third and the Fourth developed from it. Because of this, the final movement of the Fourth received "a very special, all-encompassing meaning" (BL[2] 172). In 1900 Mahler told Natalie Bauer-Lechner:

> At first glance one does not even notice all that is hidden in this inconspicuous little song, and yet one can recognize the value of such a seed by testing whether it contains the promise of a manifold life. This is particularly true in the case of "The Heavenly Life," which after the period of stagnation in Pest was the first inspiration to occur in Hamburg.

"The Heavenly Life" belonged to a series of five humoresques that came into being during the first months of 1892 in Hamburg.[2] The piano version was completed on 10 February; a little later (on 12 March) the full score was finished. In *Des Knaben Wunderhorn,* the poem (a Bavarian folk song) has the title *Der Himmel hängt voll Geigen* ("Heaven is Full of Violins").[3] The five stanzas of the poem, which Goethe characterized as "a Christian fool's paradise, not without spirit,"[4] describe the heavenly joys, draw the picture of a heavenly land of milk and honey, and end with the praise of the *musica coelestis,* the heavenly music: "*Kein Musik ist ja nicht auf Erden, die unsrer verglichen kann werden*" ("No music is there on earth that could be compared with ours"). Mahler was charmed over and over again by this poem. He saw in it an odd mixture of "knavery" and "deepest mysticism" and admired it for its imaginativeness that "turns everything upside down" and makes causality invalid (BL[2] 185).

If one keeps in mind Mahler's strong interest in metaphysical questions, one can better understand why the naive yet profound world of this poem occupied him for several years. As mentioned earlier, in the summer of 1895 he planned to let the Third Symphony, which he was then working on, conclude with "The Heavenly Life," though he was uncertain whether he should give the movement the title "The Heavenly Life" or "What the Child Tells Me." He had dropped this plan by the following summer, favoring the idea of letting a new symphony (the Fourth) end with "The Heavenly Life." A synopsis of the Fourth that was first published by Paul Bekker has the following content:[5]

Symphony No. 4 (Humoresque)

No. 1 *Die Welt als ewige Jetztzeit* (The World as Eternal Now), G major
No. 2 *Das irdische Leben* (The Earthly Life) E-flat minor
No. 3 *Caritas,* B major (Adagio)

No. 4 *Morgenglocken* (Morning Bells), F major
No. 5 *Die Welt ohne Schwere* (The World Without Gravity), D major
  (Scherzo)
No. 5. [sic] *Das himmlische Leben* (The Heavenly Life), G major

It becomes evident that for the Fourth no less than three orchestra songs were planned: "The Earthly Life" (composed at the latest in the summer of 1893), "Three Angels Were Singing a Sweet Melody" (= "Morning Bells," completed in the summer of 1895), and "The Heavenly Life." The fact that the middle song is hidden behind the laconic title "Morning Bells" prompted Paul Bekker to conjecture that plans for the Fourth Symphony were made "almost at the same time" as for the Third (that is, the summer of 1895).[6] Bekker surmised that the fourth movement of the sketch, "Morning Bells," originally was intended for the Fourth and only later found its place in the Third. The circumstances also allow another explanation. The title of the program sketch, *Symphony No. 4 (Humoresque),* rather suggests the hypothesis that the sketch was designed after the completion of the Third (that is, after the summer of 1896). Nevertheless, it is conceivable that Mahler planned initially to base the Fourth Symphony on the music of the angel choir but later dismissed this plan.

Be that as it may, the program sketch indicates that plans for the Fourth originally included three purely symphonic movements—Nos. 1, 3, and 5. Of these, it is apparent that only the first movement ("The World as Eternal Now") was realized in the final form. The Scherzo ("Dance of Death" in C minor/C major) and the slow movement (Poco Adagio in G major) of the Fourth have nothing in common with the corresponding movements of the program sketch. In this respect Mahler departed considerably from his first plan, but Paul Bekker could be correct in his assumption that the plans for the Adagio and the Scherzo occupied Mahler even after the completion of the Fourth. In a first sketch for the Eighth Symphony, the plan for a "Caritas" Adagio is evident, and it is not out of the question that in the D-major Scherzo of the Fifth the idea of a "world without gravity" still existed.

In the summer of 1899, Mahler apparently had good reason to be altogether dissatisfied with his vacation domicile. In Bad Aussee, where he spent the vacation, he felt hindered in his work by rain, cold, and the "the ghastly health-resort music" (*Kurmusik)* and he feared that the precious six weeks, the only part of the year when he was free to compose, would be wasted (BL[2] 135). He was all the happier, therefore, when he conceived of the music to "Revelge." His vacation was almost over when in the last days of July, as Natalie Bauer-Lechner tells, the Fourth Symphony "fell into his lap just in the nick of time" (BL[2] 138):

> After completing "Revelge," he had given up all work due to the many disturbances. But suddenly we could tell that in spite of it all, he had become involved in another composition. This time it was not a small work but a larger one, which meant that the noise and restlessness of the

place and the impending end of his vacation increasingly affected the poor soul. God knows what he was able to rescue during the reprieve of a mere ten days, even though we know that he can make the impossible possible. In spite of all obstacles, he is working wherever he can, even when taking a walk (either alone or with us, hanging back to be by himself), something he has not done since *Das klagende Lied*.

Remarkably, Mahler managed to draft "about half" of the first three movements in those ten days, and he even sketched the variations of the slow movement (BL² 164). His disappointment at having to stop was great. Looking back during the following summer, he expressed this regret to Bauer-Lechner:

> You can imagine with what emotions I stopped everything and left Aussee, since resuming this work seemed quite impossible. It took such a frightful amount of strength this year! I rolled up the sketches that were not legible for anyone else, threw them into the last compartment of my desk, and did not even look at them—in fact I could not even think of them without greatest, stinging pain.

In Mayiernigg, where Mahler spent his vacation in the summer of 1900, he again had difficulties in getting started on his work. This bothered him greatly. He thought he would never again write anything and already saw "his superstitious fear cruelly realized, that though he now had the house for composing, he would no longer be able to write" (BL² 157). "After the abrupt breaking off" at the end of the vacation in Aussee, it was not easy for him to find his way back to the drafts of the Fourth and to have the work "flow freely." By 7 July (his birthday) he did find his working rhythm again and was able to complete the composition on 5 August, but as Bauer-Lechner's diary tells us, "as usual, this did not make him happy but instead made him deeply upset to have lost such an important part of his life" (BL² 165).

On 19 August 1900, Mahler wrote to his friend Siegfried Lipiner: "Right! I have finished my Fourth; in the winter I will prepare the final copy" (GMB² 250). It seems that he kept his time schedule, because in the autograph (now at the Society of the Friends of Music in Vienna) we find written *Vienna, January 1901* at the end of the Scherzo.

Life After Death as a Subject

In October 1900, shortly before the completion of the Fourth, Mahler did something that amounted to denial of his symphonic work thus far by making a public statement in Munich against program music. Although he had originally been very partial to this genre, he now proclaimed that he wanted his symphonic works to be understood as absolute music, withdrawing the programs of his earlier symphonies and demanding that in the future they should be performed without programmatic explanations.

In spite of these solemn protestations, the Fourth is the exact opposite of what is commonly considered to be absolute music. The work is based on a philosophical program that Mahler did not officially reveal but nonetheless shared in conversations with friends. It is not an exaggeration to say that a full understanding of the Symphony is impossible without the knowledge of the program.

From Mahler's detailed remarks to Natalie Bauer-Lechner, to Bruno Walter, to his wife, and to Alphons Diepenbrock, it is evident that in the concept of the symphony he was guided by meditations about "life after death."[7] The subject of the work is therefore eschatological, as was the subject of the Second. In October 1901, Mahler explained this unmistakably when he described the basic mood of the Symphony to Bauer-Lechner:

> It contains the cheerfulness of a higher and, to us, an unfamiliar world that holds for us something eerie and horrifying. In the final movement ("The Heavenly Life"), although already belonging to this higher world, the child explains how everything is meant to be (BL[2] 198).

Natalie Bauer-Lechner was the first to learn more details about the Fourth. In the summer of 1900 she wrote in her diary:

> "Actually," he had already told me earlier, "I wanted to write only a symphonic humoresque, but it turned out to have the size of a normal symphony. Before, when I thought it should become a symphony, it grew into something of threefold length—my Second and Third."
>
> "The Heavenly Life" formed the final movement after the three movements Mahler had completed during this summer. He called it the top of the pyramid of this Fourth Symphony."
>
> "What I had in mind here was unbelievably difficult to do. Imagine the uniform blue of the skies, which is more difficult to paint than all changing and contrasting shades. This is the fundamental mood of the whole. Only sometimes it darkens and becomes ghostly, gruesome. But heaven itself is not darkened, it shines on in an eternal blue. Only to us it suddenly seems gruesome, just as on the most beautiful day in the woods, flooded with light, we are often gripped by a panic and fear. The Scherzo is mystical, confused and eerie so that your hair will stand on end. But in the following Adagio you will soon see that things were not so bad— everything is resolved" (BL[2] 162ff.).

Bauer-Lechner also reports on the Adagio, which Mahler also called Andante:

> He said it had the facial features of St. Ursula, who is mentioned in "The Heavenly Life" of the fourth movement. When I asked him whether he knew something about the saint and her legend, he said, "No. Otherwise I surely would not have been able or inclined to have such a definite and delightful image of her."
>
> Once he called the Andante "The Smiling of St. Ursula" and said that at the time he had a childhood image of his mother's face in mind,

recalling how she had laughed through grieving and had smiled through tears, for she had suffered unendingly yet had always lovingly resolved and forgiven everything"(BL[2] 163).

The well-known music historian Ludwig Schiedermair had asked Mahler in 1901 to explain the basic thought of the Fourth. At Mahler's request, Bruno Walter furnished the explanations in a letter to Schiedermair on 5 December 1901. His remarks agree with those of Bauer-Lechner. Walter wrote about the genesis of the work:

> Mahler, who had composed the song "The Heavenly Life" years ago, felt inspired by the delightful, childlike description of this heavenly life and felt transported into an exceedingly cheerful, distant, wondrous sphere. The thematic material, based on his own personal world of emotions, became part of the symphony. This was indeed a world of his own; probably no one else ever had breathed that air. Thus its musical reflection offered much that was new and striking.[8]

Walter described the subject of the work as follows:

> With these rather detailed reservations, let me tell you that the first three movements of the Fourth Symphony could describe a heavenly life. In the first movement, one could imagine a man getting to know this life. There is great cheerfulness, an unearthly joy that often attracts but at times seems strange. Life is bright and delightful and at times touchingly human. The second movement might be called *Freund Hein spielt zum Tanz auf* ("Friend Death is Striking Up the Dance"). Death fiddles rather strangely; his playing sends us up to heaven. Again, this is only one of several possible descriptions. *Sankt Ursula selbst dazu lacht* ("St. Ursula Stands by Laughing") could be the title of the third movement. The most serious of the saints is laughing, so cheerful is this life. Actually, she only smiles—a smile, as Mahler told me, like the ones on monuments of old knights or prelates (seen when walking through old churches), with their hands folded over their chests and the faint, peaceful smile of the departed who has found calm bliss. Solemn rest and serious, gentle cheerfulness characterize this movement, but it also contains deep, painful contrasts, like reminiscences of earthly life. At times cheerfulness grows into vivacity. If someone wonders what all this is about, a child answers in the fourth, the last movement: That is "The Heavenly Life."[9]

At the time of her engagement to Mahler, whom she married on 9 March 1902, Alma Mahler wrote:

> He told me that the Fourth Symphony was like an old picture painted on a golden background. Later he also told me that when he wrote the song *Ich bin der Welt abhanden gekommen* ("I Have Slipped Away from the

World"), he always thought of the monuments of cardinals in Italy, where the body rests with folded hands and closed eyes on flagstones in the churches.[10] I was bothered at the time by this fondness for the old; it was strange to our time. But he knew why he wanted it exactly like this because he was so naive; and at first I could not believe this. He was childlike. One could not understand this when one first heard him talk (AMML 27).

Mahler's friend Alphons Diepenbrock, a Dutch composer and conductor, wrote an essay based on authentic information about the Fourth.[11] He relates that in this work Mahler dealt "exclusively with the emotions of the soul freed from all earthly bonds, either as childlike though divinely cheerful or as the highest ecstasy to which the mystics of early times would rise in their concept of the divine." The "childlike happy mood" found expression in the first movement, the ecstatic in the third movement. The transition between these two movements was accomplished by the second movement: "It is Death who strikes up the dance and wants to lure the souls into his kingdom."

Among these explanations, Walter's comment regarding this slow movement ("Solemn rest and serious, gentle cheerfulness characterize this movement") deserves to be pointed out because it emerges, when looked at more closely, as a paraphrase of an important remark by Arthur Schopenhauer:[12] The condition of a human being who had achieved the negation of the will for life would be "unshakable peace, profound rest, and inner cheerfulness." From this it appears that Mahler's belief in divine rest and cheerfulness, at first glance seemingly naive, is based on the solid foundation of Schopenhauer's philosophy. Thus one can better understand what Mahler meant in a letter of 12 September 1903 when he wrote to Julius Buths that the strange "humor" of the Fourth "is not often recognized even by the best" (GMB[2] 282).

Considering how subtle the subject of the Fourth is, one can appreciate why Mahler refused to disclose the program of his work. Bauer-Lechner reports:

Mahler no longer wants to consider naming the individual movements of the work, as he did in earlier times. "I could think of some beautiful names for them, but I am not about to tell those nincompoops, the critics, and audiences; they would only misunderstand and twist them in the silliest ways!"(BL[2] 163).

Bruno Walter stated in the above-mentioned letter to Ludwig Schiedermair:

One cannot come to understand this work or any other of Mahler's symphonies by means of a program; it is absolute music from beginning to end, a symphony of four movements, organic in every movement, and easily accessible to anyone who has a sense for subtle humor.[13]

Design and Subject

When viewed from a distance, the Fourth strikes one as being Mahler's simplest symphony. Indeed, of all his symphonic works, it gives the impression of coming closest to the classic norm. Lasting about 52 minutes, it is, as Mahler himself remarked (BL[2] 162), no longer than the first movement of the Third.[14] It consists of four movements that are organized according to a traditional scheme: a lively first movement, a scherzo, a slow movement, and a finale (though it is an orchestra song). The form of the individual movements also seems to correspond to traditional patterns. Mahler himself, who during the summer of 1899 thought much about questions of form (BL[2] 138), said that the first movement was constructed "in spite of its freedom, with the greatest, almost pedantic regularity" (BL[2] 164). Nevertheless all movements reveal extremely original details of structure and artful variation in the sequence of musical ideas.

Further, Mahler consciously avoided employing the heaviest forces. In a conversation with Bauer-Lechner during the summer of 1900, he claimed that due to the subject matter, not one *fortissimo* occurred in the slow movement (or in the whole Symphony). "This will surprise the gentlemen who always claim that I work only with the heaviest forces" (BL[2] 163). Actually Mahler did mark several places *fortissimo* in the final version, but the fact remains that in his Fourth he made do with a relatively modest orchestra. He was content with four flutes, three oboes, three clarinets, three bassoons, four horns, three trumpets, percussion, and strings, omitting trombones and tuba. "At the end of the Adagio he would have needed them for a few measures, but he did not want to add them just for that and simply made do without them," said Bauer-Lechner. Finally, the simplicity of the themes in the first movement is so striking that the listeners at the Munich premiere on 25 November 1901 were surprised, having expected something eccentric from Mahler (BL[2] 202).

How can these special qualities of the Fourth be explained? Those who try to find an answer inherent in the music can easily be led astray. Nothing was more remote for Mahler than to render homage to classicism, that is, to write a classic work, as was attempted later by Max Reger (*Suite im alten Stil,* Op. 93) and Sergei Prokofiev (*Classical Symphony,* Op. 25). The highly individual structure of the Fourth, the economy of means, the simplicity of the themes in the first movement—these and many other things are a condition of the work's subject, the divine conditions of the soul that reveal themselves only to the one who senses the divine.

Mahler was fully aware of the novelty of his Fourth. It is "so basically different from my other symphonies," Mahler wrote on 18 August to Nina Spiegler (GMB[2] 248), adding that he had reconciled himself to having to

> explore new paths in every new work. That is why it is always so hard to get started. Whatever routine one has acquired is of no help. One has to learn afresh for every new work. Thus one remains eternally a beginner!

First Movement: *Die Welt als ewige Jetztzeit* ("The World as Eternal Now")

When one hears the first movement of the Fourth Symphony for the first time (or again after a long time), some passages are strongly reminiscent of Haydn, Mozart, Beethoven, and Schubert. One also might hear—as Adorno put it so nicely—"nonexistent children's songs."[15] This childlike character of the music (prevalent only in the exposition and recapitulation) was intentional. Mahler envisioned "unprecedented cheerfulness" and "unearthly joy,"[16] and he meant to give it expression through such music.[17] Thus he once called the first theme (mm. 4–7) "childlike, simple, and entirely non-self-conscious" (BL[2] 179). The sleigh bells at the beginning were intended to be a sign of humor (see BL[2] 202).

The music is certainly not what it pretends to be. Adorno's remark that "a masterpiece like the Fourth Symphony is an 'As If' from the first to the last note" is especially true of the first movement.[18] Mahler transforms borrowed melodic figures and stylistic means in such a way that something completely new emerges.

Mahler said about the movement, as mentioned, that it was constructed, "in spite of its freedom, with the greatest, almost pedantic regularity" (BL[2] 164). He also pointed out that the "opening theme" was followed by six further themes (seven in all) that were worked through in the development (BL[2] 198). An analysis of the composition, which is in first–movement sonata form, actually reveals seven themes, as the following outline demonstrates:

Exposition

Mm.		
	1–3	Bell motifs (*Bedächtig*) [Thoughtful] in B minor
	4–7	Theme I (*Recht gemächlich*) [Quite leisurely] in G major
	8–17	Theme II
	18–21	Theme I
	22–31	Theme II (varied)
	32–37	Theme III (*Frisch*) [Brisk]: transition to D major
	38–46	Theme IV (*Breit gesungen*) [Broadly sung]: first secondary theme in D major
	47–57	Theme V: second secondary theme
	58–72	Theme VI (*Plötzlich langsam und bedächtig*) [Suddenly slow and deliberate]: final group
	72–90	Varied repeat of the main section (false recapitulation) in G major
	91–101	Theme VII (*Wieder sehr ruhig und etwas zurückhaltend*) [Very restful again and holding back somewhat]: Epilogue in G major

Development

102–124	1st section (based on motifs of the main theme) in B minor and in E minor
125–144	2nd section: first statement of the paradise theme in A major (pastoral character)
145–154	3rd section: distorted paradise motif in C-sharp minor and E minor
155–166	4th section: includes the distorted paradise motif in E-flat minor and F-sharp minor
167–184	5th section: free treatment of bell motifs as well as of motifs from Theme II in F minor
185–208	6th section: motifs from the main theme beginning in B-flat minor
209–220	7th section: paradise theme contrapuntally combined with Theme III in C major
221–238	8th section: climax on a dissonance (BL^2 163: "panic shock"), then the *kleiner Appell* (small signal) (BL^2 164)
225–238	Transition (= hidden entry of recapitulation)

Recapitulation

239–252	Themes I and II
253–256	Paradise theme in the trumpet
257–262	Theme III
263–271	Theme IV
272–282	Theme V (*Mit großem Ton*) [With a big tone]
283–297	Theme VI (*Wieder plötzlich langsam und bedächtig*) [Suddenly slow again and deliberate]
298–322	Varied repeat of the main section
323–339	Theme VII

340–349	Coda

Looking at the distribution of the seven themes within the exposition and at the tonal disposition of this part of the movement, one readily sees that Mahler was correct when he spoke of "the greatest, almost pedantic regularity." Themes I and II form the main section, Theme III acts as a transition, the two cantabile Themes IV and V represent the secondary section, and Themes VI and VII comprise the final group or the epilogue (*Abgesang*). Except for the bell motifs of the beginning, which imply the key of B minor, the main section is in the principal key of G major; the transition modulates from G major to D major, and the secondary section as well as the final group are in the dominant key of D major. But then deviations from the classic scheme become noticeable. Following the final group there is the varied repeat of the main section (giving the impression of a false recapitulation), followed by the epilogue, in G major instead of in the dominant key. The frequent tempo changes within the exposition, of course, do not correspond with classic practice, but rather with the interpretation of a Beethoven symphony movement instituted by Richard Wagner.[19]

To determine how the impression of the "classicistic" is created in this movement, one has to point to the simplicity and treatment of themes, to the simple key relationships, to individual melodic turns (such as the chromatic suspensions in mm. 5 and 22), and to the ornamentation (occasional grace notes, written–out turns, and inverted mordents). More relevant is the unfamiliar treatment of familiar devices. Mahler shocks the listener with unexpected altered sounds, with seventh chords, and with deviations to the key of the supertonic—means that stand apart from the "classicistic" context. An example from Theme II illustrates this:

Mm. 27–29

Changes to the supertonic distinguish not only Theme II but also Theme V (see m. 50). In general, the emphasis on the second step is characteristic of "The Heavenly Life," a song whose style has strongly colored the main section, as shown by the bell motifs of the beginning.

Nevertheless, let us look a little further at the classicistic features of the music. The classic quality of several themes appears not only in the Schubert-like sound of the remarkably short Theme I, noticed by Adorno,[20] but also in a thus-far unnoticed similarity between Theme IV and Beethoven's piano sonata in E-flat major, Op. 27, No. 1:

Beethoven, first movement, mm. 8–12

Mahler, mm. 37–41

Here, too, one must speak of "unfamiliar treatment." The rather complicated metric relations (insert of a $\frac{3}{4}$ and a $\frac{2}{4}$ measure) run against the plain ductus of Theme IV and at first irritate the sense of meter of the listener familiar with classic music.

The development falls into eight sections. Its extraordinary complexity is seen not only in comparison to the exposition but throughout. Mahler commented that "the first movement begins as if it could not count to three but then goes right away into the higher multiplication table. At the end we are dealing, dizzily, with millions and millions" (BL[2] 164). Remarkable, at first, is the melodic and harmonic wealth. The exposition is almost exclusively in G major and D major, but the development continually explores new and partly distant keys, as well as the minor mode.

Aside from the bell motifs, motifs from Themes I, II, III, and VII are developed, and there are important borrowings from "The Heavenly Life." Altogether unnoticed so far is the fact that measures 113–115 of the main section paraphrase a passage (mm. 52–54) from the song. Even more significant is the anticipation and development of the paradise theme from the Finale, namely the melodic phrase sung to the words *Wir genießen die himmlischen Freuden* ("We savor the heavenly joys"). Mahler picks up the theme in the second section of the development (mm. 125–144) and transforms the passage into a typical pastorale: sustained basses in the double basses and cellos, which provide the foundation for the unison of the four flutes (Adorno spoke about the sound of a "dream-ocarina"[21]) and the complementary line for bass clarinet and bassoon.

Finale, mm. 12–14

First movement, mm. 126–131

In the following two sections (mm. 145–166) the paradise theme also maintains the lead, shortened and distorted, first in C-sharp and E minor and later in E-flat and F-sharp minor.

Mm. 148–150

A dotted scale motif (borrowed from Theme II) serves as the counterpoint for it. Muted trumpets and horns underscore the eerie character of this passage.

The two following sections of the development (mm. 167–208) are entirely in minor and contain bell motifs (the actual bells are heard only at the beginning of the development, mm. 102–108) and motifs from Themes I and II that lead toward a climax. The accumulated tension dissolves abruptly with the entry of the somewhat noisy, extremely bright, very radiant C major passage (mm. 209–220), in the course of which the first trumpet plays the paradise theme in yet another variation. The horn motifs are taken from Theme III.

Mm. 211–215

The movement's climax (mm. 221–224 occurs on an unexpectedly harsh dissonance, the minor ninth chord with a lowered fifth (G—B—D-flat—F—A-flat), which seems even more blatant after the serene C major. The voice leading paints the picture of a fall from great height. The trumpets quote the shortened, distorted paradise motif in upper and lower range:

Mm. 221–224

With this—the D-flat above middle C—the final note of this phrase becomes the beginning note of a fanfare by the trumpets and horns, a fanfare (mm. 224–236) that coincides with the artfully disguised beginning of the recapitulation. Mahler once said that "they will not find out until later how artistic this return is" (BL[2] 202).

The strange as well as unexpected happenings at the end of the development defy strictly musical explanation. In conversations with Bauer-Lechner, Mahler explained them hermeneutically but without identifying the passages. As he expressed it, "the uniform blue of the skies is the fundamental mood of the whole.[22]

Mahler further disclosed that in the first movement a kind of "small military signal, a companion piece to the large one in the last movement of the Second" occurs:

When the confusion and the pushing and shoving of the troops, who had moved out in orderly fashion, becomes too much, a signal by the commander immediately gathers them to the accustomed order under his banner (BL² 164).

These explanations can be related to the music: the C major passage of the development corresponds to the image of floods of light, the dissonant chord at the climax expresses "panic shock," and the trumpet fanfare is the "small military signal."

Scherzo: *Todtentanz—Freund Hein spielt zum Tanz auf* ("Dance of Death—Friend Death is Striking Up the Dance")

Mahler conducted his Fourth Symphony twice on the evening of Sunday, 23 October 1904, in Amsterdam.[23] Regarding the second movement, one could read in the printed program: *Scherzo. In gemächlicher Bewegung.* (*Todtentanz*) [Scherzo. Unhurried. "Dance of Death"].[24] According to this, the name *Todtentanz* (missing in both the autograph and the first edition that was published in 1902) is authentic. Mahler's remarks to friends and acquaintances also indicate that he thought of the movement as a "dance of death." As mentioned in Bruno Walter's letter to Ludwig Schiedermair (quoted above) and according to an instruction printed in the first edition, the solo violin is to play "like a fiddle." Natalie Bauer-Lechner relates that Mahler specified the scordatura of the solo violin (tuned one tone higher), "so that the violin would sound screeching and rough, as if Death would strike up [the music]" (BL² 179).[25] According to Alphons Diepenbrock, it was Mahler's intention to achieve "a shrill and frightening effect" by means of the scordatura.[26] "It is Death who strikes up the dance and seeks to lure the souls into his realm."

The subject of the ominous street player was popular in nineteenth-century visual arts and music. Donald Mitchell[27] rightfully pointed out Franz Grillparzer's 1847 novella *Der arme Spielmann* (*The Poor Street Player*) and Arnold Böcklin's impressive *Self Portrait with Fiddling Death* of 1872.[28] We do not know whether Mahler was familiar with these works, but it is certain that he received important inspiration from the *Danse macabre* by Camille Saint-Saëns, a symphonic poem (based on a poem by Henri Cazalis) that was very popular during the nineteenth century. It has scherzolike features, specifies scordatura for the solo violin, contains reminiscences of the Dies irae, and also includes the xylophone.

Mahler's Scherzo (this term is used even though it appears only in the autograph) presents a clear, five-part structure: Part A (mm. 1–68)—Part B (mm. 69–109)—Part A¹ (mm. 110–200)—Part B¹ (mm. 201–280)—Part A² (mm. 281–341)—Coda (mm. 342–364). The A parts, aside from minor deviations, are written in C minor/C major; the B parts are written in F major or D major; and the piece closes in C major. To point out that the first two parts show significant changes at every repeat (including rearrangements and combinations of ideas) should be superfluous after what has been said thus far: Mahler spoke of "variations" (BL² 202).

If we consider the first part more closely, we can recognize a five-division mirror arrangement that adheres to the following scheme:

Mm.   1–6   "Prelude" (key undefined)
      6–33   Section A in C minor
      34–45   Section B in C major
      46–63   Section A' in C minor
      64–68   "Postlude" (beginning in a Phrygian-like C minor modulating
              to F major)

"Prelude" and "Postlude" presented the same material: a horn call motif and a characteristic trill motif. The scherzolike parts leave the listener with a mostly grotesque, eerie impression. This is due not only to the scordatura of the solo violin, but also to the intervals that give preference to diminished fourths and fifths and to a preference for the tone F-sharp, for Phrygian and chromatic sounds, and for augmented chords (for instance, mm. 3, 30, 43–44). It is also due to the sounds produced by the strings (with mutes, pizzicato, col legno). Only the B section is brighter, but even there Mahler occasionally provides eerie effects, as in measures 153–154 and 185–190, where horns are prominent in their low range. He originally had thought (as the autograph indicates) to reinforce the horns at this point with the tuba. Presumably he dismissed this idea because he does not use the tuba or the trombones anywhere else in the Fourth.

The trio sections have a distinct ländler character. In several places, bourdon basses stand out and woodwind timbre dominates. At this point Mahler intertwined contrasting ländler melodies (an "unhurried" and a "slow" ländler).[29] There are free quotations from "The Heavenly Life" and an anticipation of the Cecilia theme:

Finale, mm. 158–163

Cä - ci-lia mit ih - ren Ver-wand - - - ten sind treff-li-che Hof- mu-si - kan-ten!

Scherzo, mm. 78–83[30]

There is also an anticipation of the "heavenly music" theme:

Finale, mm. 124–127

Scherzo, mm. 254–261

In the lied this theme is performed *sehr zart und geheimnisvoll* (very gently and mysteriously) and *ppp,* while in the trio it is presented in a more rustic form.

As first noted by Adorno, an instructive example of Mahler's "montage technique" is offered in measures 185–191 at the end of part A[1] where the horn call motif and the characteristic trill motif are added to material taken from section B. In the process, the trill motif experiences a metric displacement:

Similarly artful are the modulations at the beginning of Part A[2] (m. 281ff.). Part B[1] closes in D major and prepares B minor. However, the key at the beginning of Part A[2] cannot be clearly defined. Here Mahler prefers the vague, wanders through various keys, touches C minor (m. 284), G minor (m. 286), and B major (m. 290), then reaches B minor (m. 294) only to leave it right away, roams again through various keys (D minor, G minor, D major, G minor, C minor), and finally reaches C major in measure 314. Some measures later he provides another surprise: In measures 332–335, flutes, bassoons, and horns play a G-flat major signal over a sustained low C. The eerie passage has a bitonal touch accentuated by the tam-tam and bass drum roll. The final cadence in the Coda is typical for the movement's ambivalence. The C major sound alternates in measures 350–361 with unrelated sounds that take the place of the dominant:

Mm. 349–355

Nothing symbolizes the ambivalence of the movement better than the expression mark *lustig* (merrily), which Mahler specifies in three places (m. 71 for the clarinet, mm. 128–129 for the first horn, and m. 170 again for the first horn). The appropriateness of this mark is clear when one remembers that for many people and many nations, Death is Janus-faced. "The Hindus," Arthur Schopenhauer writes, "attribute two faces to the death god Yama: a very dreadful one and a friendly and merciful one."[31] And in death-dance verses of the Middle Ages, the sound of bagpipes, which Death plays, is described as being dissonant, frightening, deceiving, but also alluring.[32]

Ruhevoll (Poco adagio)—*Das Lächeln der heiligen Ursula* (Restful—"The Smile of Saint Ursula")

In the summer of 1900 Mahler spoke of the third movement of the Fourth Symphony sometimes as an Adagio and other times as an Andante, which irritated Natalie. When she asked him about this, he answered that he could just as well call it Moderato, Allegro, or Presto, "for it includes all of these" (BL[2] 163). He also stated that the variations of this movement "were the first proper ones he had written; that is, the first ones that are varied through and through, as he imagined variations to be."

As Paul Stefan[33] recognized first, the movement consists of variations on two themes and presents a five-part structure (according to the scheme A—B—A[1]—B[1]—A[2]) with Coda:

First section (Part A)

Mm. 1–16 Main theme
     17–36 Variations on the main theme (with inclusion of a modified contrapuntal restatement
     37–50 *Abgesang*
     51–61 Final part with bell-like motif (reminiscent of *Parsifal*)

Second section (Part B)

62–75	First part in E minor
76–92	Second part beginning in E minor and closing in D minor (plungelike climax)
93–106	*Abgesang* in D minor

Variation of the first section (Part A¹)

107–170	*Anmutig bewegt* [Graceful and lively] (At the beginning very moderate, in the course of the variation gradually a little more lively)
171–178	Transition (*Klagend*) [lamenting]

Variation of the Second section (Part B²)

179–191	First part beginning in G minor
192–211	Second part beginning in C-sharp minor and closing in F-sharp minor (plungelike climax)
212–221	*Abgesang*

Further variation of the first section (Part A²)

222–282	Agogically increasing variations of the main theme:
222–237	Andante in $\frac{3}{4}$ meter in G major
238–262	Allegretto subito in $\frac{3}{8}$ meter in G major
263–277	Allegro subito in $\frac{2}{4}$ meter in E major
278–282	Allegro molto in $\frac{2}{4}$ meter in G major
283–287	Andante subito in $\frac{3}{4}$ meter (*Ganz plötzlich das Anfangstempo der Variation*) [Very suddenly the beginning tempo of the variation]
288–305	*Abgesang* (Poco adagio) in $\frac{4}{4}$ meter
306–314	Final passage with bell-like motif

Coda

315–325	Poco più mosso: anticipation of the Finale; intonation of the "heavenly music" in E major
326–353	*Sehr zart und innig* (Very gentle and heartfelt): a fading conclusion with eternity motifs

Two ideas determine the arrangement, the character, and the course of the movement: the idea of great contrast between two basically different theme complexes and the idea of the intensifying variation.

The marking *Ruhevoll* (restful) refers exclusively to the first part of the movement and characterizes it precisely. The music flows along with great restfulness, the dynamic level is *pianissimo,* and apart from several temporary modulations, the music remains in G major. This part of the movement shows a bar form arrangement: *Stollen* (mm. 1–16)—*Stollen* (mm. 17–36—*Abgesang* (mm. 37–50), and Appendix (mm. 51–61). The theme, a sixteen-measure cantilena of the cellos, is played and immediately repeated, But this repeat already is a variation: the theme is melodically paraphrased, extended, and contrapuntally combined with a distinctive counter–melody in the second violins and later in the oboe. The following *Abgesang* in the first two measures quotes the bell motif of the pizzicato double basses (from the theme) but is otherwise thematically completely independent. It also contains a reminiscence of the phrase *Mit Flügeln, die ich mir errungen* ("With wings that I have achieved for myself") from the Finale of the Second Symphony:

Second Symphony, Finale, mm. 679–682

Fourth Symphony, third movement, mm. 45–47

In the Appendix, the bell motif of the cellos and double basses stands out significantly. Its form is reminiscent of the bell motif from Wagner's *Parsifal*.[34] The conclusion is formed by alternating tonic and dominant chords that are orchestrated in the most sophisticated way. The delicate change of tone color between woodwinds and strings caused Rudolf Stephan[35] to speak of a *Klangfarbenmelodie* (tone-color melody), a term that was used by Arnold Schoenberg.

The second part forms the strongest contrast imaginable to the first part. It presents a minor complex, beginning in E minor and ending in D minor. Its distinguishing feature is not restfulness but rather lament (the remark *klagend* [lamenting] at measure 62 in the oboe part is original), excitement, great tension, and then deep depression. The complex has three sections; their structure also resembles bar form. In the first, the 14-measure theme is stated. Its expressiveness and intensity result in part from sighlike figures, large intervals, chromatic and rapidly falling figures (mm. 74–76). In the second section, the theme is freely varied while the music sounds urging and passionate. A great increase in intensity leads to a plunging *fortissimo* climax, after which the volume decreases rapidly. The chromatically falling line of the horn in the *Abgesang* (mm. 97–105) is symbolic of deepest mourning.

The third part is a variation of the first. Outlines of the shapes of themes and phrases, number of measures, and harmonic framework are mostly, but not always, maintained. Thus measures 45–50 of the first complex are dealt with in a free manner (see mm. 151–160). The complex acquires a different character by its faster tempos. The tempo specifications read *Anmutig bewegt* (Graceful, lively) and Allegretto grazioso, and Mahler's instruction to increase the tempo in the course of the variation is important.

Considerable changes can be noticed in the fourth part; it is a very free variation of the second. The keys (G, C-sharp, and F-sharp minor instead of E and D minor) and the instrumentation are changed, along with partial rearrangement of the thematic material. Thus the chromatically descending line of the horn, which originally gave profile to the *Abgesang,* now appears in the first section (mm. 183–188). This part far exceeds the second in intensity.

In the fifth part the main theme undergoes four agogically increasing variations that change its character completely: Andante—Allegretto subito—Allegro subito—Allegro molto (subito). According to a notation by Mahler, the tempo change should occur "suddenly and surprisingly." The third of these variations (Allegro subito) is exceptional in that it is in E major, and the fourth (Allegro molto) breaks off after five measures.[36] With an elegiac phrase of the horns (mm. 283–287), the music suddenly returns to the beginning tempo of that part (Andante). Following this is a varied form of the *Abgesang* and the closing passage with the bell-like motif of the double basses.

Formal analyses of this movement may be indispensable and informative, yet the deeper meaning of the music is revealed by Walter's remarks to Schiedermair: "Solemn rest and serious, gentle cheerfulness" comprise the mood of this movement, which also includes "deep, painful contrasts" (as reminiscences of earthly life) and intensification of the mood from cheerful to vivacious. The two basic ideas of the movement (the harsh contrast between the theme complexes and the principle of intensification in variations) are thus derived from a poetic concept. In Mahler's imagination, restfulness and the gentle cheerfulness of the heavenly life can rise to boisterousness, but this gaiety is contrasted with the misery of earthly life. It is evident from this that Mahler in fact did realize his original intention to bring out in his Fourth the contrast between the heavenly and the earthly life. (See also the program sketch discussed at the beginning).

Finally, let us look at the Coda. As the end of the fifth part is fading away, the most splendid passage of the movement and of the entire Symphony immediately follows. Winds, harp, and divided strings (the latter in arpeggios and figurations) play the E major chord triple *forte*; the timpani and double basses bring the bell-like motif; horns and trumpets present the theme of the heavenly music in an interesting "mixed version":

Mm. 320–323

Then the volume decreases rapidly. Eternity motifs[37] appear in the violins and later in the harp and double basses. The chord sequence is rather exceptional: E—C—F$^6_4$—D—G—E minor—G—E minor—D. An area of resolution is clearly defined, and the music becomes slower and fades away. The performance indication at the end reads *Gänzlich ersterbend* (completely dying away). Mahler described the passage: "The fading away at the end is ethereal, churchlike, Catholic in mood" (BL[2] 163).

Finale: *Das himmlische Leben* ("The Heavenly Life")

The five verses of the Bavarian folk song *Der Himmel hängt voll Geigen* ("Heaven is Full of Violins") deal with four subjects. The first verse, which describes the "heavenly joys," implies something that only seems to be a paradox: the "most gentle restfulness" of heavenly life does not exclude cheerfulness and boisterousness:

> *Wir führen ein englisches Leben,*
> *Sind dennoch ganz lustig daneben,*
> *Wir tanzen und springen,*
> *Wir hüpfen und singen,*
> *Sankt Peter im Himmel sieht zu.*

> We are leading an angelic life,
> Are nevertheless altogether cheerful,
> We dance and we leap,
> We skip and we sing,
> Saint Peter is heaven is looking on.

A contrast to the altogether idyllic imagery of the poem is provided only by the first lines of the second verse, which hint at the story of the death of the "dear little lamb."[38] In the final five lines of the second verse, and in the third and fourth verses, the heavenly land of milk and honey is described as having, of course, a "cellar," a "garden," and a "pond." The poem closes (fifth verse) in praise of the heavenly music.

When setting the piece to music, Mahler, as was his custom, changed details of the poem. Mainly he omitted four lines from the fourth verse:

> *Willst Karpfen, willst Hecht, willst Forellen*
> *Gut Stockfisch und frische Sardellen?*
> *Sankt Lorenz hat müssen*
> *Sein Leben einbüßen*

> Would you like carp, hake, or trout,
> Good dried fish, or sardines?
> St. Lawrence had
> To forfeit his life

and combined the third and fourth verses, which are related in content, so that the setting consists of only four verses.

Mm. 1–11   Prelude (*Sehr behaglich*) [very comfortable]; in G major
      12–39   Verse 1, beginning in G major and closing with an A minor triad without a third
      40–56   Interlude with bell sounds (*Plötzlich frisch bewegt*) [suddenly fresh and lively], beginning with a B minor triad without a third and closing in E minor
      57–75   Verse 2 (*Etwas zurückhaltend*) [somewhat slower] in E minor
      76–79   Interlude with bell sound (*Wieder lebhaft*) [lively again]
      80–114   Verse 3 (= verses 3 and 4 of the poem) (Tempo I) beginning in G major and closing with a D major triad without a third
      115–121 Interlude with bell sound (lively again) beginning with a B minor triad without a third and leading to E major
      122–141 Interlude (Tempo I. *Sehr zart und geheimnisvoll bis zum Schluß*) [Very gentle and mysterious to the end] in E major, like a pastorale
      142–174 Verse 4 (= Verse 5 of the poem) in E major
      175–184 Postlude, fading away

The outline shows that the verses are connected by lively interludes, characterized by bell and triangle sounds. An analysis of the setting shows the combination of strophic and through-composed form found in many Mahler songs: the musical substance of the first verse partially reappears in the following verses. This musical substance functions as a kind of model that nevertheless is changed and enlarged and occasionally abandoned altogether.[39] Thus the following verses are based in part on their own thematic substance. I will sketch the relation of the verses to each other.

The first verse, corresponding to the text, is clearly divided into two sections (mm. 12–24 and mm. 25–39). While the first section, during which the main theme of the song is stated, is governed by the image of "gentle restfulness" found in heaven, the more lively second section describes the "cheerfulness" of the "angelic life." It closes with two characteristic turns that also play a role in the following verses: a clause with the distinctive interval of the diminished fifth (mm. 33–34) and a choralelike figure in archaic harmonization (mm. 35–38).[40]

The second verse has painful moments. Written in E minor, it is based mostly on its own thematic material, though it also closes with the (varied) choralelike figure.

The third (musical) verse is longer than the others, since it is comprised of two verses of text. It begins with the theme of the first verse but then develops independently. Its close is similar to that of the first, with the phrase containing the diminished fifth and the choralelike figure returning.

Finally, the concluding verse is built initially upon the first half of the first verse, the praise of heavenly music corresponding with the image of "most gentle restfulness", but then changes to a new theme that was first played in the preceding interlude by the flute and the muted violins.

Mahler called *Das himmlische Leben* "the top of the Symphony's pyramidal structure" (BL[2] 162). He originally thought of the song as a humoresque rather than as a parody. To prevent misunderstandings, he inserted a note in the score of the first edition: "to be sung with childlike, cheerful expression; entirely without parody!"[41] Of course, many of his contemporaries could not and would not take this Finale seriously and suspected a persiflage.[42] Yet the song—in retrospect, one might say—reveals the deeper meaning of the entire Symphony. An insider as well as a listener who did not know any of Mahler's explanations could conclude from the text of the Finale that life after death is also the subject of the three previous movements. A reviewer for the New York performance of the Fourth in January 1911 concluded quite correctly:[43]

Mahler's symphony is more or less a puzzle. The composer did not provide titles for the individual movements or for the Symphony as a whole. Through the artistic device of connecting the movements thematically and through the employment of a solo voice in the last movement Mr. Mahler admits, voluntarily or involuntarily, that his work is to be counted as program music.

The Middle Symphonies

The "Completely New Style"

> The Fifth is finished—I had to reorchestrate it almost completely. It is hard to believe that at the time I could have written again like a beginner, as though I had completely forgotten the routine of the first four symphonies. A completely new style demanded a new technique.   GMB² 403f.

Mahler's Fifth Symphony, which (for the time being) was completely orchestrated in 1903, opens the group of the middle symphonies that display common characteristics. Three works (the Fifth, Sixth, and Seventh) are purely instrumental, in contrast to the three Wunderhorn symphonies (the Second, Third, and Fourth) which are symphonic cantatas. The former do without words, singers, or choirs. They also do without symphonic arrangements of pre-existent songs, and they were supposed to be played, according to Mahler's wish, "without a program."

Between the Fifth and the preceding Fourth there are strong contrasts in character, expression, timbre, and style. Measured by the large orchestra of the Fifth (but also of the Second and the Third), the Fourth almost seems scored for chamber orchestra. More importantly the Fifth distinguishes itself by brilliance of sound, by virtuosity of orchestral writing, and by a clear turn toward polyphony. Movements like the Scherzo and the Rondo-Finale of the Fifth have no counterpart among Mahler's early symphonic works. Hearing the Rondo-Finale for the first time, one is quite astonished by the many fuguelike passages and the numerous contrapuntal voices it contains. It seems therefore important to point out that in the spring and summer of 1901, Mahler busied himself intensively with Bach[1] and did not tire of praising Bach's amazing art of polyphony. From the many remarks that Natalie Bauer-Lechner reports, two especially deserve to be quoted here: "In Bach, all the seeds of music are combined, as God encompasses the world. There has never been greater polyphony" (BL² 184), and the confession "I can't describe how I continually learn from Bach (like a child, sitting at his feet) because my way of working is inherently Bach-like!" (BL² 189).

135

Mahler was aware that with the Fifth he had created a new style. In a letter to Georg Göhler dated 8 February 1911 (see quote at the beginning of this chapter), Mahler confessed that this new style posed new problems for his orchestration technique, and it is a fact that he did much more retouching of the orchestration here than in any other work. As Erwin Ratz explains, three versions exist that differ in many details[2] After a reading session with the Vienna Philharmonic in the spring of 1904, Mahler reduced the percussion part considerably because in desperation Alma accused him of having written "a symphony for percussion" (AME 95). Elsewhere she recalled:

> Since the Fifth, he was continuously dissatisfied with himself; the Fifth was reorchestrated for almost every performance[3] and he returned to the Sixth and Seventh over and over again. It was a turning point. Not until the Eighth was he again sure of himself, and in *Das Lied von der Erde,* which is posthumous, I cannot imagine that he would have changed a single note. That is how economically he proceeded in that work (AME 180).

According to Hans Ferdinand Redlich, the relationship between the three purely instrumental symphonies is not "ethical and metaphysical," as that of the first four symphonies, but rather "physical."[4] This is clearly manifested in the Sixth and Seventh. The close connection is evident in the use of the "major-minor seal," (a C-major chord immediately followed by a C-minor chord) and in the use of cow bells. There is no question that the characteristics pointed out by Redlich are superficial and that the three symphonies have other more far-reaching qualities in common. Mahler compensated for his decision not to use pre-existing songs by composing movements in the character of songs without words. The Adagietto of the Fifth, the Andante moderato of the Sixth, and the Andante amoroso of the Seventh can be considered as such. All three form, in a certain sense, symphonic equivalents to the Friedrich Rückert songs.

A comparison of the symphonies of the first two periods shows that Mahler's stylistic development follows the law of evolution. Certain phenomena, already somewhat noticeable in the early works, appear fully developed in the second period, including a fondness for harshness of sound, linear friction, sharp contours in voice leading; for bitonal or pseudo-bitonal effects; for obliterating the difference between major and minor modes; for certain cadences; and for certain tonal devices. Unlike his protege Schoenberg, Mahler did not follow the road to atonality, yet he modernized his own tonal language in a different way and by other means.

According to Jean Matter, Mahler did not reveal himself to be a composer of the twentieth century until the Seventh[5] Whether one shares this opinion or not, it is indisputable that several very progressive features of compositional technique stand out in the Seventh, and for good reason it aroused Schoenberg's admiration. Three features deserve especially to be pointed out, since until now they have not been recognized: The development section of the first movement at times modulates so boldly that tonal centers can no longer be distinguished; the third movement (*Schattenhaft*) [Shadowlike] offers one of the earliest examples of Mahler's montage technique and of his unique method of inserting material parenthetically; one portion of a movement is loosened up by interpolating sections in a different tempo. Repeated abrupt changes in tempo, dynamics, and genre often result.

The Fifth Symphony

> The Scherzo is an accursed movement! It will have a
> long history of suffering! For fifty years conductors
> will take it too fast and make nonsense of it. The
> public—oh, heavens—how should it react to this
> chaos that is eternally giving birth to a world that
> then perishes in the next moment, to these primordial
> sounds, to this blustering, bellowing, roaring ocean,
> to these dancing stars, to these shimmering, flashing,
> breathing waves?   AME 315f.

> The Fifth is a cursed work. No one comprehends it.
>   AME 336

Origin

In the summer of 1901 Mahler was especially productive. He composed no
less than eight songs and three movements of the five-movement Fifth
Symphony. In view of this, his remark in a letter to Nina Spiegler of 20
August—"With the harvest of this year one can really be quite content"—is
quite an understatement (GMB² 263).

Natalie Bauer-Lechner's diary once more provides valuable information
about the work of that summer.[1] She tells us that on 10 August Mahler
played seven songs for her in his little cabin in the woods of Maiernigg at the
Wörthersee, "songs he had composed in fourteen days (each one being composed on one day and orchestrated on the next)" (BL² 193f.). These included
Der Tamboursg'sell ("The Drummer") from *Des Knaben Wunderhorn,* six
songs to poems of Friedrich Rückert, two or three of the *Kindertotenlieder*
("Songs on the Death of Children"), and the songs *Blicke mir nicht in die
Lieder* ("Do Not Look at My Songs") and *Ich atmet' einen linden Duft* ("I
Breathed a Gentle Fragrance"). A few days after Mahler had completed his
"vacation work," he set the poem *Ich bin der Welt abhanden gekommen* ("I
Have Slipped Away from This World") to music. The keyboard sketch of

this song (now at the Pierpont Morgan Library) is dated 16 August 1901.

Natalie reports further that Mahler spoke to her about the Fifth for the first time at the end of July or beginning of August (in any case before 5 August), "namely about the third movement, on which he is now working" (BL² 192). This statement is worded so that one has to assume that the first two movements of the work had been drafted by this time. Incidentally, the Fifth was originally planned to have four movements. Mahler told Natalie, "It will be a proper symphony with four movements, each one complete in itself, all connected only by their similar moods" (BL² 193).

In November 1901, Mahler met Alma Schindler, daughter of a Viennese landscape painter. This important event is also significant to the origin of the Fifth. According to a credible report of Willem Mengelberg, the Adagietto was conceived as a declaration of love to Alma and was apparently composed in November 1901.² Since the Adagietto is thematically most closely connected with the Rondo-Finale, one can assume that the Finale was not composed until the summer of 1902.

After the 9 June 1902 premiere of the Third Symphony in Krefeld, Mahler and his wife went straight to Maiernigg, where their lives were "very quiet but also very busy." Alma tells about the work of this summer in her memoirs (see AME 57):

> Mahler had the sketches of the Fifth Symphony with him. Two movements were completed, the rest were being drafted. I tried to play the piano softly, but when I asked him, he [said that he] had heard me, although his working cabin was located far away in the woods. Therefore I changed my activities. I always copied everything of the Fifth Symphony as soon as it was completed, so that I finished my manuscript only a few days later than he finished his work. He became more and more accustomed to having me write out the parts, except for the first few measures, and in so doing, I learned to read a score and hear it while writing. In the process I gradually became a real help to him."³

If one compares and evaluates both Natalie's and Alma's observations, it becomes certain that in the summer of 1901 Mahler completed only the first two movements of the Fifth. The Scherzo sketch, as will be explained later on, received quite a few elaborations and modifications during the following summer. Incidentally, what Alma recorded about her working with Mahler applies to the clean copy of the score sketch. Unfortunately neither preliminary sketches to the Fifth nor the score sketch itself have been discovered.

According to Alma's information, Mahler completed the Fifth "in the autumn" of 1902 and played it for her (AME 64):

> It was the first time that he played a new work for me. Arm in arm we walked solemnly up to his studio in the woods. Soon afterward the vacation was over, and we moved to Vienna. The Fifth was completed, and he worked all winter on the final copy.⁴

The Symphony had its premiere on 18 October 1904 in Cologne and, according to a letter of Mahler, had a mixed reception (AME 317). The Adagietto and the Rondo-Finale were appreciated the most. Richard Strauss, however, preferred the first three movements. On 5 March 1905 he wrote to Mahler:

> At the dress rehearsal, your Fifth Symphony again brought me great pleasure, which was dimmed for me only by the little Adagietto. It serves you right that precisely that movement was liked the most by the audience. The first two movements especially are quite splendid; the ingenious Scherzo seemed a bit too long. How much this is the fault of the inadequate performance is beyond my judgment.[5]

The Inner Program

All those who view Mahler's symphonic works as models of "pure, absolute music" like to refer especially to the Fifth. They point out that there is no detailed program for this work.[6] Bruno Walter, for instance, states that neither conversations with Mahler nor anything in the music suggested that "extra-musical thoughts or emotions" had exerted any influence on the music of the Fifth.[7] It was "music—passionate, wild, pathetic, sweeping, solemn, gentle, full of all emotions of the human heart, yet 'only' music. No trace of any metaphysical question enters into its purely musical course." Whoever adheres to this opinion, however, does not realize the nature of the Fifth, which, like all of Mahler's music, makes a statement—one that is based on an *inner* program that is kept secret. Several things point to this "ideal" program: the number and sequence of movements; their character; the division into three parts (movements one and two form the first part, movement three the second part, movements four and five the third part); the choice of keys of the movements (C-sharp minor—A minor—D major—F major—D major); the thematic connections existing between movements one and two and likewise between movements four and five; and many other things. Thus the Symphony begins with a dark funeral march in C-sharp minor and ends with an airy, cheerful Rondo-Finale in D major which, significantly, is marked Allegro giocoso.[8] This harsh contrast seems to suggest a new, poetic rephrasing of the old motto *per aspera ad astra,* as well as the philosophical idea of transcendence and of overcoming suffering—the basis of the First and Second.

The *inner* program of the Fifth does not merely relate to the polarity between the first and last movements. It also extends to the middle movements, each expressing a poetic idea. Just to touch briefly now on the results of the semantic analyses: the second movement modifies the idea *Dall' Inferno al Paradiso* inasmuch as paradise (unlike the Finale of the First) ultimately is not reached. The brilliant chorale is and remains only an episode in the midst of a world governed by despair and mourning. Regarding the idea for the Scherzo, Mahler advised Bauer-Lechner "It is mankind in the bright light of day, at the zenith of life" (BL² 193). Later he also gave this movement features of a dance of death and with that the meaning of *media vita in morte sumus* (in the midst of life we are in death). As to the Adagietto, the allusions, until now ignored, to the "gaze" motif from Wagner's *Tristan* support Mengelberg's statement that the movement was meant as a confession of love to Alma.

Trauermarsch: Wie ein Kondukt ("Death March: Like a Funeral Procession")

Mahler was especially fond of marches and of death marchlike music. The *Marche funèbre* type occurs several times in his work. The fourth Wayfarer song, *Die zwei blauen Augen von meinem Schatz,* begins in a death march tempo. The "Death March in Callot's Manner" from the First Symphony combines the *Marche funèbre* character with the basic feature of an Andante marziale. In the first movement of the Third, death marchlike passages play an important role, and in the summer of 1901 Mahler set *Der Tamboursg'sell* to music, a death marchlike song for solo voice and orchestra from which the violins and violas strangely enough have been omitted.

Mahler's first symphonic death march on a grand scale is the first movement of the Fifth, composed at the same time as "The Drummer." A death march at the beginning of a symphony? Mahler's procedure appears less bold if one considers that works by Berlioz and Tchaikovsky begin similarly. Berlioz's *Symphonie funèbre et triomphale* Op. 15 of 1840, composed for large military band, consists of three movements: a "Marche funèbre," an "Oraison funèbre" (with trombone solo), and "Apotheose."

Whether Mahler was familiar with Berlioz's work is uncertain, but he shares with Berlioz a preference for brass sound, which dominates several passage of the death march.⁹ Typically the movement begins with an *Appell* (a kind of military fanfare) by the solo trumpet, an instrument that stands out in several places. Regarding this fanfare, Mahler noted in the score: "The upbeat triplets of this theme should always be played somewhat hurriedly (quasi accel.), in the manner of military fanfares."¹⁰

The movement shows a clear five-part structure: Main section (Part A)— Trio I (Part B)—Main section (Part A¹)—Trio II (Part B¹)—Coda (Part A²). The following is an outline of the structure:

Main section (Part A) in C-sharp minor

Mm.		
	1–34	First part beginning with trumpet solo
	34–60	Second part, elegiac character
	61–88	First part again (altered)
	88–120	Second part again (altered)
	120–154	Third part beginning in A-flat major and closing in D-flat major/D-flat minor

Trio I (Part B) in B-flat minor
Plötzlich schneller. Leidenschaftlich. Wild.
(Suddenly faster. Passionate. Wild.)

155–172 First part
173–194 Second part beginning in E-flat minor
195–232 Third part (linked to the first) in B-flat minor

Main section (Part A^1) in C-sharp minor

233–262 First part (altered)
262–294 Second part (altered)
294–316 Third part (altered) in D-flat major
317–322 Transition

Trio II (Part B^1) in A minor

323–336 First part
337–356 Second part beginning in D minor
357–376 Third part in A minor with collapselike climax (*klagend*)
         [lamenting]

377–415   Coda (Part A^2) in C-sharp minor

The basic idea of this movement is the contrast between the ceremonial formality of the main sections and the intensification of expression in the trios. *In gemessenem Schritt. Streng. Wie ein Kondukt* (At a measured pace. Stern. Like a funeral procession) is how Mahler characterized the basic tempo of the movement. Massive brass sounds, faltering rhythms, but also threnodic elegiac passages characterize the main sections.[11] In the trios, where subjectivity breaks through, the tempo is accelerated. In the first trio, the expression rises to *Leidenschaftlichkeit* (passion) and *Wildheit* (wildness)—Mahler's performance markings. Pain and grief speak in this music with such intensity that the marking *lamenting* at the high point of the movement (No. 18) seems almost superfluous.

The formal scheme merely hints at what one only recognizes after a thorough analysis, namely, that every recurrence of a part or section is greatly changed—nothing stays the same. A few examples may clarify this: The solo trumpet plays its fanfare four times (mm. 1–20, 60–80, 232–254, and 376–409), each time taking on a different form. The beginning of the fanfare often remains unchanged, but the continuation proceeds differently, so that one must speak of four different versions.

A concise four-measure phrase, with which the first parts of the main sections end, is not only melodically and rhythmically altered, but also orchestrated in different ways. In measures 31–34 and 57–60 it is played by the horns or the trombones:

In measures 84–88 it occurs in the trombones:

In measures 258–262 the tuba finally takes over this phrase one octave lower.

The threnodic, elegiac melody of the violins and cellos (mm. 34–56) characterized the second section of the main parts.[12]

Mm. 34–42

It appears in Part A[1] in a completely new version to which the term "variant" cannot do justice:

Mm. 262–270

A comparison of the two trios is especially instructive. Although the second trio is for the most part based on the thematic substance of the first, Mahler creates something completely different from the material. The two trios differ from each other in key (B-flat minor in the first, A minor in the second), the accompanying figures, and their characters. In addition, the sequence and form of the thematic ideas differ so strongly that there seem to be two completely different parts. In but one example, the trumpet phrase at the beginning of the first trio appears at the beginning of the second trio in this astonishing transformation:

Mm. 154–160

Mm. 322–327

Common to both trios are indeed several surges of intensification that lead to climaxes (mm. 221 and 229 or 369ff.) They soon lose intensity, and it is instructive to observe in both cases the seamless transition to parts A¹ and A². The transition from Part A¹ to the second trio is no less artfully shaped. Serving as bridge are measures 316–322, a timpani solo in the rhythm of the military fanfare from the beginning.

The strictly symmetrical structure and the formal perfection of the movement should also be noted. The death march begins softly with the trumpet solo and also ends very softly with signals of the muted solo trumpet and first flute. The closing suggests that the music is disappearing into the distance, completely beyond hearing.

Stürmisch bewegt. Mit größter Vehemenz ("Turbulently Rough. With Greatest Vehemence")

In reviewing the second movement of the Fifth Symphony, Paul Bekker did not hesitate to use superlatives. He considered the movement to be among Mahler's most magnificent creations and called it "a piece of such eruptive strength of passion and intensification of content that one has to count it among the greatest achievements in symphonic art."[13] As to its "formal significance and force of ideas," he found that the movement "towers considerably above" the death march. Not only was it conceived more broadly, but also (like other opening movements) it displayed an ingeniously organized sonata form.

Those wishing to comprehend the movement and find the key to its meaning (Mahler considered it the symphony's main movement[14]) must first investigate its structure.

Exposition

Mm. 1–64   Main section in A minor, divided into two parts of 30 and 34 measures (in the course of the second part a significant trumpet motif is prominent)

64–74   Transition (tritone motif in the trumpets and inferno figures in the woodwinds)

75–140   Secondary section in F minor (= a new setting of the second trio from the death march)

Development

141–145 Diminished seventh chord with inferno figures
146–174 Development and combination of the motifs from the main section
175–188 Tritone motifs in the trumpets and later in the trombones; inferno figures in the woodwinds; the sighing motif in the strings
188–213 Monody of the "lamenting" cellos in E-flat minor
213–253 New setting of the secondary section in E-flat minor (m. 230ff: contrapuntal combination with motifs from the main section)
254–265 Motifs from the main section
266–287 Return to the "main section" of the death march (mm. 294–311), now beginning in B major
288–315 *Più mosso subito:* marchlike section beginning in A-flat major, growing in intensity
316–322 Pesante (*plötzlich anhaltend*) [suddenly stopping]: anticipation of the chorale (in A major)

Recapitulation

322–351 Main section beginning in A minor and leading to E minor
352–427 Secondary section beginning in E minor and leading to E-flat minor
428–463 *Wuchtig* (Weighty): contrapuntal combination of motifs from the secondary sections
464–519 Pesante: Chorale in D major (Vision of Paradise)

Coda

520–525 Diminished seventh-chord over a nonchord B-flat, main motif of the movement, inferno figures, sighing motifs
526–556 First part of the main section in D minor (a surge of intensification leads up to a collapselike climax)
557–576 Area of resolution in A minor

The above outline shows clearly that Bekker was right when he spoke of the "ingeniously organized sonata form." The movement is indeed cast in normal sonata form. It contains everything considered typical: the division into three main parts and a coda, the contrasting themes, a clear disposition of tonalities, and finally the thematic treatment in the development. The division into four clearly distinguishable part is evident: exposition (140 measures), development (182 measures), recapitulation (197 measures), and coda (57 measures). Like a landmark, a diminished seventh chord appears at the beginning of each part. In the very first edition of the study score there were even repeat signs at the end of the exposition, as Ernst Nodnagel reports.[15] According to Nodnagel, Mahler hurried to do away with this kind of "atavism" in later editions because he "clearly sensed the psychological untruthfulness of returning, at this point in the music's emotional development, to the 'already dealt-with,' overcome moods."

Further, the movement offers a perfect example of the dualism of thematic contrast. A group of first themes, to be performed in a *wuchtig* manner and "vehemently" (Mahler's instructions), is contrasted by an elegiac second theme. In the exposition the first theme complex is in A minor and the second theme is in F minor. The recapitulation modifies the key relationship to A minor and E minor.

Finally, in the development (and also in the recapitulation) the movement's themes are given a thorough workout. They are contrasted with one another, treated imitatively, and combined contrapuntally. Some examples: At the beginning of the development, measures 155–159, the *wuchtig* main motif in the double basses and cellos is contrapuntally combined with a striking motif that was originally given to the trumpet (mm. 43–46). A little later (mm. 157–162) this motif is treated imitatively.

Still later (mm. 230–253 and 428–444) motifs from the first theme complex and from the secondary theme are linked together. Beside this, new thematic material develops from elementary motifs, such as the gripping monody of the "lamenting" cellos in E-flat minor (mm. 188–213) and the marchlike theme in A-flat major (mm. 288–306). To trace the metamorphoses and interweavings and "fate" of the individual themes and motifs in this movement in detail would require an extended treatise.

The movement, however, also contains peculiarities that do not necessarily correspond to traditional sonata form. In this context three features are of interest:

1. The first two movements of the Fifth Symphony are thematically so closely related to each other that one might speak of linkage. Passages of the second theme group of the second movement borrow their thematic substance from the trios of the death march. Obviously we are not speaking here of exact duplication: the trios are newly composed. Here and there, Mahler does quote the first movement literally: the B major passage (mm. 266–287) of the second movement refers to measures 294–311 of the death march. Adorno spoke of "inserts" and "interpolations" from the death march.[16] The word *interpolation* (there is something pejorative about it) does not really

do justice to the circumstances: elegiac feelings that change into passion are not foreign to the climate of this movement. The passages from the death march are integrated into the second movement.

2. At the end of the recapitulation, a magnificent chorale of the winds resounds in D major (*Pesante*, mm. 464–519). It appears somewhat out of place in these somber surroundings. Motivically and thematically this chorale (Bekker spoke of "chorale sun,"[17] Adorno of "chorale vision"[18]) cannot be derived from the material heard at the beginning of the movement. Nevertheless the breakthrough accomplished by this chorale does not occur without preparation. A short passage in a bright A major, resembling this breakthrough, can already be found at the close of the development *(Pesante,* mm. 316–322).

3. Heinrich Schmidt[19] and Bernd Sponheuer[20] have pointed out that the skeleton of sonata structure in the movement is overlayed by a "peripeteia" (sudden change) character. Accordingly, the peripeteia process moves in several phases (or relays), the chorale being nothing other than the target of the peripeteia.

Essential clues for the interpretation and the semantic deciphering of the movement can be gained by comparing it with the Finale of the First and with several passages from the Finale of the Second. The comparison brings out important and surprising connections and a striking similarity in gesture and also to some extent in the motivic material. *Stürmisch bewegt* is the performance instruction not only for the second movement of the Fifth, but also for the Finale of the First, and both movements have in common their impetuosity, indeed, their wild passion.[21] Furthermore, chromatically falling eights and triplet figures known from the Finale of the First occur in the second movement of the Fifth at several places;[22] there they have inferno character:[23]

First Symphony, Finale, mm. 21–24

Fifth Symphony, second movement, mm. 322–325

In several places the trumpets play tritonic motifs.[24] In nineteenth-century music and also in Mahler, the tritone is the symbol of evil or impending doom.[25]

Mm. 65–67

The motiflike outcry that characterizes the main theme and appears for the first time in the second trio of the death march can be related to similar formations in the Finale of the Second:

Second Symphony, Finale, mm. 195–197

Fifth Symphony, Death march, mm. 323–327

Fifth Symphony, second movement, mm. 6–10

Most importantly, the second movement of the Fifth shares the peripeteia character with the Finale of the First, and the breakthrough in both movements occurs in a chorale.

All of this indicates that the basic programmatic idea of the Finale of the First, as well as of the second movement of the Fifth, is the comparison of inferno and paradise, of reality and utopia, of boundless despair and the promise of another, better world. The realm of paradise, however, is not reached, in this movement, unlike the Finale of the First. The chorale appears like a vision from another world; it cannot bring about a real change. A catastrophic climax (mm. 544ff.) characterizes the ghostly ending of the movement.

Scherzo

The third movement of Mahler's Fifth Symphony is the first movement that he explicitly marked *Scherzo* when it was published, though the movement is not a scherzo in the traditional sense. It is a composition enormously rich in contrasts and thematic qualities of a dancelike and songlike nature, and its rather complicated form inspired various attempts, some very sweeping, to interpret it.[26] Let us therefore begin with a new, detailed outline:

Main section

Mm.		
	1–15	First period (main theme)
	15–26	Second period (main theme with modified contrapuntal restatement)
	26–39	Third period (variation of the main theme)
	40–72	Fourth period (with a new eighth-note theme and a concise rhythmic counter theme beginning in B minor and leading into the substance of the main theme)
	73–82	Fifth period
	83–120	Sixth period (beginning with the eighth-note theme and leading into the substance of the main theme
	121–135	Seventh period

Trio I (in B-flat major)

136–173 Two periods of 15 and 23 measures

Main section (shortened recapitulation)

174–200 Two periods of 14 and 13 measures
201–221 Fugato on the eighth-note theme

Trio II

222–240 First section (of preparatory character)
241–276 Second section (beginning *langsamer* [slower] and *ruhig* [restfully], with growing intensity)
277–307 Third section: four-line episode in G minor
308–336 Fourth section (molto moderato): new version of the theme (the strings pizzicato); measures 329–334 a reminiscence of Trio I (*schüchtern*) [timidly]
337–388 Fifth section: imitative treatment of the theme
389–428 Sixth section (*nicht eilen*) [do not rush]: new version of the theme (with added reminiscences of Trio I and the main theme)

Development

429–489 Development and contrasting of the motifs of Trio I and the main theme

Recapitulation (greatly modified)

490–562 Main section (four periods of 15, 12, 10, and 36 measures)

563–578 Trio I
579–632 Trio II combined with the eighth-note theme
633–699 *Kräftig* (strongly): motifs of Trio I and of the main theme developed in two large waves of intensification (the climax occurs on an unresolved eleventh chord)
700–763 New version of the episode from Trio II

Coda

764–819 Stretta

This outline reveals the structure of a scherzo with two different trios (going back to Robert Schumann), as well as some features of a sonata movement. Adorno hit the nail on the head when he spoke of the "novelty of the development-scherzo."[27] He also praised the "orchestral mastery," the "full instrumentation," the polyphonic texture, and the dynamic enrichment of the form—the result of ingenious interaction between the parts.

In a conversation with Natalie Bauer-Lechner during the summer of 1901, Mahler compared the Scherzo with the "tail of a comet" and also said, "It is thoroughly kneaded, so that not even one grain remains unmixed or unchanged. Every note is full of life and everything is whirling in a dance" (BL[2] 193). This description particularly fits the main section, which is, in fact, like a whirling waltz. Other statements by Mahler seem to refer primarily to the main section (and maybe to Trio I). On 5 August he reiterated to Bauer-Lechner:

> You cannot imagine how difficult it [the movement] is for me. I continually run into obstacles because of the simplicity of its themes, which use only tonic and dominant harmonies. Nobody else would dare do this nowadays. The chord progressions are, therefore, difficult, especially since I always insist that nothing must be repeated—everything has to develop organically. The individual parts are so difficult that they require players of solo ability. With my thorough knowledge of the orchestra and instruments I couldn't help including some very daring passages and figures (BL[2] 192f.).

Strangely enough the main section consists of seven periods of different lengths, with most of the cadences in D major. Only the fifth and the seventh close with a deceptive cadence in B minor.

While the main part of the Scherzo is bursting with strength, the gentle first trio has the character of a *valse*[28] in B-flat major. The second trio represents an elaborately divided complex in minor. In the six sections it is very instructive to observe how Mahler keeps gaining new versions from a songlike model.

In the first section (mm. 222–240), the two original motifs of this model are presented, one rhythmically concise, the other like a sigh:

Mm. 222–228

In the second section (mm. 241–276), a cantabile theme emerges from the sighing motif. The rhythmically concise motif appears now as a counterpoint:

Mm. 241–247

The third section (mm. 277–307) is the well-known four-line episode in G minor, which Vladimir Karbusicky related to Mahler's early musical impressions and discussed extensively:[29]

Mm. 277–285

In the fourth section (mm. 308–336), the theme takes on a completely new character, especially by means of the instrumentation. Adorno called this pizzicato episode Mahler's "prototype of the shadowlike":[30]

In the fifth section (mm. 337–388), the theme first appears in major:

In the sixth section (mm. 389–428), it finally shows this form:

In the conversation with Bauer-Lechner mentioned earlier, Mahler discussed the Scherzo:

> There is nothing romantic or mystical in it, only an expression of extraordinary strength. It is mankind in the full brightness of day, at the zenith of life. That is also how it is orchestrated: no harp and no English horn (BL[2] 193).

This comment apparently was made long before the movement was completed, because the final version contains, as we have seen, romantic and mystic passages. The sighing motif at the beginning of the second trio is typically played by the English horn. These observations lead to the conclusion that Mahler did not compose the second trio until the summer of 1902.

Richard Specht called attention to some very important information about the Scherzo that strangely enough has gone completely unnoticed. In his small monograph of 1905,[31] which was authorized by Mahler himself, Specht mentions that Bruno Walter, "in a felicitous inspiration" related the basic mood of the movement to Goethe's *An Schwager Kronos:*[32]

> *Spute dich, Kronos!*
> *Fort den rasselnden Trab!*
>
> *Frisch, holpert es gleich,*
> *Über Stock und Steine den Trott*
> *Rasch in's Leben hinein!*
>
> *Ab denn, rascher hinab!*
> *Sieh', die Sonne sinkt!*
> *Eh' sie sinkt, eh' mich Greisen*
> *Ergreift im Moore Nebelduft,*
> *Entzahnte Kiefer schnattern*
> *Und das schlotternde Gebein.*
>
> *Töne, Schwager, in's Horn,*
> *Raßle den schallenden Trab.*

> Hurry up, Kronos!
> Continue the rattling trot!
>
> Briskly he bumps along,
> Over stick and stone trotting,
> Quickly into life!

> Go on, faster down!
> See, the sun is setting!
> Before it goes down, before I the gray-beard
> Am caught by the fog in the fen,
> Toothless jaws are clattering
> And bones are rattling.
>
> Sound your horn, stagecoach driver!
> Rattle the resounding trot.

It is possible that Walter's reference to the well-known poem in the last analysis goes back to Mahler himself.[33] In any case, the Scherzo and poem are closely related in mood. Let us consider the following: The Scherzo, a composition with obbligato horn ("Sound your horn, stagecoach driver") takes on features of a dance of death at the end of the development (mm. 462–489), where the Glockenspiel and later the wooden rattle play the ostinato rhythm $\frac{3}{4}$ ♫♩ ♩ | ♫♩ ♩ | . *Media vita in morte sumus* could stand as a motto above the Scherzo.

Adagietto

The fourth movement of the Fifth Symphony, which is Mahler's most famous thanks to Luchino Visconti's film *Death In Venice,* is a song without words. Written for harp and strings, its mood and certain melodic turns are related to the Rückert song *Ich bin der Welt abhanden gekommen.* The directions *seelenvoll, mit innigster Empfindung* (soulful, with deepest emotion) and *mit Wärme* (with warmth) that Mahler supplies for the performance of the Adagietto convey only a pale impression of the soulfulness and intimacy of this music, which here and there suggest Schumann.[34]

In the score he used, the conductor Willem Mengelberg made some notations that are of inestimable value for a deeper understanding of the Adagietto.[35] He wrote: "This Adagietto was Gustav Mahler's declaration of love for Alma! Instead of a letter, he sent her this manuscript without further explanation. She understood and wrote back that he should come!!! Both have told me this!" On the left margin of the page, Mengelberg entered a poem, the words of which are meant to go with the melody of the first violins:

> *Wie ich dich liebe,*
> *Du meine Sonne,*
> *ich kann mit Worten Dir's nicht sagen*
> *Nur meine Sehnsucht*
> *kann ich Dir klagen*
> *Und meine Liebe*
> *Meine Wonne!*

How I love you,
You, my sun,
I cannot find words to tell you.
Only my longing
Can I lament to you,
And my love,
My delight!

On the lower margin also in Mengelberg's writing, we read "If music is a language, then this is proof. He tells her everything in *tones* and *sounds,* in music."

One no longer questions the correctness of those remarks once one realizes that in the middle section of the Adagietto[36] Mahler quotes the "gaze motif" from Wagner's *Tristan* and paraphrases it several times:[37]

Wagner, *Tristan und Isolde,* Prelude to Act I, mm. 45–48

Fifth Symphony, Adagietto, mm. 61–71

Alma was a good musician and talented composer; she was bound to understand the hint.[38]

When was the Adagietto written? Mahler met Alma at a social gathering on 7 November 1901. In a letter of 5 December, he was still using "*Sie,*" the formal form of address, but on 8 December he used the familiar form "*Du*" (AME 256–259). On 7 December he and Alma had become secretly engaged. He did not announce his engagement to the general director of the Court Opera until 28 December.

Rondo-Finale

The final movement of the Fifth Symphony can be classified from every point of view as the counterpart to the funeral march. The pain and lament of that march is opposed by a cheerfulness that rises to boisterousness.

Opinions regarding the value of the movement vary greatly. While older interpreters rated it positively, critical voices have emerged in recent times, under
the influence of Adorno's philosophy.

Let us begin with some prime examples. Richard Specht took slogans of
Friedrich Nietzsche and spoke of the resounding "will of life" and "will for
power."[39] Similarly, Paul Bekker saw in the movement a "crowning affirmation of life."[40] Rudolf Mengelberg apostrophized it as an "anthem of jubilation in praise of earthly life,"[41] Dika Newlin emphasized the "busy optimism
of the fugal rondo,"[42] and Heinrich Kralik characterized it as a "musical
declaration of joy."[43] On the other hand, Theodor W. Adorno thought that
the Finale, "while containing many fresh details and new ideas about form,
such as fast motion (as in film technique)," lacked substance in contrast to
the first three movements.[44] Bernd Sponheuer felt that Mahler's music here
was "exceedingly affirmative."[45] Adorno accused Mahler of going to emotional extremes: "Mahler was a bad yes-man. His voice breaks like
Nietzsche's when he proclaims values, when he himself practices this dis-
gusting concept of "overcoming," pounced on by musical analysts. He makes
music as though joy ruled the world."[46]

Mahler called the movement a Rondo-Finale. More precisely stated, we
are looking at a Rondo that has sonata traits and contains numerous fugal
sections.

Introduction

Mm.   1–23   Presentation of several motifs that play a role in the fugal
              passages

Exposition

24–56   Main section, arranged in bar form = Rondo theme in D
          major: Allegro giocoso. *Frisch* (fresh)
56–135   Fugal Part I (Principal key: D major)
136–166   Main section = Rondo theme in D major
167–190   Fugal Part II (B-flat major, D major, F-sharp major)
191–233   Secondary section (Grazioso) in B major
233–240   Epilogue in B major

Development

241–272   Introductory section (*Fließend*) [flowing]
273–306   Fugal Part III
307–336   Section beginning in C major
337–372   Section beginning in B major and modulating to D major
373–414   Secondary section (Grazioso) in D major, partly treated
          imitatively and partly provided with counter melodies
415–422   Epilogue
423–496   Fugal Part IV

Recapitulation

Coda

Elements resembling a rondo in this structure are the triple appearance of the main section (Rondo theme), which serves as a refrain in D major, and the development of formally and tonally self-contained sections, serving as couplets. (The secondary section also reappears three times.) Elements resembling a sonata are the existence of numerous development passages, the manner of treatment, and above all the tonal disposition. While the main section and the secondary section are tonally stable (in the exposition in D major or B major and in the recapitulation in D major or G major), the development brings bold modulation.

Alternating the songlike and playful virtuoso passages lends a unique quality to the movement. The main section and the secondary section are cantabile and lyrical, whereas the fugal sections almost always have a bravura tint. Such concerted writing points to what Paul Hindemith did thirty years later. Some passages contain pedal points, with brass players competing with each other (e.g., mm. 479–496 and 538–580). There the music displays great brilliance.

Mahler based the Finale on several themes and motifs of his own (the motif played by the bassoon in mm. 3–5 corresponds note for note with the beginning of the *Wunderhorn* song *Lob des hohen Verstandes* ["In Praise of High Understanding"] but also linked it to the second movement and the Adagietto. The chorale theme of the second movement, there performed brightly and *pesante,* appears here in diminution and in a remarkable rhythmic transformation, which reminded Adorno of film technique and caused him to speak of "fast–motion composition" (*kompositorischen Zeitraffer*):

Second movement, mm. 499–519

Rondo-Finale, mm. 72–75

The chorale theme seems to have been robbed of all its weight and dignity.[47] Much less radical is the metamorphosis that the theme from the middle section of the Adagietto undergoes in the secondary section of the Rondo-Finale. Nevertheless, it loses its highly expressive, longing character and now assumes graceful features:

Adagietto, mm. 50–53

Rondo-Finale, mm. 191–197

Mahler marked the main theme at the beginning of the exposition "Allegro giocoso. *Frisch*."[48] This direction appropriately characterizes the mood and thought content of the entire movement, which typically does not have any sections in minor. Even the development lacks minor keys; "major" happiness reigns supreme. There are no eerie moods. The tam-tam—the idiophonic symbol of fright, horror, and death that is heard several times in the first two movements of the Symphony—is left out here altogether. The mood of the movement is at times reminiscent of the second *Wayfarer* song and its wholesome world, as well as of the first movement of the Fourth with which the Rondo-Finale shares some childlike figures. One is inclined to speak of a musical vocabulary of cheerfulness.[49]

Fourth Symphony, first movement. mm. 32–33

Fifth Symphony, Rondo-Finale, mm. 79–82

In spite of the exclusive use of the major mode, the music, rich in shades of color, is not lacking in tension. Using unexpected turns, Mahler knows how to keep his listeners in suspense. In this movement the art of *imprévu,* of the deceptive cadence, celebrates a real triumph.[50]

In the fugal sections the chorale theme, as previously explained, assumes a light and playful quality, but at the end of the recapitulation (mm. 711–748), the chorale appears in its original, splendid form. Alma Mahler reports in her memoirs that in a conversation with Mahler immediately after the completion of the Fifth she had expressed concerns about the "ecclesiastical, uninteresting" chorale (AME 64). Mahler replied with a reference to Bruckner, to which she responded: "*He* may, but *you* may not!" She continues: "I tried, as we were walking down through the woods, to make clear to him the difference between his character and Bruckner's. His strength, in my opinion, was *not* the incorporation of church chorales." Unfortunately, Alma does not tell us what she considered to be the character differences between Mahler and Bruckner.[51]

In the very boisterous final stretta, the trombones once again play the chorale melody, now in shorter note values (mm. 759–771). Even more interesting is the form that the chorale melody assumes in the horns:

Mm. 748–755

Incidentally, regarding the character difference between Mahler and Bruckner: Bruckner did not end any of his symphonies with a virtuoso, boisterous coda, and he would never have thought of treating a chorale melody in such a playful way.

According to Adorno's well-known observations, "brokenness" was the "core of experience" for thoughtful Mahler.[52] Yet he composed movements that show no trace of brokenness. When, in the summer of 1902, he composed the Rondo-Finale of the Fifth, he was in a very euphoric mood because he strongly believed he had found the greatest happiness of his life.

A page from the short score of the first movement of the Sixth Symphony
Bavarian State Library (Munich)
First Publication
Measures 93–122

The Sixth Symphony

My Sixth will be asking riddles that can be solved
only by a generation that has received and digested
my first five.   GMB² 295

People always remain the same. Now, all of a
sudden, they like my first five symphonies. The Sixth
will have to wait until my Seventh has appeared.
                                        GMB² 306

All things considered, [the Fifth] is more suitable for
an introduction than the Sixth. Both are tough nuts
for the Parisians.   GMB² 314

Origin

Mahler's Sixth Symphony, composed during 1903 and 1904, has become
known as the "Tragic." According to Bruno Walter, this dark title goes back
to Mahler himself.[1] Be that as it may, it is certain that the symphony was
already performed under this title during Mahler's lifetime and that it characterizes the content of the work correctly.[2]

If one's concept of tragedy in general is the unavoidable, fateful downfall
of a person in the battle with overpowering forces, then the title is appropriate for the Sixth.[3] As Paul Bekker pointed out, it is Mahler's only
symphony that ends somberly rather than victoriously (as do the First,
Second, Fifth, Seventh, and Eighth) or transfigured (as the Third, Fourth,
and Ninth).[4] The overall impression the work has on the listener is determined by the coda of the Finale. The passage marked *schwer* (heavily), No.
165–166 (imitation between trombones and tuba, with timpani roll) clearly
has the character of a requiem. It is also significant that in the Finale Mahler
calls for a hammer, which, in the first version, strikes in three places. All who
felt they had to make crude jokes about this sound effect have completely
misunderstood the hammer's symbolic meaning. Here, too, Paul Bekker

realized correctly what Mahler had in mind: It signifies "an interference by something outside this world, something of a supernatural, crushing effect that mankind can no longer fight against."[5]

Since numerous symbolic tonal features of the Sixth point toward programmatic intentions, it seems strange that the work has been widely regarded as absolute music. In response to the remarks of Theodor W. Adorno, one often comes across the opinion that the splendid "form immanence" of the Sixth constitutes its content.[6] Actually the Sixth takes its place—together with Tchaikovsky's Sixth Symphony (1893) and Richard Strauss's *Ein Heldenleben* ("A Hero's Life") (1898) and *Sinfonia domestica* (1903)—among the great symphonic works that have been autobiographically conceived. Alma Mahler states in her memoirs that the Sixth is based on an autobiographical programmatic concept.

Mahler began work on the Sixth during the summer of 1903 in Maiernigg at the Wörthersee, where he spent the vacation together with his wife and his little daughter (Maria Anna Mahler, born 3 November 1902). He was in a good frame of mind: "He often played with the child, dragging her all over, taking her in his arms, dancing and singing. He was so young back then and so unencumbered" (AME 78). According to Alma, two movements of the Sixth were completed during that summer, "and the idea for the other movements was completed in his head" (AME 79). Unfortunately she did not reveal which movements of the work were completed.

In June of the following year Mahler left his wife, who was again expecting, "in the care of her mother" in Vienna and went "utterly alone" to the lake. "You know why? It is simply my duty," he wrote to Arnold Berliner on 19 June (GMB[2] 291). On 15 July, Alma gave birth to their second daughter, Anna Justina,[7] then travelled to join Mahler. "The summer was delightful, without any conflicts, happy," Alma writes in her memoirs. Mahler completed the Sixth Symphony and "added three further songs to the two *Kindertotenlieder,* a fact that I could not understand" (AME 91–93). Alma's discomfort about these songs is understandable, and the reasons for her disliking them seem plausible.

> I can well understand that one might compose such terrible texts if one does not have any children or if one has lost children. After all, these shocking verses did not come to Friedrich Rückert out of nowhere; he wrote them after he experienced the most cruel loss of his life. I cannot understand how one can sing about the death of children if a half hour before one has hugged and kissed those who are cheerful and healthy. At the time I said immediately: "For heaven's sake, don't tempt fate!"

At the end of the vacation Mahler played "the now completed" Sixth for Alma: "We again went arm in arm up to his little house in the woods, where we were undisturbed. All of this always took place with great solemnity."[8] At the end of this statement Alma provides the following extremely important hermeneutical remarks:

After he had finished the first movement, Mahler came down from the woods and said, "I have tried to capture you in a theme; I do not know whether I have been successful. You will have to put up with it."

It is the long, sweeping theme of the first movement of the Sixth Symphony. In the third movement he describes the arrhythmic playing of the two children, staggering through the sand. Horrible—those children's voices become more and more tragic, and at the end there is one fading little voice, whimpering. In the last movement he describes himself and his downfall or, as he said later, the downfall of his hero. "The hero who receives three blows from fate, the third of which fells him like a tree." These are Mahler's words.

No other work has flowed so directly from his heart as this one. We both cried at the time; we felt so deeply what this music meant, what it forebodingly told us. The Sixth is his most personal work and is also a prophetic one. In the "Songs on the Death of Children" and in the Sixth, he "musically anticipated" his life. He, too, received three blows from fate, and the third did fell him. At the time, however, he was cheerful, conscious of the greatness of his work, and his branches leafed and blossomed.

One can hardly understand the deeper meaning of these expressions without knowing something about Mahler's intellectual world. According to Richard Specht's testimony, Mahler was an "utter determinist"; he was convinced "that the creative person is lifted up by his inspiration to a higher, anticipatory level of existence, and that in his creative work he would anticipate the experience that everyday life would later bring."[9] Not until we completely understand this concept can we comprehend Alma's account of the dress rehearsal for the first performance of the Sixth in Essen on 16 May 1906, after which Mahler was totally shocked, "sobbing, wringing his hands, and not in control of himself" (AME 127). No work, according to Alma, touched him so much at the first hearing. He conducted the performance "almost badly because he was ashamed of his excitement and afraid that his emotions would cause him to lost control of himself while conducting. He did not want anyone to suspect the truth of this horrible, last *Anticipando* movement." It seems as though Mahler indeed foresaw the tragic events that the year 1907 would bring to him and his family: the death of his older daughter, his resignation from the Vienna Court Opera, and the diagnosis of heart disease. One does not have to be an advocate of in-depth psychological interpretation of works of modern art to acknowledge that the visions of downfall oppressing Mahler at the conception of the Finale of this prophetic symphony were derived from deeply rooted fears. Not surprisingly, by November of 1898 he already identified with the fate of Coriolan (BL^2 126), and he felt understood by Arthur Schnitzler, who was particularly gripped by "the awful, somewhat dehumanized and soulless" aspects in the gloomy Finale of the Sixth.[10]

Thematic Connections and Symbols

Mahler's concept of the symphony was closely connected with the idea of a cyclical form. In all of his symphonies, individual, several, or all movements are connected with each other, either thematically or in some other way. Mahler attributed great importance to those connections and from time to time pointed them out in letters or conversations.[11]

In the Sixth, thematic connections exist between the movements. In the Andante moderato, for instance, the horns (mm. 165–168) quote the choralelike theme of the first movement (mm. 61–63).[12] In addition, a comparison of the first movement with the Scherzo and the Finale (all three are in A minor) shows that some themes have been developed from the same nucleus. We might speak of a "common substance" or even of thematic "association" in the sense of Werner F. Korte.[13] Yet more important is the emotional relationship existing between these three movements, which can be attributed to the recurrence of certain characters of expression (march, chorale, stirring, or even hymnic music, music from far away), to the use of various idiophones, and last but not least, to the use of two devices (a rhythmic and a harmonic one) that capture the tragic element in the Sixth.

A kind of motto is formed by basic rhythm and the following well-defined sequence of major-minor chords:

First movement, mm. 57–60

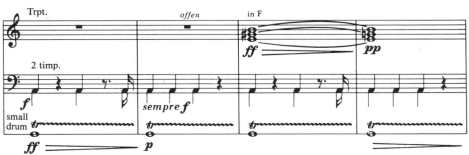

The chord sequence often returns in the first movement, Scherzo, and Finale, holding the three movements together like an iron clamp and preventing any breakthrough (e.g., from despair to triumph).[14] Mahler said nothing about the meaning of these two devices, but Paul Bekker[15] (following Richard Specht[16]) described the chord sequence as an "unchangeable verdict of fate." He was undoubtedly correct.[17] If one considers that the concept of the tragic, according to the classic view, includes the working of a super-powerful, inescapable fate, then this interpretation makes sense and Adorno actually says very little when he points out that the term *tragic* had been degraded to a "cultural educational reminiscence."[18] After all, the Sixth does prove impressively how much the category of the tragic meant to Mahler.

The first movement, Scherzo, and Finale belong together inasmuch as their range of expression includes the frightening. The tam-tam, sound symbol of horror and death, is left out in the Andante moderato and used quite sparingly and purposefully in the three other movements. It is heard six times in the first movement (mm. 181, 185, 376, 377, 379, and 381), ten times in the Scherzo (mm. 228–234, 250–251, 401–405), and five times in the Finale (mm. 395–396, 401–402, 479, 520–523, and 773–777). It is revealing that in the Scherzo the tam-tam accentuates the fatal aspect of the basic rhythm, as well as twice punctuating the major-minor seal in the Finale and accompanying one of the hammer blows.

The cowbells are used in the first movement, in the Andante moderato, and in the Finale of the Sixth as well as in the first "Night Music" of the Seventh. As Mahler explained on the occasion of the Seventh's first performance in Munich, he did not use the bells as a pastoral symbol, but to create the mood of "the loneliness of being far away from the world."[19] He wanted only to create "a sound of nature, echoing from a great distance." This passage sounded to him "as though he stood on the highest peak, in the face of eternity."[20] These extremely meaningful remarks underscore again the metaphysical dimension of Mahler's symphonic work. They are all the more credible if one recalls that cowbells are heard in the outer movements of the Sixth in passages meant to sound as if the music is coming from far away.

Among other instruments used symbolically in the Sixth, the bells, the hammer, the whip, and the wooden rattle are reserved for the Finale. The xylophone, generally recognized as sound symbol for the macabre after the *Danse macabre* of Saint-Saëns, is used only in the first movement and Scherzo. The large array of idiophones in the Sixth understandably caused concern and forced Mahler to announce to the Vienna Court Opera orchestra on the occasion of a dress rehearsal:

> Nowhere do I intend merely to make noise, even though I enlist so many percussion instruments. If you listen, you will notice that I always use only one percussion instrument at a time, never several. By employing various percussion instruments, I sought merely to achieve variety in timbre.[21]

This statement is not entirely correct, since in a number of places the score does call for the use of several percussion instruments simultaneously.

Allegro energico

The first movement of the Sixth Symphony has always been praised for the regularity of its sonata structure. Paul Bekker spoke of a "textbook example of symphonic sonata structure"[22] and of clear, "paradigmatic" structure.[23] These judgments are hardly overstated. In comparing the movement with the distinctly more irregular structure of the first movements of the Second and Third Symphonies, it becomes evident that in the Sixth Mahler comes closer to the conventional idea of sonata structure. The movement is clearly divided into exposition (122 measures), development (163 measures), recapitulation (88 measures), and coda (107 measures). The exposition even has repeat signs, and the movement is based on three contrasting themes or theme complexes that are manipulated and developed most ingeniously. There is a marchlike energetic first movement (the indication Allegro energico refers to the first theme complex), a choralelike theme, and a *Schwungvoll* (sweeping) second theme written in the key of the parallel subdominant (F major). Examining it more closely, of course, the movement also has many special features that need our attention. Let us begin with a formal outline.

Exposition

Mm.		
	1–56	Main section in A minor of marchlike character (following 5 measures of introduction, two sections of 19 and 32 measures)
	57–60	Lead rhythm, major-minor seal
	61–76	Chorale theme in A minor (8 + 8 measures)
	77–90	Secondary section (*schwungvoll*) in F major
	91–98	Insert with motifs of the main section
	99–115	Continuation of the secondary section in F major
	115–122	Epilogue in F major

Development

123b–177 First Part: Development of motifs from the main section: marchlike character (the lead rhythm mm. 123b–153 five times and mm. 152–174 nine times in the timpani and small drum)

178–196 Second Part: Development of motifs from the secondary section and main section (two tam-tam beats)

196–250 Third Part (*Allmählich etwas gehaltener*) [gradually a little more sustained]: music from far away with cowbells (motifs from the second section, chorale, and main section, adding a signallike call of a fourth; mm. 203–204 and 208–209 the major-minor seal)

251–285 Fourth Part: (Tempo I. Subito. *Sehr energisch* [Very energetic]): motifs from main section and chorale

Recapitulation

286–333 Main section in A minor (mm. 314–315: the major-minor seal)

332–335 Lead rhythm, major-minor seal

336–347 Chorale theme in diminution: Music from a distance

348–351 Transition with motifs from the secondary section

352–365 Secondary section (*unmerklich drängend*) [slightly faster] in D major

365–373 Epilogue in D major

Coda

Jean Matter wondered how Paul Bekker, who wrote his book about Mahler shortly after World War I, could interpret the march rhythms of the Sixth as an anticipation of the terrible happenings of the war. Matter spoke of an *obsession de la marche*.[24] Although Mahler's obvious love for marchlike rhythms allows for various interpretations, the word *obsession* is well chosen for the Sixth. The idea of the march does indeed determine the character of large passages in the outer movements. At the same time, other characteristics hold their own. In this symphony the balance of forces is well maintained.

The first theme complex of the Sixth is quite extensive, consisting of no less than fifty-six measures divided into two sections of twenty-four and thirty-two measures. They begin similarly, both ending in half cadences besides corresponding in other ways. One might speak of a gigantic period in two parts. The second brings a new motif, which a few measures later experiences a rhythmic and diastematic change.

Mm. 29–31

Mm. 34–36

Toward the end, the second section reaches a climax on a dissonance, an altered dominant-ninth chord (E—G-sharp—B-flat—D—F), a climax having the effect of a collapse. This is immediately followed by the tragic symbols of the lead rhythm and the major-minor seal.

The chorale theme that follows—strictly symmetrical, even square (eight + eight measures)—is performed by the woodwinds and later by the first horn.[25] It is placed exactly halfway between the main and secondary sections, the position that is normally occupied by the transition in classic sonata form. The theme, however, does not modulate to the key of the secondary section, but rather rests (established in A minor), so to speak, within itself. A trombone figure from the Finale of the Second Symphony (mm. 82–84) seems to have supplied the motivic nucleus of this theme:

Second Symphony, Finale, mm. 82–84

Sixth Symphony, first movement, mm. 61–68

Guido Adler criticized the theme of the secondary section as "melodically weak."[26] Such esthetic judgments tend to be subjective. Nonetheless, it is certain that the broadly arched *schwungvoll* theme, which Mahler himself considered to be a portrait of his wife, forms a strong contrast to the main theme. Mahler's interruption of the theme and interpolation of an eight-measure passage with motivic material from the main theme complex (mm. 91–98) represents an ingenious artistic device. According to Paul Bekker the stylistic change that begins with the Fifth is clearly reflected in Mahler's new tendency toward "thematic work," a procedure that until then was perhaps unimportant to him, certainly not crucial or even intentional.[27] This exaggerated statement does not do justice to a composition such as the first movement of the Fourth Symphony, but there is some truth to it. If one compares the first movement of the Sixth with that of the Third, the traditional ideas regarding thematic work do seem to fit the former more than the latter. For a deeper understanding of Mahler's style, it is more important to note that in the Sixth he does not give up his earlier manner of including passages that are distinctive and self-contained.

The development of the first movement of the Sixth is clearly divided into four parts, each of which has an unmistakable appearance. The marchlike first part (mm. 123b–177) consists exclusively of motifs from the main section. Surprisingly it shows a marchlike structure following the scheme A (mm. 123b–143) + B (mm. 144–151) + A′ (mm. 152–177). Two similar outer sections quite clearly reveal A minor as a tonal center and frame a shorter section in E minor. It is typical of the three-part structure that in the outer sections, timpani and the small drum play the basic rhythm of the symphony five or nine times; it is only here that a concise motif often stands out, though it was presented only once in the exposition:

Mm. 20–21

Mm. 129–130

Mahler now adds trills to the motif and mostly entrusts it to the woodwinds and the xylophone. No wonder that largely due to this timbre the music at times sounds eerie and anticipates the general mood of the Scherzo.

Marchlike rhythms also play a large role in the second part of the development (mm. 178–196), but its thematic material is mostly dominated by the main motif of the sweeping secondary theme, which now in fact loses its major character and moves into the minor mode:

Mm. 179–185

The way in which Mahler connects the two first parts of the development reveals great artistry. The accompanying motif of trombones and tuba introducing the second part (mm. 177–179) (taken from the first four notes of the sweeping theme) is already played at the end of the first part (mm. 173–174 by bassoons, cellos, and double basses. The trill motif of the woodwinds at the beginning of the second part (mm. 178–179 and 182–183) is a leftover, so to speak, from the eerie trill motif of the first part.

The third part (mm. 196–250) occupies a special place within the development by interrupting it to a certain extent. It seems to introduce sounds from another world. (Karl Weigl and others spoke of a "dream world".[28]) The tempo becomes slower, the dynamic level almost never leaves *pianissimo,* and harmony and instrumentation show exceptional character— all characteristics of "music from far away" are there.[29] This part also is in three sections according to the scheme A + B + A[1]. In the two outer sections during which cowbells and celesta are heard, chorale and Alma motifs dominate, as well as a new call-like motif of a fourth; but in the middle section (mm. 217–233), a grazioso in G major and E-flat major, motifs from the main movement and second sections are contrasted and contrapuntally combined. Surprising is the metamorphosis of a very energetic motif from the main section by means of diastematic inversion and by changes of dynamic level and articulation:

Mm. 26–27

Mm. 217–220

Mahler here achieves startling and completely new coloristic sounds through the mixing of tone colors and seemingly bitonal effects:[30]

Mm. 209–215

After the *morendo* ending of the third part, the thread is picked up again. The fourth part (mm. 251–285) enters ("very energetic") in the first tempo with that striking trumpet motif from the main section (mm. 29–31):

Mm. 250–254

The motif had not been developed so far and is now processed in every conceivable way, including contrapuntal interweaving with the chorale theme. A short intensification leads to the recapitulation, which strangely enough begins in A major but after only four measures reaches A minor, the main key of the movement. It is hardly necessary to point out that the shortened recapitulation shows numerous alterations and practically amounts to a new composition compared with the exposition.

The exceptionally long coda is rich in motivic and thematic work and amounts to a second development. Clearly divided into three parts, it primarily contains motifs from the main and secondary sections.[31] Right at the beginning, Mahler provides a surprise. Along with the pulsating march rhythm of the double basses and contrabassoons, the trombones play *pianissimo* motifs from the main theme, mainly in E minor and F-sharp minor (mm. 376–381). Low notes of the horns and four tam-tam beats underscore the requiem-like character of the passage. In a sudden change of expression, the orchestra responds to the eerie *pianissimo* with a *fortissimo* outburst. Mahler's instruction in the score is Più mosso subito (*Wie wütend dreinfahren*) [Entering furiously]. The passage undoubtedly has programmatic meaning (possibly chasing away thoughts of death); quite logically the *fortissimo* outburst is followed by a marchlike passage, highly energetic and demonic in nature, presenting the first motif of the main theme simultaneously in its basic form and in its inversion:[32]

Mm. 402–405

The third section of the coda deserves special attention, since it was conceived as an apotheosis of Alma. At the beginning the trumpets play in unison and *fortissimo,* along with emphatic timpani beats, the first motif of Alma's theme in augmentation:

Mm. 444–448

After that, motifs of the main and secondary sections alternate in dialogue and are also contrapuntally combined:

Mm. 466–470

Nevertheless, Alma's motifs have the last word; they supply the affirmative, indeed, triumphant (almost operatic) ending. If one interprets the Sixth as a drama in four acts, then this jubilant ending marks its high point by which one can later realize the extent of the fall.

Mahler's remarks regarding the musical portrait of his wife in the secondary section will become more understandable if one takes into consideration that in Richard Strauss's tone poem *Ein Heldenleben* Op. 40, completed in 1898, one section was originally entitled "The Hero's Companion." Mahler followed closely the symphonic work of his friend and rival Strauss, and it is quite likely that in the conception of his Sixth he received various impulses from Strauss's autobiographical compositions. We will have to return to this point later.

Scherzo

Compared with the Scherzo of the Fifth, that of the Sixth is constructed with considerably greater clarity.[33] The five or six parts into which it is divided reveal the disposition that is familiar from the Scherzo of the Fourth: A—B—A^1—B^1—A^2—Coda. Three structural peculiarities of the movement deserve to be mentioned from the outset: The Scherzo is developed from relatively few motifs; the trio and the main parts are connected through artful transitions and interludes; and the second trio is in a different key (D major) than the first (F major). For Mahler, it is a matter of course that every part of the movement is greatly varied at every return.

Main movement (Part A) in A minor

Mm.	1–41	First section
	42–61	Second section
	62–96	Third section (= modification of the first) (mm. 87–91 the major-minor seal)

Trio (B) in F major

	97–113	First section
	114–128	Second section
	129–145	Third section
	146–172	Fourth section
	173–182	Transition (with parallel major thirds)
	183–198	Interlude in F minor

Main movement (Part A^1) in A minor

	199–238	First section (mm. 228–231 the lead rhythm with tam-tam)
	239–272	Second and third section (the two sections are interwoven); mm. 261–265 the major-minor seal

Trio II (Part B^1) in D major

	273–290	First section
	291–306	Second section
	307–319	Third section
	320–335	Fourth section
	336–344	Fifth section
	345–354	Transition
	355–371	Interlude beginning in E-flat minor

372–411   Main movement (Part A²) in A minor

Coda

412–419   First section
420–432   Second section (with threefold statement of the major-minor
          seal)
433–446   Third section (with threefold statement of the major-minor
          seal)

It is immediately apparent that the moods of the main parts are similar to several passages in the first movement. The throbbing rhythms of timpani, cellos, and double basses are reminiscent of the first movement's beginning; the weighty first motifs of the violins are derived from the same core as the beginning of the first theme of the first movement.

Scherzo, mm. 1–6

In addition, the trill motif of the woodwinds and the xylophone, measures 15–19, clearly points to the first part of the development of the first movement:

First movement, mm. 129–130

Scherzo, mm. 15–19

The major-minor seal appears several times (once in the first part, once in the third, and six times in the coda), and in approximately the middle of the movement, the timpani, reinforced by harps, and tam-tam play the lead rhythm:

Mm. 228–231

The second movement of the Sixth is possibly the most demonic of Mahler's scherzos. The performance instructions—*wuchtig* and *wie gepeitscht* (as if whipped)—give an impression of the generally eerie character of the main sections. By way of contrast, some of the thematic material of the trio sections (Mahler labels them *altväterisch* [jovial] and grazioso) sounds like children's songs. The demonic quality of the movement results not only from this extremely strong contrast, but also from the thematic material of the main sections, the compact way of writing, the massive instrumentation, and from certain performance indications.

For this Scherzo, Mahler calls for an almost full orchestra: all woodwinds, eight horns, four trumpets, three trombones and tuba, timpani, Glockenspiel, xylophone, bass drum, triangle, cymbals, tam-tam, harps, and strings. Almost nowhere else does he have the brass play so often with mutes; often he divides the groups of instruments and has half play muted or stopped while the other half play open.[34] Here and there during the interludes, the strings are to play *col legno* (mm. 183–194 and 355–358).

Certain passages sound especially eerie. Among the most impressive are the sequences of parallel major thirds in the horns during the transitions:

Mm. 176–182

Similar parallel thirds in the last of the *Songs on the Death of Children* serve as description of an eerie mood: *In diesem Wetter, in diesem Braus* (In this weather, in this storm). Equally eerie is the passage with the tuba (mm. 227–238), which Mahler takes down as low here as Wagner did in the second act of *Siegfried*:

Mm. 231–238

The character of the trios contrasts strongly with that of the main section, as has been indicated. Therefore it is all the more surprising that a phrase from the middle part of the main section (mm. 50–54) forms the core of the trio theme.

Mm. 50–54

Mm. 96–100

Though strongly contrasting in character, this close motivic connection between the main section and trio of a scherzo is very unusual for Mahler.

The obvious change of meter in the trio sections has often elicited comment. Adorno wrote: "The irregularity of the meter is not limited to the surface, the sequence of the metric units, but rather reaches down to the essence, the structure of the music."[35] That the trio sections present constant tempo changes has gone unnoticed. In the first trio, the regular tempo (*altväterisch*) is superseded no less than three times by passages marked *drängend* (urgent, pressing). Mahler's instructions read:

Mm. 98–110 *Altväterisch.* (Poco meno mosso.) Grazioso
    111–113 *Tempo natürlich drängend* (naturally urgent)
    114–122 *Tempo wieder angehalten* (restrained again)
    123–128 *Tempo natürlich drängend*
    128–140 Again *altväterisch*
    140–145 *Natürlich drängend*
    146–172 Suddenly again as before (*altväterisch*)

Mahler mentioned to his wife that in the Scherzo he was describing "the arrhythmic playing" of the two little children "who were staggering through the sand." So far no one has given this comment the consideration it deserves. It clarifies that the meter and tempo changes, which stand out so much in the trio sections, are there for programmatic reasons. The situation is even more revealing when one realizes that Mahler's trio theme, which the oboe plays in the second trio in D major, is quite similar to the theme of the oboe d'amore or the oboe from the Scherzo of the *Sinfonia domestica* by Richard Strauss:

Mm. 273–280

Strauss, *Sinfonia domestica*, Scherzo (*munter*) [lively]

Significantly enough, Strauss's Scherzo originally was subtitled *Kindliches Spiel, Elternglück* ("Childlike Play, Parental Happiness").[36]

The score of the *Sinfonia domestica* was published by Bote and Bock in March 1904.[37] To judge by his letter to Peters, Mahler became acquainted with it no later than July 1904.[38] From this we can conclude that he did not complete the Scherzo of the Sixth until the summer of 1904—especially because he also remarked that the Scherzo represented the playing of *both* little children.

Andante moderato

Like the Adagietto of the Fifth and the Andante amoroso of the Seventh, the first part of the Andante moderato of the Sixth is also a song without words. In tone it is similar to the fourth of the *Songs on the Death of Children*: "*Oft denk' ich, sie sind nur ausgegangen!*" ("Often I Think They Just Went Out for a Walk"). It is presented in three-part song form: A (mm. 1–20)—B (mm. 20–27)—A¹ (mm. 28–42)—*Abgesang* (mm. 42–55).

Paul Bekker said that the main theme was not among the "most original manifestations of Mahler's mind."[39] Bekker believed that the beginning, with the "languishing rise of a sixth," had something "almost ironically popular," and that Mahler himself most likely did not completely enjoy this theme. One can hardly share these opinions. The melody is marked to be performed *zart, aber ausdrucksvoll* (gently, but expressively); any intent of irony seems most unlikely. And as to its being "popular," Arnold Schoenberg pointed out in the 1912 memorial speech in Prague that the 10-measure theme departed from the conventional.[40] Melodic structure and harmonization also display ingenious features. The E-flat major theme vacillates between major and minor; as a result, the third and the sixth steps are often lowered. More importantly, all other steps of the scale are subject to alteration. F-flat occurs next to F, G-flat next to G, C-flat next to C, and D-flat next to D. This shows that Mahler, whom David Josef Bach called the "last proponent of the diatonic," now and then tempered diatonicism in a special way.[41]

Mm. 1–10

In the middle section of this song without words (set in an Aeolian-tinted G minor), the English horn, and later first flute and first clarinet, prominently carry the melody. The instrumentation takes the melancholic character of the melody into account, the English horn (not heard in the first movement and Scherzo) being the instrument of lament par excellence:

Mm. 22–26

The *Abgesang,* closing *morendo* on a pedal point on low E flat, has a pastoral tint. Its two motifs—a rocking motif (called "cradle motif" by Paul Bekker) and an eighth-note motif[42]—considerably affect the structure of the whole movement:

Mm. 42–46

Viewed from a distance, the Andante moderato of the Sixth shows the familiar five-part structure A—B—A^1—B^1—A^2, but on closer inspection it becomes clear that the movement is based on a formal concept that is totally different from, for instance, the slow movement of the Fourth Symphony.

While the Fourth's Poco Adagio is based on two theme complexes of strongly contrasting character (one in major, the other in minor), in the Andante moderato the parts are motivically connected. In other words, the B parts differ considerably in character from the first part, yet they contain and develop motifs and themes from the first part.

Part A

Mm.   1–55   Three-part song form according to the scheme A + B + A' + *Abgesang*. Section B establishes an elegiac theme in G minor; a rocking motif and an eighth-note motif are important in the *Abgesang*. Tonic key: E-flat major

Part B

56–83   First section: after four introductory measures in C major, the elegiac theme in A minor; symphonic development of the eighth-note motif and other motifs in E minor and B minor

84–99   Second section: Pastorale in E major with harps, celesta, and cowbells (rising motif and rocking motif)

Part A¹ (shortened)

100–114   Main theme in E-flat major (with another voice in counterpoint)

Part B¹

115–128   First section: *Misterioso* in C major (derived from the eighth-note motif)

129–138   Second section: Pastorale in A major with celesta (rocking and eighth-note motifs)

139–145   Third section: Elegiac theme in A minor

146–159   Fourth section: Elegiac theme in C-sharp minor, then climax in F-sharp major with cowbells

Part A²

159–201   Main theme, first in B major, then in E-flat major; ending fades away

The development-like character of the B parts is seen in the disposition of keys. The circle of keys continually widens. We reach not only the keys of A, E, and B minor, but also the bright keys of A, E, B, and F-sharp major. The alternation between more elegiac passages in minor and bright passages in major is striking, as is Mahler's tendency to connect rather than actually to modulate to different key areas.[43]

The second part of the movement opens with a high, bright interval (E^3–G^3) in the flutes and strings. After four introductory measures (the oboe playing the rocking motif and the first clarinet the eighth-note motif), the elegiac theme in A minor sets in. Very intensive developments of the eighth-note motif follow.

Mm. 65–67

E minor and B minor motifs are also developed. The ending is formed by a splendidly orchestrated passage of pastoral character in E major in which the cowbells and celesta are heard for the first time in this movement. An ascending motif in the horns and the rocking motif in the trumpets characterize the passage:

Mm. 85–89

Paul Bekker rightfully pointed out that the passage reminds one vividly of the E-major breakthrough in the slow movement of the Fourth.[44] E major occurs here as "the transfiguration key, an expression of ecstasy, vision of the supernatural," just as it did in the slow movement and in the Finale of the Fourth. Note that the ascending horn motif is strikingly similar to the hymn-like *Blicket auf* (glance upward) motif from the second part of the Eighth Symphony (No. 176).

After the first two quite broadly conceived parts, the short third part (the main theme here has a counter melody) seems more like a transition to the fourth part, which brings a contrasting thought. Of the four sections of this part, the first three (in C major, A major, and A minor) are *pianissimo*. The marking *Misterioso* (No. 56) refers to all three. At the beginning of the *Misterioso* the cellos and violas are to play "without expression." In the fourth section, however, the long-restrained emotion breaks through. The elegiac theme enters *forte* in C-sharp minor, and the tension-filled music quickly escalates to a triple *forte*. At the high point (mm. 154–159), cowbells ring out again, and suddenly the main theme appears. It is played by the cellos in B major, to be performed *Immer mit bewegter Empfindung (auf und abwogend)* (Always with great emotion [rising and falling]), and it leads back to E-flat major in measure 173. The intensity diminishes little by little, and the movement fades away, morendo *ppp*.

Finale

> The new as a cryptogram is the image of
> decline; only through its absolute negativeness
> does art express the inexpressible, the utopia.[45]

The Finale of the Sixth Symphony is surrounded by a special aura. Paul
Bekker considered it to be ("next to the Finale of the Eighth") the greatest
music Mahler had written,[46] and Adorno called it "the center of Mahler's
entire œuvre."[47] Three qualities explain the high ranking of this movement:
the monumentality of its plan; its vast range of expression (visionary,
choralelike, marchlike, ecstatic, dramatically moving, music from far away,
and hymnic) and the speed at which the most varied characters follow each
other; its gloomy closing.

The movement has been extensively reviewed. Erwin Ratz presented a
thematic, motivic analysis that is as detailed as it is exhaustive.[48] Adorno
provided revealing discussions, and Bernd Sponheuer discussed it in depth
(72 printed pages) under the heading "Failure as Success: The Construction
of Negative Formal Content (*Formimmanenz*)." So far semantic questions
have not been considered. They will be at the center of the following
investigation.

The structure of the movement corresponds to normal sonata form. An
introduction precedes each section: exposition (228 measures), development
(291 measures), recapitulation (253 measures), and coda (110 measures). In
the exposition, recapitulation, and coda, the introductory theme leads into the
major-minor seal, played together with the lead rhythm. Especially noteworthy are the passages in the exposition, development, and recapitulation
that follow the introductory theme or the major-minor seal (mm. 16–48, 67–
95, 237–270, and 537–574). They show Mahler's characteristic type of
"music from far away" and are exceptional in every way. The dynamic level
seldom exceeds *pianissimo*; the strings (if they do not have pizzicato figures)
play mostly with mutes and favor tremolo figures; the harps mostly use the
plectrum; low bells and cowbells sound only here and at no other time; there
are many sustained voices and pedal points, which means that harmony
changes often take place in the middle voices. Elements from the main theme
and secondary theme complexes (and other motifs as well) are merely hinted
at. Thus the tuba intones a motif consisting of three notes that are later
important as part of the main theme (mm. 19–22).

Mm. 19–22

Motifs suggesting calling or sighing follow:

Mm. 19–24

In measures 27–40 the tuba, and the fourth and first horns play in succession the first motifs from the secondary section:

Mm. 27–40

Then (again in succession) another three-note motif is heard in celesta, tuba, and first oboe; it is borrowed from the main theme. A sighing motif and another motif with skips of an octave and a tenth follow:

Mm. 39–43

The motivic material seldom goes beyond beginnings. As Debussy did at the same time, Mahler employs an almost impressionistic technique of suggestion. A comparison of these passages with the actual exposition, development, and recapitulation confirms what an initial hearing may have suggested; namely, the music operates on two basically different levels. One is unreal, dreamlike, and far removed; the other is in the foreground and real. Recognizing these levels makes it easier to comprehend what Mahler meant when he said that the passages in which the cowbells ring made him feel "as though he stood on the highest peak, facing eternity." This vision suggests a comparison with Strauss's tone poem *Death and Transfiguration,* Op. 24, or to be more precise, with the poem of Alexander Ritter upon which the composition is based, in which a doomed person is thinking of his bygone life.[49]

Let us examine the structure and characteristics of this colossal movement more closely. Here in particular an overview can replace long descriptions and discourses.

Exposition

Mm. 1–15 Introductory theme (*Sostenuto*) with lead rhythm and major-minor seal
16–48 Music from far away (*Etwas schleppend*) [Somewhat dragging]: suggestion of exposition motifs, call-like sighing motifs, and a motif with an interval of a tenth; harps and celesta; mm. 29–33: *tiefes Glockengeläute in der Ferne* (low bell sounds in the distance)
49–64 Brass chorale (Heavy. Marcato) beginning in C minor
65–66 Lead rhythm and major-minor seal
67–95 Music from far away (*Etwas fließender*) [A little more flowing]: suggestions of exposition motifs
96–97 Major-minor seal
98–113 Transition to the main section (Allegro moderato), beginning *pianissimo* and building to *fortissimo*
114–140 Main section (Allegro energico) in A minor
141–175 *Pesante*: choralelike theme contrapuntally combined with main section motifs
176–190 Conclusion of the main section
191–228 Secondary section in D major

Development

229–236 Introductory theme
237–270 Music from far away: Reminiscences of exposition motifs along with the call-like sighing motif; mm. 239–249 cowbells, mm. 253–259 *tiefes Glockengeläute stets in der Ferne* (low bell sounds, always in the distance)
271–335 First part of the development
271–287 Signallike motifs from the secondary section and call-like sighing motifs
288–335 Development of the secondary section material (sweeping in character)
336–396 Second part of the development (m. 336: first blow of the hammer)
336–363 Work with motifs from the choralelike theme (the strings accompany with motifs from the main section)
364–396 *Etwas wuchtiger. Alles mit roher Kraft* (Somewhat more weighty. Everything with brute strength). Dramatic "battle scene" with main section motifs, ostinato rhythms, and harsh dissonances; mm. 395–396 the major-minor seal and a first tam-tam beat
397–478 Third part of the development
397–457 *Kräftig, aber etwas gemessen* (Strong, but somewhat restrained): at the beginning, work with the marchlike main

theme (the whip is used only in this section; mm. 401–402 the second tam-tam beat)

458–468 *Allmählich sich beruhigend* (Gradually settling down): section of hymnic character in A major, derived from the introductory theme and from secondary section motifs

469–478 *Noch mehr zurückhaltend* (Even more restrained): transition (~mm. 86–95)

479–519 Fourth part of the development (m. 479 the second hammer blow and the third tam-tam beat): elaboration mainly of choralelike motifs

Recapitulation

520–536 Introductory theme with lead rhythm and major-minor seal (m. 520 the fourth tam-tam beat)

537–574 Music from far away: reminiscences of exposition motifs; mm. 549–554 *tiefes Glockengeläute in der Ferne* (low bell sounds in the distance) and mm. 554–560 *Herdenglocken in der Ferne* (cowbells in the distance)

575–641 *Grazioso*: Secondary section beginning in B-flat major and leading to A major (here and there coupled with choralelike and main section motifs); mm. 622–625 the lead rhythm

642–669 Main section in A minor (mm. 668–669 the lead rhythm and the major-minor seal)

670–727 Development and contrapuntal treatment of motifs from the main and secondary sections, along with choralelike motifs (mm. 720–725, 385–394)

728–753 *Abgesang* of hymnic character

754–772 Motifs from the secondary and main sections (mm. 754–759 the lead rhythm)

Coda

773–789 Introductory theme with lead rhythm and major-minor seal (m. 773 the fifth tam-tam beat; (m. 783 the third blow of the hammer in first version only)

790–815 Imitative section for trombones, tuba, and horns (= epitaph)

816–822 Closing (mm. 820–821 the lead rhythm)

The actual exposition operates with three richly differentiated themes: a marchlike main theme in A minor, a periodically constructed chorale theme, and a sweeping secondary theme in D major that starts *piano* and ends in a triple *forte*. Note that the chorale theme is contrapuntally combined with motifs from the main section and that the actual transition from A minor to D major takes place in a section (mm. 176–190) following the chorale theme.

Bernd Sponheuer pointed out that these three themes correspond entirely

in their character with the three themes of the first movement.[50] Both times
the themes are marked Allegro energico. He also pointed out some similari-
ties between the individual motifs. The interrelationships in fact go further.
The main motif of the sweeping Alma theme from the first movement returns
almost note for note in the secondary theme of the Finale:

First movement, mm. 76–78 (transposed to G major)

Finale, mm. 205–208

It is also remarkable that the contrapuntal combination of main and
secondary section motifs does not occur in the first movement or in the
development of the Finale (which would have been likely). Instead it occurs
in the coda of the first movement and in the recapitulation of the Finale. All
of this leads to the conclusion that in the Finale (as in the exposition and in
the recapitulation) Mahler picks up and treats anew the subject of the first
movement. One also wonders whether the sweeping secondary theme of the
Finale is semantically related to the Alma theme. (In regard to the expression of this Finale theme, Adorno stated that it moved "between light-headed
good fortune and high-surging ecstasy.")[51]

   Be that as it may, the insistent quality of this Finale results (as was
suggested at the beginning) from the abundance of contrasting modes of
expression. (To do justice to this fact, Ratz talked about "positive" and
"negative" situations.[52]) It is worthwhile to study how one and the same
theme can totally change its character, when it is only slightly modified but
incorporates changes in tempo and instrumentation. Thus toward the end of
the recapitulation (mm. 728–753) the dark introductory theme (also
appearing in inversion) takes on virtually hymnic features because of its turn
to D major, but a little later, in the requiem-like trombone passage of the
coda (mm. 790–808), it appears in a more lugubrious form than at the
beginning.

Mm. 3–6

Mm. 566–569

Mm. 728–731

Mm. 745–750

Mm. 791–795

Special relevance for the Finale's meaning has to be given to the five tam-tam beats and the three blows of the hammer. The first two tam-tam beats (mm. 395–396 and 401–402) accentuate the major-minor seal, which becomes a tragic symbol. The third tam-tam beat occurs at the beginning of the fourth development section (m. 479), the fourth at the beginning of the recapitulation (mm. 520–523), and the fifth at the beginning of the coda (mm. 773–777). The hammer blows fall (in the first version) at the beginning of the second and fourth development sections (m. 336 and m. 479) and in the coda (m. 783).[53] In a later, drastic change of instrumentation Mahler crossed out the third hammer blow (it coincides with the major-minor seal and the lead rhythm) because it would have, as Erwin Ratz suspects, "exaggerated the feeling of an ultimate ending, which actually is no ending."[54]

What gave Mahler the idea to use a hammer in the Sixth? Several factors suggest that he was inspired by Ritter's poem for Strauss's *Death and Transfiguration,* in which the following verses are found:

> *Da erdröhnt der letzte Schlag*
> *Von des Todes Eisenhammer,*
> *Bricht den Erdenleib entzwei,*
> *Deckt mit Todesnacht das Auge.*

> Now booms the final blow
> By the iron hammer of death,
> Breaking in two the earthly body,
> Covering the eye with the night of death.

In conclusion, Mahler's Sixth reveals itself to be counterpart to Strauss's *Ein Heldenleben*. Richard Strauss, disciple of Friedrich Nietzsche, the adversary of Christianity, would probably never have thought of the idea to describe his own downfall in a symphonic work.[55] After the premiere of the Sixth he made the following typical remark to Alma: "I do not understand why Mahler forfeits the greatest effect in the last movement, right at the beginning giving the greatest strength and then continually becoming weaker and weaker" (AME 128).[56] But Alma, who harbored many resentments against Strauss, reacted properly:

> [Strauss] has never understood him [Mahler]. Here and always, the man of the theater was speaking. That Mahler had to make the first blow the strongest, the second weaker, and the third the weakest (the death blow of the dying hero) is obvious for everyone who has even vaguely comprehended the Symphony. Perhaps the momentary effect would have been stronger in reverse dynamic, but that is not what he was after.

Mahler was quite conscious of the fundamental differences between his character and Strauss's. On 16 July 1906 he wrote to his wife: "His character will always remain alien to me. His way of thinking and feeling is worlds apart from mine" (AME 367).

Sketches for the third movement of the Seventh Symphony
The New York Public Library
First Publication
Note the word *Belfast*

The Seventh Symphony

In spite of this I have decided that in New York for
now I will not perform the Seventh but the Fourth.
For an audience that does not yet know anything I
have written, the work is too complicated. AME 420

It is my best work and predominantly of a cheerful
character.   GMB² 336

Origin

As has been explained, Mahler composed several of his symphonies in two-
year cycles: the Third in 1895 and 1896, the Fourth in 1899 and 1900, the
Fifth in 1901 and 1902, the Sixth in 1903 and 1904. The Seventh does not
quite fit into this pattern, insofar as the two *Nachtmusiken* ("Music of the
Night") were already written in 1904, during or after work on the Sixth, and
the other movements were completed in 1905. "In the summer of 1905,"
Alma writes in her memoirs, "Mahler wrote the Seventh Symphony in *one*
go. By the middle of the summer of 1904 he had already designed the 'ground
plan' " (AME 115).

Mahler himself elaborated on the history of the Seventh. In a letter to his
wife (June 1910), he emphasized that in art as in life, he was completely
dependent upon "spontaneity." "If I was supposed to or had to compose, I
probably would not manage to write a single note." He exemplified this by
referring to the genesis of the Eighth and Seventh Symphonies:

The summer before [1905] I had intended to complete the Seventh, for
which both Andantes were done.[1] For two weeks I tortured myself to the
point of melancholy, as you must remember, until I ran off to the
Dolomites! There the same circus, and finally I gave up and went home,
convinced that the summer would be wasted. You did not meet me in
Krumpendorf because I had not announced my arrival. I stepped into the
boat to be rowed over. At the first stroke of the oars, I hit upon the theme

189

(or rather the rhythm and the style) of the introduction to the first movement, and within four weeks the first, third, and fifth movements were completely finished! Do you remember that? (AME 451).

The score of the first movement of the Seventh bears the date "Maiernigg, 15 August 1905."[2] On that day, Mahler reported the completion of the work to his friend Guido Adler:[3] *"Septima mea finita est. Credo hoc opus fauste natum et bene gestum."*[4] Mahler locked up the completed score in his desk and did not initially consider a performance. At this time the Sixth had not yet been performed, and three more years would go by before the premiere of the Seventh (19 September 1908 in Prague). Alma reports that he made minor corrections in the orchestration right up to the dress rehearsal. Many of his friends who had especially come to Prague (e.g., Privy Councilor Neisser, Arnold Berliner, Ossip Gabrilowitsch, Alban Berg, Artur Bodanzky, Gerhard von Keussler, and Otto Klemperer) helped him to transfer corrections into the full score and parts "because he noticed discrepancies up to the dress rehearsal and was constantly making changes, as long as there was a chance before the score was printed" (AME 180). Alma, who went to Prague a little later, found Mahler's room "covered with the written-out orchestra parts. . . . He mercilessly made changes—not, of course, in the composition, but only in the orchestration."

Alma goes on to tell that the work "was hardly understood by the Prague audience, although there was something like a *success d'estime* (AME 181). It is therefore all the more remarkable that Arnold Schoenberg found access to Mahler's symphonic writing through the Seventh. The letter he wrote to Mahler on 29 December 1909 (after the Vienna premiere of the Seventh) is an unconditional testimony to Mahler's art (AME 446–449). Schoenberg wrote that he could not say "which of the movements [he] liked best." Everything seemed so "transparent"; at a first hearing he had sensed so many "subtleties of form" and had always been able to follow a "main line." He added that he could not understand why he had not "related" to this music before.[5] These remarks become especially significant if one considers that at this time Schoenberg had already set out on the road to atonality.[6]

Mahler's Hermeneutic Instructions

Mahler did not announce a program for his Seventh, so all the more attention should be given to the hermeneutic suggestions that he made in conversations with his wife and friends. According to Alma, "while composing his *Nachtmusiken,* he had visions of Eichendorff's poetry, rippling fountains, German Romanticism. Other than that, this symphony is without program" (AME 115). Regarding the introduction of the first movement, he remarked, "here nature roars [like a stag in rut]."[7] He compared the mood of the first *Nachtmusik* to the painting "The Night Watch" by Rembrandt,[8] and he explained the Rondo-Finale with the aperçu: "The world is mine!"[9]

Further statements by Mahler about the Seventh are found in a letter from Alphons Diepenbrock to his friend Johanna Jongkindt of 17 October 1909:

> There are still passages in the first movement that I do not like and that I wish were shorter. There is no true Adagio. In the first movement, we again find several heavenly moments, along with these beautiful, lamenting, stifled bird voices. There are also typically Jewish things (You know that I am a Jew!) such as the trombone solos *Wir gehn nach Lindenau, dort ist der Himmel blau!* ("We go to Lindenau, there the sky is blue!"). The fourth movement, a serenade, is indescribably charming, a confession of love to the universe. [Movements] one, two, three are all moods of the night; so is four, but there only the delightful is reigning. Three is spooky, as is two here and there, although quite cozy and jovial Mahler melodies also appear. (It is not true that he wanted to describe "The Night Watch" here. He only mentioned the painting as a comparison. It is a nocturnal journey; he says he thought of a *Scharwache* [a small group of watchmen]. By the way, he says something different every time. Certainly it is a march with a fantastic *clair obscur,* so that an analogy with Rembrandt is appropriate. The fantastic colors lead one's fantasy automatically into the past and suggest pictures of mercenaries and soldiers.) The first movement begins very gloomily with a tenor horn solo (*Ein riesengroßer Schatten*) [A gigantic shadow]. The third movement in D minor is very ludicrous; all kinds of demons are laughing and shrieking in it. In the fourth movement, the serenade, a mandolin and a guitar, which unfortunately get a little drowned out by the other instruments, create a very pleasant effect, heightening the *amoroso* character. But the fifth movement is the climax: C major, radiant sun, night is gone. This movement is immensely long but grand, even if it is too noisy here and there.[10]

In his introduction to the first performance of the work in Vienna on 3 November 1909, Richard Specht provided additional valuable information regarding the Seventh:

> As is known, Mahler did not like to give titles to his symphonies and their individual movements, to avoid even a hint of programmatic meaning. Yet the heading *Nachtwanderung* ("Walk by Night"), occasionally suggested by admirers of the composer for the premiere in Prague, is not to be rejected as an indication of general mood. It could be valid for the whole work or only for the first movement. The three-movement intermezzo could be called "Voices of the Night," and "Into the Morning" might describe the final movement. Recently Bruno Walter revealed the only possible meaning of such descriptions, so there is no danger that these remarks could be misunderstood and be interpreted in the sense of "program music."[11]

Specht's statements once again document Mahler's fear of being identified with the popular trend of illustrative program music in the manner of Strauss. Some of Specht's remarks in conversations with friends confirm that

Mahler always spoke of the same metaphors regarding individual movements of the Seventh. This is why Specht also compares the first *Nachtmusik* with the "procession of a ghostly watch, moving to long-forgotten march rhythms and wistful songs of long ago." He called the Andante amoroso a night piece, "full of sweet voices of love, mysterious whispering, rippling of fountains, and rustling of linden trees in the moonlit square of a quaint little old town."

After what has been said, it is no wonder that many spoke of the Seventh as a Romantic symphony. Bruno Walter felt that "in the three middle movements of the Seventh, meaningfully and humanly revealing, we hear music embodying a romanticism that we thought had been overcome."[12]

First Movement

Mahler's resentment against a note-for-note recapitulation was derived from well-defined convictions regarding the philosophy and theory of art. He, who called every repeat "inevitably a lie," was of the opinion that a work of art, like life, had to keep developing (BL[2] 158).[13] This attitude affected not only individual movements and symphonies but also Mahler's entire symphonic writing. Although from time to time we come across similar situations in different works, Mahler never repeats himself. There is probably not a single movement of his that duplicates the form of another or that could even be interpreted as a variant of another.

An instructive example of this is offered in the first movement of the Seventh Symphony. In structure and in several details of form it shows some similarity to the first movement of the Third. At the same time it differs fundamentally from it in countless details. Both movements open with slow introductions, aside from the entrance of the theme in the Third, and in both cases the introductions are completely integrated into the movements as they reappear in the development and the recapitulation. Moreover, recitative and arioso-like passages appear in both introductions, accompanied over long stretches by tremolos and funeral march rhythms. Nevertheless the specific difference lies in the fact that in the first movement of the Third the actual exposition is based solely on a marchlike theme, while in the first movement of the Seventh it is based on three contrasting theme complexes.

Exposition

Mm.		
	1–44	Slow introduction
	1–18	Arioso, accompanied by funeral-march rhythms (*Langsam*) [slow]
	19–26	March theme (*Etwas weniger langsam, aber immer sehr gemessen*) [A little less slow, but always very measured]
	27–44	Again arioso (*Nicht schleppen, später Tempo I*) [Not dragging, later Tempo I]

45–49   Transition with formations of fourths (Più mosso)
50–109   Main section in E minor (Allegro con fuoco)
110–117   Transition
118–133   Secondary section in C major (*Mit großem Schwung*) [With great sweep]
134–144   Final section (based on the march theme)
145–162   Main section (Tempo I)
163–173   Transition

Development

174–195   First section: Variation of the arioso from the slow introduction (~mm. 1–18)
196–211   Second section (Moderato): Based on the secondary theme in B minor/B major
212–227   Third section (Again Tempo I): Based on exposition motifs
228–244   Fourth section (♩ = ♩)
245–255   Fifth section: Based on exposition motifs; mm. 247–251 fanfares and signals of the trumpets
256–265   Sixth section (*Gemessener* [More measured]. Meno mosso): religious vision: The march theme changed to a solemn chorale; reminiscences of *Urlicht*; tonal center: E-flat major
266–297   Seventh section (Subito Allegro I. *Ziemlich ruhig* [Fairly quiet]): Episode with solo violin in G major/G minor
298–316   Eighth section (*Etwas gemessener* [Somewhat more measured] ♩ = ♩): religious vision with trumpet fanfares, chorale lines, and reminiscences of *Urlicht*
317–337   Ninth section (*Sehr breit*) [Very broad]: Might be considered the center of the movement in B major

Recapitulation

338–372   Arioso (Adagio), beginning with funeral march rhythms and trombone solos
373–464   Main section (Maestoso)
465–486   Secondary section (♩ = ♩) in G major
487–522   Closing section (*Frisch*) [Brisk] (mm. 495–522 more or less corresponding to mm. 27–44)

Coda

523–547   Tempo I (Allegro)

The grouping of the contrasting theme complexes into threes (called the first, secondary, and closing sections in the formal outline) is consistent in the exposition of this movement, as it also is in the first movement of the Sixth. Even so, these two movements differ further from one another, not only in their entire form and in details, but also in the variety of expression. The first movement displays greater variety, and Adorno certainly was right about this movement when he said that the orchestral range of colors includes everything "from the brighter-than-major to gloomy shadows."[14] The palette indeed extends from the funeral march to Allegro con fuoco, from the march to the visionary chorale, from extremely austere passages to sweeping music.

When analyzing the movement, one immediately marvels at the way the "fiery" E minor-theme of the first movement emerges (Allegro con fuoco, mm. 50–109). The preceding slow introduction can be understood as a lengthy process that leads to the development of this main theme. Let us follow it step by step.

At the beginning of the movement, the slow introduction clearly consists of three sections (mm. 1–18, 19–26, and 27–44); two passages with the character of an arioso frame a marchlike section. The theme is presented at the beginning by the tenor horn with a "grand tone":

Mm. 2–4

It is picked up a few measures later by the trumpet:

Mm. 7–8

and it is reiterated a little later by the tenor horn:

Mm. 12–13

In the process it not only is shifted metrically but its intervals and rhythm are also altered. The changes are such that one can indeed speak of a "developed variation" in the sense of Arnold Schoenberg.[15]

After the marchlike section, the arioso begins again. Now the trombones perform new thematic material:

Mm. 27–29

It is picked up a little later by the tenor horn (again the metric shifts are characteristic):

Mm. 32–35

From this material Mahler gains the "fiery" main theme in E minor, but its second motif is derived from the very first notes of the tenor horn:

Mm. 50–55

One recognizes the relevance of this main motif when observing that Mahler also derived from it the very characteristic motif of a fourth for the main theme:

Mm. 79–82

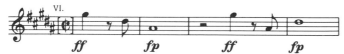

It appears in whole chains of fourths in the basic form and in inversion:

Mm. 106–111

Mm. 531–535

It is easy to see that Schoenberg, whose first Chamber Symphony Op. 9 was composed in 1906, must have been pleased with these formations of fourths and many other "modern" features of the Seventh.

The slow introduction and the main section are also connected rhythmically: the funeral march rhythm at the beginning changes into the lively accompanying rhythm (m. 50ff.). And regarding the relation of keys in this movement, the six-five chord

on B at the beginning cannot obscure the fact that B minor is the primary
tonal center of the introduction, though the main key of the movement is E
minor.

Mahler titled the actual sonata movement Allegro con fuoco, a description that does not only refer to the first main theme complex. A detail of
instrumentation is symptomatic for the rather fiery character of long stretches
of the movement: The cymbals are heard more often than in any other
Mahler work. At the cymbal crash in measure 331, Mahler even writes "with
fire!"

The unique effect of the movement is fundamentally due to the wealth of
contrast. The first theme complex vacillates between E minor and B major. It
is basically diatonic, sharp-edged, and rhythmically tight, while the extremely
gentle second complex (C major in the exposition and G major in the
recapitulation) includes many chromatic elements and requires rubato (many
fermatas). The leading melody of the violins (marked "with great sweep"),
beginning *pianissimo,* repeatedly reaches ecstatic high points and is often set
to dissonant chords, which caused Adorno to speak of a radiant "super-
major."[16]

Nowhere else does Mahler come so close to the idiom of Strauss's tone
poem *Also sprach Zarathustra,* Op. 30 (1896) as in this secondary section
and in passages in which individual string players appear as soloists.

The final section at first works with the marchlike theme of the introduction, which previously was deliberate but now is to be played *flott* (swiftly):

Mm. 136–139

This is followed by a variant of the main theme.

The nine sections of the development (174 measures) differ from one
another in tempo, character, and instrumentation. While some are
dynamically lively and modulate through several keys, others are tonally
stable. The opening section (mm. 174–195) consists of a variation of the first
arioso (mm. 1–18) while the second (mm. 196–211) is in B minor/B major
and is treated like chamber music. Solo string players and individual woodwind players execute chromatic motifs from the secondary theme. Here the
music is strikingly reminiscent of a passage in Strauss's *Also sprach
Zarathustra:*

Mm. 203–209

Strauss, *Also sprach Zarathustra*

The third (mm. 212–227), fourth (mm. 228–244) and fifth (mm. 245–255) sections modulate extremely boldly and mix and combine the motifs of the exposition. Here Mahler ventures to the borders of atonality. In contrast to this, the four final sections, which form a complex, are solidly tonal.

At the end of the fifth section (ritenuto, m. 255) the music, up until then urgent and pressing, suddenly stops. The tempo becomes broader (more deliberate in m. 257 and Meno mosso in m. 258). While the first trumpet plays a signal on one note, the second trumpet enters with a concise, three-note motif repeated several times, which in the following will have an important part and which is reminiscent of a passage (the angel scene) from the *Urlicht* movement of the Second Symphony.[17] The clarinets, bassoons, and low strings play the augmented main motif from the marchlike theme *feierlich* (solemnly), which now reveals its chorale-like core. Again trumpet fanfares resound (the three-note motif now moves to the flutes), as well as the chorale-like chords.

Second Symphony, *Urlicht,* mm. 36–40

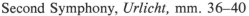

Seventh Symphony, first movement, mm. 257–259

After the abrupt entrance and apparent interpolation of the Allegro episode, which is in the style of chamber music in G minor/G major (mm. 266–297)[18] there is a renewed pause (mm. 298–316). Again we hear trumpet fanfares, the call-like three note motif and chorale-like sounds, first in the bassoons and low strings (mm. 304–307), then in the bassoons and horns (mm. 310–311), and finally in the horns and trombones (mm. 313–316 *sehr*

weich geblasen [very soft]). A harp glissando introduces the last section in B
major (mm. 317–337), which combines the most important motifs and in a
sense forms the core of the whole movement. The motivic symbolism and the
instrumentation—the music in general—all show clearly that the development ends with a religious vision.

Nachtmusik I

According to Richard Specht, admirers of Mahler recommended the title
Nachtwanderung at the premiere of the Seventh in Prague, thinking of it as a
suggesting a mood. The title certainly applies to the second movement, a
marchlike composition with the title *Nachtmusik*.[19] The idea of a walk at
night was a popular topic of Romantic and late Romantic poetry. In
Nietzsche's *Also sprach Zarathustra,* a book that Mahler valued for its
musicality, we find the statement: "Come! Come! Come! Now let us walk! It
is the hour: Let us walk into the night!"[20]

Mahler's *Nachtmusik I* shows an original variant of the typical marchlike main section with two different trios. The movement has an arch form,
indeed, even a mirror structure, something that has gone completely
unrecognized.

Mm.		
	1–29	Introduction, flowing into the major-minor seal
	30–82	Main section (three-part song form) in C major-minor
	83–121	Trio I (divided into three sections) in A-flat major
	122–140	Intermezzo (with cowbell and tam-tam)
	141–178	Trio II beginning in F minor
	179–188	Introduction, leading into the major-minor seal
	189–211	Trio II (continuation) in C minor
	212–222	Intermezzo
	223–261	Main section
	262–293	Trio I (mm. 280–282 and m. 286: cowbell in the orchestra)
	294–317	Main section
	318–343	Introduction with major-minor seal

As is obvious from the outline, an introductory section returns twice with
modifications. The second introductory section (mm. 179–188) comes to the
approximate middle of the movement and divides it into two mirrored halves.
In the first half, the marchlike main section follows the introduction. After
this comes the first trio; an intermezzo; the marchlike main section again; and
finally the second trio, which is interrupted by the middle introductory section and then continued. The individual sections then return in reverse order.
There is one flaw in the regularity of the retrograde: after the second trio, the
order of intermezzo and main section is reversed.

The *Nachtmusik* begins with a dialogue of the horns. After "calling" and
"fading-away" motifs of the first horn, the second horn gives a muffled

answer.[21] A highly original contrapuntal section for the first oboe and first clarinet follows, into which the call-like motif intrudes. This section gradually develops into a confusion of sounds interspersed with trill motifs. Mahler himself revealed that this was to resemble a nocturnal bird concert because at the final return of the introduction, measures 319–320, he indicated *wie Vogelstimmen* (like bird calls) in the score. In all three cases the confusion of voices flows into the well-known major-minor seal with the chord sequence C major/C minor, which here obviously is a nocturnal symbol. It is interesting that the seal appears the first two times combined with a chromatic slide from high to low while the major third and minor third sound at the same time (m. 29 and m. 187).[22]

Theodor Adorno saw Mahler's love for tonal ambivalence as a progressive aspect of his composing: "Tonality that sharpens itself through continuous major-minor shifts becomes a modern medium."[23] There is no question that the characteristic light-dark effects of the movement go back to Mahler's major-minor manner and that they suggested the comparison with Rembrandt. The theme of the marchlike first section certainly thrives on this manner; its mode is "major-minor." The minor third alternates with the major third, and the sixth step is to be found both in its major and minor form:

Mm. 30–37

Of course, the traditional modes are not neglected. The folklike melody of the first trio is clearly in major:

Mm. 82–88

The second trio is in minor with the marking *sehr ausdrucksvoll u. hervortretend* (very expressive and prominent):

Mm. 164–168

In spite of the contrasting modes, the different sections hang together. This can in part be attributed to the unifying effect of the introductory motifs from which Mahler derives a phrase in triplets contrapuntally combined with the marchlike main theme (mm. 62–82, 141–154, and 239–261). These motifs carry over into the second trio (mm. 173–176 and 192–206: clarinet signals marked *quasi Tromba* [like a trumpet]).

Finally, the intermezzos or transitional sections (mm. 122–140 and 212–222) in the above outline are worthy of consideration because of the extremely thin scoring. Here the calls of the winds surrounded by utter silence give the effect of someone calling out loudly in the still of the night.

Schattenhaft ("Shadowlike")

The third movement of the Seventh Symphony, with the rare and therefore striking marking *schattenhaft,* is placed between the two *Nachtmusik* movements.[24] It has repeatedly been called a nocturnal piece.[25] Hans Ferdinand Redlich considered it to be the most original of the five movements of the Seventh,[26] and Jean Matter called it one of Mahler's most remarkable examples of the demonic.[27] In view of these characterizations it seems strange that the movement, a mixture of an eerie scherzo and a fantastic dance scene, has never been discussed in more detail.

Main section

Mm.	1–12	Introduction
	13–37	First Part
	38–53	Second part (*klagend*) [lamenting]
	54–71	Third part (*etwas flotter*) [somewhat faster]: Waltz in major-minor
	72–85	Introduction (Variant)
	86–107	First part (Variant)
	108–115	Second part (*Lamenting*): Variant (shortened)
	116–159	Major-minor waltz (expanded)
	160–178	Last part

Trio

179–209	First part
210–246	Second part: Development of the first motif from the first movement
246–260	Third part

Main section

261–276	First part (Variant)
277–292	Second part, now in E-flat minor

As this outline indicates, the movement is arranged and constructed quite simply: A main section and a Trio (designated expressly by Mahler himself) alternate twice. It is probably unnecessary to point out that the parts undergo considerable changes at the return. According to Adorno, the movement "again is a development scherzo as in the Fifth, yet reduced by the necessity to place a third piece of special character between the two Night Music movements."[28] The appropriateness of the classification "development scherzo" is debatable. Although here and there development-like passages occur, the movement in no way reaches the complexity of the Scherzo of the Fifth. Of the main section's nine parts, the first four return in the same sequence, with modifications, shortenings, and expansions. The introduction (mm. 1–12) can be viewed as a rhythmic play between timpani and the pizzicato of the cellos and double basses, producing a grotesque, eerie effect. Horns, clarinets, and flutes later join this play. The first part (mm. 13–37) bears the features of a *perpetuum mobile*. The constant triplet motion that develops here forms the basis of the second section as well (mm. 38–53), during which flutes and oboes strike up a lamenting melody. The subdued mood of this music results from the instrumentation (strings and trumpets are muted) and from the dynamic level that remains *piano,* with sforzati, accents, and short crescendos and diminuendos. It also includes figures containing sighs (mm. 26–32) and polyrhythmic formations (hemiolas in mm. 30–33, as well as duplets against triplets). The first bassoon plays in a remarkably high range (mm. 39–53). This bassoon passage further illustrates Mahler's previously mentioned remark: "I often have basses and bassoons squeak in the highest register" (BL[2] 176).

The music of the third part forms a strong contrast to the first two parts: A violin melody in typical major-minor manner has a waltzlike accompaniment (strings without mutes):[29]

Mm. 52–59

The dancelike character of this passage forms a contrast to the scherzo-like parts and underscores the ambivalence of the movement, which Karl Weigl characterized quite accurately when he wrote: "There is a constant, restless scurrying away, a rushing and chasing that is then interrupted by a vigorous dance rhythm and a gently dreamy melody (Trio)."[30] Along with the restless scurrying we hear much stumbling, tumbling, and falling. Probably no other movement by Mahler has so many tumbling passages.[31]

What does the heading *schattenhaft* mean? Jean Matter thought that the movement evokes a dance of shadows and evil spirits.[32] Some light might be shed upon the matter by the observation that in Strauss's composition *Till Eulenspiegels lustige Streiche* (Till Eulenspiegel's Merry Pranks) Op. 28, the death sentence (mm. 386–393) is followed by a passage marked *schnell und schattenhaft* (fast and shadowlike) in which the violins, violas, and trombones are muted.[33] For Mahler the title may refer not only to the ghostlike, eerie, and nocturnal, but also to the unfathomable and, therefore, the threatening.

All in all the Trio has a lighter timbre than the main section. The major mode is not unequivocal, alternating with minor passages or containing minor elements. Thus the cadence of the oboe melody, which sets the mood for the first part (mm. 179–209), has a Phrygian figure:

The second part (based on the first motif of the first movement and developed in three waves of increasing intensity) oscillates between minor and major.

Mm. 209–217

In the third part (mm. 246–260), the leading melody of the cellos is in major-minor:

The main section and Trio are connected in an ingenious way. In numerous inserted measures in the Trio (marked *Più mosso. Subito*[34]) the *kreischende* (shrieking) waltzlike motif from the main section is picked up and varied:

Mm. 154–157

Mm. 185–188

These poetically meaningful interpolations may be seen as musical parentheses.

The recapitulations of the main section and Trio (to the extent that one can speak of recapitulations) are, as mentioned, strongly altered. Thus in measures 277–292, the lamenting section appears transposed to E-flat minor. Especially instructive in terms of Mahler's manner of montage are measures 417–427, marked *wild*. The final melody of the Trio, now played by trombones and tuba(!), is combined with a variant of the major-minor waltz from the main section:

Mm. 417–426

In the relatively short coda, Mahler uses variants of the first motif and the shrieking waltz motif, which becomes shorter and shorter.[35]

Nachtmusik II: Andante amoroso

The serenade character of the Seventh's fourth movement is so strongly defined that there would be no doubt about it even without the headings *Nachtmusik* and Andante amoroso.[36] Guitar and mandolin occur only in this movement, which is orchestrated like chamber music.[37] Trumpets, trombones, tuba, and percussion are left out, and the wind instrumentation is reduced. Mahler restricts himself to two flutes, two oboes, English horn, two clarinets, two bassoons, contrabassoon, two horns, two harps, and strings. Long stretches of the movement constitute a song without words—a song, however, where ecstatic moments are not foreign to the lyrical quality and intimacy. Mahler tried to capture the mood of the *Nachtmusik* with such eloquent indications as *Mit Aufschwung* [with sweep] (at the beginning), *Graziosissimo* (m. 56), *melancholisch* (m. 89), and *excited* (m. 320). The instructions *steigernd* (building up) and *drängend* (urgent) need not be mentioned here, since they are not specific.

The structure of this Andante amoroso represents a modification of the standard three-part form—main section, trio, and varied recapitulation of the main section—the trio being preceded by a relatively long development-like section:

Main section

Mm.	1–4	Refrain
	4–7	Accompanying figures
	8–27	First part (A)
	28–37	Second part (B)
	38–55	Third part (A^1)
	56–75	Fourth part: Graziosissimo (C)
	76–98	Fifth part (A^2)

Development

99–125	First part (beginning with chromatic progressions)
126–165	Second part (beginning in A-flat major with a new theme and building up)
166–186	Third part (Again a tempo) in G-flat major

Trio

187–210	First part in B-flat major
211–227	Second part
228–259	Third part in F major

Recapitulation

259–263	Refrain
264–282	First part
283–294	Second part
295–310	Third part
311–331	Fourth part (great climax)
332–353	Fifth part

354–390   Coda

As the outline suggests, the main section shows a rondo-like disposition with the Scheme A—B—A^1—C—A^2, which is underscored by the repeated return of a short ritornello (Richard Specht[38] spoke rightly of refrain):[39]

Mm. 1–4

The special aspects of form come to light if one analyzes the micro structure. The accompanying parts of first clarinet and first bassoon (mm. 4–10)
are typical of the approach. They are written in an independent, linear
manner but also have thematic importance:

Mm. 4–9

The clarinet and bassoon figures are derived from the following theme:

Mm. 7–17

Those wishing to study Mahler's variation technique should compare this
theme with the metamorphoses it undergoes in sections A^1 and A^2. In the last
section, individual segments are rearranged, and some motifs even appear in
inversion:

Mm. 76–85

The musical examples show that the theme is nine measures long and that the
main section is in the major-minor mode.

A dark timbre is peculiar to the two (corresponding) sections of the
development (mm. 99–125 and mm. 166–186). Chromatic progressions are

all the more obvious here since they are atypical for Mahler. At the beginning of the middle section (mm. 126–133) the mood brightens temporarily. The horn, seconded by bassoon and mandolin, brings a new, lively form of the theme. After this the music becomes more subdued. Several interrupted crescendos signal an impending outburst of passion that is immediately suppressed.

The two main sections of the trio also correspond with each other (mm. 187–210 and mm. 228–259). In both sections, cellos and horn or bassoons and violins play broadly flowing cantilenas in B-flat major or F major. The darker timbre of the middle section (mm. 211–227) is marked by extreme contrasts. Its key at first is ambiguous, floating between G-flat major, E-flat minor, and B-flat minor.

Like the exposition, the recapitulation is in five sections but (as usual for Mahler) differs greatly from the exposition. It would go too far to list all the changes; suffice to say that the *Graziosissimo* section of the exposition is now extended to a grand climax (mm. 311–331).

As mentioned earlier, Alma Mahler reports that Mahler had in mind "visions of Eichendorff's poetry, rippling fountains, German Romanticism." The mention of rippling fountains points to the second *Nachtmusik*. The *Nachtlied* from Nietzsche's *Also sprach Zarathustra* contains sentences that apply directly to Mahler's remarks and above all to this Andante amoroso:

> *Nacht ist es: nun reden lauter alle springenden Brunnen.*
> *Und auch meine Seele ist ein springender Brunnen.*
> *Nacht ist es: nun erst erwachen alle Lieder der Liebenden.*
> *Und auch meine Seele ist das Lied eines Liebenden.*

> Night it is: Now all the fountains are speaking louder.
> And my soul also is a leaping fountain.
> Night it is: Only now all the lovers' songs awaken.
> And my soul is also the song of a loving one.[40]

In his commemorative speech in Prague (1912), Arnold Schoenberg also counted the middle movements of the Seventh "with their guitar, harp, and solo sounds" among the movements that present us with what is "amazingly new."[41] Regarding the guitar in the Andante amoroso he said that it was not chosen for a single effect; rather the entire movement was dependent upon this sound. Undoubtedly Schoenberg's seven-movement *Serenade* Op. 24 (1921), which also includes guitar and mandolin in its instrumentation, reflects his esteem of Mahler's second *Nachtmusik*.

Rondo-Finale

The Finale of the Seventh, like the Finale of the Fifth, provoked controversial evaluations and interpretations. Older critics understood it as an expression of "glad, sun-happy, lighthearted joyfulness";[42] a "piece full of blinding daylight"; a "supreme affirmation of life"; and even a "C-major Dithyrambus."[43] Several younger interpreters, however, consider it to be a weak or at least puzzling composition.

The decisive turn in the history of its interpretation was brought about by Adorno's book on Mahler. Adorno, who admired the "negativeness" of Mahler's music, was offended by the positiveness of this Finale.[44] He criticized the "meager content of the whole thing," the "persistent diatonicism," the "strained happy tone," and the "pomp." He writes:

> The movement is theatrical; only on a stage set can the sky be so blue above the nearby festival meadow.[45] The positiveness of the *per aspera ad astra* [literally, through adversity to the stars] of the Fifth, which is even surpassed by this Finale, reveals itself only as a tableau, as a colorful, turbulent scene.

Karl Schumann went one step further when he expressed the hypothesis that "maybe the movement is a gigantic persiflage of the pompous, turn-of-the-century style, a bizarre summary of orchestral effects not unlike the manner of the American Charles Ives."[46] Peter Ruzicka suspected "a documentary summation of and confrontation with unreflected positiveness, a kind of inventory of the musical environment that was in the process of falling apart."[47] Hans-Klaus Jungheinrich said that in this context Mahler's C-major sounded like a quote, like "a compositional attitude that is being criticized at the same time."[48] The symbolic strength of the key becomes the "stigma of the deep questionability of the symphonic concept."

Any attempt to understand Mahler's intentions has to begin with a close look at the music. Let us begin with an overview of the form:

Mm.		
	1–52	First ritornello (sections 1–16) in C major
	53–78	First secondary theme in A-flat major (*behaglich*) [comfortable]
	79–99	Second ritornello (sections 3 and 4) in C major
	100–115	Second secondary theme (*Grazioso*) and variant of section 4 of the ritornello
	116–119	*Pesante*
	120–152	Third ritornello (sections 2, 4–6) in C major
	153–185	First secondary theme in A minor (*Etwas zurückhaltend*) [somewhat restrained]
	186–188	*Pesante:* Suggestion of the unison theme
	189–209	Fourth ritornello (sections 3 and 4)
	209–219	First secondary theme (*Nicht eilen—recht gemessen*) [Not rushed—quite deliberate]
	220–248	Second secondary theme (Grazioso)
	249–268	Unison theme followed by *unmerklich drängend* (slightly faster), leading to a tritone
	269–290	Development-like passage (motifs from the ritornello and the second secondary theme)

291–308 Fifth ritornello in A major (sections 1, 2, and 4 combined vertically); mm. 295–297 a quote from the second secondary theme
309–359 First secondary theme in G-flat major (*gemütlich*) [comfortable]
360–367 Sixth ritornello (section 2) in B-flat major (Tempo I subito); loud bell ringing (low)
368–402 Unison theme, a slightly faster passage leading to a tritone
402–433 Second secondary theme (mm. 425–431: the first trumpet plays section 2 of the ritornello)
434–442 Unison theme in the strings (now accompanied by winds)
443–445 *Zurückhaltend* (restrained) (*molto pesante*)
446–454 Seventh ritornello (section 2) in D major; soft bell ringing
455–485 The main theme from the first movement, in D minor, C-sharp minor, and C minor (mm. 476–485: Bell ringing *crescendo*
486–491 Unison theme in B major (*flott*)
492–499 Main theme from the first movement in B-flat minor
500–505 *Breiter (plötzlich)* [Broader (suddenly)]
506–516 *Strahlend* (radiant) main theme from the first movement, in D-flat major, the second secondary theme added as counterpoint
517–536 Second secondary section
536–538 Accelerando
538–590 Eighth ritornello (complete) in C major (bells and cowbells)

Mahler entitled the movement Rondo-Finale, like the last movement of the Fifth. However, the rondo character is far more pronounced here than in the Fifth. In the Finale of the Fifth the actual rondo theme is heard only three times; here it occurs seven times. Another difference is that the Finale of the Seventh, unlike that of the Fifth, is not a sonata-like rondo. Attempts to designate parts of the movement as corresponding to exposition, development, recapitulation, and coda are not convincing because typical development-like passages hardly occur (mm. 269–290 are an exception) and because sections of urgent, pressing-forward character are rare (mm. 249–268 and mm. 368–402).[49] The structure of the movement can be understood as sequential, as Sponheuer remarked, and not as developmental.[50] The movement operates with the ritornello and the two secondary themes, which change appearance. To say that the ritornello lacks originality would be euphemistic. Its surprisingly conventional, even archaic style (considering the time it was composed) is partly due to the triadic and fanfare melodies. Clearly Mahler wanted to achieve a festive, panegyrical mood. All six sections of the ritornello are in C major.

The first section is clearly introductory in character and is based on the fanfare motif first played with bravura by the timpani:

In the second, choralelike section (mm. 7–14), the first trumpet melody goes up to the C above the staff:

The third section (mm. 15–22) paraphrases Wagner's *Meistersinger* prelude:

The sequential passages of the fourth section (mm. 23–37) are march-like in character.

The fifth and the sixth sections (mm. 38–44 and mm. 45–52) are again characterized by a fanfare style:

There has been so much criticism about this Rondo-Finale that the art with which Mahler handled the ritornello all the more deserves to be recognized; none of the repeats are exactly alike. The ritornello recurs in complete form at the end of the Symphony (though even there with some modifications), so that one might say that the experience at the end hardly differs from the experience at the beginning. Other than that, the ritornello occurs in shortened and variously modified forms; one or several sections, often transposed to other keys, take the place of the whole.[51] The second section of the ritornello is clearly preferred. In measures 360–367 it takes on the form of a massive brass chorale. In the A-major section (m. 291ff.) Mahler manages to combine sections 1, 2, and 4 vertically.

Of the two secondary themes, the first shows all characteristics of a pastorale, with the musette-like basses being especially obvious.

Mm. 56–59

The first secondary theme appears in A-flat major (mm. 53–78) and G-flat major (mm. 309–359), marked *behaglich* and *gemütlich* (comfortable). It also has two variants in minor (mm. 153–185 and 210–219) that depart considerably from the original model.

The graceful second secondary theme (often marked grazioso) bears minuet features:

Mm. 100–105

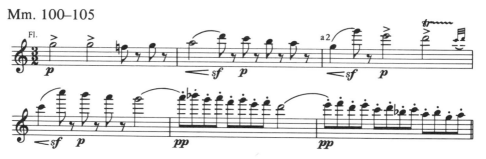

Evidence of this trait is the marking *Graziosissimo, beinahe Menuett* (almost minuet) at No. 276. The theme appears in C major (mm. 100–105); A major (mm. 220–240); D-flat major (mm. 241–246); again in C major (mm. 411—430); and finally in D-flat major (mm. 506–516), where it is contrapuntally combined with the radiant main theme from the first movement.

The change of themes and keys results in a kaleidoscopic profusion of color. The remark about a "colorful, turbulent scene" is justified. To observe that segments from different thematic areas are frequently contrapuntally combined is more important for an understanding of the composition. To cite only two examples: within the fifth ritornello (mm. 295–297), the second secondary theme appears; and the trumpet theme from section 2 of the ritornello is heard in the middle of the Graziossimo theme (mm. 425–431). At times Mahler's music reaches a complexity that is beyond description.

Even so, looking at it as a whole, the Rondo-Finale seems conventional compared with the first movement, which is forward-looking. The panegyrical tone and the will to be happy at all costs resulted in a remarkably brilliant orchestral sound but hindered Mahler from stepping out into truly new territory. The movement's "weakness" (if one may call it that) results less from the "meager content" and the "persistent diatonicism" than from the oppressive dominance of C major and the other major keys. The minor mode is definitely under-represented. Apart from the two pastoral sections in A minor (mm. 153–185 and 210–219), it is not until the return to the main theme from the first movement, beginning with measure 455, that some minor keys are touched upon (D minor, C-sharp minor, and B-flat minor).

What was Mahler's purpose—what did he want to express with this Rondo-Finale? Did he perhaps really see the movement as "a gigantic persiflage of the pompous?" This assumption can be refuted. Let us remember that persiflage was totally foreign to Mahler. We learn from Bruno Walter that Mahler, who had such a sense of humor, greatly disapproved of the telling of jokes.[52] In a letter to Emil Gutmann he described the Seventh as a work of "primarily cheerful character" (GMB[2] 336). This statement undoubtedly refers to the Andante amoroso and the Rondo-Finale, where such significant markings as *Maestoso* (m. 7),[53] *Solemn* (m. 506), and *Somewhat solemn. Magnificent* (two measures after No. 290) are found.[54] *Loud bell-ringing* appears for the first time at the massive brass chorale (mm. 360–367). At the end of the movement, cowbells and other bells sound repeatedly. Bells were Mahler's sound symbols for eternity.[55]

The panegyrical tone of the Rondo-Finale, the distinct rondo-like structure of the movement, and the fact that the ritornello returns no less than seven times lead to the conclusion that Mahler understood the movement as a parable for the eternal return. What he expressed in 1905 symphonically had been conceived in 1881 by Friedrich Nietzsche. "Nietzsche wrote that the basic concept" of Zarathustra is the "thought of eternal return, the highest form of affirmation ever to be achieved."[56] This thought is poetically expressed in the chapter "The Seven Seals" from *Also sprach Zarathustra*. This "Yes and Amen Song" is constructed as a rondo, which in itself is surprising. Of the seven lines that make up each of the seven verses of the poem, the final three express belief in the eternal return and are treated as a refrain. In a conversation with Bernard Scharlitt in 1906, Mahler confessed that he appreciated Nietzsche very much as a poet. "His *Zarathustra*," he said, "originated in the spirit of music; indeed it is almost symphonically constructed."[57]

Mahler's handwritten text of the Pentecost Hymn
(for the Eighth Symphony)
The New York Public Library
First Publication

Veni creator spiritus,
Mentes tuorum visita
Imple superna gratia
quae tu creasti pectora.
Qui paraclitus diceris
Donum Dei altissimi,
Fons vivus ignis charitas
et spiritalis unctio.
Accende lumen sensibus
infunde amorem cordibus
hostem repellas longius
pacemque dones protinus
ductore sic te praevio
vitemus omne noxium.
Gloria Patri Domino

Deoque qui a mortuis
surrexit ac Paraclito
in saeculorum saecula.
Amen

4 In firma nostri corporis
virtute firmans perpeti

3 In septiformis numere
dignus tui munere dexterae
tu rite promissum Patris
sermone ditans guttura

6 Per te sciamus da Patrem
noscamus atque filium
teque utriusque spiritum
credamus omni tempore

The Eighth Symphony

> Here I am immersed in *many notes!* I have just com-
> pleted my Eighth. It is the greatest I have composed
> thus far. It is so unique in content and form that it
> does not lend itself to description. Imagine that the
> universe begins to sound and ring out. These no
> longer are human voices, rather planets and suns that
> are circling. MB[2] 312

> All my previous symphonies are merely the preludes
> to this one. In the other works everything still was
> subjective tragedy, but this one is a source of great
> joy. To Richard Specht[1]

Comments by Mahler

The Eighth Symphony, composed in 1906, was the first work that actually
brought Mahler a triumphant success. Ever since the enthusiastic response it
received at the Munich premiere on 12 September 1910, it has been
(although not altogether undisputed[2]) Mahler's "chief work."[3] Several
aspects contributed to this reputation: An enormous force of instrumentalists
and singers is required; the expression "Symphony of the Thousand," coined
by the Munich concert agent Emil Gutmann, is not an exaggeration when one
considers that 858 singers and 171 instrumentalists took part in the Munich
premiere.[4] The combination of the Latin Pentecost hymn *Veni Creator
Spiritus* ("Come, Holy Ghost, Creator") with the final scene of Goethe's
Faust II was noteworthy, given the incredibly high standing that Goethe's
Faust—and especially this last scene—enjoyed among German-speaking
people. The distinctive character of the work (symphony, oratorio, music
drama, and redemption mystery) and the fundamentally impressive music
itself—all these contributed to the work's reputation.

Mahler himself considered the Eighth to be his major achievement. He
called it his Mass,[5] as well as "a gift to the entire nation."[6] In a conversation

with Richard Specht[7] in August 1906 in Salzburg, he substantiated the special qualities of the Eighth in so much detail and with such precision that it would be neglectful not to quote his statement here:

> Just think: Within the last three weeks I have completed the sketch for a totally new symphony, something that makes all my other works seem like preparatory efforts. I have never composed anything like this. In content and style it is altogether different from all my other works, and it is surely my greatest accomplishment. I have probably never worked under such compulsion; it was a vision that struck me like lightning. The whole immediately stood before my eyes; I had only to write it down, as if it had been dictated to me. . . . This Eighth Symphony is noteworthy, for one thing, because it combines two works of poetry in different languages. The first part is a Latin hymn and the second nothing less than the final scene of the second part of *Faust*. Are you surprised? I had longed to combine the hermit scene and the Finale with the *Mater Gloriosa* in a way that would be different from all the sugary, weak ways it has been done, but I had forgotten all about it. Then the other day I came across an old book. I opened it to the hymn *Veni Creator Spiritus,* and immediately the whole thing was there: not only the first theme, but the entire first movement. In response to this I could not possibly find anything more beautiful than Goethe's words in the hermit scene! Its form is also something altogether new. Can you imagine a symphony that is sung throughout, from beginning to end? So far I have employed words and the human voice merely to suggest, to sum up, to establish a mood. I resorted to them to express something concisely and specifically, which is possible only with words—something that could have been expressed symphonically only with immense breadth. But here the voice is also an instrument. The whole first movement is strictly symphonic in form yet is completely sung. It is really strange that nobody has thought of this before; it is simplicity itself, *The True Symphony,* in which the most beautiful instrument of all is led to its calling. Yet it is used not only as sound, because the voice is the bearer of poetic thoughts.

Origin

There is much about the Eighth's history that is unusual and apt to be misinterpreted, leading to confusion and astonishment. One is therefore obligated to trace its history (which unfortunately reveals several gaps) as precisely as possible.

In Maiernigg during June 1906, Mahler fell prey to "the typical first two weeks of creative paralysis. Almost every year this let him feel the fears of being unproductive" (AME 129–131). Suddenly, as he stepped into his cabin where he worked in the morning, the idea came to him: the *Veni Creator Spiritus*. As Alma relates:

He wrote the whole opening chorus with the half-forgotten text from memory. But text and music would not fit; the music had turned out more broadly than the words. In great excitement, Mahler sent off a telegram to Vienna and had the complete text of the old Latin hymn telegraphed to him. The complete text fit the music perfectly. He had intuitively composed the complete verses.

Alma's account regarding the composition of the first part agrees basically with other reports except for one important point: She says that Mahler wrote down the "half-forgotten text from memory." In his conversation with Specht, as mentioned, Mahler says that an "old book" had accidentally fallen into his hands and that he had opened it to the Pentecost hymn. In an extremely informative report, Ernst Decsey supplies a similar version:[8]

> He set the old hymn *Veni Creator Spiritus* to music, for which he had gotten the text from somewhere. While composing he realized that the music was pouring out beyond the text, overflowing like water from a full basin; in other words, the structural concept of the music did not coincide with the verses. He told a friend of his misery and this friend, a philologist, pointed out to him that this was natural because in the version he had, the text was incomplete, with about one-and-a-half verses missing. Mahler then saw to it that the complete text was sent to him as quickly as possible by the court music director Luze in Vienna. When the hymn arrived, Mahler was surprised to find that the words coincided exactly with the music and that his sense of form was responsible: every one of the new words fit easily into the whole.

The friend to whom Mahler had turned for advice was the archeologist Dr. Fritz Löhr. On 21 June,[9] Mahler requested that he translate two verses of the hymn, asked him how two words (*paraclitus diceris*) were to be scanned, asked whether there was "a beautiful translation (maybe even one that *rhymes*)," and begged for an immediate answer: "Otherwise it will come too late. I need it as creator and creature!" (GMB[2] 308). From this letter we can conclude that Mahler had the text by 21 June and was composing the first part. Four weeks later, around 18 July, he expressed apprehension that "this cursed old church book" from which he had taken the text of the *Veni Creator Spiritus* was not quite "flawless" and asked Löhr for the "authentic text of the hymn" (GMB[2] 310).

It is not known precisely whether Mahler had thought all along of letting the final scene of *Faust II* follow the Latin Pentecost hymn or at what time he started composing this final scene. From a letter to Willem Mengelberg we can conclude that he finished sketching the whole symphony by 15 August, at the latest. "Here I am, immersed in many notes! I have just completed my Eighth," he wrote to Mengelberg in a letter that arrived in Amsterdam on 18 August (GMB[2] 312). From 16–18 August he was in Salzburg, where he conducted *The Marriage of Figaro* during the Mozart

Festival.[10] It was there that the quoted conversation with Specht took place, in which he mentioned that during the last three weeks he had finished the sketches of a completely new symphony. In view of these precise dates, the reports of the critic Julius Korngold, whom Mahler had met in Salzburg, are less significant:

> He was full of visions of a new symphony, full of happy anticipation, almost boisterous. A well-thumbed little book was peeking out of his coat pocket: *Faust*. The sequences of the medieval religious poet had been set; they were to occupy the first part of the symphony (it became the Eighth). Now Goethe's corresponding sections were to be composed (AME 130).

Alma reports that upon returning to Maiernigg from Salzburg, Mahler continued to work on the Eighth "as if in a fever" (AME 131). Before departing for Salzburg, Mahler had played and sung the *Chorus mysticus* for Alma. She goes on to say that she was "completely under the spell of this work and after a few days sent him the entire sketch, written down from memory, fully harmonized" (AME 131).[11]

Thus the sketch of the score of this gigantic work seems to have been completed in ten weeks, from the middle of June to the end of August 1906,[12] because at the beginning of September, according to Alma, Mahler had to "join the troops" in Vienna (AME 131).

The Spiritual Unity of the Two Parts

The more one becomes engrossed in the Eighth Symphony, the more vividly the following questions present themselves: How did Mahler hit upon the idea, which initially seems so strange, to base the two parts of the work on two such heterogeneous texts as the Latin Pentecost hymn and the final scene from *Faust II*? How did he perceive these texts and how did he interpret them musically? Finally, what constitutes the unity of the two parts of the Symphony? The questions are justified, especially when one realizes that a thousand years separate these two texts. Hrabanus Maurus (d. 856), one of the most respected scholars of his time, wrote the hymn *Veni Creator Spiritus,* most likely in Fulda after 809, whereas Goethe completed *Faust* in 1830–1831.

Hans Mayer spoke of this "tremendous discrepancy" between the two texts and set up two hypotheses for discussion.[13] First, Mahler considered the hymn of Hrabanus Maurus "within the context of a religious experience of its time and geographic area, as a poetic statement of faith from the town of Fulda during the early ninth century." In that case, no music, not even Mahler's, could succeed in establishing "spiritual unity" with Mahler's *Faust* interpretation. A *concordia discors* would result.

In that case the two parts of the Eighth Symphony embody two worlds:

One, which is irrevocably gone and is quoted as a rejection, and another, the world of the late Goethe, which is also gone but to which one can still relate intellectually. Looking at it this way, the unity of this "Symphony of the Thousand" might be seen in the unsolved parataxis, in a side by side that in reality is a conflict.

The second hypothesis asserts that Mahler was intent on unity, that is, on a synthesis of Hrabanus Maurus and Goethe "accomplished by music." "In that case, *Faust* and especially the Latin hymn were reinterpreted by the imperious composer" and became a composition of "total religious and poetic misuse." According to Mayer, there is much evidence to support this theory.

In contrast to Hans Mayer, Stefan Strohm expressed the opinion that Mahler did not intend to "psychologize" the Latin hymn but that the music of the first part was absolute in that "it seeks the absolute as content."[14]

How then do the two parts of the Eighth relate to each other? Are we dealing with parataxis or synthesis? Numerous observations (some not considered until now) definitely indicate that Mahler understood and interpreted the two texts in a very personal way and that by means of music he achieved a remarkable synthesis:

1. The differences between the two texts are evident and undeniable. At the same time, it cannot be ignored that both contain certain theological concepts, including thoughts of grace, love, and illumination. The final scene of *Faust,* which expresses Goethe's personal credo, has a firmly theological foundation. On 6 June 1831, Goethe confessed to Eckermann:

   You must admit that the end, when the saved soul ascends, was very difficult to do. I could easily have gotten lost in vagueness, treating such transcendental, hardly definable matters. But by means of sharply defined figures and concepts of the Christian church I was able to give a concise, formal aspect to my poetic intentions.[15]

2. H. J. de Marez Oyens[16] referred to Goethe's translation of the Latin Pentecost hymn, which Goethe himself characterized in a letter to Zelter (18 February 1821) as an "appeal to the universal world genius."[17] The assumption of Marez Oyens that Mahler did not come across the hymn until he was reading Goethe was verified by Alma in March 1917.

3. According to a sketch sheet discussed by Paul Bekker, Mahler originally planned the Eighth to have four movements. Two hymns, *Veni Creator Spiritus* and *The Birth of Eros,* were meant to enclose two middle movements: a scherzo and an Adagio entitled *Caritas.*

This sketch proves clearly that Mahler intended from the very beginning to connect the medieval hymn with a completely different, pagan hymn. *The Birth of Eros* may be the end of the classic *Walpurgisnacht* from Goethe's *Faust II*.[18]

4. In the quoted conversation with Richard Specht, Mahler felt that "in response" to the Pentecost hymn he could not find "anything more beautiful" than Goethe's words in the hermit scene. In his concept there actually was a close connection between the two texts. On the occasion of the Munich dress rehearsal of the Eighth in September 1910, Mahler made an extremely informative statement (transmitted by Anton von Webern): "At the passage *accende lumen sensibus,* the bridge extends over to the close of *Faust*. The passage is the pivotal point of the entire work."[19]

5. In June 1909, three years after beginning work on the Eighth, Mahler wrote a long letter to his wife that contained an informative interpretation of the *Chorus mysticus* (AME 436–438).[20] Here he constructed a polarity between the "ever-manly," which he described as "eternal longing, striving, moving ahead," and the "ever-womanly," which he characterized as "resting, the goal." He explicitly interprets the figure of the *Mater Gloriosa* as the personification of the ever-womanly. He also clarified the contrast between the "appearances" and the "imperishable" and emphasized that the imperishable in "its earthly appearance is inadequate." The idea of redemption "from the body of earthly inadequacy" is important here, and this formulation can contribute considerably to a deeper understanding of his conception of the line *Infirma nostri corporis* in the Pentecost hymn.

6. Mahler successfully achieves the spiritual unity between the two parts of the Symphony by musical means or, more precisely, through the leading themes and motifs that permeate the entire work. With them the composer furnishes an instructive and impressive musical exegesis.

Part I—Hymn: *Veni Creator Spiritus*

According to the research of Heinrich Lausberg, *Veni Creator Spiritus* was most likely written by Hrabanus Maurus on the occasion of a synod in Aachen during the year 809, a synod at which theological questions dealing with the Trinity were addressed.[21] The number of the original seven verses has symbolic meaning as an allusion to the seven gifts of the Spirit, which, according to Isaiah 11:2, are spirit, wisdom, knowledge, counsel, strength, insight, and fear of the Lord.

The hymn has been transmitted in several versions that differ from each other in details.[22] As always, Mahler took many liberties in accommodating the text. He rearranged some verses, exchanged the couplets in one verse, omitted some words, and replaced some. Beyond this, he used only the first couplet of one verse. The text that he set to music contains seven and a half verses and is given here with the English translation:[23]

Veni creator spiritus,	Come, Holy Ghost, Creator come,
Mentes tuorum visita,	From Thy bright heavenly throne.
Imple superna gratia,	Come, take possession of our souls,
Quae tu creasti pectora.	And make them all Thine own.
Qui Paraclitus diceris,	Thou who art called the Paraclete,
Donum Dei altissimi,	Best Gift of God above,
Fons vivus, ignis, caritas	The Living Spring, The Living Fire,
Et spiritalis unctio.	Sweet Unction, and True Love!
Infirma nostri corporis	With Thy strength which ne'er decays
Virtute firmans perpeti	Confirm our mortal frame,
Accende lumen sensibus,	And guide our minds with Thy blest light,
Infunde amorem cordibus.	With love our hearts inflame.
Hostem repellas longius	Far from us drive our hellish foe,
Pacemque dones protinus.	True peace unto us bring,
Ductore sic te praevio	And through all perils guide us safe
Vitemus omne pessimum.	Beneath Thy sacred wing.
Tu septiformis munere	Thou who art seven-fold in Thy grace,
Dextrae paternae digitus.	Finger of God's right Hand,
[Tu rite promissum Patris,	[His promise, teaching little ones
Sermone ditans guttura.]	To speak and understand.]
Per te sciamus da patrem,	Through Thee may we the Father know,
Noscamus [atque] filium,	Through Thee the Eternal Son,
[Te utriusque] spiritum	[And Thee] the Spirit of them Both
Credamus omni tempore.	Thrice-blessèd Three in One.
Da gratiarum munera,	Give unto us the joy of heaven,
Da gaudiorum praemia.	Give us Thy grace divine.
Dissolve litis vincula,	And may the fetters of our strife
Adstringe pacis foedera.	In pacts of peace combine.
Gloria Patri Domino,	All glory to the Father be,
Natoque, qui a mortuis,	And to the risen Son;
Surrexit, ac Paraclito	The same to Thee, O Paraclete,
In saeculorum saecula.	While endless ages run. Amen.

A page formerly owned by Bruno Walter, now in the New York Public Library, documents that Mahler wrote down the Latin text before he began or while he wrote the composition. As a comparison shows, he used the accepted liturgical version. In that version the last line of the fourth verse (according to the numbering of Mahler's "definitive version") reads *Vitemus omne noxium* (not pessimum), and the second line of the sixth verse reads *Noscamus atque filium*. Moreover, the text of the fifth verse (which Mahler finally shortened by half) is complete in this copy. The text of the seventh verse, which Mahler most likely received from Löhr, is missing in this copy and in the usual liturgical version.

In the conversation with Richard Specht that has been quoted several times, Mahler said the first movement was strictly in symphonic form even though it was sung throughout. "In symphonic form" means that the movement is constructed in first-movement sonata form rather than in strophic from, though it displays numerous irregularities.

Exposition

Mm. 1–45   Main section (Verse I, first couplet)
      1–20   First main theme
     21–30   Second main theme
     31–45   Transition (first main theme)
     46–107   Rondolike secondary section (Verse 1, second couplet, and Verse 2; principal keys: D-flat and A-flat major
    108–123   Intermezzo: new setting of Verse 1 (at the beginning the *Veni* theme)
    124–140   Orchestral interlude (mm. 135–144: low bell in A)
    141–168   Closing section (Verse 3, first couplet)

Development

    169–216   First section (Allegro, *etwas hastig*) [somewhat hasty]: Orchestral interlude: Music from far away, shadowlike in character (muted brass, low bell in A-flat); primarily development of the *Veni* theme.
    217–257   Second section (*Noch einmal so langsam als vorher*) [Twice as slowly as before]: New composition of Verse 3
    258–261   Transition (*Plötzlich sehr breit und leidenschaftlichen Ausdrucks*) [Suddenly very broad and with passionate expression]
    262–289   Third section (*Mit plötzlichem Aufschwung*) [With sudden impetus]; new theme (Verse 3, second couplet); marchlike character
    290–311   Fourth section: Dramatic scene above a basso ostinato (Verse 4, first couplet)
    312–365   Fifth section: Double fugue on the two main themes (Verse 4, second couplet, Verse 5 and 6); marchlike character
    366–412   Sixth section (Verse 3, second couplet); corresponding at the beginning with the third section

Recapitulation

413–431 First main theme (Verse 1, first line)
432–473 *Gehaltener* (More subdued): Sections from the secondary
         section (Verse 2 first couplet, Verse 7, and the second line of
         Verse 4); mm. 431–441 ~mm. 80–89
474–489 Final section (Verse 4)
488–507 Orchestral interlude (contrapuntal development of the *Veni*
         theme)

Coda

508–580 Statements of almost all themes of the movement; at the end
         the *Accende* and *Creator* themes

Focusing on the proportions of the individual parts, one begins to realize
how irregular the form of the movement is: the exposition has 168 measures,
the development 244, the recapitulation only 95, and the coda 73. Nevertheless, the composition (or, with some bias, the adaptation of the text to the
music) is generally speaking so felicitous that it is not easy to identify the
one-and-a-half verses Mahler adapted after he had sketched the music. If one
traces the relationship of text and music, it becomes evident that he was not
guided by the abstract idea of absolute music, as has recently been
emphatically claimed, but that he continually had the text in mind. The key
passages of the music are all tailored to the text.

Viewed from a distance, the exposition reveals the usual sonata-like outline: main theme, transition, contrasting secondary theme, and *sui generis* a
closing theme. Nevertheless, at a closer look, several abnormalities become
obvious: two main themes can be distinguished, the secondary theme is
followed by a transition that brings back the first main theme, and the closing
section is preceded by an orchestral interlude.

The two main themes of the movement were surely created with a view to
their being modified and combined in the development. Mahler used them for
the double fugue. Both appear with the same text—the first line of the hymn,
which is *Veni, creator spiritus*—but the accents are placed differently: In the
first theme, the word *Veni* is repeated:

Mm. 2–5

In the second theme, the word order is turned around (*Spiritus, O
Creator, veni*), and the word *creator* is repeated:

Mm. 21–27

The invocation is apparently at the center of the first theme, whereas the second theme refers to the Creator-Spirit Himself.

The arrangement of the verses is also informative. Mahler executes the exposition with two-and-a-half verses. One might assume that he devoted the first verse to the main section, the second verse to the secondary section, and the two lines of the third verse to the closing section, but this is not so. The actual distribution of the text looks like this:

Main themes:	*Veni, creator spiritus*
Transition:	*Mentes tuorum visita*
Secondary section:	*Imple superna gratia,*
	Quae tu creasti pectora.
	Qui Paraclitus diceris,
	Donum Dei altissimi,
	Fons vivus, ignis, caritas
	Et spiritalis unctio.
Intermezzo:	Verse 1
Closing section:	*Infirma nostri corporis*
	Virtute firmans perpeti

Mahler apparently perceived the second couplet of Verse 1 and the four lines of Verse 2 as a unit because he obviously believed that the subjects belonged together (the highest mercy and the characteristics of the spirit, which are the fountain of life—fire, love, and spiritual balm). In this way he succeeded in bringing out the strong contrast between the impetuous main section (the performance marking *Allegro impetuoso* primarily refers to the main section) and the tender secondary section. This contrast does justice to the symphonic form and to the text's meaning. The contrast is also accentuated by dynamic means. The main section and the transition passage are sung *fortissimo* by both choirs: the actual secondary theme is performed *piano, dolce,* and *espressivo* by soloists:

Mm. 46–54

Later the secondary theme is also given to the choirs.

Looking more closely at the movement's themes, one will easily recognize that they are more vocal than instrumental in spite of their agility and expansiveness, but they are dealt with symphonically in the way they are repeated, transposed, varied, inverted, augmented, combined with each other, and given new coloring.

The closing section offers an informative example. It is based on the first main theme with some secondary ideas.[24] The once radiant *Veni* theme appears in its original form (mm. 152–153 in the basses of the first choir) and in inversion (mm. 165–168), as well as in a surprising variant in which it appears as a shadow of itself due to the changed dynamic, the transposition to a lower register, and its rhythmic and melodic transformation:

Mm. 141–145

This metamorphosis is related to the meaning of the text that speaks here of the weakness (mortality) of the body (*Infirma nostri corporis*).[25] Mahler emphasized these words through the exceptional musical treatment and gave them a transcendent meaning. In measures 145–152, the choirs are accompanied by a solo violin that is directed to play *stets etwas flüchtig* (always somewhat fleetingly), its cantilena imitating the call of the *Bird of Death* from the apocalyptic vision of the Finale in the Second Symphony.[26] The passage's meaning is also reflected in the preceding intermezzo (m. 135ff.), in which a low bell rings out several times—Mahler's aural symbol of transcendence.

The development documents perhaps even more impressively than the exposition that Mahler was anxious to give musical expression to the text's meaning. Of the six sections into which it clearly divides, the first (mm. 169–216) is an interlude to be performed *etwas hastig* (somewhat hastily). It provides a symphonic illustration of the *Infirma* thought. Intended to sound like music from far away and mostly built on a pedal point on A-flat, it primarily develops the *Veni* theme that now appears like a shadow. Horns, trumpets, and trombones are muted, and the high strings at first play pizzicato. Again a low bell sounds.

After this interlude it is appropriate that in the second section (mm. 217–257) the soloists again sing the *Infirma nostri corporis*. Although Mahler uses existing thematic material, the composition of the verse is altogether new (its entire text now being performed). The *Veni* theme appears in a minor variant that bears little resemblance to the archetype:

Mm. 218–222

The darkly tinted C-sharp minor of the beginning gives way (m. 227) to a friendly F major. As soon as the word *lumen* is sung, brighter keys appear: D major (m. 231), C major (m. 235), and G major (m. 241). One can clearly recognize that even in details of key symbolism Mahler never lost sight of the text's meaning.

The second couplet of Verse 3 expresses the request for enlightenment and love (more precisely, for love to flow into the hearts): *Accende lumen sensibus / Infunde amorem cordibus*.[27] Mahler must have considered these verses to be the hymn's central message. It was not enough for him to set the lines of the second section of the development (mm. 231–254) to gentle music, underlining the prayerful character of the passage; he also used them as the basis for the third section (mm. 262–289). This passage functions as a breakthrough, providing the movement's first climax and combining ecstatic traits with marchlike features. The soloists, the two mixed choirs, and also the boys' choir (appearing here for the first time) again sing the two verses, at first in unison, "with sudden impetus" in a radiant E major *fortissimo*. Their theme can, with some effort, be derived from the *Veni* theme, which subsequently becomes the principal theme in the second part of the Symphony:

In the fourth section of the development (mm. 290–311, *Hostem repellas longius / Pacemque dones protinus*) we also find an admirable congruity between text and music. Mahler was led by the notion of the enemy (not of peace) and shaped the section as a highly dramatic scene. An eight-measure chorale is extended to fourteen measures by strange interpolations that sound like an outcry. The orchestral accompaniment is remarkable: groups of seven notes and other rhythmic formations in the basso ostinato go against the $\frac{4}{4}$ beat and attract attention:[28]

Mm. 290–295

Not surprisingly, this passage made a strong impression on Igor Stravinsky.

In the development so far, the meaning of the text has dictated the shape of the music, but in the fifth section (mm. 312–365) musical principles of construction are in the foreground. Here Mahler combines the two main themes of the movement:

Mm. 314–320

The result is a grand double fugue, quite regular in construction, the entries always coming on E-flat and B-flat. It "consumes" much text (the second couplet of Verse 4 and Verses 5 and 6).

It is, however, typical of Mahler's concept of the text that he does not close the development with this double fugue, providing instead a sixth section (mm. 366–412) that picks up the *Accende* theme and develops it along with other motifs. Thus a kind of da capo structure is achieved: the third and the sixth sections of the development correspond with each other and enclose the highly dramatic scene and double fugue.

After a long pedal point on B-flat, the recapitulation begins (m. 413) with a cymbal crash and the sound of the organ. With relatively few changes the first main theme is heard (*Veni, creator spiritus*). The secondary and closing sections are completely new, though they are based on the first couplet of Verse 2 and on Verses 7 and 4.[29] Here Mahler contrapuntally combines voices (m. 463ff.) that have texts from different verses, a procedure that is not arbitrary. The second line of Verse 4, *Pacemque dones protinus,* and the last line of Verse 7, *Adstringe pacis foedera,* both express the thought of peace, which is now at the center. The close of the recapitulation (mm. 479–89), however, deals with the thought of victory over evil: *Ductore te praevio / Vitemus omne pessimum.*[30]

The coda (based on Verse 8 of the hymn, the glorification of the Trinity) combines the themes of the movement. In succession we hear the *Infirma* theme, the *Veni* theme, the *Imple* theme, then the *Accende* theme, and finally the *Creator* theme. The *Accende* theme is given special emphasis, not only because it is sung by the boys' choir (to the words *Gloria, in saeculorum saecula, Patri*) but because it is played by four trumpets and three trombones located away from the other players. Thus Mahler gave to the entire movement the central thought of enlightenment and love.

Part II—The Final Scene from Goethe's *Faust II*

The final scene of Goethe's *Faust II* owes its fame to the metaphysical subject, the fantastic elements in its conception, and the musicality of the verses and their suggestive power. The scene tells the story of Faust and Gretchen to its end and at the same time offers a solution for the "puzzle of this world." The abundance of characters (three patres, three women in deep sin, Doctor Marianus, the *Mater Gloriosa,* Gretchen, choirs of holy anchorites, angels, and the blessed young boys) is remarkable without being confusing.[31] As Erich Trunz describes it, "The scene shows mountains and trees, hermits [anchorites] and hovering angels; it is a picture in which vertical movement is strongly emphasized. The action gradually moves from the lower to the upper regions."[32]

It is easy to imagine that Mahler, who deeply honored Goethe and had a liking for metaphysical themes, was especially attracted to this scene. As previously mentioned, he told Richard Specht that it had been his desire for a long time to compose this hermit scene and the closing with the *Mater Gloriosa*. But it is also understandable that the composition presented distinct problems.[33]

Both parts of the Eighth Symphony are closely connected by their themes and motifs, yet one can generally say that the second part is stylistically different. While the first part is cantata-like, the second comes noticeably closer to the realm of music drama and the redemption mystery reminiscent of *Parsifal*. The different styles are conditioned by form and content of the poetry, as well as by the numerous vocal solos in the second part, which demand a completely different style of composition than the verses of the Latin Pentecost hymn and are performed exclusively by choirs or by soloists. The second part also presents a large array of musical genres most of which do not appear in the first part. This applies especially to the recitative and arioso; to the hymn, chorale, and song; and to the *Religioso* character.

Two examples may serve here. Mahler set the song of the Pater ecstaticus *Ewiger Wonnebrand* (Eternal flame of rapture) as a musical hymn (mm. 219–261). He divided it into five periods (four with eight measures and one with ten), all beginning with the same motif and giving the impression of verses. The singing of the three women in deep sin (mm. 868–1016), however, is set like chamber music. It is quite songlike and anticipates the style of *Das Lied von der Erde.*

To obtain an overview of the organization of this gigantic movement, which lasts about one hour, and to understand Mahler's compositional principles, it is first necessary to study the structure of this movement. In his thematic analysis of 1912, Richard Specht was the first to state that one could easily divide the movement into Andante, Scherzo, and Finale.[34] The Andante or Adagio (mm. 1–384) is followed by an intermezzo (mm. 385–442, beginning with the chorus *Gerettet ist das edle Glied* [Rescued is the noble member]), a Scherzo (mm. 443–611), and the Finale (beginning with m. 612). However, closer analysis will reveal that the structure of the section is too complex for such a relatively simple scheme. Specht's outline ignores two things: At three places in the second part Mahler borrows music from longer sections of the first part—borrowings that are also important for a semantic analysis. Moreover, within the second part we find anticipations of later passages and a return to earlier ones, while additional connections exist between different passages. If we keep this in mind, we need not be surprised that a detailed analysis shows manifold interconnections:

Mm.	1–146	Poco Adagio, later Allegro moderato: instrumental Arioso (basic key: E-flat minor)
	147–162	Four-line chorale = instrumental version of the choir of the younger angels *Nebelnd um Felsenhöh* (Like mist around the rocky heights) (~mm. 580–593)
	163–167	End of the instrumental Arioso
	168–218	*Wieder langsam* (again slowly): instrumental Arioso as foundation of the choir (and echoes) of the holy anchorites (basic key: E-flat minor)
	219–260	Moderato: Pater ecstaticus (*sehr leidenschaftlich* [very passionate]): Hymn in several musical verses (basic key: E-flat major)
	261–265	Allegro: Intonation of the love theme (trumpet)

166–362	Allegro appassionato: Pater profundus: Arioso (basic key: E-flat minor)
361–384	Hymnlike transition (motivic material from the song of Pater ecstaticus)
385–420	Allegro deciso: Choir of angels and later choir of blessed young boys, largely borrowed from the first part (corresponding are II, mm. 385–410 and I, mm. 262–281)
418–442	Allegro mosso: Transition (trumpet and horn announce Faust's spiritual reincarnation and anticipate a theme from the choir of blessed young boys that is to follow later)
443–519	Scherzando: Choir of the younger angels (*Jene Rosen*) [Those roses]; basic key: E-flat major
520–539	Intermezzo (at the beginning the love theme played by the trumpets)
540–580	*Schon etwas langsamer und immer noch mäßiger* (Already somewhat slower and more moderate): Introduction and choir of the more perfected angels. Borrowing from the first part (corresponding are II, mm. 540–580 and I, mm. 135–168)
580–611	Choir of the younger angels: Chorale of several lines (inclusion of the Glockenspiel); m. 604 entry of Doctor Marianus, who at first is only to accompany and should not be prominent
612–638	Allegro deciso: Choir of blessed young boys and Doctor Marianus: Faust's reincarnation (*Freudig empfangen wir diesen im Puppenstand*) [Joyfully we receive this man in the pupal stage]; inclusion of the Glockenspiel; mm. 613–626 ~ mm. 422–435
639–757	Praise of the *Mater Gloriosa* by Doctor Marianus (main keys: E major and E-flat major)
758–779	Poco più mosso: Intermezzo modulating from E-flat major to E major
780–867	*Äußerst langsam* (Extremely slow). Adagissimo: Floating on high of the *Mater Gloriosa*: mixed choir and choir of the penitent women (main keys: E major and B major)
868–905	*Fließend* (Flowing): Magna Peccatrix: song style (beginning in B major and closing in E-flat major)
906–956	*Immer dasselbe Tempo* (Always the same tempo): Mulier Samaritana: Song style (beginning in E-flat minor and closing in E-flat major)
956–967	Intermezzo (at the beginning the love theme played by the trumpets)
968–1016	*Immer fließend* (Always flowing): Maria Aegyptiaca: song style (main keys: G minor and E-flat major); the

passage mm. 970–978 is borrowed from the Rose chorus (mm. 474–482)

1017–1093	*Sehr fließend, beinahe flüchtig. Wie ein Geflüster* (Very flowing, almost hurried. Like a whisper): Trio of three women in deep sin, at first in the form of a canon (mm. 1058–1079 are borrowed from the Rose chorus, mm. 443–461); Keys: C major, A major, A minor, F major
1093–1141	Prelude and song of the Una Poenitentium with mandolin solo (basic key: D major); Theme of the *Mater Gloriosa*
1141–1185	Choir of the blessed young boys (theme of the *Mater Gloriosa,* basic key: D major)
1186–1212	Allegro: Choir of the blessed young boys (with Glockenspiel), later Una Poenitentium. Return to the music of mm. 613–638 (Faust's spiritual life)
1213–1243	Again in Tempo: Una Poenitentium: quotation from the first part (corresponding are II, mm. 1213–1243 and I, mm. 46–61 and mm. 108–122)
1243–1248	The love theme treated imitatively by horns and trumpets
1249–1276	*Very slow:* Mater Gloriosa *dolcissimo* (basic key: E-flat major)
1277–1383	*Hymnlike:* Doctor Marianus and choir (basic key: E-flat major)
1384–1420	*Flowing*: E-flat major postlude using the *Blicket auf* (glance upward) motif (Glockenspiel and tam-tam); at the end *diminuendo bis zum Verlöschen* (diminuendo to the point of dying away)
1421–1448	Slowly: Transition (with harmonium, celesta, piano, and harps)
1449–1528	Beginning very slowly: Chorus mysticus
1528–1572	Postlude with the *Veni* theme from the first part

If one studies this scheme and ignores the more detailed relationships, one may say that the first "movement"—including the symphonic prelude, the choir of the anchorites, and the singing of the Patres ecstaticus and profundus—is a Poco Adagio building to an Allegro appassionato (mm. 1–384). The dominant characteristics of the movement, which is in E-flat minor or major, are the Arioso and the Hymnus. The Rose chorus of the younger angels takes the place of the Scherzo, which Mahler marks *Scherzando* in measure 444. In Specht's view it extends to the transition "Joyfully we receive" (m. 612); actually it goes only to measure 519. A Finale is clearly recognizable. It does not begin at measure 612, as Specht presumed, but at measure 639 (No. 89) at the unexpected entrance of Doctor Marianus, *Höchste Herrscherin der Welt* (Highest ruler of the world). From here on the theme of the *Mater Gloriosa* dominates. Just how strongly the entire structure is interconnected is evident when one realizes that the music of the three women in deep sin, which begins (mm. 868–871) and closes (mm. 1005–1012) with the theme of the *Mater Gloriosa,* at times (especially in the Trio) returns to the theme of the Rose chorus. Thus measures 474–482 correspond to measures 970–978, and measures 443–461 correspond to measures 1058–1079. At least the latter correspondence reflects a textual connection, because the younger angels state expressly that they received the roses *aus den Händen liebend-heil'ger Büßerinnen* (from the hands of loving, holy repenting women).

The more one studies the Eighth, the more one realizes that Mahler employs Wagner's *Leitmotif* technique in a highly individual way. The borrowings from the first part, the anticipation of that which is to come, the return to that which was, and the interrelated sections of the second part—all these serve to bring about profound emotional and intellectual connections. The second part of the Eighth is full of references to past and future. The Wagnerian categories of *Ahnung* (foreboding), of *Vergegenwärtigung* (bring to mind), and of *Erinnerung* (remembrance) definitely are applicable.[35] These factors preclude an approach to this music based on formal analysis; only a semantic analysis can discover Mahler's intentions and compositional principles.

Four basic poetic and musical ideas guided Mahler in his conception of the second part: the ideas of eternal love, divine grace, earthly inadequacy, and spiritual reincarnation (the continuation of life after death). Let us investigate how these ideas are reflected in the work.

Of all the themes of the first part, the *Accende* theme recurs most often in the second part. It occurs in instrumental as well as vocal versions and, in imitative sections, in a mixed version. An examination of all passages where it appears with text or as commentary reveals that Mahler considered it a theme of enlightenment and love.

At first it supplies the motivic substance for the first movement of this final scene, the Arioso and the Hymnus. Played by the first trumpet, it then rounds off (mm. 261–265) the singing of Pater ecstaticus. His final words are *daß ja das Nichtige alles verflüchtige, glänze der Dauerstern, ewiger Liebe Kern"* (that indeed what is empty will vanish, and radiant is the lasting star, core of eternal love). It introduces the song of Pater profundus, who, abiding in lower regions, is still bound to the sensual. Mahler used the *Accende* theme for no less than three passages from the music of this Pater, three passages that speak emphatically of love and enlightenment. He emphasized all three with special performance markings: *Gehalten* and *leidenschaftlich* (sustained and passionate), *Maestoso,* and *Mit Inbrunst* (with fervor). In all three cases the vocal version of the theme is treated in imitation with an instrumental variant:

Mm. 284–293

Mm. 316–320

Mm. 357–362

Extremely important for the further understanding of the theme's meaning is the borrowing of a section from the first part. Mahler based the angel choir's *Gerettet ist das edle Glied* on the music that in the third section of the development (with sudden impetus) was inspired by the verses *Accende lumen sensibus, / Infunde amorem cordibus.* Corresponding with each other are I, measures 262–281 and II, measures 385–410. The *Accende* and the *Infunde* themes now appear with the following text:

Mm. 384–389

Mm. 396–402

In this context, the wordier [German] text of the angelic choir acts as a kind of commentary to the two Latin lines.

> *Gerettet ist das edle Glied*
> *Der Geisterwelt vom Bösen:*
> *Wer immer strebend sich bemüht,*
> *Den können wir erlösen,*
> *Und hat an ihm die Liebe gar*
> *Von oben teilgenommen,*
> *Begegnet ihm die selige Schar*
> *Mit herzlichem Willkommen*

> Rescued is the noble member
> Of the spirit-world from evil.
> Whoever endeavors with constant striving,
> He it is whom we can redeem!
> And if love has touched him even
> From above,
> The blessed host meets him
> With a hearty welcome.

On 6 June 1831, Goethe told Eckermann that the verses of the angelic choir contain the key to Faust's salvation:

> Within Faust himself [there is] an increasingly higher and purer activity until the end, and from above eternal love is coming to his aid. This is

entirely in harmony with our religious ideas, according to which we are redeemed not only through our own strength, rather through the added divine grace.[36]

Faust therefore owes his redemption just as much to his own endeavor as to eternal love and divine grace.

If one keeps this exegesis in mind, one better understands why in measures 520–526 the trumpets enter with the *Accende* theme, after the last words of the Rose chorus: *es ist gelungen* (it was not in vain). It also seems quite logical that Doctor Marianus, the representative of spiritual love, addresses the *Mater Gloriosa,* who is the personification of eternal love, as "Highest ruler of the world" (mm. 639–641), using a melodic figure derived from the *Accende* theme:[37]

It is just as logical that by making minor changes to this musical statement, Mahler gains the theme of the *Mater Gloriosa,* the principal theme of the Symphony's Finale:

Mm. 780–783

As previously explained, in the Christian religion as well as in Goethe's *Faust* the idea of eternal love is closely connected with the concept of divine grace. Mahler must have been conscious of this connection. The concept of grace was important for Mahler, for he set the verses of Gretchen *Er ahnet kaum das frische Leben* . . . (He barely senses the new life . . .) to music of the secondary section in the first part. The corresponding passages are I, measures 46–61 and measures 108–122 and II, measures 1213–1243. The texts of both sections express the thought of grace. In the first part the words are *Imple superna gratia / Quae tu creasti pectora* (Fulfill with heavenly grace / The hearts you have created) while in the second part Gretchen says the following about Faust's transfiguration:

> *Er ahnet kaum das frische Leben,*
> *So gleicht er schon der heiligen Schar.*
> *Sieh, wie er jedem Erdenbande*
> *Der alten Hülle sich entrafft,*
> *Und aus ätherischem Gewande*

Hervortritt erste Jugendkraft!
Vergönne mir, ihn zu belehren!
Noch blendet ihn der neue Tag!

He hardly senses the fresh, new life,
As he is already resembling the sacred host.
See how he departs from every earthly connection,
From the old shell,
And out of the ethereal garment
Fresh, youthful strength is coming forth!
Grant me to teach him!
He is still dazzled by the new day!

Gretchen is able to teach Faust only if it is granted to her, that is, through grace. It is significant for the intellectual connection between love and grace that after Gretchen's final words the horns and later the trumpets (mm. 1243–1248) play the *Accende* theme. This suggests that the new day, which is still blinding Faust, is the realm of love.

A further meaningful connection exists between the choir of the more perfected angels and the *Infirma* thought. Mahler adapted the text of this angelic choir to the music he had composed for the conclusion of the first part. Corresponding are I, measures 135–168 and II, measures 540–580. Thus the following texts correspond: *Infirma nostri corporis / Virtute firmans perpeti* (The weakness of our body / Strengthen with your miraculous power) and

Uns bleibt ein Erdenrest
Zu tragen peinlich,
Und wär' er von Asbest,
Er ist nicht reinlich.
Wenn starke Geisteskraft
Die Elemente
An sich herangerafft,
Kein Engel trennte
Geeinte Zwienatur
Der innigen beiden;
Die ewige Liebe nur
Vermag's zu scheiden.

An earthly remnant remains for us,
Painful to bear,
And even if it would be indestructible,
It is not pure.
When by strong power of the mind
The elements
Have been snatched up,
No angel will separate

The unified double nature
Of the intimate two;
It is only eternal love
That is able to separate it.

Both texts have in common the thought of the earthly dimension of existence, the weakness of the body or the earthly remainder, something that is
painful for the more accomplished angels to bear. This is probably what
Mahler had in mind in the June 1909 letter to his wife quoted earlier, when
he spoke of redemption "from the body of earthly inadequacy," a necessary
redemption, so that the inadequacy referred to in the *Chorus mysticus* can
become reality (AME 438).

Nevertheless, that which is denied to the more accomplished angels—to
keep apart the "united double nature" of the elemental and the spiritual in
Faust and to grant him the "life of the spirits" (line 11969) or the "new life"
(line 12086)—is successfully accomplished through eternal love by the
blessed young boys. Mahler, in fact, succeeded in expressing this musically:
He based the choral lines of the blessed young boys, occurring in two places
quite distant from one another, on the same music. Therefore, measures 613–
638 and 1187–1212 correspond to each other, as do their texts:[38]

Freudig empfangen wir
Diesen im Puppenstand;
Also erlangen wir
Englisches Unterpfand.
Löset die Flocken los,
Die ihn umgeben!
Schon ist er schön und groß
Von heiligem Leben.
Er überwächst uns schon
An mächtigen Gliedern,
Wird treuer Pflege Lohn
Reichlich erwidern.
Wir wurden früh entfernt
Von Lebechören;
Doch dieser hat gelernt:
Er wird uns lehren.

Joyfully we receive
Him in a pupal state;
Thus we will gain
An angelic pledge.
Loosen the ties
That surround him!
Immediately he is beautiful and great,
Filled with holy life.

He already outgrows us
With powerful limbs
And will respond abundantly
To faithful care.
At an early age we were separated
From among the living;
But this one is learned:
He will teach us.

It is very typical for Mahler's concept that already in measures 422–425 of the Allegro mosso the trumpet and later the horn (without the use of text) announce the spiritual reincarnation of Faust. The two choirs of the blessed young boys display an especially refreshing tone, emphasized by the inclusion of the Glockenspiel to which Mahler attached symbolic meaning. In October 1900 he had stated to Natalie Bauer-Lechner (in connection with the *Urlicht* movement of the Second Symphony) that "the stroke of the little bell reminds me of the soul in heaven, where it would have to begin anew childlike, in a pupal state" (BL[2] 168). Several years before the composition of the Eighth, Mahler evidently had completely familiarized himself with the world of Goethe's final scene.

The thematic symbolism as well as the symbolism of instruments and keys are of paramount importance in the Eighth. A few references may suffice: The sound of harps and harmonium is assigned to the *Mater Gloriosa*. Typically the first harp chord occurs (m. 639) at the address of Doctor Marianus, "Highest ruler of the world." Similarly the harmonium enters in measure 780 at the appearance of the hovering *Mater Gloriosa*. It establishes the characteristic sound of the *Religioso*. The mandolin is used only during the *Una Poenitentium* (mm. 1095–1141); appropriately enough Gretchen speaks here of the return of the *früh Geliebten, nicht mehr Getrübten* (early beloved, no longer saddened one).

Regarding the symbolism of keys: the basic key of both parts of the Eighth is E-flat major, but it is obvious that in both parts Mahler attached special meaning to E major. It is the key of the sudden upward impulse *Accende lumen sensibus* in the development of the first part and also of the *Mater Gloriosa* in the second part. Doctor Marianus's praise of the *Mater Gloriosa* begins, of course, in E major but modulates to E-flat major in measure 704ff, as soon as the sudden alleviation of the glowing fire is mentioned *(wenn du uns befriedest)* [when you pacify us].

At the end of the Symphony (m. 1528ff.), the brass repeatedly brings the *Veni* theme from the first part, at times in imitation. These statements not only serve as a formal rounding off but are surely meant to be symbolic as well. The Symphony ends, as it began, with an invocation of the Creator Spirit.

Why did Mahler connect the Latin Pentecost hymn with the final scene from *Faust*? A Goethe commentator indirectly gave a plausible answer. As Erich Trunz states, God appears to human eyes as a male.

But all earthly things long to return to the highest light and will again be lifted up to it. Here, however, where the godly reveals itself as loving and merciful, human eyes view it as female. Therefore a line leads from the earthly Gretchen to the Una Poenitentium, to the three holy repenting women, to the *Mater Gloriosa,* and into the primeval light of divine strength of love.[39]

It can be considered certain that the dialectic of the ever-manly and ever-womanly played a role in the conception of the Eighth.

Mahler dedicated the Eighth Symphony to his "dear wife," Alma Maria.[40] Many later remarks lead to the conclusion that he projected his idea of the ever-womanly upon his wife. For him the term *ever-womanly* meant, as mentioned, "the resting, the goal" (AME 437). After his psychoanalytical conversation with Sigmund Freud in August 1910, he found Freud's diagnosis to be correct. On 4 September 1910, he wrote to his wife from Munich: "Freud is right. For me you have always been the light, the central point!" (AME 466). And in poems and letters he addressed to her in August and September of 1910 he referred to her as the "harbor" he now had reached: "Hail to me—I have died to the world—I am in the harbor" (AME 460 and 471).

PART THREE

The Late Symphonies

Regarding the Late Style

Mahler's late style has aroused interest among researchers at least since Paul Bekker. This is not surprising if one considers that many viewed Mahler's last symphonies as examples of the New Music. For Theodor W. Adorno, the Ninth was the first major work of New Music.[1] An attempt to determine the style of these works scientifically entails considerable difficulties that already manifest themselves in the choice and formulation of suitable terminology. The style has been regarded as "dissolution," as "decay," as having a tendency toward "disassociation" and "disintegration." It was thought that concepts such as free atonality, linear polyphony, musical prose, "analytical instrumentation," open form, and the principle of "avoiding repetition" might indicate the trend.[2]

As one considers how best to arrive at a scientific understanding of the late style, three problems become evident. First, several of the adopted terms (for instance, the concept of free atonality) prove to be inappropriate. Second, there is the acute danger of over-generalization in applying terms such as *dissolution* and *decay*. Third, some stylistic characteristics of the late period are already present in earlier symphonies. With these factors in mind, some phenomena that can be considered typical for the late works will be pointed out:

1. In the late works, Mahler constructs some movements (such as the first movements of the Ninth and Tenth Symphonies) with such freedom and originality that their form allows different interpretations. Isolated instances of this can already be observed in the first two periods, but Mahler now goes one step further. The term "avoiding repetition" is inappropriate for the late works because it implies that every thought must be followed by a completely different one. Actually, Mahler constructs his movements economically, basing them on a few thoughts. His manner consists of letting the earlier thoughts always appear in a new "illumination," carrying variation to the extreme.

2. In a letter to Mahler, Bruno Walter appropriately described the horizontal and vertical relationships in the middle symphonies (Fifth through Eighth) as follows:

> In your later works you are less and less inclined explicitly to harmonize your melodies. Instead, you develop several melodic lines that seem to be completely independent and hence achieve a purely horizontal texture. Their vertical meeting results in harmonic progressions that are as economical as possible and yet as full as necessary. In that way you arrive at an extremely complicated polyphonic style, whose necessary artistic contrast could only be provided by occasional, very simple homophony.[3]

The later symphonies continue these tendencies, sometimes to the extent that here and there one may speak of a purely horizontal style. Some movements and passages from *Das Lied von der Erde,* the *Misterioso* from the first movement of the Ninth, and the fugatos from the Rondo-Burlesque of the Ninth all seem to anticipate the linear style of the Twenties. They show Mahler as an artist far ahead of his time. Yet even in the late symphonies, passages that are conceived more homophonically occur beside the linear-polyphonic ones.

3. Some writers like to speak of a tendency toward a chamber music style in Mahler's late works. This formulation is vague and therefore inappropriate. It would be more fitting to say that in his later works Mahler intentionally includes passages that are scored as chamber music. Examples exist in *Das Lied von der Erde,* the *Misterioso* from the first movement of the Ninth, and the development in the first movement of the Adagio from the Tenth. However, sections orchestrated as chamber music also occur in works from the early and middle periods, the difference between these and the late works being one of degree.

4. It is typical for the late works that none closes in a glorifying, affirmative manner, an apotheosis. *Das Lied von der Erde* as well as the first and last movements of the Ninth and the Tenth die away, fade away, subside *pianissimo.* Their codas express the thought of *morendo.* Their endings are, so to speak, ethereal. Mahler himself spoke of the ethereal ending of the slow movement of the Fourth Symphony. This manner results from a poetic rather than programmatic intention.

Das Lied von der Erde
("The Song of the Earth")

> I have been very industrious (which tells you that I
> have 'acclimatized' quite well). I do not know what
> the whole work might be named. A wonderful time
> was granted to me and I think it is probably the most
> personal [composition] I have created thus far.
>
> GMB² 347f.

Autobiographical Background

The above sentences from a letter by Mahler to Bruno Walter refer to *Das Lied von der Erde*. Mahler composed it during 1907 and 1908, under circumstances that support his statement that it was probably the most personal work he had created up until then. More than with most of his other works, a knowledge of the autobiographical background is essential for a thorough understanding of the composition.

The year 1907 no doubt marked a turning point in Mahler's personal and creative life. It would not be an overstatement to say that the happenings of that year profoundly influenced his fate.

By May of 1907, Mahler had already toyed with the idea of resigning from his position as Vienna Court Opera director to accept an attractive offer from New York in order to have more time to compose. In June he met in Berlin with the director of the Metropolitan Opera, Heinrich Conried, and negotiated with him.[1] In Vienna he then asked for his release, which was promptly granted. In the second half of June, like every year, the Mahler family went to Maiernigg. There Maria Anna, Mahler's oldest little daughter, became sick with scarlet-fever diphtheria. In spite of a tracheotomy, she died on 12 July (AME 153f.). Alma's memoirs help us understand the extent of the traumatic shock suffered by Alma, Mahler, and his mother-in-law on account of this sad happening. A few days later the district physician in Maiernigg, Dr. Blumenthal, diagnosed a grave heart condition for Mahler, which troubled the composer deeply. He took the next train to Vienna to consult Professor Kovacs[2] The famous professor verified Dr. Blumenthal's diagnosis ("bilateral valvular defect from birth, although compensated") and recommended to Mahler, who was a passionate athlete, a "terrain treatment (*Terrainkur*), in order to get used to 'walking'" (AME 155).

To get some distance from these happenings, the Mahler family left Maiernigg and fled to Schluderbach in Tyrol. Here Mahler engrossed himself in *The Chinese Flute* by Hans Bethge, a collection of freely translated Chinese lyrics published in 1907 by Insel-Verlag in Leipzig[3] Mahler already had greatly enjoyed these poems and had "put them aside for later" (AME 156). According to Alma,

> Now, after the death of the child, after the terrible diagnosis of the doctor, in the mood of frightful loneliness, away from our house, away from his place of work (from which we had fled)—now these exceedingly sad poems took hold of him. Already in Schluderbach, on long, lonely walks, he sketched the orchestra songs that one year later were to become *Das Lied von der Erde*.

We do not know how far Mahler got with the sketching of the songs during that summer. However, we hear from Alma that he worked on them "feverishly" the entire summer of the following year[4] The work grew as he composed:

> He connected the individual texts, composed interludes, and the enlarged forms pulled him more and more to his original form—the symphony. When he realized that this would again be a kind of symphony, the work soon acquired its shape and was completed before he knew it (AME 175).

Alma also reported that he did not dare call it a symphony because he had an outright, superstitious "fear of the idea of a Ninth Symphony" (AME 145). He firmly held to the superstition "that no great symphonic writer was to live beyond his Ninth" (AME 146). Therefore, even after the completion of the work (as is evident from the letter to Bruno Walter quoted at the beginning) he was not sure what he should name it. At first he thought of the title *Das Lied vom Jammer der Erde* ("The Song of the Misery on Earth") (AME 176); later he provided the subtitle "Symphony for Tenor and Alto Voice and Orchestra."[5]

Alma Mahler, Richard Specht, and Bruno Walter all confirm that Mahler's condition after the diagnosis of his heart problem decisively affected the concept of *Das Lied von der Erde*. "All of his sorrow, his fear, he put into this work," according to Alma (AME 176); and Specht, who was well informed, writes that at the time in question, Mahler was overwhelmed by the feeling of "having to say farewell."

> "Frightened by the carelessly brutal words of a physician, he thought of himself as being close to death. In this mood, everything about life appeared to him to be painfully and intensely colored. This mood brought

him to the quietly subdued yet hardly bearable words and sounds of his work, which, with its pantheistic feeling toward nature and the world, might be called *Das Lied von der Erde* but just as well might be called *Das Lied vom Irdischen* (meaning mortal), the earthly to which one must say farewell.[6]

Bruno Walter called *Das Lied von der Erde* "a creation *sub specie mortis.*"[7]

Arrangement of the Poems

The Chinese Flute consists of no less than 83 poems.[8] It is possible that Mahler read them all. At any rate, he chose seven eighth-century poems from the collection of Bethge that contrast strongly with each other in thought and mood and yet still form a whole. He undertook numerous changes, gave new titles to some, and added verses of his own.

Four poems are by Li-Tai-Po (701–763), the most famous ancient Chinese lyric poet: No. 1 *Das Trinklied vom Jammer der Erde* ("The Drinking Song About the Misery of the Earth"), No. 3 *Von der Jugend* ("Regarding Youth"), No. 4 *Von der Schönheit* ("Regarding Beauty"), and No. 5 *Der Trunkene im Frühling* ("The Drunkard in Spring"). Three of these poems bear other titles in Bethge: No. 3 is called *Der Pavillon aus Porzellan* ("The Porcelain Pavilion"), No. 4 *Am Ufer* ("At the Shore"), No. 5 *Der Trinker im Frühling* ("The Drunkard in Spring"). Mahler replaced the "realistic" titles by more general or more poetic ones.[9] The author of No. 2 (*Der Einsame im Herbst*) ["The Lonely One in Autumn"] is Tchang-Tsi, and No. 6 (*Der Abschied*) ["The Farewell"] is based on two poems, one by Mong-Kao-Jen and the other by Wang-Wei, the two poets being friends. Bethge's titles are *In Erwartung des Freundes* ("Expecting the Friend") and *Der Abschied des Freundes* ("The Friend's Farewell").

How did Mahler combine these poems? A careful reading reveals various correspondences between Nos. 1 and 6, between Nos. 2 and 5, and between Nos. 3 and 4.

The basic theme of *Das Lied von der Erde* (the title is Mahler's) is the love of nature and life, the futility of all things, but above all the mortality of mankind who cannot enjoy even for a "hundred years" "an all dem morschen Tande dieser Erde [all the decayed trinkets of this earth]" (No. 1), while the "dear earth" again grows green and blossoms everywhere in spring (No. 6). Looking back, nostalgia and saying farewell are the central emotional and spiritual themes of the work. *Dunkel ist das Leben, ist der Tod!* (Dark is life, is death!)—this maxim of Li-Tai-Po forms the center of the first song. *Nur Ein Besitztum ist dir ganz gewiß: das ist das Grab, das grinsende, am Ende* (You can be sure of but one possession: that is the grave, grinning, at the end). Mahler did not set these verses by Li-Tai-Po to music![10]

Regarding Li-Tai-Po, Hans Bethge wrote:

"Transience" is the name of the continually admonishing imprint of his feelings. He drinks to stun his melancholy, but in reality he only drifts into new melancholy. He drinks and reaches for the stars, full of longing. His art is earthly and at the same time supernatural.[11]

Nos. 2 and 5 correspond to each other through their opposite nature, as paradoxical as this may sound: No. 2 is an autumn song, full of melancholy; No. 5 is a spring song. For dramaturgical reasons Mahler placed it as No. 5 because he needed a strong contrast before his requiem-like Finale.

Nos. 3 and 4, both idyllic, belong together in a certain way. The youth and beauty they sing about are pretense and remembrance. Life is a dream (No. 5); the drunk one seeks to forget in wine. The verses inserted by Mahler in No. 6 offer a kind of key for a deeper understanding of the cycle. They are taken from a poem of his youth (December 1884)[12] and read: *Die müden Menschen geh'n heimwärts, um im Schlaf vergess'nes Glück und Jugend neu zu lernen!* (The tired people go home to learn bliss and youth anew in their sleep).

Mahler's numerous changes of the original texts reveal a fine literary sense.[13] Most of them deepen the content of the poetry. For example, in No. 5 Mahler replaced the rather pale verse *Ich seufze tief ergriffen auf* [I sigh in deep emotion] with *Aus tiefstem Schauen lauscht' ich auf* (From profound observation I harken attentively). A few verses earlier he made a seemingly unimportant change, which, however, is very significant. While Li-Tai-Po says *Und wenn ich nicht mehr trinken kann, / Weil Leib und Kehle voll* (And when I cannot drink anymore, / Because body and throat are full), Mahler writes *Und wenn ich nicht mehr trinken kann, / Weil Kehl' und Seele voll* (And when I cannot drink anymore, / Because throat and soul are full). Finally, there is the extremely suggestive verse inserted in No. 6: *O Schönheit! O ewigen Liebens—Lebens—trunk'ne Welt!* (Oh beauty! Oh world drunk with eternal loving and living!).

Except for the letter to Bruno Walter quoted at the beginning, we have no written comment by Mahler regarding *Das Lied von der Erde*. A sentence from a letter to his wife (10 September 1908) refers to it indirectly. Alluding to a comment made by a trumpeter who had difficulties with his part while Mahler was rehearsing the Seventh in Prague, Mahler writes:

This comment immediately made me think of the inner being of this man. He cannot comprehend his own *life of misery,* always struggling with the highest muted tones; he cannot see what this is all about and how this screeching fits into the symphony of the world, into the great chord" (AME 414).

When Mahler wrote this letter in Prague he had already completed the composition of *Das Lied von der Erde*.

A Symphony of Songs, Small and Large

As mentioned, Mahler considered *Das Lied von der Erde* to be a symphony rather than a song cycle. Investigating what might have moved him to give the work the subtitle *A Symphony* may help us to understand his concept of symphonic writing.

As we all know, it is not easy to define the term *Lied* (song). Nevertheless the term suggests a piece of moderate dimensions, basically lyric in mood, clearly melodious, and fairly simple. The middle movements of *Das Lied von der Erde* (Nos. 2–5) contain some of these characteristics: the dimensions are easily comprehended, Nos. 2–4 (No. 4 only in part) are lyrical, and in many places the vocal melody is clearly songlike. Beside this, the music of Nos. 2 and 5 displays strophic structure.

In contrast, the outer movements cannot be considered to be *songs*; "vocal pieces" (*Gesänge*) seems more appropriate. Their dimensions are considerable (with 405 and 572 measures they last approximately 10 and 30 minutes, respectively); both present a sonata-like structure; both contain development-like passages and fairly long orchestral interludes, all of which exceeds normal song dimensions. The mood of the concluding song (a movement that begins like a dirge) is hardly songlike in character, and fairly long interludes acting as developments also characterize the middle section of No. 4.

Larger dimensions, important orchestral interludes, the sonata-like structure of the outer movements—these features surely made Mahler aware of the symphonic concept of his work. Alma confirms this indirectly when she says: "He connected the individual texts and provided interludes, and the extended forms drew him more and more to his original form—to the symphony" (AME 175). The symphonic character of the cycle also is underscored by the motivic, thematic connections between the movements. Some of these reminiscences and allusions so far have been ignored.

Thus *Das Lied von der Erde* can indeed be understood as a kind of symphony: two massive outer movements framing a slow movement (No. 2) and three interludes, one of which (No. 3) has a distinct scherzando character.

Musical Material and Exoticism

The strong impression of unity and compactness that *Das Lied von der Erde* makes on the listener is largely due to the choice of musical material. Pentatonic scales and certain three-note constellations occur in all movements. Josef V. von Wöss had recognized this in 1912.[14] He noticed that the "pentachord" characterizes certain passages of Nos. 3 and 4, and he spoke of a "basic motif" (consisting of a major second and a minor third) found in all parts of the work, "sometimes clearly exposed as such; sometimes disguised or as a part of another related motif; sometimes enlarged, diminished, or rhythmically changed or inverted or in retrograde, but always clearly recognizable." Several decades later, Dieter Schnebel noted that these tone rows provided "in quasi serial form the material for the most varied structures."[15] More recently Uwe Baur pointed out two things: first, pentatonic formations occur in five movements (No. 2 is an exception); second, three measures after No. 68 "the complete pentatonic scale C—D—E—G—A occurs simultaneously.[16]

Undoubtedly Mahler gave a special place to pentatonicism in the structural plan of *Das Lied von der Erde* to establish the ancient Chinese tonal coloring. However, pentatonicism is by no means the domineering tonal system. It would be better to say that it holds its own next to major-minor tonality. Aside from movements and passages that are clearly in major or in minor or both, there are those that display the ambiguity of mode so typical of Mahler.

What are the roots of Mahler's exoticism? Uwe Baur believed that Mahler surely had some knowledge of Chinese music, since music history books at the close of the nineteenth century dealt with this music. The turn of the century also witnessed a great vogue of Chinese literature, which had also put Bethge's text rewritings into Mahler's hands. It is far more likely that he received the decisive stimulus from Giacomo Puccini's *Madama Butterfly* (1904), a work Mahler performed for the first time at the Vienna Court Opera on 31 October 1907.[17]

One might also mention that *Das Lied von der Erde* contains three whole-tone passages. They do not represent exoticism, as one might think, but serve as illustration and tone painting. As Adorno already noticed, the first passage (No. 1, mm. 317–319) accompanies the "decayed trinkets" of this earth.[18] The second, a unison figure in the strings (No. 1, mm. 366–367), is less significant. The third passage (No. 6, mm. 453–459) illustrates the roaming to faraway places which was mentioned shortly before.

Das Trinklied vom Jammer der Erde ("The Drinking Song About the Misery of the Earth")

Hans Bethge's text version of *The Drinking Song about the Misery of the Earth* consists of four stanzas of seven, eight, eight, and seven lines. The four stanzas all close with the refrain: *Dunkel ist das Leben, ist der Tod* (Dark is life, is death). The song ends with the invitation to empty the golden goblets to the bottom. The actual toast, however, is a "Song of Sorrow" focused on the *Vanitas* thought, the vanity of everything mortal:

> *Ein voller Becher Weins zur rechten Zeit*
> *Ist mehr wert als die Reiche dieser Erde.*
> . . . .

> *Das Firmament blaut ewig, und die Erde*
> *Wird lange feststeh'n auf den alten Füßen.*
> *Du aber, Mensch, wie lange lebst denn du?*
> *Nicht hundert Jahre darfst du dich ergötzen*
> *An all dem morschen Tande dieser Erde.*

> A goblet full of wine at the right time
> Is worth more than all the kingdoms of this earth!
> . . . .
> The firmament is eternally blue, and the earth
> Will long endure upon its ancient feet.
> But you, oh man, how long do you live?
> Not even a hundred years can you enjoy
> The decayed trinkets of this earth.

In the last stanza Li-Tai-Po provided a shrill accent with the image of a wild, ghostlike figure, a monkey that squats in the moonlight on the graves and whose howling pierces the sweet fragrance of the evening.

Mahler replaced the last word, *evening,* with *life* and also made numerous other changes. He rearranged verses and words and changed several parts of lines. Thus he substituted "und die Erde / Wird lange fest steh'n und aufblüh'n im Lenz (and the earth / Will long endure and blossom in spring) and, most importantly, he left out three lines of the third stanza:

> *Nur Ein Besitztum ist dir ganz gewiß:*
> *Das ist das Grab, das grinsende, am Ende.*
> *Dunkel ist das Leben, ist der Tod.*

> There is but one possession you can be sure of:
> That is the grave, the grinning one, at the end.
> Dark is life, is death.

In this manner he contracted the last two stanzas of the original into one that is considerably longer than the first two; they include six or eight lines; the contracted stanza totals twelve. Mahler most likely did not use the three lines quoted for two reasons, one being that the musical refrain was to be repeated only twice (not three times). Second, the aphorism of the grinning grave was incompatible with his religious world view. He believed strongly in the continuation of life after death.

The form of the composition can be described as a kind of synthesis of strophic structure and sonata-allegro form. The movement clearly has four parts: exposition, varied repeat of the exposition, development, and varied recapitulation. The first two stanzas correspond with the two exposition parts, while the lines of the more extensive third stanza are spread over development and recapitulation.

First Exposition (= first stanza)

Mm.   1–32   First section in A minor
      33–52   Transition
     353–80   Secondary section in D minor and G minor
     381–88   Refrain in G minor

Second Exposition (= second stanza)

     89–124   First section
    125–136   Transition
    137–152   Interpolated passage beginning in B-flat major and ending in
               C-flat major
    153–182   Secondary section in E-flat minor and A-flat minor
    183–202   Refrain in A-flat minor/A-flat major

Development (Arioso character)
(third stanza, lines 1–2)

    203–229   First section
    230–260   Second section
    261–284   Third section
    285–292   Transition

Recapitulation (third stanza, lines 3–12)

    293–325   Secondary section beginning in B-flat minor
    326–372   First section
    373–392   Refrain in A minor/A major
    393–405   Postlude

The sonata-form model is maintained in that during the expositions a
transitional passage connects the first and secondary sections. Furthermore,
the secondary section is followed by a conclusion, provided by the refrain.
Even at a first hearing one notices that the strong contrast between first and
secondary sections is established motivically, thematically, dynamically, and
by their respective characters. The first section is quite expansive, bringing
call-like motifs in the horns and three-tone or pseudo-pentatonic constellations in the strings:

Mm. 1–9

The tender secondary section, however, revolves around but a few notes:

Mm. 56–65

A detailed analysis reveals that Mahler employed the following compositional principle: the active, enthusiastic, and energetic lines are assigned to the first sections, and the reflecting, meditative lines occur in the secondary sections. This explains why he reversed the parts in the recapitulation and placed the secondary section first ("But you, oh man, how long will you be living?"). The image of the wild, ghostly figure, however, was set to music from the first section.

The development is clearly divided into three sections and a transition and is for the most part treated as an orchestral interlude that bears the character of an instrumental arioso. Over a tremolo foundation in some of the strings, the first trumpet, English horn, first violins, and first clarinet perform call-like motifs or arioso melodic arches that are at times contrapuntally combined.[19] *Forte* and *fortissimo* outbursts are remarkably rare, *piano* being the prevailing dynamic of the development, which is not geared toward a climax, but rather an aura of mystery.

The refrain offers a key to a fuller understanding of the tectonic and tonal disposition. At the close of the first exposition, it is heard in G minor, A minor being the basic key of the movement:

Mm. 81–89

At the end of the second exposition (mm. 183–202) it returns in A-flat minor/A-flat major, and at the end of the recapitulation (mm. 373–392) in A minor/A major. This progression brings about an intensification and at the same time determines the key relationships of the secondary sections in the two parts of the exposition.

Der Einsame im Herbst ("The Lonely One in Autumn")

The four stanzas of the poem by Tchang-Tsi relate an autumn landscape to the psychic condition of a lonely person. The poetic images suggest winter, sleep, and death, although winter and death are not explicitly mentioned. The need of the lonely one to sleep and rest may, however, be interpreted as a longing for death: *Sonne der Liebe, willst du nie mehr scheinen / Um meine bittern Tränen mild aufzutrocknen?* (Sun of love, will you nevermore shine / To tenderly dry my bitter tears?)"[20] The question is rhetorical, and the mood in which Mahler's composition fades away is bleak.

Among the songs and other vocal pieces of *Das Lied von der Erde,* "The Lonely One in Autumn" occupies an exceptional position, not only because the song is scored in chamber style, calling for a very modest number of players,[21] but because it also demonstrates a kind of linear polyphony that is unique even when one considers that Mahler set a precedent for it in the third of the *Kindertotenlieder* (Songs on the Death of Children).

In No. 2 of *Das Lied von der Erde,* the voices seem to have been set in a completely linear way, independent of each other. The manner of writing is mostly characterized by melodic lines in the woodwinds and the first horn set off against a background. This background is often provided by the *etwas schleichend* (somewhat stealthy) eighth-note movement of the muted first violins, symbolizing circling, indifference, sameness. A somewhat monotonous but very expressive melody of the first oboe determines the physiognomy of the movement:

The first four measures of this melody are later taken up by the first clarinet:

Mm. 25–28

Here in the fourth measure, the note A is changed to A-flat. This lowering, along with the entire disposition of the melody, points to its distant archetype: the *traurige Weise* (sad tune) of the English horn in the third act of *Tristan*, the symbol of immeasurable sorrow and bleakness.[22]

The construction of the song is simple and clearly arranged:

Mm.   1–24   Prelude
      25–49   First Stanza
      50–77   Second Stanza
      78–101   Third Stanza
     102–137   Fourth Stanza
     138–154   Postlude

Mahler based the four stanzas of the poem on a musical model stanza containing one minor and one major complex, a stanza that is strongly modified at every repeat, indeed newly realized. This means that the material of the stanza is newly arranged, regrouped, changed, developed further, illuminated in a new way, scored differently, and equipped with other new features. All stanzas are musically different. As a composer of songs, Mahler discovered a unique path between strophic structure and through-composition, a path that establishes his own uniqueness.

The unprecedented fluctuation of expression in this song is also reflected in the numerous performance markings. Melodies in the minor complex are to be played *molto espressivo* (m. 3, first oboe; m. 9, first clarinet) or *with great expression* (m. 29, first oboe). For some motifs Mahler indicates *without expression*.[23] Phrases from the major complex, however, are marked *warm* (m. 37, oboes and clarinets), *zart leidenschaftlich* (with gentle passion) (mm. 70–71, violins), *innig* (tender) (m. 92, voice), and *mit voller Empfindung, leidenschaftlich* (with full emotion and passion) (m. 121–123, voice).

The dynamic and emotional climax of the song occurs at measures 128–135, the passage being marked *with great impetus*. It is followed immediately (mm. 136–137) by a passage marked *without expression*. The musical answer to Tchang-Tsi's question is: The sun of love does not shine. The song fades away in grief, *morendo*.

Von der Jugend ("Regarding Youth")

Among the four Li-Tai-Po poems that Mahler set to music in *Das Lied von der Erde,* "The Porcelain Pavilion" is undoubtedly the daintiest and most elegant. The pavilion made of green and white porcelain symbolizes culture, youth, beauty, and an elegant way of life. In the pavilion, beautiful and extravagantly dressed friends meet, drink, converse, and write verses.

The structure of the poem is musical. The first two stanzas describe the pavilion and the bridge that leads to it. The next two stanzas indicate what happens in the pavilion, while the final three deal with the appearance of the reflected image. Just as in a recapitulation, the motifs of the bridge, the friends, and the pavilion return.

This graceful poem inspired Mahler to compose a picturesque genre painting that has primarily a scherzando character. In many places woodwind timbre is dominant in music distinguished by agility and charm. The piccolo determines the tone color of the whole. The preferred articulation markings are *staccato* and *saltando,* and the music operates mostly in middle or high ranges. Those who have referred to Mahler's music as being "without bass" would enjoy this movement. The lower range is only rarely explored; the double basses add only individual dots of pizzicato.

The composition presents a da capo layout according to the scheme A (mm. 1–34)—B (mm. 35–96)—A¹ (mm. 97–118): two similar but not identical outer parts frame a longer middle part. The pentatonic coloring of the outer movements is unmistakable, yet there is no pure pentatonic writing.

Mm. 3–6

Mm. 13–18

In the middle part, the first four measures of the vocal line take on the function of an instrumental refrain. They also appear in variations and alternate with melodious, *legato* sections.

Mm. 39–47

The predominantly scherzando character of the music disappears in the fifth stanza (mm. 70–96, *Ruhiger* [more quiet]); Mahler sets the story of the strange reflection image in minor. In this piece he is fond of writing chains of broad harmonic areas in an impressionistic manner, at times through harmonies with common thirds. The harmonic rhythm is quite slow, and the tonal scheme is B-flat major (m. 6), G major (m. 35), E major (m. 55), E minor (m. 59), G major (m. 68), G minor (m. 70), G major (m. 92), G minor (m. 94), and B-flat major (m. 97).

The orchestra does without trombones and timpani while the triangle adds a special touch to the piece. Bass drum and cymbals are used very sparingly, and the trumpet is heard in only four measures (mm. 35–36 and mm. 47–48).

Von der Schönheit ("Regarding Beauty")

Li-Tai-Po's poem *At the Riverbank* tells of young girls picking lotus flowers, of handsome lads that trot along on valiant horses, and of yearning love. Mahler made so many changes in this poem that Ernest W. Mulder rightly spoke of it as a paraphrase.[24] Especially the pictures of lads trotting along and horses dashing away must have been very important to Mahler because he made two stanzas out of Li-Tai-Po's third stanza. His text therefore contains five stanzas instead of the original four. Let us compare the third stanza of Li-Tai-Po to the two stanzas by Mahler:

Li-Tai-Po
Sieh, was tummeln sich für schöne Knaben
An dem Uferrand auf mutigen Rossen?
Zwischen dem Geäst der Trauerweiden
Traben sie einher. Das Roß des einen
Wiehert auf und scheut und saust dahin
Und zerstampft die hingesunkenen Blüten.

Oh, see what handsome lads are playing
There on the edge of the shore on valiant steeds.
Among the branches of the weeping willows
They trot along. The steed of the one
Whinnies, shies and dashes away
And tramples the fallen blossoms.

Mahler
O, sieh, was tummeln sich für schöne Knaben
Dort an dem Uferrand auf mut'gen Rossen,
Weithin glänzend wie die Sonnenstrahlen;
Schon zwischen dem Geäst der grünen Weiden
Trabt das jungfrische Volk einher!

Das Roß des einen wiehert fröhlich auf,
Und scheut und saust dahin,
Über Blumen, Gräser wanken hin die Hufe,
Sie zerstampfen jäh im Sturm die hingesunk'nen Blüten
Hei! Wie flattern im Taumel seine Mähnen,
Dampfen Heiß die Nüstern!

Oh, see what handsome lads are playing
There on the edge of the shore on valiant steeds,
Glistening from afar like rays of the sun;
Between the green branches of the willows
The lively, young folk are trotting along!
The steed of the one whinnies happily,
Shies and dashes away;
Over flowers and grasses the hooves are moving,
They suddenly trample the fallen blossoms as in a storm.
Ho! Its mane flies in a frenzy,
With nostrils hotly steaming!

Mahler constructed the movement in three parts. He used the first two stanzas for the main section, the two following stanzas for the development-like middle section, and the last stanza for the varied recapitulation. The following presents a formal outline:

Main section

Mm.	1–6	Introduction
	7–13	First (pentatonic) theme in G major
	13–22	Second theme in G major
	22–29	Again the first theme in G major
	30–42	Third theme in E major and B major

Development-like middle section

43–52	First section (developed from motifs of the introduction)
53–61	Second section: Più mosso subito (marchlike): pentatonic theme and the lads' theme from the third movement
62–74	Third section: *Noch etwas flotter* (Still a little faster) (lads' theme)
75–87	Fourth section: Allegro (modification of the pentatonic and the lads' theme)
88–95	Fifth section

Varied recapitulation

96–103	First theme in B-flat major
104–114	Third theme in G major
114–124	Second theme in G major
124–144	Postlude

The main section musically paints the picture of the flower-gathering girls. As the outline indicates, it consists of an introduction and three themes that are unified though each has its own character. The charm of the introduction is reminiscent of the flower movement from the Third Symphony.

The first theme is pentatonically tinted (the melody of the first flute, first oboe, and first clarinet heard simultaneously, is purely pentatonic).

Mm. 6–13

The second theme is folklike,

Mm. 13–22

Wave lines characterize the third theme:

Mm. 32–35

The development-like middle section, clearly divided into five parts, is directed toward a climax as the tempo markings indicate. Strangely enough it has so far escaped notice that Mahler not only develops the pentatonic theme of the beginning but also states and develops the lads' theme of No. 3. A few examples may demonstrate the connections:

Von der Jugend, mm. 41–44

Von der Schönheit, mm. 61–63

Mm. 82–84

Mm. 87–90

Here then Mahler's music combines the pentatonic girls' theme with the impetuous lads' theme and generally accomplishes the ultimate in tone-coloring and drastic expression. The picture of trotting is musically expressed by repeated notes of the muted horns and trumpets (mm. 70–71); harsh voice leading and dissonance suggest ugliness, and trombones and tuba play the once-so-gentle pentatonic theme, but now *roh* (roughly) and in minor (mm. 74–79). Josef V. von Wöss stated with good reason that the Allegro section of the movement was among Mahler's most realistic creations.[25]

For this middle section, Mahler needed the full orchestra: piccolo, triple woodwinds, four horns, two trumpets, three trombones, tuba, timpani, tambourine, bass drum, cymbal, mandolins, harps, and strings. During the entire *Das Lied von der Erde* the timpani play only at this point.

A few further comments regarding the recapitulation: Bethge's last stanza consists of five lines while Mahler's has eight. Mahler wrote one additional line (*In dem Dunkel ihres heißen Blicks* [In the darkness of her fervid glance]) and preceded the whole by two lines that he took from the second stanza: *Gold'ne Sonne webt um die Gestalten, / Spiegelt sie im blanken Wasser wider* (The golden sun weaves around the forms / Reflecting them in the still water). He thus emphasized the effect of recapitulation served by the stanza. It is typical that Mahler reversed the sequence of the themes in the recapitulation: the first theme is followed by the third and then the second theme.

Der Trunkene im Frühling ("The Drunkard in Spring")

Li-Tai-Po's poem "The Drunkard in Spring" is a thoughtful humoresque, a drinking song against the backdrop of the *Vanitas* idea. The realization that life is a dream and that all striving is in vain drives a person not only to drink but also to indifference toward everything, even toward spring. He drinks excessively in order to forget. Of the poem's six stanzas, the first two describe the drunken condition. The two middle ones introduce the motif of the bird who announces the arrival of spring, while the last two stanzas, which seem to function as a recapitulation, make it clear that even this news cannot awaken the drunk one.

Of all movements of *Das Lied von der Erde,* the fifth is the brightest. The sharp key, A major, has a special brightness of its own, and Mahler's instrumentation shows that he was eager to achieve an especially brilliant, intense sound. The violin and harp glissandi (mm. 15–16 and mm. 72–73) serve this purpose, along with the running passages in the postlude (mm. 87–89). Subtle connections with the first movement reveal that Mahler understood the movement to be a kind of companion piece to *The Drinking Song About the Misery of the Earth.* Thus a horn call attracts attention at the beginning of several stanzas:

Mm. 1–2

The formal organization of the movement is determined by the structure of the stanzas. Mahler based the whole on a model stanza, musically bilateral, that (returning five times) is varied, paraphrased, and reshaped. It consists of a main thought and a contrasting secondary thought; small intervals and pronounced rhythms determine the character of the main thought, and large intervals (sixths, sevenths, and octaves) determine the character of the secondary thought. Here are four measures of the secondary thought:

Mm. 8–11

Stanzas	Main thought	Secondary thought
1st stanza (mm. 1–14)	A major/B-flat major	F major
2nd stanza (mm. 15–28)	A major/B-flat major	F major
3rd stanza (mm. 29–44)	A major	A major-minor
4th stanza (mm. 45–64)	F major/B-flat major	D-flat major
5th stanza (mm. 65–71)	—	C major
6th stanza (mm. 72–87)	A major/B-flat major	F major
Postlude (mm. 87–89)	A major	—

It should be mentioned that the first, second, and sixth stanzas are by no means identical, in spite of their similar basic structure. Mahler composes a new model stanza each time, and in the fifth stanza he altogether omits the main thought. For those who wish to study Mahler's variation technique, this movement presents excellent material.

Li-Tai-Po's poem offers ample opportunities for musical illustration, and Mahler makes good use of them. Thus the somewhat strange modulation from A major to B-flat major (at the beginning of the first, second, and sixth stanzas) illustrates the staggering of the drunkard. Likewise there are prominent bird-call motifs in the third and fourth stanzas. The motifs of the solo violin (mm. 31–33), piccolo (mm. 41–44), and woodwinds (mm. 51–64) serve that purpose. Interestingly enough, the solo violin plays fragments from the Andante amoroso of the Seventh Symphony:

Seventh Symphony, *Andante amoroso,* mm. 76–80

Das Lied von der Erde, mm. 31–33

Der Abschied ("The Farewell")

> The basic motif of all tragic situations is the
> actual passing away, and there is need for
> neither poison nor dagger, neither spear nor
> sword. Having to depart from a familiar,
> beloved, rightful condition, caused more or less
> by coercion, by a hated power, is a variation on
> that same theme.
>
> Goethe[26]

The two poems by Mong-Kao-Jen and Wang-Wei that Mahler combined
in the final song of *Das Lied von der Erde* were entitled *In Expectation of
the Friend* and *The Friend's Farewell* by Bethge. They have the same origin.
As Bethge explains, Wang-Wei was the friend whom Mong-Kao-Jen
expected; he had addressed his poem to Mong-Kao-Jen. Therefore the
second poem refers to the first.[27]

Mahler made numerous changes in these two poems and enlarged them
as well. Ernest Mulder, who compared the versions, again spoke of
paraphrases.[28] It is certain that Bethge's texts gained much through Mahler's
interventions. While Wang-Wei leaves it open whether the described farewell
is a farewell from the friend or from life in general. Mahler's text seems to be
more definite. Let up compare the crucial passages of the text:

Wang-Wei
Wohin ich geh? Ich wandre in die Berge,
Ich suche Ruhe für mein einsam Herz.
Ich werde nie mehr in die Ferne schweifen,
Müd ist mein Fuß, und müd ist meine Seele,
Die Erde ist die gleiche überall,
Und ewig, ewig sind die weißen Wolken ...

Whither shall I go? I wander to the mountains;
I seek rest for my lonely heart.
I will nevermore roam afar.
Tired is my foot and tired is my soul,
The earth is the same everywhere,
And eternal, eternal are the white clouds ...

Mahler
Wohin ich geh'? Ich geh', ich wandre in die Berge,
Ich suche Ruhe für mein einsam Herz!
Ich wandle nach der Heimat, meiner Stätte!
Ich werde niemals in die Ferne schweifen.
Still ist mein Herz und harret seiner Stunde!
Die liebe Erde allüberall blüht auf im Lenz und grünt

Aufs neu! Allüberall und ewig blauen licht die Fernen.
Ewig . . . ewig . . .

Whither shall I go? I go, I wander to the mountains,
I seek rest for my lonely heart!
I wander to my homeland, my home!
I will never roam afar.
My heart is quiet and awaits its hour!
Everywhere the dear earth blossoms in spring and becomes green
Anew! The blue horizon shines everywhere and eternally
Eternally . . . eternally . . .

Mahler's additions, according to which the one departing goes toward home awaiting his hour, are significant, as is the reference to the blooming of the "dear" earth in spring, to the eternal cycle. Mahler's music makes it even clearer that the departure spoken of here is the one from life: the two long sections marked *schwer* (heavy) (mm. 1–54 and 303–429) in part remind one of a funeral procession or even a requiem. In both, the tam-tam determines the music's somber mood.

"The Farewell" is not only the longest movement of *The Song of the Earth* (it takes almost as long as all the previous movements together), it is also the most substantial. It therefore seems logical that Mahler structured it according to the model of sonata form which, however, here is basically in two parts. The exposition is followed by the recapitulation, which contains aspects of a development. This dualism arises from the correspondence of the two poems that Mahler combined.

Exposition

Mm.		
1–54	First section (*Schwer* [heavy], four-four meter)	
1–18		First part
19–54		Second part (beginning like a recitative)
55–165	Secondary section (*Sehr mäßig* [very moderate], Alla breve)	
55–97		First part
98–136		Second part
137–157		Third part
158–165	Recitative with flute solo	
166–287	Closing section (*Fließend,* [flowing], three-four meter)	
166–198		First part
199–244		Second part
245–287		Third part
288–302	Epilogue (*Mäßig* [moderate], Alla breve)	

Varied recapitulation

303–429	Development-like extended first section	
303–373		First part

374–429   Second part (recitative-like beginning)
430–459 Secondary section (shortened)
460–508 Closing section
460–489   First part
490–508   Second part
509–572 Coda (in the voice part the word *ewig* [eternally] occurs seven times

As the outline demonstrates, the sonata-like structure is evident.[29] The correspondence between exposition and varied (partly extended, partly shortened) recapitulation is obvious. In the exposition, three theme-complexes are quite clearly defined. These differ in tempo, meter, and key. While C minor is the basic key of the first section, the secondary section is in F major, and the closing section is in B-flat major.

Mahler's manner of distributing the verses of the first poem over the sections of the exposition is worth studying. The first section consists of a prelude and a recitative and arioso-like section that musically pictures the evening mood. Among the three parts of the secondary section, the first one illustrates the singing of the brook, the second represents the longing that wants to dream now and the tired people who are going home. The third part at first imitates bird-calls[30] and then pictorially evokes an image of the world asleep.[31] The actual waiting for the friend is set as a recitative. The final movement gives expression to the longing for the friend and the "drunken world."

To find out what creates the incomparable urgency of this movement, one might begin by observing the extreme contrast existing between the first section on the one hand and the secondary and closing sections on the other, a contrast that can only be inadequately described as one between heaviness and lightness, darkness and brightness, elegy and lyricism, halting tunes and endless melody, heaviness or metric and rhythmic instability.

To state it more concretely: The first section does not modulate, but is bound to the basic key of C minor (and also to C major). The low C is sustained over long stretches like a pedal point. The threnodic melody (interspersed with rests) develops from a "turn" figure of the oboe and of sighs (in thirds) in the accompanying instruments.

The voice enters with a unique recitative that is accompanied by the low C of the cellos and a rhythmically free cantilena of the first flute:

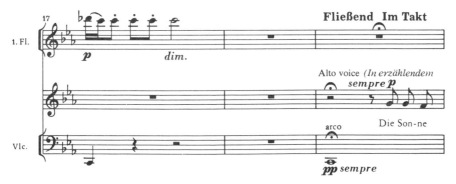

The mood is temporarily lightened with the reference to the rising moon.

Secondary and closing sections are clearly distinct, yet they have much in common. Both are divided into three sections, each beginning in the same key (F major or B-flat major), but frequently modulating. In both cases the basically subdued emotion at times takes on passionate, even ecstatic features. Both furnish examples of Mahler's unmistakable linear polyphony, both are characterized by polyrhythms, and in melody and rhythm both ignore the bar lines. Two short examples follow, the first from the secondary section:

The second is from the closing section. Note the deceptive cadences that emphasize the impression of "unending melody":

The recapitulation is partly extended and partly shortened. The first section now numbers 127 measures (only 54 in the exposition); but the secondary and closing sections are much shortened.[32] The changes (which in part are due to the brevity of Wang-Wei's poem) do not affect the correspondence between exposition and recapitulation. The parallels among the sections as to their themes and forms are unmistakable.

In comparing the two first sections (mm. 1–54 and mm. 303–429), one recognizes that they relate to each other just as a sketch relates to a full realization. Not only are the motifs treated more broadly, but the expressive content is greatly increased. The elegiac mood of the beginning gives way to funereal music, threnodic in character and containing long, eloquent rests (mm. 318, 320, and 322). This *grave* movement undoubtedly belongs among Mahler's most moving passages.

As in the exposition, the first section in the recapitulation is divided into two sections. The first is an orchestral interlude, the second presents the music for the actual farewell. The verse *Ich wandle nach der Heimat, meiner Stätte!* (I wander to my homeland, my home!) and the two following verses are set to the music of the secondary section, while the closing section contains Mahler's personal testimony concerning the eternal life cycle: *Die liebe Erde allüberall blüht auf im Lenz und grünt / Aufs neu! Allüberall und ewig blauen licht die Fernen* (Everywhere the dear earth blossoms in spring and becomes green / Anew! The blue horizon shines everywhere and eternally). How important the aspect of eternity was to him is also shown at the end of coda: The alto sings the word *eternal* seven times. The use of seven word repetitions is surely intentional.

Mahler never heard *Das Lied von der Erde*. The premiere took place on 20 November 1911, after his death, under the baton of Bruno Walter in Munich. The performance profoundly impressed Alban Berg and Anton von

Webern, who had traveled to Munich especially for the performance. On 23 November Webern wrote to Berg:

> What you write about *Das Lied von der Erde* is wonderful. As I told you, it is like the procession of life or, better yet, of that which has been experienced, before the soul of the dying. The work of art is intensified; that which is mere fact evaporates, but the idea remains. That is what these songs are like.[33]

The Ninth Symphony

> I have been very diligent and am just putting the
> finishing touch on a new symphony. . . . As far as I
> know it, the work is a nice addition to my small
> family. Thus far I have just kept on writing blindly,
> and now, when I am just beginning to orchestrate the
> last movement, I have already forgotten the first one.
> This symphony says something I have had on the tip
> of my tongue for the longest time. As a whole it may
> be closest to the Fourth, yet it is altogether different.
>
> GMB[2] 368

Origin

When Mahler took on responsibilities in the New World, his way of living
underwent some change. He spent half a year conducting in New York, and
the remaining months he lived in Europe. In one respect, he continued his
Viennese lifestyle: he dedicated the summer months exclusively to composing, and during winter mornings he went over his works and finished their
orchestration.

On 8 or 9 June 1909,[1] Alma Mahler took her husband to Toblach and
traveled on with their child to Levico, where she had to undergo some health
treatment (AME 191). Mahler remained in the large home (called Villa
Altschluderbach) "utterly alone" (GMB[2] 361), but he corresponded often
with his wife. Those very revealing letters discussing Goethe, *Faust,* the purpose of life, and the *Chorus mysticus* (AME 436–442) date from June 1909.
On 13 June he wrote to his wife that as long as "this ghastly weather continues" he would not go to his composing lodge (AME 435). Nevertheless it
must have been soon after this that he began working on his Ninth; otherwise
he would not have told Theodor Spiering in August that some time ago he
had begun "a major work" and that he was "completely buried" in it (GMB[2]
367). He certainly could not have reported the completion of the symphony's
draft to his friend Bruno Walter in the letter cited at the beginning of the

271

chapter (GMB² 368). "I wrote the score," he adds, "quite rapidly, in maddening haste. As a result it probably is indecipherable for strangers' eyes. I only hope that I may be granted time this winter to prepare a clean score." Actually the score Mahler refers to is the truly hard-to-read score sketch of the Ninth, the first three movements of which came into the possession of Alban Berg in 1923 and which Erwin Ratz edited in 1971 in a beautiful facsimile edition.² If this sketch was completed at the end of August 1909, then Alma's account, according to which the sketches for the Ninth date from the summer of 1908, is believable (AME 180).

In October Mahler took the score sketch along to New York, boarding the boat in Bremen on 12 October, but several weeks passed until he could begin preparing the clean copy. On 18 or 19 December he wrote to Bruno Walter: "Before long I hope to start my Ninth" (GMB² 374). Not until 1 April 1910, the day before his departure for Europe, was he able to report to his friend the completion of the full score (GMB² 383).

Mahler's superstitious fear of a Ninth has already been mentioned. In her memoirs Alma traces the title *Das Lied von der Erde* to this fear, saying that Mahler originally shied away from naming the Ninth Symphony by its numerical title (AME 192). Richard Specht also gives us to understand that after completion of *Das Lied von der Erde* Mahler sometimes felt that he had warded off the fateful danger.³ But he was not sure of himself. "I can hear him," writes Specht, "as, thinking of Beethoven's Ninth, he said about his own: 'And it is also in D! But at least in major.' " How well Mahler's contemporaries understood these and similar trains of thought is documented in Schoenberg's memorial speech of 1912.⁴

> It seems that the Ninth is a limit. He who wants to go beyond it must pass away. It seems as if something might be imparted to us in the Tenth which we ought not yet to know, for which we are not yet ready. Those who have written a Ninth stood too near to the hereafter.

Farewell, Death and Transfiguration—The Central Topics of the Work's Reception

The posthumous premiere of the Ninth occurred on 26 June 1912 in Vienna, under the direction of Bruno Walter. It occasioned vivid response from the press. In Austrian newspapers and journals alone, seventeen reviews appeared; they were partly positive, partly negative, and partly aloof.⁵ They clearly show that hermeneutic points of view already played an eminent role and that some topics received special attention: The subjects of farewell and of death and transfiguration briefly governed discussions of the Ninth Symphony, even until the Sixties.

Let us begin with a representative selection. Dr. Moriz Scheyer, one of the reporters attending the premiere, perceived the Finale of the Symphony as the "resigned farewell of an unsteady person who finally went to his rest."⁶

Richard Specht, Mahler's intimate friend and biographer, wrote in the *Illustrirtes Wiener Extrablatt*:

> Of these four movements, the first is surely the most captivating, with its evening sun and farewell mood reminiscent of *Das Lied von der Erde,* indulging in feelings of death, of anxious and sweet rapture. We shall discuss it in more detail after the excitement has died down.[7]

Another critic felt that Mahler's Ninth and Bruckner's Ninth[8] had "the farewell from life" in common, and added:

> It will be up to a future Mahler biographer to demonstrate how Mahler, always the proponent of a powerful philosophy of life and one who doggedly insisted on his own will, gradually arrived at a philosophy of life that sought bliss in self-sufficiency and forever had made peace with all things on which the curse of earthly weight was resting. Out of this wisdom his last great work was born. If someone wants to learn to weep he should listen to the first movement of this Ninth, the great, magnificent song of the ultimate farewell![9]

As early as 1913, Guido Adler stated that in the Ninth, Mahler, "after changing images of life, said farewell to it" and that the work closed "dying."[10]

William Ritter, an enthusiastic Mahler fan, interpreted the Ninth under the motto *death and transfiguration,* applying the two concepts to the first movement and the Finale. "Un être en qui l'humanité entière trouve sa plus complète expression, dit toute sa tendresse. La mort l'attend."[11] (In this person, all mankind finds its most complete expression, all its tenderness. Death is waiting.) With this metaphor he explained the first movement, and he interpreted its syncopated opening rhythm as the arrhythmic beat of a diseased heart.

William Mengelberg's interpretation was even more specific. After extensive studies of Mahler's sketches and manuscript, he entered numerous hermeneutic notes into his score, which assume a quite detailed program for the four movements of the work. Thoughts of leave-taking and death are central. The following is Mengelberg's "program":[12]

Das Lied von der Erde is: Farewell from the "Friend!" (from Mankind!!)
The Ninth Symphony is: Farewell from all whom he loved
—and from the world
—! and from his art, his life, his music
—1st movement   Farewell from "his loved ones" (his wife and child—longing! deepest)
—2nd movement   "Dance of the Dead" ("You must go down into the grave!") Since you live, you perish. Grim humor.
—3rd movement   Gallows humor—! Working, striving, all are futile attempts to escape death!!
                 trio—: a warped ideal (original motif)

—4th movement   Mahler's song of life

Mahler's soul sings its farewell! He sings from his innermost being. His soul sings—sings—its final farewell: "Good-bye!" His life, so full and rich—will soon be over! He feels and sings: "Farewell, my music" (*Mein Saitenspiel*).

Paul Bekker's interpretation is similar.[13] For him also farewell and death were the basic themes of the Ninth. "Life, love, creative power are viewed in retrospect by one who inwardly is already in the hereafter. Death for him is the fulfillment of all that the struggle for life and the longing for life once offered as a goal." As Bekker sums it up: " 'That Which Death Tells Me' is the unwritten title of the Ninth Symphony."[14]

The theme of death is also central to Alban Berg's extremely subtle interpretation. For him, the first movement of the Ninth "is based upon the foreboding of death." In an undated letter to his wife, Berg wrote:

Once again I played through Mahler's Ninth Symphony. The first movement is the most wonderful music Mahler wrote. It is the expression of remarkable love for this earth, the longing to live upon it in peace, to enjoy nature to its greatest depths before death enters. Because death does come, inexorably. This whole movement is based on a foreboding of death. It appears over and over. All earthly enchantment reaches a peak; therefore we continually have these rising outbursts, always after the tenderest passages. This foreboding is strongest at the tremendous moment when in this profound, yet painful joy of life, death forcefully announces its arrival. Then there are these eerie viola and violin solos and knightly sounds: Death in armor! There is no rebellion against him! What comes after this seems to me like resignation. The thoughts about the *hereafter,* which appear on pages 44–45, are always *misterioso,* like very thin air—even *above* the mountains—in a rarefied sphere (ether). And once again, for the last time, Mahler turns toward earth—not to battles and deeds, which he brushes off (as he did in *Das Lied von der Erde* with descending chromatic *morendo* runs), but rather totally and only to nature. He wants to enjoy whatever treasures earth still offers him for as long as he can. He wants to create for himself a home, far away from all troubles, in the free and thin air of the Semmering Mountain, to drink this air, this purest earthly air with deeper and deeper breaths— deeper and deeper breaths,

so that the heart, this most wonderful heart ever to have beaten among men, widens—widens more and more—before it must stop beating.[15]

Bruno Walter also thought that the title of the final song from *Das Lied von der Erde* ("The Farewell") could be the heading for the Ninth.[16] Originating from the same mood, the first movement had turned out to be

a tragic, strangely moving, noble paraphrase of farewell emotions. An unparalleled hovering between the sadness of leave-taking and the vision of heavenly light (not floating fantasy, rather immediate emotions) lifts the movement into an atmosphere of utmost transfiguration.

Finally, Karl H. Wörner compared Mahler's Ninth to Tchaikovsky's *Pathétique* and thought that coming to terms with death was the subject of both works.[17]

Bernd Sponheuer openly declared his dislike of several of the interpretations mentioned, especially those of Bekker and Wörner. He talked about a "vague death-mystique" and about "outrageously superficial, trivial metaphysics" and stated:

The strongest argument against such interpretations that see the Ninth only one-sidedly from an eschatological viewpoint is this: In spite of the underlying mood of farewell and mourning, the work displays magnificent constructive, tectonic strength, which justifies referring to it as the first example of the New Music.[18]

As understandable as this reaction might seem, it nevertheless represents a swing of the pendulum to the other extreme. It is possible to appreciate the Ninth's compositional innovations without disregarding the semantic features.

All in all, we must remember that Mahler himself inspired these reactions to the work. We must not lose sight of the fact that the first edition of the score, published in 1912 before the first performance, was consulted by many reviewers and contained numerous hermeneutic indications in the first movement that suggested specific content: *Mit Wut* (with ire), *Schattenhaft* (shadowlike), *mit höchster Gewalt* (with greatest force), *Wie ein schwerer Kondukt* (like a solemn funeral procession). Beside this, the score draft contains most revealing autograph exclamations clearly showing that Mahler associated remembrances of the past and thoughts of farewell with this piece. The notations in the first movement are especially instructive: *O Jugendzeit! Entschwundene! O Liebe! Verwehte!* (O Youth! Lost! O Love! Vanished!) (p. 29) and *Leb' wol! Leb' wol!* (Farewell! Farewell!) (p. 52). No doubt the more detailed hermeneutic interpretations of Willem Mengelberg and Alban Berg (both of whom had studied the draft of the score) were in part based upon their awareness of these markings.

Sequence of Movements and Disposition of Keys

Paul Bekker called the Ninth a "strange" work.[19] Its many new aspects are most evident in the unusual sequence of movements and in the disposition of keys. Two slow movements frame two lively ones: an Andante comodo in D major is followed by a dancelike movement in C major, a ghostly Rondo-Burlesque in A minor, and a highly expressive Adagio in D-flat major that begins with lively expression and ends "dying" in triple *piano*.

In the summer of 1896 at the latest, Mahler thought about the sequence of the movements. Measured by the Allegro, he considered the Adagio to be a "higher form" (BL[2] 68). By that time he had already decided that his Third Symphony (as the Second) should close with an Adagio, "contrary to the usual." Accordingly, what is new about the Ninth is not the Adagio ending but the Andante beginning. (This is noteworthy, even though the Fifth opens with a funeral march.) Here we have a break with the long–standing symphonic tradition, which Mahler invalidated little by little. He consistently continued on this path with the composition of the Tenth.

Let us stay with the Ninth. A further point worthy of consideration is the parallel structure of the movements. "Every movement," as Paul Bekker put it, "is there for its own sake. Symphonic unity is established only by the overall picture."[20] Motivic and thematic connections between the movements in which Mahler otherwise placed so much value and which are also evident in the Tenth, are quite rare. The Burlesque is quoted in the Finale, but there are no connections between the outer movements except for the one-time use of the main rhythm in the Adagio (mm. 122–124).[21]

The better acquainted one becomes with the Ninth, the stronger one senses a certain parallel with Tchaikovsky's famous *Symphonie Pathétique,* Op. 74 of 1893. This work, as is generally known, begins with a short Adagio, the introduction to a lively movement in sonata form. Then follow a dancelike second movement (Allegro con grazia), a third movement that is something between a scherzo and fast march (Mahler's Burlesque also contains marchlike features), and an Adagio lamentoso that dies away in quadruple *piano*. It must be mentioned that in 1901 Mahler had spoken contemptuously to Natalie Bauer-Lechner regarding the *Pathétique*; he called it "a shallow and extroverted, terribly homophonic work" (BL[2] 186). Nevertheless he must have received a lasting impression from it.

The Ninth belongs to those Mahler symphonies that close in a different key from the one in which they begin. The Fifth begins in C-sharp minor and ends in D major; similarly the Seventh begins in B minor and ends in C major. In the Ninth we can observe the opposite process: The Andante comodo is in D major, but the Adagio is in D-flat major. The key relationships that were traditional in multi-movement works since the Classic period no longer apply.

Mahler's decision to write the Adagio of the Ninth in D-flat major probably had several reasons. Paul Bekker hinted at key symbolism when he said: "D major, key of life fulfillment, drops to D-flat major, key of solemnity."[22] Certainly, D-flat major has an altogether different expressive quality than D major (Mahler's Adagio would be unimaginable in D major!). In choosing this key, Mahler enriched his work by a new dimension.[23]

First Movement

The first movement of the Ninth Symphony has always been praised as a most original composition, particularly in terms of form. Paul Bekker in 1921 spoke of a "rhapsodically free structure,"[24] while recent scholars have tried to understand the movement's structure either in terms of double variation or of sonata form. Heinrich Schmidt,[25] Hans Tischler,[26] Helmut Storjohann,[27] and finally Carl Dahlhaus[28] defended the thesis that the movement was based on two alternating theme complexes that were varied over and over again. On the other hand, Erwin Ratz,[29] to whom we owe the most comprehensive analysis thus far, interpreted the movement as a variation of sonata form without disregarding the factor of the double variation. A new analysis arrives at results that for the most part verify Ratz's insights, though differing in details. This leaves us with the following formal scheme:

Exposition

Mm.	1–6	Introduction (main rhythm, three-tone motif)
	7–26	Songlike main theme in D major
	27–46	Contrasting theme in D minor
	47–79	Main theme (extended and modified, basic key: D major)
	80–107	*Etwas frischer* (A little more brisk): closing section in B-flat major

Development

108–147	First part: m. 110 *Tempo I. subito (aber nicht schleppend)* [but not dragging]: at the beginning the main rhythm and the three-tone motif; horns, trombones, and strings are often muted; mm. 128–129 the first tam-tam beats
148–210	Second part: new version of the main theme (at first in D major) and developing of the material from the closing section; mm. 201–203 climax with a subsequent fall
211–266	Third part (*Leidenschaftlich*) [passionate]: development of material from the contrasting theme
267–318	Fourth part (*Tempo I.* Andante): new version of the main theme (in D major) and developing of material from the closing section; mm. 314–318 the lead rhythm, (*mit höchster Gewalt*). *fff* [with greatest force] in trombones and tuba (tam-tam beats)
319–346	Fifth part (mm. 327–328 *Wie ein schwerer Kondukt* [Like a

solemn funeral procession]): three-tone motif, sighing motifs, signals of the trumpets, tam-tam beats, and later ringing of bells

Recapitulation

347–371 Main theme (at the beginning in D major)
372–375 Contrasting theme (four measures)
376–390 Episode as parenthesis (*Misterioso*)
391–406 Continuation of the contrasting theme (*Nicht mehr so langsam*) [Not so slowly] and *Etwas belebter* [somewhat livelier]

406–454   Coda

To begin, the proportions of the movement are unusual: The exposition has 107 measures, the development has 239 measures, and the drastically shortened recapitulation with the coda has 108 measures. Thus the development is at least twice the length of the exposition. Looking more closely at the exposition, one can clearly discern three theme complexes: a lyrical songlike main theme in D major contrasted with a darker, passionate secondary theme in D minor and with a lively closing section in B-flat major. Assuming the movement to be in sonata form, it is irregular that Mahler returns to the main theme after the contrasting theme and then changes and develops it.

Those who explain the movement as a double variation like to point out that the secondary theme and closing section are partly based on the same motivic material. Thus Carl Dahlhaus perceived the closing section as a variation of the secondary section and said that the seemingly irregular exposition (A^1—B—A^2—C) actually was regular, with a modified and therefore written-out repeat (A^1—B^1—A^2—B^2). This concept, however, does not do justice to the actual tectonic relations. First of all, the closing section is not exclusively based on the material of the secondary theme but introduces a number of new elements such as the characteristic trill motifs (mm. 86–90). Second, the closing section is in a different key (B-flat major) and above all in a different mode than the secondary section (D minor). Third, it brings about a remarkable agogic intensification.[30] And most importantly, its mood is euphoric in contrast to the main and secondary themes. The exposition, which begins very gently and lyrically, closes full of verve and *fortissimo* with a fanfare!

The structure of the movement departs from regular sonata form in that the songlike main theme, though varied, returns several times in the development, at first in the original key, D major. In the course of the movement we come across no less than seven songlike passages in D major.[31] This frequent return to the main theme gives a rondo flavor to the movement.

In comparing these passages, one marvels at Mahler's unparalleled variation technique. No passage is altogether like another; one gets the impression that the composer moves further and further away from the model he had set up at the beginning. At the same time, the comparison gives us an instructive insight into the micro-structure of music.

The songlike theme that is first performed by the second violins (mm. 6–16) is simply structured. Strictly diatonic, it consists of short, mostly one-measure motifs separated from one another by rests and never leaving D major. The manner in which this theme is treated, however, is revealing. From the beginning Mahler combines it contrapuntally with a rhythmic, often similar melody in the second horn. He leaves the accompaniment to harp, divided cellos, and double basses, which execute very simple progressions while the divided violas persist in bringing the three-tone motif of the introduction (mm. 3–4).

Mm. 6–12

Even more interesting is the second section of the songlike theme (mm. 17–26). One might view it as a supplementary or consequent phrase. The primary melody, now in the first violins, is joined by the two independently developed counter-melodies in the second violins and cellos. While the individual melodies are simple, their combination results in a complex, netlike fabric. Diether de la Motte stated this precisely when he called it "complicatedly simple."[32]

Since Adorno it has become customary to employ the terms *disassociation* and *disintegration* in describing Mahler's late style. Further analysis of the final group will surely show that its seemingly heterogeneous motivic components (including sighing motifs, a distinctive chromatic motif, trill motifs, and others showing great verve) penetrate and cross each other (voice crossing being characteristic of Mahler's late style), harmonizing with each other in spite of all their disparity. The integration occurs at the highest level.

What about the music's specific meaning? Peter Andraschke has dealt with this question.[33] In contrast to Arnold Schoenberg who, strangely enough, underestimated Mahler's subjectivity, Andraschke held that in view of its background, this work was closely tied to the person of Mahler and to his concept of his own death. Andraschke tried to assign specific meanings to the first two themes of the first movement. He came to the following conclusion:

> To the short phrases of the first movement's main theme one might appropriately assign the words *Leb wol*!, jotted down by Mahler in the recapitulation (score sketch I/52 above the descending intervals of a second). Quite possibly the theme was invented with these words in mind. The musical gesture as a whole, the eloquence of this theme, which is primarily made up of stepwise descending intervals (sighing motifs), expresses farewell and mourning.

Let us see to what extent precise statements can be made beyond these observations regarding the movement's meaning.

The meaning of several basic elements of the composition is most easily accessible by examining the development section, which moves between extremes. Those who have heard it often and attentively are apt to note that songlike, quiet, or even weary passages alternate with full-sounding, euphoric, ecstatic, or highly excited passages. It is symptomatic that the two high points of the development (at the end of the second and the fourth section, mm. 197–204 and 307–320) end like a collapse. After the first climax the musical image suggests a plunge.

The first section of the development (mm. 108–147) is of decisive importance for its further course and its end. After the bright closing of the exposition, the first section appears strangely dark. Muted trombones, strings, and muted horns determine the timbre. Tam-tam beats are added (for the first time in mm. 128–129).

The development begins with three elements that originate in the beginning of the movement but now are darkly colored:

Mm. 108–113

Over a timpani roll, the horns perform the syncopated rhythm. Then the timpani play the three–note motif of the harp (mm. 3–6; F-sharp—A—B—A) but modify it diastematically (G-flat—B-flat—C—B-flat). In the next measure the horns take over the motif, again changing its articulation, dynamics, and intervals (B-flat—D—E-flat—D). It is an artful variant, implying the sighing motif of the main theme.

The sighing motif, with intervals of major and minor seconds, assumes a leading role in the third part of the development, where it is played by the horns, first in unison:

Mm. 237–243

and then in "horn fifths." Daring harmonies result because these horn fifths are imitated by the clarinets and later, on different steps, by the bassoons:

Mm. 245–250

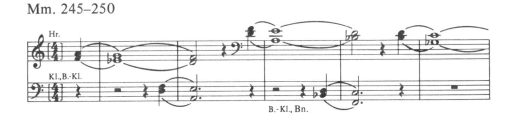

This passage shows such an obvious similarity to the "Farewell" motif from Beethoven's sonata *Les Adieux,* Op. 81a and its imitative treatment in the first movement that one might well consider it a conscious allusion. Here is the particular passage from Beethoven's sonata:

All this suggests that the *Leb' wol* exclamations in Mahler's score sketch may indeed be related to the main theme of the Symphony's first movement.

The importance of the elements presented at the beginning of the development does not become apparent until the end of that section. In measures 314–317 the trombones now play *fff* the syncopated main rhythm of the beginning *mit höchster Gewalt* (with utmost force). In measure 317ff. the timpani present an ostinato of the three-note motif followed by the cellos and double basses. Tam-tam beats and sighing motifs in the bassoons and later in the horns add to the picture.

In measure 327ff. follows the passage marked "Like a solemn funeral procession." It is based on sighing motifs in the woodwinds and signal calls of the trumpets. The three-note motif of the timpani serves as the foundation; it is taken over by three low bells in measures 337–346. In the recapitulation, tam-tam and Glockenspiel are left out, and the syncopated main rhythm (the symbol of death) understandably is no longer heard.

The major changes in the recapitulation (in comparison with the exposition) were the result of Mahler's ideas regarding the theory of art, already discussed, but they also resulted from non-musical considerations. The main theme appears in a new version, and the sweeping closing section is dropped altogether according to the changed situation. A 15-measure episode, marked *Misterioso* and orchestrated as chamber music, has been interpolated into the contrasting section. It offers a superb example of Mahler's linear polyphony.

Mm. 376n381

Its material is partly derived from measures 32–33 of the exposition and in part freely invented. Style, physiognomy, and timbre of some lines are reminiscent of bird calls,[34] and Alban Berg's interpretation of this passage as a vision of the hereafter is quite appropriate.

The coda represents the type of *morendo* ending so characteristic of Mahler's late works. The marking *morendo* occurs three times in the score (mm. 409, 419–420, and 450–451). The coda brings reminiscences of two motifs from the closing and secondary sections, as well as *sehr zögernd* (very hesitant) calls of farewell in the flutes and oboes, later in the clarinets, and ultimately in the horns. The calls eventually fade away. Inserted is a highly original cantilena of the flute (mm. 419–434) based on sigh motifs and to be performed *schwebend* (floating). A solo violin responds to the farewell calls of the wind instruments. The harmonic rhythm is extremely slow.[35]

Paul Bekker was the first to see in Mahler's late works a "style of disintegration" and of "decay."[36] The only passages to which these rather unfortunate terms apply are the *morendo* endings.

Second Movement

The second movement of the Ninth Symphony was categorized by Adorno as *Todtentanz* (Dance of Death)[37] and had already been characterized by Paul Bekker as a composition dominated by the idea of death.[38] It is easier to understand these associations if one remembers that the movement relates at least in one respect to the Death-Dance Scherzo of the Fourth. The violins are to play the first theme "like fiddles," as the solo violins did in the Fourth.

More appropriately one might speak of this movement as the *summation* of Mahler's dance styles. All Mahler's dance styles (described elsewhere in detail[39]) are represented here: the unhurried (*gemächlich*) ländler, the two types of waltz, and the slow ländler. They are clearly distinguished from one another by different tempos.[40]

The variety of contrasting styles at first seems to have confused Mahler himself. He was initially undecided about a title for the movement. In the score sketch he marked it as a scherzo, but he then crossed out that word and substituted *Menuetto infinito*[41]—a designation that does not fit either.

The four dance styles of the movement differ from one another typologically as well as structurally. Thus the unhurried ländler *Tempo I, etwas täppisch und sehr derb* (somewhat clumsy and very crude) is in a clearly diatonic major. At first it does not depart from the tonic key of C major, if one disregards brief excursions to F major. The main theme of the violins is simple, yet the texture becomes complex due to the added contrapuntal voices, which, by their linear quality, provide sharp contours.

The main theme of the first type of waltz (*Tempo II,*. m. 90ff.) belongs to the major-minor mode (E major/E minor). While the first six measures are relatively simple harmonically, the structure of the last seven measures is significantly more complicated. An old model of classic harmonic progressions, the chain-of-fourths cadence I—V—VI—III—IV—I, is altered to the point of being unrecognizable:

Mm. 96–100

Many similar alterations occur in this movement, as well as in the Rondo-Burlesque and the final Adagio.

The theme of the second type of waltz (for which the persistent accompaniment of quarter-note after-beats is typical) is introduced in an unusual way. Trombones and tuba present the melody of the first five measures, which presumably caused Adorno to speak of "wild vulgarisms":[42]

Mm. 147–154

The simple theme of the slow ländler (*Tempo III*) begins in F major but is then continued in whole notes and harmonized with a sequence of at times altered dominant seventh chords:[43]

Mm. 252–259

The uniqueness of the movement results from the strong contrast between the different styles. In this multifaceted composition, Mahler includes the crude (unhurried ländler) and the gentle (slow ländler), sprightly waltz melodies, and scherzando-like passages (m. 339). There are mournful sections (mm. 515–516), and the grotesque is not excluded. At several points the horns quote a phrase from the *Fischpredigt*:

Mm. 576–578

The following outline demonstrates the rondolike structure of the movement, which originally was a little longer:[44]

Mm.   1–89   Unhurried ländler (*Tempo I*); basic key: C major
      90–167   Waltz (*Tempo II*); basic keys: E major and E-flat major

168–217 Waltz (*Tempo II*), at first with the inclusion of elements from the slow Ländler, beginning in E-flat major

218–229 Slow ländler (*Tempo III*) in F major

230–251 Interpolation: insertion of a passage mostly made up of elements from the unhurried ländler (*Tempo I*)

252–260 Continuation of the slow ländler (*Tempo III*)

261–312 Waltz (*Tempo II*: "But a little faster than the first time"); basic key at the beginning: D major

313–332 Waltz ("Still a little more lively")

333–368 Slow ländler (*Tempo III*) in F major

369–404 Unhurried ländler (*Tempo I*), enriched with elements from other sections

405–422 Gradually moving to *Tempo II*

423–485 Waltz (*Tempo II*); basic key: E-flat major

486–515 "Still a little more brisk": waltz in B-flat major

516–522 Reminiscences of the slow ländler ("lamenting") and of the unhurried ländler

523–621 Unhurried ländler (*Tempo I* subito), in part contrapuntally combined with elements from the other dance styles. Basic keys: G major and C minor

The new aspects of this movement are found within the details; they become apparent on closer study. This is why one should not blame many reviewers of the premiere for not understanding the movement. They were offended by its length, its "noisy" instrumentation, and by its "senseless brutalities."[45] They did not notice that the so-called vulgarisms were intentional and that through the medium of music Mahler wanted to show a mirror of the world.[46] Not until half a century later could Adorno[47] define one aspect of the movement, the method of musical montage.[48] The poetic concept of the movement also remained misunderstood. It begins *sehr derb* (very crudely) and, after a minor episode (mm. 576–598), ends in an extremely discreet *pianissimo* with reminiscences of the first ländler motifs. As Bruno Walter formulated it, one senses that "the dance is over."[49]

Rondo-Burlesque

As a literary genre, burlesque (from *burla,* meaning "joke") is inseparably tied to parody, travesty, and the grotesque. Characteristic of the genre are derision and distortion to the point of buffoonish caricature. The burlesque in music cannot be defined so clearly and so uniformly, but it is certain that the end of the nineteenth and the beginning of the twentieth century had a tendency toward it and that several humoresques and burlesques are characterized by rhythmic complications, hidden quotes and hints, and by paraphrases of many themes. Richard Strauss's *Burlesque* for piano and orchestra (four timpani), composed in 1885, was a work that Mahler probably knew.[50] In 1901 Max Reger composed his *Six Burlesques* for four–hand piano, Op. 58, and in 1906 the dancelike *Burla,* Op. 37, No. 2 by Ludwig Thuille was published.

In the score sketch of the Ninth, Mahler originally designated the third movement as *Burlesque in Form of a Rondeau* (note the French spelling of the last word). Later he crossed out the words *in Form of a Rondeau* and placed the word *rondeau* at the beginning: *Rondeau-Burlesque.* The rondolike structure of the movement is quite strongly pronounced, as the following outline shows:

Mm.   1–78   First section (Allegro assai. *Sehr trotzig* [Very stubborn]); basic key A minor
      79–108   Fugato I (= first development of the first section motifs); basic key: D minor
    109–179   Secondary section (= song in four stanzas) marked *leggiero*; basic key: F major; new timbre: triangle
    180–208   First section in A-flat minor and A minor
    209–261   Fugato II with real answer to the themes at the fifth
    262–310   Secondary section (= song in three stanzas); basic key: A major; new timbre: Glockenspiel
    311–346   Fugato III in the manner of a "circular fugue" (themes enter on D-flat, A-flat, E-flat, and B-flat)
    347–521   Episode (= music from far away), based on the two thoughts from the third fugato: the cantus-firmus-like idea and the turn motif; performance markings: espressivo and *Mit großer Empfindung* (With great feeling); basic key: D major
    522–616   Varied recapitulation of the first section with the inclusion of the fugato themes
    617–667   Coda (Più stretto and later Presto)

A first section that serves as a kind of refrain alternates with a secondary section and a long episode that strikes one as phantasmagoric. Added to this are three fugatos that are partly based on motivic material from the first section. The contrasts between the energetic, "very stubborn" first section, the light-footed secondary section, and the rapturous episode are very abrupt.

A kind of relentless linear polyphony is shown not only by the three fugatos, but also by the first section itself: no voice seems to be considering the other. In the fugatos, the fugal style of the 1920s is anticipated. The polyphonic sections involve the use of a sequential technique otherwise rejected by Mahler.[51]

A careful analysis of the first section shows that it is clearly divided into an introduction (mm. 1–6), a three-part structure according to the A—B—A scheme (mm. 7–22, 23–43, and 44–63), and a marchlike second theme (mm. 64–78).

The three fugatos can be considered to be developments of the first section. They work with its abundant thematic material, but little by little they also introduce new thoughts. In the brightly orchestrated first fugato, the equality of the voices has been carried to such an extent (mm. 79–108) that it is difficult to determine what is theme and what is counterpoint:

Mm. 78–82

Incidentally, the parts of the four flutes and piccolo are gleaned from measures 14–18 (oboes and clarinets), the line of the three trombones and the tuba is derived from measures 8–12 (oboes), and the violins pick up the main theme (mm. 6–9).

With the beginning of the secondary section (m. 109), the mood suddenly changes. A stroke of the triangle (it lends the specific color to the whole secondary section) marks the change; the tense tone of the fugato is replaced by a popular song idiom. The violins play a leggiero melody, rhythmically simple and featuring whole-tone sequences, causing it to sound like a hit tune from the beginning of the century. The harmonization follows the pattern of the cadence based on chains of fourths modified by deceptive cadences.

Mm. 109–118

At a closer look the entire secondary section reveals itself as a song without words in four stanzas: Stanza I (mm. 109–130), Stanza II (mm. 131–146), Stanza III (mm. 146–168), Stanza IV (mm. 169–179). The second, third, and last stanzas (this one being incomplete) are obvious variations of the model stanza.

The trivial character of the secondary section is so blatant that it would be surprising if it had *not* been noticed. Adorno was reminded of Lehár (specifically of his *Merry Widow* of 1905),[52] and Dieter Schnebel spoke of a Lehár parody.[53] The sketches indicate that Mahler's intention in this dallying secondary section was indeed ironic. On one sheet he notated the first three measures of the theme, and on another sheet he notated a phrase that is reminiscent of popular music:

The importance of rapidly changing expression as a principal characteristic of the Burlesque can be realized if one traces the rest of the movement. The fourth stanza of the first fugato is suddenly broken off after 11 measures. The music changes abruptly to the first section, first in A-flat minor and then in A minor. A cymbal crash marks the sudden change.

The second fugato (mm. 209–261) seems more conventional than the first because theme and counterpoint can now be clearly distinguished:

Here the voice leading deserves attention. The first four measures of the theme are borrowed from the first section; the rest is freely invented. The opposite applies to the counterpoint, where the first three measures (the head) are freely invented and the rest is based on certain motifs from the first section. The four entries of the theme occur in the usual manner at the fifth and octave. The last measures of the second fugato (mm. 251–261) lead to the secondary section (mm. 262–310), which is, of course, varied and now reduced to three stanzas. Here the Glockenspiel marks the change.

The third fugato (mm. 311–346) enters with the counterpoint of the second, which now becomes the theme, enlarged by a kind of prefix (the characteristic jump of a sixth). Alongside appears a more or less freely invented contrapuntal part, whose head, a characteristic turn figure, plays an important role in the continuation of the movement:

Mm. 319–325

Of the three fugatos of the Burlesque, the third is compositionally the most progressive because the entrances of the themes occur consistently on the steps of the circle of fifths rather than at the fifth and octave (as in the traditional fugue): The first entrance is on D-flat, the second on A-flat, the third on E-flat, the fourth on B-flat. Before Mahler, the technique of the circular fugue (or the circular fugato) is found in Brahms's motet *Why is the Light Given to the Weary,* Op. 74, No. 1 of 1878;[54] in Tchaikovsky's *Pathétique* (first movement) of 1893; and in Strauss's *Also sprach Zarathustra* of 1894 ("Regarding Science"). After Mahler we find it in the work of Bartók and Hindemith.

The inserted D major episode (mm. 347–521) seems like a foreign body within the Burlesque. It follows the third fugato and starts suddenly with a cymbal crash and a tremolo of the violins and flutes (flutter-tongue) on high A.[55] The dynamic, timbre, and resonance give it an unreal and dreamy character. The dynamic level is *piano* and *pianissimo* with isolated *forte* and *fortissimo* passages. For the strings, horns, trumpets, and trombones, the mute is often required; the violins must partly play *sul ponticello*; several harp glissandi stand out. The tempo becomes slower (mm. 354–355: *Etwas gehalten* [somewhat restrained]).

The themes of the episode are based on the two ideas of the third fugato: the cantus-firmus-like thought and the turn motif from which Mahler gains long, expressive arches.[56]

Mm. 352–359

The cantilena of the violins (m. 394ff.) is to be performed *Mit großer Empfindung* (with great sensitivity). A variant to page 33 of the score sketch exists (containing mm. 482–511) on a loose sheet on which the turn motif is noted several times with markings such as "like a shadow" or simply "shadow."

If distortion to the point of caricature is part of the nature of a burlesque, then Mahler's movement is a true burlesque. So far, the turn motif was treated most expressively. Now, in the midst of the ethereal episode, the E-flat and A clarinets present it in reduced form with a sudden triple *forte*—surely a gross distortion (m. 444ff. and 454ff.). Julius Korngold[57] and Rudolf Mengelberg[58] spoke correctly of something "satanic," a "horrible grimace," putting an end to all longing for softness and intimacy. Though not so suddenly, the phantasmagorical episode is followed by the varied recapitulation of the first section and a coda that rises to the point of frenzy.

The episode does help us understand the deeper meaning of this strange movement: that which makes it burlesque is the contrast between three basically different levels of expression, between the reality of a trivial surrounding and a dreamed-of, beautiful world, which (so far) remains unattainable.

Adagio

Given only a superficial examination, the Finale of the Third Symphony, the slow movement of the Fourth, the Andante moderato of the Sixth, and the Adagio of the Ninth may impress us as having the same form and a similar layout. Two contrasting theme complexes take turns several times, as is often the case with Bruckner. However, if one compares the movements more closely, it becomes evident that Mahler provides a different content every time and changes the scheme according to the underlying poetic idea. The structure of the Adagio of the Ninth Symphony can be roughly outlined as follows:

Part 1

Mm.	1–2	Opening
	3–27	First-theme complex in D-flat major (in mm. 11–12 an anticipation of the secondary theme as an interpolation)
	28–48	Secondary theme in a Phrygian-tinted C-sharp minor

Part 2

	49–72	New version of the first theme complex (basic key: D-flat major)
	73–76	Quote of a passage from the Burlesque (mm. 394–409)
	77–87	Spinning–out of motifs from the first theme complex
	88–107	New version of the secondary theme (basic keys: C-sharp minor and F-sharp minor)

Part 3

	107–125	Build-up with climax (motivic material from the first theme complex)

Part 4

Coda

What is unique about this movement? In the first place, the idea of contrast has been pushed to the limit. The two theme complexes contrast not only in regard to the mode (major-minor), form, harmonization, dynamics, and character of expression, but in every other way imaginable, and so strongly that one has to speak of two poles.

The first theme complex contains as its constructive element the turn figure of the Burlesque. It is played by the strings—highly expressive, full sounding and richly harmonized.

As the example shows, Mahler extends the D-flat major framework by the use of quasi-deceptive cadences, by altering the cadence of chains of fourths, and by turning to remote scale steps (F—C—A in mm. 8–9). The four-part, strict writing known from Bruckner's music (using fundamental progressions) undergoes a remarkable modernization.

The formal structure is also noteworthy. The first theme complex is in three-part song form with an addition: Introduction (mm. 1–2)—A (mm. 3–10)—B (mm. 13–16)—A¹ (mm. 17–23)—Addition (mm. 24–27). Typical of Mahler's late works is the interpolation in measures 11–12; here the secondary theme is anticipated. In the added passage, the second violins quote the turn motif from the Burlesque note-for-note:

Mm. 24–25

Kurt von Fischer rightly characterized the beginning of this movement as showing "expressive pathos."[59] The distinctly thin setting of the secondary theme forms a very harsh contrast:

First violins and cellos (supported by contrabassoon and, later, double basses) play a two-voiced phrase in a Phrygian tinted C-sharp minor, *pianissimo* and *ohne Empfindung* (without emotion). They move in extreme registers (high and low) and seem not to be related to each other. The absence of lines in the middle range creates the impression of a vacuum. Later in the movement (m. 34ff.) there is occasional three-part writing, but it remains thin. A few woodwinds and violin and viola solos provide a chamber music sound. The secondary theme also appears shadowy at its varied recurrence (mm. 88–107).

In contrast, the first theme complex appears in new versions that intensify harmonically and dynamically, while the instrumentation becomes richer each time. Mahler reaches the climax of the movement by treating elements from the first theme complex very freely. At the high point (mm. 118–122), the trumpets play the chromatic nucleus of the complex *fortissimo* (with bells up) and in augmentation.

The idea of contrast—working with extreme opposites—characterizes not only the Adagio's themes but also its dynamics. We hear numerous expected and unexpected contrasts between *fortissimo* and *pianissimo*. Thus the interpolation of a thought from the secondary theme in measures 11–12 appears like a *pianissimo* island within the full sound of the music. Elsewhere the first return of the first theme complex (mm. 49–72) closes *drängend* (pushing forward), *molto crescendo,* but it is a broken-off crescendo; the expected high point is not reached. In measure 73 the quote from the Burlesque appears *pianissimo subito.* The reverse process can be noticed in measure 107, at the link between the second and third parts of the movement. After the secondary theme has faded away *pianissimo,* there follows the increasingly intense passage with thematic material from the first theme complex, *heftig durchbrechend* (violently bursting out) and *fortissimo.* One final example: The second reappearance of the first theme (m. 126), beginning *fortissimo,* contains several broken-off crescendos (mm. 132–133 and 137–138) and a diminuendo (mm. 144–147) that leads to an area of dissolving sound (mm. 148–158). This prepares the written-out *morendo* ending of the Adagissimo (mm. 159–185).

In the letter to Bruno Walter quoted at the beginning of this chapter, Mahler wrote regarding the Ninth (GMB[2] 368): "This symphony says something I have had on the tip of my tongue for the longest time. As a whole it may be closest to the Fourth, yet it is altogether different." The reference to the Fourth so far has remained without comment, but it deserves attention. A remarkable similarity exists between the slow movement of the Fourth and the Adagio of the Ninth. Both are on two rondolike theme complexes, alternating and contrasted, but both close *morendo.* There is, however, a subtle difference. In the slow movement of the Fourth, the *morendo* is restricted to the closing part, which Mahler compared with an "ethereal" mood (BL[2] 163). In the Adagio of the Ninth, the *morendo* is the clue to the whole movement. In addition to the threefold remark *ersterbend* (dying), the indication *morendo* appears no less than eight times.[60]

The interpretation of the Adagio as a musical quotation is very telling. In measures 163–170 of the Adagissimo the first violins play *mit inniger Empfindung* (with tender feeling) and *morendo,* a phrase from the fourth of the *Kindertotenlieder:*

Song, mm. 62–69
In the sunshine! The day is beautiful up in yonder heights!

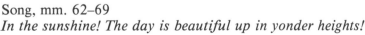

Adagissimo, mm. 163–171

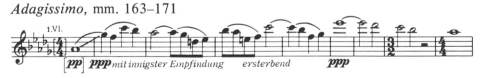

The quote, first discovered by Julius Korngold,[61] was further investigated by Monika Tibbe.[62] Her opinion that Mahler "included the text quoted from *Kindertotenlieder* without saying so" is to be accepted. With the ethereal ending of the Ninth Symphony, Mahler once again testified to his faith in the continuation of life after death.

Short score of the Purgatorio movement of the Tenth Symphony
The exclamations *O Gott! O Gott! Warum hast du mich verlassen?* and *Dein Wille geschehe!* are almost exact quotes of Matthew 27:46 or 6:10.

The Tenth Symphony

Fate of the Work—Deryck Cooke's "Concert Version"

The Tenth Symphony that Mahler left behind underwent a strange fate: Mahler had verbally expressed the wish that after his death the manuscript be burned, but Alma Mahler could not bring herself to fulfill her husband's wish. To the contrary, she allowed herself to be persuaded to make the manuscript accessible to the curious public. In 1924, a facsimile edition of the autograph was published by the prestigious Zsolnay Verlag.[1] Since then, interest in the work has continued to grow. In 1967, forty-three years later, the publisher Walter Ricke issued a considerably more complete facsimile edition.[2]

Those who condemn Alma Mahler for reasons of piety should remember that she sought advice from experts and friends of her husband. Thus Richard Specht, whom she allowed to inspect the manuscript, discovered to his "complete" surprise that "two movements of the work, an Adagio (which represents a first movement) and an Intermezzo, were completely finished with every instrumental part precisely notated—the sketch could be made into a score without changing a note."[3] Even though Specht's account is not quite correct in all details, it cannot be denied that Mahler's Tenth is not a fragment but a torso *sui generis*. Of the five movements, the first two are complete or almost complete in the score sketch. The third movement (*Purgatory*) is written on three loose sheets as a short score; moreover the first 30 measures are also written out in the score sketch. The two final movements exist as a short score on four staves, with sparse indications of the instrumentation. Mahler's manuscript consists of seventy-two pages of a fully written-out draft and ninety-three pages of short score. Deryck Cooke rightfully stated that the thematic lines are "pure Mahler"[4] and that this also applies to about ninety percent of the counterpoint and harmonies.

Keeping this in mind, one can understand more easily why in 1924 Alma Mahler asked Ernst Krenek whether it would be possible to complete the work and to orchestrate it. Krenek restricted himself to furnishing a clean copy of the full score of the beginning Adagio and a performable score of the *Purgatory* movement. On the basis of these scores the first performances of the two movements took place in Vienna during 1924 and shortly afterward in Prague.[5] Approximately thirty years were to pass before musicologists working independently in various countries (Joe Wheeler in England, Clinton Carpenter in North America, Hans Wollschläger in Germany, and Deryck Cooke in England) undertook the difficult but fascinating task of producing a concert version of the Tenth.[6] Cooke's version turned out to be the most successful. After many revisions and tests it began a few years ago to succeed in the concert hall.

Opinions differ as to the legitimacy of attempting a "completion" or "reconstruction" of the Tenth. While some Mahler fans categorically rejected the idea, the efforts were approved and even welcomed by others. The opponents (among them Bruno Walter, Theodor W. Adorno, and Erwin Ratz) liked to draw attention to the fact that even the opening Adagio is "incomplete" and that it was Mahler's habit, even in completed works, to retouch them over and over again. On 10 November 1923, Bruno Walter wrote to Alma Mahler:

> No composer was more resentful than Mahler about allowing an incomplete work to become known—you know this as well as I. I much regret that you disregarded this aversion, deeply rooted in his character and work, and expose to the public a torso that lacks the corrections and finishing touches that only the composer could have provided—especially for the premiere at a location with acoustics that are most unsuitable for a symphonic work.[7]

Erwin Ratz also expressed great reservations about the reconstruction efforts: "As is well known, Arnold Schoenberg, Anton von Webern, Alban Berg, and Ernst Krenek have declared it impossible to reconstruct the complete work, since the existing sketches merely represent an early stage of the work, the final form of which can only be surmised."[8] Deryck Cooke, on the other hand, made it clear that Mahler's manuscript did not consist of sketches, but contained a comprehensive, fully developed layout. Beyond this, the short scores seemed to him to be "unambiguously orchestral." However, he did not want his work to be considered a "completion" or "reconstruction" and admitted that a true completion really was unattainable:

> Mahler himself, in bringing it to its final form, would have revised the draft—elaborated, refined, and perfected it in a thousand details; he would also, no doubt, have expanded, contracted, redisposed, added, or canceled a passage here and there (especially in the second movement); and he would finally, of course, have embodied the result in his own incomparable orchestration.[9]

Cooke's accomplishment is having made Mahler's manuscript readable and performable. The more intensively one studies the "concert version," the clearer it becomes that Cooke worked very cautiously. His work is based on a profound knowledge of Mahler's late style and orchestration. The greatest problems occurred where the texture presented gaps, where contrapuntal voices or chord sequences are not written down. Cooke studied the parallel corresponding passages but occasionally had to make additions. He called his method "substitute composing," "imitational composing," or "Pastiche composing" [a work to which more than one composer contributed—TRANS.]

Origin

Mahler's Tenth was written during the summer of 1910. Unfortunately the history of the work can be reconstructed only in part because many relevant documents are undated, and a number of significant events from this period need clarification.

Under the heading "summer 1910" Alma Mahler writes in her memoirs:

> I took Mahler to Toblach and then had to go on to Tobelbad, as prescribed by the physician, to cure my ailing nerves. Mahler remained in Toblach, looked after by old, dependable domestic servants, and he began to sketch the Tenth (AME 215).

This must have occurred in May 1910 because on 2 June he visited his wife in Tobelbad (GMB[2] 383f.). He could not have gotten very far with his work during May or especially June because he had to conduct preliminary rehearsals for the Munich premiere of the Eighth. For this purpose he went to Leipzig and Munich in June after he rehearsed with the Viennese *Singverein,* at the end of May.[10]

A severe marriage crisis cast a shadow over the summer of 1910. It had apparently been smoldering for some time but was aggravated by the appearance in Toblach of a long-time admirer of Alma, Walter Gropius. Mahler feared that he would lose his wife to Gropius. During this period he was, as Alma writes in her memoirs, "in deepest turmoil" (AME 218):

> That is when he wrote all those exclamations and words addressed to me into the sketch of the Tenth Symphony. He recognized that he had led the life of a psychopath and suddenly decided to see Sigmund Freud (who was then staying in Leyden in Holland).

The conversation with Freud took place on 26 August. Freud diagnosed a "compulsion neurosis" and a strong mother fixation ("Mary complex") and explained to Mahler that he was seeking his mother in every woman.[11] This conversation seems to have calmed Mahler greatly, though he rejected the idea of a mother fixation. On 4 September he wrote to his wife from Munich (AME 466): "Freud is right. For me you have always been the light, the central point!"

The manuscript of the Tenth documents that during the summer of 1910 Mahler was also haunted by thoughts of departure and death and that the events of his personal life did not remain without influence on his concept of the work. The following jottings are of special significance in this context: "You alone know what it means. Ah! Ah! Ah! Farewell, my music! Farewell. Farewell. Farewell" (at the end of the fourth movement); "To live for you! To die for you! Almschi!" (at the end of the Finale).

If one considers that Mahler went to Munich at the beginning of September 1910 to conduct rehearsals for the Eighth, several things support the assumption that the manuscript of the Tenth came into being for the most part during the months of July and August. However, contrary to his habit, Mahler did not return to the manuscript of the Tenth during the winter of 1910–1911. As Alma reports, "a kind of fear kept him from busying himself with it" (AME 233).

The Cyclical Concept

The Tenth Symphony, like the Second, Fifth, and Seventh, consists of five movements. Mahler established their definitive sequence in the manuscript with Roman numerals (written with blue pencil). The first movement, an Adagio, is followed by a Scherzo, an intermezzo-like third movement that bears the title *Purgatory,* a fourth movement, and the Finale. It is quite unlikely that this numbering would have been changed later because the work, as Cooke already mentioned, presents in this form a symphonic development of five movements that would be meaningless in any other sequence.[12] Mahler's contradictory and later rejected indications for placement of the fourth movement show, however, that at first the sequence of movements was not clear to him.

It is important to the overall structure of the Symphony that it begins with an Adagio and ends with a slow movement: The Finale is clearly divided into a slow introduction, an Allegro moderato, and a slow section. In so doing, Mahler continued along the path of the Ninth without repeating himself: The last movement of the Tenth greatly differs from the Adagio of the Ninth, not only in structure but also in content.

The disposition of keys in the Tenth is less daring than in the Ninth. The opening Adagio is in F-sharp major, the second movement is in F-sharp minor (ending in F-sharp major), and the third movement is in B-flat minor. The fourth movement, strangely enough begins in E minor and closes in D minor, and it is also unusual that the Finale begins in D minor but closes in F-sharp major. Originally Mahler intended to end the Symphony in B-flat major[13] but he abandoned that plan.

The thematic connections between the movements are much tighter and more varied in the Tenth than in the Ninth. The Finale works to a great extent with *Purgatory* motifs and also uses material from the first and fourth movements. (Only the second movement of the Tenth is somewhat isolated.) The way in which the Finale is connected to the fourth movement, as well as the thematic borrowings, indicate that this movement was the last to be completed.

Adagio

The Tenth's first movement is so unusual in form and content that it is difficult to define its uniqueness precisely and to describe it analytically. Eberhardt Klemm, who made the first extensive analysis, was of the opinion that the Adagio was based on two alternating themes that reappear in innumerable variations, and that their alternation constituted the form. The chief characteristic of the whole movement was "that almost all melodic happenings can be attributed to arch forms and that all melodic material appears in variants of arches." Klemm's conclusion:

> The dynamics of the movement move in a constant up and down, an "on the way" without ever getting there, in keeping with the idea on which the whole movement is based. The intersecting counterpoint, the extreme ranges, the arch structure of themes and complexes, the shifting of high points and the bow sforzati at the beginnings of the measures, the strange sounds and painful dissonances: all of these form the image of frozen space, a kind of historical space in which the acting subjects are locked up.[14]

The list of themes that Tyll Rohland[15] provided in a detailed study is more comprehensive: it includes an introductory theme, two theme complexes, a sixteenth-note motif, and a pizzicato motif. Rohland studied Mahler's variation technique more closely and noted that the introductory theme appears (with variants) five times, the first theme appears twenty-one times, and the second theme appears fourteen times. He believed that the structure of the Adagio, in contrast to the character variation of the Classic and Romantic periods, could be designated as "morphological variation." In other words, in this kind of theme variation, only the outward appearance of the theme changes, while the meaning, the character, the content remain the same.

A new analysis may result in some new insights. If we take the themes' characters into consideration there can be no doubt that we must speak of three contrasting themes (referred to in the following as I, II, and III).

Theme I (with the tempo marking Andante) is performed as a solo by the violas in its first appearance (and in two later ones). Later in the movement it occurs several times in a two-part version. It is tonally ambiguous (beginning in B minor and ending in E-sharp major[16]), and it has a lonely character:

Mm. 1–15

Strangely enough, it has gone unnoticed that the archetype of this theme is the melody of the English horn, the "sad tune" of the shepherd from the third act of *Tristan*.

Theme II (Adagio) is constructed quite differently. Two highly expressive melodies dominated by large intervals unfold and cross each other above a chordal, somewhat choralelike background. The quality of this theme, which returns in free inversion and numerous variants, reminds one of the expressiveness and ecstasy of Bruckner, though it already appears expressionistic:

Mm. 16–23

The theme is in F-sharp major, though the tonal framework is expanded by the inclusion of distant keys (for instance, A major in m. 20, B-flat major in m. 21). In the harmonization of this theme, Mahler loves sounds containing tension and dissonances[17] such as ninth chords. He often includes two different alterations of the same tone in one chord![18]

Klemm concedes Theme III to be a variation of Theme I; Rohland thought both themes were "closely related." A closer look reveals, however, that the similarity pertains only to the structure of the beginnings of themes; the continuation, which is the part that matters, is different. The distinctive pizzicato accompaniment lends Allegretto features to Theme III (m. 81, Mahler marks it *fliessend* [flowing]), and the trill motifs appear like a Scherzando:

Mm. 31–34

This example should clarify that Mahler knew not only the "morphological" kind of variation but also the type in which the character changes—and he used both in the Adagio of the Tenth.

As to the Adagio's structure, Specht[19] was of the opinion that it came closest to free rondo form; Klemm did not supply an outline; Rohland assumed an A—B—C form (Part A, 80 measures; Part B, 97 measures; Part C, 98 measures). If one compares the Adagio with other movements by Mahler and also considers the tonal relationships, one will find that it goes considerably beyond aspects of sonata form.[20]

Part 1 (Exposition)

Mm.		
	1–15	Theme I (Andante), key not clearly defined
	16–27	Theme II (Adagio), basic key: F-sharp major
	28–39	Theme III, basic key: F-sharp minor

Part 2 (varied repeat of the Exposition)

	40–48	Theme I (Andante come prima)
	49–80	Theme II (Tempo Adagio), basic key: F-sharp major; mm. 75–80 in the first violins a segment from Theme I
	81–104	Theme III (flowing) in F-sharp minor, then in B-flat minor

Part 3 (Development)

	105–111	Theme I
	112–140	Working with motifs from Themes II and III

Part 4 (varied Recapitulation)

	141–152	Themes II, basic key: F-sharp major
	153–171	Theme III, basic key: F-sharp minor
	172–177	Material from the development (mm. 118–125)

178–183   Theme II
184–193   Theme I (*Etwas zögernd*) [Somewhat hesitant]

Part 5 (Climax)
194–212   Chorale, then nine-tone chord

Part 6 (Coda)
213–275   Area of dissolution (motifs from all three themes)

As the outline shows, the three themes are exposed and then repeated, though in varied form. The development (mm. 105–140) differs in several ways from this double exposition: first, by the renewed entry of the lonely viola theme in B-flat minor; second, by the imaginative development of motifs from Themes II and III; third, by the instrumentation that is partly in chamber music style (both the violin and viola stand out in solo parts); and fourth, by the modulations. While the exposition is in F-sharp major, F-sharp minor, and B-flat minor, the development explores other keys.

It is not surprising that the recapitulation (mm. 141–193) is varied. It begins with Theme II in F-sharp major, then rearranges the sequence of themes (Theme III, II, I). Between Themes III and II, a section from the development is inserted: measures 172–177 correspond to measures 118–125.

The two most important, unique happenings of the Adagio occur between the recapitulation and coda in a very unexpected way, or, in the words of Adorno, "beyond the music's own motion":[21] a chorale (mm. 194–199) and a nine-tone chord (mm. 203–208). The chorale, after a *ppp* section, enters *fortissimo* with the A-flat minor triad.[22] Due to the masterful orchestration, this passage has an organlike fullness of sound. A few measures later, also unexpectedly, the famous nine-tone chord follows,[23] surely a number with a fateful meaning.[24]

Phrases, motifs, counterpoints, and other elements derived from the three themes alternate in the long coda (mm. 213–275).[25] In this process the motivic material of Theme II dissolves more and more. The fading out is ethereal.

Scherzo

In the manuscript, the second movement of the Tenth Symphony is marked *2. Scherzo-Finale.* Because of handwriting discrepancies between the word *Finale* and the word *Scherzo,* Cooke assumed with good reason that Mahler added the word later, possibly before the composition of movements II, IV, and V, with the intention of leaving the work as a two-movement symphony.[26]

Be that as it may, the movement is certainly one of Mahler's most original scherzos. Built according to the well-known scheme A—B—A¹—B¹—A²—Coda, it employs the principle of contrast: the distinction between metric regularity and metric irregularity. The music of the A parts is asymmetric:[27] it knows no strict meter and thrives on metric changes. The music of the B parts which have a trio character, is mostly in $\frac{3}{4}$ meter. Because of this the music of the A parts is primarily determined by rhythm; the music of the B parts is primarily determined by melody.

Meter changes had already occurred in the Scherzo (to be more precise, in the Trio) of the Sixth Symphony, but the Scherzo of the Tenth goes a good deal farther. The extremely frequent meter changes irritate the listener and cause Mahler to look like one of the fathers of New Music.

Part A

Mm.   1–22   First section (F-sharp minor)
      23–59   New version of the first section (F-sharp minor)
      60–75   Transition
      76–130 Secondary section (F major)
     131–164 New version of the first section (F-sharp minor)

Part B

     165–185 First part (E-flat major)
     186–201 Second part (G minor)
     202–211 Third part (E-flat major)
     212–223 Fourth part (B major)
     224–234 Fifth part (E-flat major)
     235–245 Sixth part (E-flat minor)

Part A¹

     246–255 Ideas from the first section
     256–269 Ideas from the secondary section
     270–278 Ideas from the first section
     279–299 Ideas from the secondary section

Part B¹

     300–319 First part (D major)
     320–330 Second part (C major)
     331–348 Third part (D major)
     349–365 Fourth part (D major-minor)

Part A²

     366–415 Ideas of the first and secondary sections (F major)

Coda

416–522   Alternating between ideas from the A and B parts, also
montage; closing in F-sharp major

Looking closely at Part A¹ one can discover sonata-form features. A first
section (more precisely a double first section) is followed by a transition, a
secondary section, and a new version of the first section. First and secondary
sections are strongly contrasted, beginning with their key relations (first section: F-sharp minor; secondary section: F major). Then there is metric contrast. There is no discernible order in the succession of different kinds of
meter in the first section, but most of the periods in the secondary section
begin with a $\frac{5}{4}$ measure. There is also contrast in the instrumentation: In the
score sketch Mahler indicates mostly strings and brass for the first section but
mostly woodwinds for the secondary section. Here are the incipits:

Beginning of first section, mm. 1–5

Beginning of secondary section, mm. 76–80

Part B is clearly in the character of a ländler.²⁸ Of its six sections, four
are in major and two are in minor. The principal major subject is quite
expansive:

Mm. 167–174

In the minor section, mode and harmonies are not clearly established,
and there is some harshness of timbre. Here, too, Mahler prefers sounds that
show different alterations of the same tone:

Mm. 185–193

In the following sections the thematic material is changed, moved around, arranged in new layers; it appears in different timbres and is developed and transposed into different keys. (Thus Part A² appears, strangely enough, in F major.) At the same time, the parts are getting shorter: Part A, 164 measures; Part B, 81 measures: Part A¹, 54 measures; Part B¹, 66 measures; Part A², 50 measures. The coda (107 measures), however, presents the biggest surprise, since here Mahler introduces thoughts from both parts in rapid succession and also in contrapuntal combinations.

In 1912 it was said that the Tenth was "altogether cheerful, even boisterous."[29] These characterizations (which probably go back to Alma Mahler) really apply only to the second movement.

Purgatorio

As mentioned before, many of Mahler's late works bear distinct autobiographical features. This is especially true of the three final movements of the Tenth Symphony. The deep sighs, exclamations, and intimate entries appearing in the manuscript on the opening pages of sections and between the notes indicate that Mahler went through a serious crisis as he composed these movements.

On the front page of the section containing the third movement, Mahler wrote in ink: *Nro. 3* and underneath *Purgatorio oder Inferno* (Purgatory or Inferno). The word *Inferno* is crossed out and the lower half of the page is cut off. It probably contained an important entry of so private a nature that Mahler himself or his wife cut off that half of the sheet.

The third movement of the Tenth is the shortest symphonic movement Mahler wrote, lasting approximately four minutes. Clear and simple in structure, it represents a da capo form: Part A, measures 1–63; Part B, measures 64–121; Part A¹, measures 122–170. In the manuscript (short score) the da capo is not written out. Mahler contented himself with merely writing down the measures of the short coda. For Mahler, the recapitulation always meant a new composition, so this da capo is quite unusual. We cannot know whether he would have left it at that in the final copy or would have varied it.

Richard Specht, who was the first to investigate the movement, noticed a certain similarity with one of Mahler's *Wunderhorn* songs, *Das irdische Leben* ("Earthly Life").[30] Specht saw a remarkable correspondence between the beginning of the song and the beginning of the movement: "the relentless grinding of the mill of life, this busy revolving that is without soul, is expressed in both by the same onward-pressing configuration." Actually, the similarity goes beyond this: song and symphonic movement have the same $\frac{2}{4}$ meter, in both the strings are muted (in only the outer parts of *Purgatory*), both express anxiety, and in both the ending is eerie. The lied ends *pianissimo* with a stroke of the cymbal; *Purgatory* ends with a beat of the tam-tam.

Yet Mahler never copies his own work. The structures are different (the song has a modified strophic form), as is the musical content as a whole: motifs; harmonies; and the shaping, overall and in detail. In the *Purgatory* movement the brighter passages are longer. The movement begins in B-flat minor (mm. 1–24), then changes to B-flat major (mm. 25–40), returns to B-flat minor, and modulates to F minor. The middle section has the basic key of D minor but also contains a brighter passage in D major (mm. 70–81).

The motivic style is strange and at the same time revealing. It conveys the impression of a *perpetuum mobile* resulting from the constant accompaniment figuration and also from the motifs of the main sections that are characterized by anapestic trill motifs and fast sixteenth-note motifs. In the middle section, Mahler does much with these motifs, which he changes, enlarges, and continues differently. Two new observations are important for a deeper understanding of the movement. The even motion of the middle section is stopped or interrupted in four places by highly expressive, sighing figures. Furthermore, Mahler's very strange verbal sighs and exclamations refer precisely to these four retarding passages.

For the first passage, there is no verbal commentary in the manuscript:

Mm. 83–89

However, after the second passage Mahler wrote the words *Tod! Verk.!* (the abbreviation *Verk.* could stand for *Verkommen,* "to perish"):

Mm. 91–95

To the third passage (marked in the manuscript *Gehalten* [restrained]) Mahler adds the exclamations *Erbarmen!! O Gott! O Gott! Warum hast du mich verlassen?* (Mercy! Oh God! Oh God! Why hast thou forsaken me?).

Mm. 106–109

Between the notes of the fourth passage (marked *Rit.*) are the words *Dein Wille geschehe!* (Thy will be done!).

Mm. 112–115]

The last two exclamations (which quote Matthew 27:46 or 6:10) prove that Mahler understood Purgatory to be not only the "purification" in the sense of the Catholic dogma of faith, but above all a condition full of suffering and torture. Mahler tells of his concept of Purgatory in an undated letter to Carl Moll, written either in the summer of 1909 or of 1910:

> I am doing fine. As you know I enjoy solitude as much as a drinker likes wine. I even believe that all people need it once a year. A kind of Purgatory—or maybe a purging of the mind—both are right (GMB[2] 390).

Those who are acquainted with Mahler's intellectual world and creative process will not be surprised to find out that the Purgatory movement of the Tenth owes its origin to a definite occurrence. What this experience was is not known, but in her memoirs Alma Mahler describes an event that certainly could qualify. According to her report, Walter Gropius, who loved Alma, had written a letter to her and asked her to leave everything behind and join him. It is understandable that Mahler, who read the letter because it was addressed to him, was deeply hurt. While staying in Toblach expecting an answer to his letter, Gropius was brought to the house by Mahler himself so that he could talk to Alma. Alma reports:

> The short conversation I had with him, I interrupted after a few minutes because I suddenly was afraid for Mahler. Mahler was walking back and forth in his room. Two candles were burning on his table. He was reading in the Holy Scriptures. He said: "What you do will be right. Decide for yourself!" But then I did not have a choice! (AME 218)

Fourth Movement: *Der Teufel tanzt es mit mir* ("The Devil is Dancing with Me")

The positioning of some of his movements was a problem that at times occupied Mahler intensively. An extreme case is the fourth movement of the Tenth Symphony. Remarks in the autograph indicate that he was uncertain whether he should place the movement at the beginning of the Symphony, in second place, or at the end. On the front of the folder are these markings, written in ink: *2. Satz,* underneath this: *Finale,* and again underneath: *1. Scherzo* (*I. Satz*). All three were crossed out, partly in ink, partly in blue pencil. Then Mahler wrote the word *Finale* in blue pencil, but again crossed it out and finally wrote IV in blue pencil.

The further entries on the front of the folder show that in the summer of 1910 Mahler's condition from time to time bordered on insanity; a kind of title of the movement is the remark *Der Teufel tanzt es mit mir.* Below this is written

> *Wahnsinn, faß mich an, Verfluchten!*
> *Vernichte mich*
> *Daß ich vergesse, daß ich bin!*
> *Daß ich aufhöre, zu sein*
> *Daß ich ver.*

> Insanity, grab me, the accursed one!
> Destroy me
> That I forget that I am!
> That I stop existing
> That I *ver.*

The abbreviated word at the end could mean *verende* or *verkomme* (perish) or *verrecke* (perish like a beast). Let us examine whether and to what extent these entries offer a kind of commentary to the music. A formal outline may be of help.

Mm. 1–122 Main section, divided into three parts: A (mm. 1–56); B (mm. 57–106); A¹ (mm. 107–122); basic key: E minor
123–165 Trio (basic key: C major)
166–218 Main section varied and shortened, culminating in a climax suggesting a sigh
219–225 Brief Trio hint in C major
226–247 Main section (varied and shortened)
248–379 Trio (new version), basic key: A major
380–409 Main section (varied and shortened)
410–443 Trio (new version in B major culminating in a climax suggesting a sigh)
444–494 Main section (new version based on elements from section

B) culminating in a climax with a sigh
495–504   Brief Trio hint
505–578   Coda (based on material from the Main section and the Trio)

The movement can be seen as a mixture of a demonic scherzo and a tender, happy waltz. The frequent changes between main section and trio are characteristic for the structure. The regularity in the sequence of the sections is deceptive, however, as the trios sometimes are only suggested.

Main section and Trio contrast strongly in regard to mode (minor or major); to harmony (unlike the main section, in which complicated chordal sequences are often revealed, while the harmony in the Trio is at times reduced to the simplest functions); and, above all, to the character of expression. While the music of the main section is often full of tension, the Trio appears to be relaxed.

The chord sequence $F_7 < F$–sharp$_7$ at the beginning is typical of the tension prevalent in the main section. It serves as a seal or characteristic imprint of the movement, and it returns at various points:[31]

Mm. 1–4

The beginning of the Trio, on the other hand, is rhythmically attractive (using hemiolas) but harmonically very simple:

Mm. 122–130

It is interesting to observe that at a later return (Trio hint) this passage takes on even simpler features (parallel sixths with tonic-dominant change) and that Mahler, in the short score from which we quote, defined them, this time explicitly, as *Dance*.

Mm. 219–225

He marked a passage from the first section *sehr klagend* (very lamenting):

Mm. 184–192

For the basic character of this quite ambivalent movement it is no less typical that three passages (mm. 210–218, 432–443, and 486–495) culminate in sighing climaxes, two of which are followed by very simple dance music:

Mm. 210–220

The example demonstrates that the abrupt change from the tragic to the trivial is a trait that can be traced in virtually all of Mahler's works, all the way from *Das klagende Lied*[32] and *Todtenmarsch* of the First Symphony to the Tenth.

The programmatic content of the movement does not become completely evident until the coda (mm. 505–578). It is significant not merely because it mixes motifs from the first section and the Trio, but because it leads into a key that is alien to the movement (beginning in E minor and ending in D minor) and because the music seems to move more and more into the distance, closing with the stroke of a "completely muted" drum (as Mahler indicates in the short score). Regarding this ending, which at first glance seems strange, Mahler remarked in the short score: "You alone know what it means. Ah! Ah! Ah! Farewell, my music!"

In her memoirs Alma Mahler lets us know the meaning of this ending:

The young arts and crafts student Marie Uchatius was once with me in the Hotel Majestic. Something caught our attention. On the broad street along Central Park there was hustle, bustle, and noise. We leaned out of the window; below us was a great crowd of people. A funeral procession was approaching. We then learned from the newspapers that it was a fireman who had been killed while fighting a fire.[33] The procession stopped. The head fireman stepped forward and gave a short speech. On the eleventh floor we mostly guessed that he was speaking. A short pause, then a beat on the muffled drum. Everyone stood in silence—then the procession moved on. The end.

This strange memorial service forced tears from our eyes. Concerned about him I looked at Mahler's window. He was also leaning far out and his face was covered with tears. The scene had made such an impression on him that he used this short beat on the drum in his Tenth Symphony (AME 170).

As in the second movement of the Ninth, here the dance music also stops at the end. Death has the final say.

Finale

One of the most astonishing discoveries one makes in looking more closely at the Finale of the Tenth is the fact that the movement draws to a great extent on the thematic material of the *Purgatory* movement. Its motifs are quoted, modified, and developed to the extent that in retrospect one might consider the short *Purgatory* movement to be the symphony's central movement. The Finale, to be sure, also brings new themes, including a sweeping theme in D major and two melodious Adagio themes that determine the end of the movement.

Apart from the close connections with the *Purgatory,* there are also thematic ties to other movements. The Finale quotes the fourth movement and turns to three places in the first movement. These reminiscences help underline the cyclical character of the Symphony and support the conclusion that the Finale was the last movement to be written.

Part I (Introduction)

Mm. 1–29   First section: funeral music with strokes on the large muffled military drum (*Purgatory* motifs)

30–71   Second section: two cantilena themes (in the sequence I, II, and I) in D major and B major

72–83   Third section: funeral music

Part II (Allegro moderato)

84–144   First section: development of the *Purgatory* motifs (basic key: D minor)

145–178 Second section: exposition of a sweeping D major theme, formed in measures 98–103

179–186 Climax containing a sighing motif = reminiscence from the fourth movement (mm. 210–218)

187–244 Third section: repeated statements of the first cantilena theme of the Finale

245–250 Transition

251–266 Fourth section: return to elements of the first and second sections (mm. 251–259) ∼mm. 104–114)

Use of material from the first movement

267–274 ∼I, measures 188–193

275–283 ∼I, measures 203–208

284–298 ∼I, measures 1–15

Part III ($\frac{4}{4}$ meter)

299–384 Further modification of the two cantilena themes in B-flat major, F-sharp major, G major, and again F-sharp major (the seventh stands out as an expressive interval)

385–400   Coda

As the outline indicates, the structure of the movement is complex and in many ways unique. Apart from reverting to material from the first movement (mm. 267–298), the two slow sections (83 and 86 measures in length) frame a lively middle section of 185 measures. In the short score, Mahler marks the first part *Introduction* and the second part expressly Allegro Moderato. Tempo markings for the first and third parts are missing in the manuscript, yet Deryck Cooke surely labeled the two parts correctly as *Langsam, schwer* (slowly, heavily) and *Sehr ruhig* (very quietly).

The introduction, clearly divided into three sections, includes contrasting material. While the two outer sections (mm. 1–29 and mm. 72–83) are among Mahler's most lugubrious passages (both representing funeral music), the considerably brighter middle section (mm. 30–71) sounds comforting. The Finale begins as the fourth movement had ended, with a sound symbolizing a funeral—the beat of a muted drum. In the first section of the introduction and in the third section, this beat is followed by five more drum beats. In between, motifs from the *Purgatory* movement are heard. Their effect is quite different, however, due to the much slower tempo, the augmentations, and above all to the transposition into a low register; they seem dark, dragging, eerie. Here are the first eight measures of the Finale in the notation of the short score:[34]

The introduction literally quotes two of the four musical sighs from the middle section of the *Purgatory* movement, namely, the two insertions that Mahler associated with death and with the pleas of mercy:

Finale, mm. 11–14 and mm. 21–24

Both quotations also appear in the third section of the introduction (mm. 76–78 and 80–83) but in reverse sequence.

The middle section of the introduction differs from the others in mode (the dark D minor of the beginning is replaced by D major and B major), harmony (the pedal-point harmonies of the beginning give way to a more regular manner with frequent chord changes), and above all in the two cantilena themes that dominate the higher ranges and are to play an important role as the movement progresses. According to Mahler's indications in the short score, the first ethereal theme, strikingly and attractively harmonized, was intended for the flute, and the second for the violins:

Mm. 29–37

Mm. 44–49

In the Allegro moderato, contrasting levels of expression account for the section's uniqueness. The motivic material of the *Purgatory* movement forms the first level (somewhat mysterious and spooky but also strident), which Mahler develops here in a symphonic, virtuoso manner. The sweeping D-major theme comes from a completely different, euphoric mood, introduced here as contrast:

Mm. 144–152

The melodious first theme represents a third realm of expression and is played several times (mm. 186–244), here and there combined contrapuntally with *Purgatory* motifs.

Three references back to the first movement constitute a decisive turn, especially the restatement of the nine-tone chord (mm. 275–283) and the lonely theme now played by the horns (mm. 284–298). Those who now expect a kind of recapitulation will be disappointed. The lugubrious music of the beginning does not return: death is transcended.

The third part of the movement (mm. 299–384) appears like a long *Abgesang*. The two cantilena themes on which it is based are elaborated upon in the manner of an "endless melody." The expressive power of the music partly results from the frequent use of the interval of a seventh. Mahler discovered its expressive power in this Finale:[35]

Mm. 315–321

The passage at measure 353ff., with all violins (according to Mahler's indications in the short score) playing the first cantilena theme *fortissimo* and with "big sound," represents the expressive climax of the whole movement and is one of the most beautiful passages of all symphonic literature.

The extremely tender coda (mm. 385–400) fades away *pianissimo*. Mahler's words in the short score "To live for you! / To die for you!" refer to this music. Seven measures before the end we hear a last, flaring-up gesture: The melody suddenly rises, reaches an accentuated high note, and slowly sinks back down. As commentary to this musical "address," Mahler wrote into the short score the nickname of his wife: *Almschi!*[36]

Abbreviations

AME   Alma Mahler. *Gustav Mahler: Erinnerungen und Briefe*. 2nd ed. Amsterdam, 1949.

AMML   Alma Mahler-Werfel. *Mein Leben*. Frankfurt am Main/Hamburg, 1963 (Fischer Bücherei 545).

BL[1]   Natalie Bauer-Lechner. *Erinnerungen an Gustav Mahler*. Leipzig/Vienna/Zurich, 1923.

BL[2]   Natalie Bauer-Lechner. *Gustav Mahler in den Erinnerungen von Natalie Bauer-Lechner*. Diary entries, Herbert Killian, ed. Hamburg, 1984.

DKW   *Des Knaben Wunderhorn. Alte deutsche Lieder gesammelt von L. Achim von Arnim und Clemens Brentano*. Complete ed. (according to the text of the 1st ed., 1806/1808.) 3 vols. Deutscher Taschenbuch Verlag, Munich, 1963.

FL 1   Constantin Floros. *Gustav Mahler*. Vol. 1, *Die geistige Welt Gustav Mahlers in systematischer Darstellung*. Breitkopf and Härtel, Wiesbaden, 1977.

FL 2   Constantin Floros. *Gustav Mahler*. Vol. 2, *Mahler und die Symphonik des 19. Jahrhunderts in neuer Deutung. Zur Grundlegung einer zeitgemässen musikalischen Exegetik*. Breitkopf and Härtel, Wiesbaden, 1977.

GMB[1]   Alma Maria Mahler, ed. *Gustav Mahler: Briefe 1879–1911*. Berlin/Vienna/Leipzig, 1924.

GMB[2]   Herta Blaukopf, ed. *Gustav Mahler Briefe: 1879–1911*. Rev. and enl. ed. Publications of the International Gustav Mahler Society, Vienna/Hamburg, 1982.

GMUB   Herta Blaukopf, ed. *Gustav Mahler: Unbekannte Briefe*. Publications of the International Gustav Mahler Society, Vienna/Hamburg, 1983.

HLG 1   Henry-Louis de La Grange. *Mahler,* vol. 1. New York, 1973.

M. (mm.)   Measure (measures).

No.   Rehearsal number in score.

Other abbreviations according to *Riemann-Musiklexikon, Sachteil* (Mainz, 1967), p. 10ff.

Notes

Introduction to the English Edition

1. Reprinted in L. Stein, ed. *Style and Idea,* p. 136.

Introduction

1. See Floros, *Gustav Mahler,* vol. 1, Chapter 1 (hereafter cited as FL 1).
2. See also Friedrich Schiller, *Über die ästhetische Erziehung des Menschen*; and Robert Schumann, *Rezension der* Symphonie fantastique *von Berlioz* (1835).
3. Strauss answered him: "You may be right regarding the program of the *Domestica;* in this you agree with G. Mahler, who condemns the program altogether. But regarding the *Symphonia Domestica,* (1) I have not added a program, and (2) I believe that you yourself have a somewhat incorrect concept about the purpose of such a program" (qtd. in Erich H. Mueller von Asow, *Richard Strauss. Thematisches Verzeichnis,* vol. 1[Vienna/Wiesbaden, 1959], p. 341).
4. The manuscript of the Tenth Symphony presents an extreme case.
5. Pfohl, *Gustav Mahler.,* p. 68; Manfred Wagner, *Geschichte,* pp. 392, 396; Worbs, "Gustav Mahlers Sinfonien," pp. 4–8.
6. Regarding the method of semantic analysis, see Floros, *Gustav Mahler,* vol. 2. (hereafter cited as FL 2); and Floros, "Verschwiegene Programmusik," pp. 204–225.
7. Lindt, ed., *Bruno Walter: Briefe,* p. 115.
8. Casella, "Gustav Mahler," p. 240f. See also Casella, "Festrede," pp. 415–419.
9. Stefan, *Gustav Mahler: eine Studie,* p. 86f.

Fundamentals of "Tetralogy"

1. See FL 1, pp. 167–172. See also Floros, "Weltanschauung," pp. 29–39.
2. See Adorno, *Physiognomik,* p. 31ff.
3. Bekker, *Gustav Mahlers Sinfonien,* p. 32f.
4. Anonymous [Natalie Bauer-Lechner], "Aus einem Tagebuch über Mahler," *Der Merker* 3 (March 1912), p. 188.

The First Symphony

1. Mahler to Fritz Löhr on 1 January 1885: "I have written a cycle of songs, six so far, which are all dedicated to her" (GMB[2] 35).
2. Mahler to Fritz Löhr on 22 June 1884 (GMB[2] 30).
3. Adler, *Gustav Mahler,* p. 98f.
4. Fritz Löhr in GMB[1] 478, footnote 39; and GMB[2] 413, footnote 39.
5. Steinitzer, "Gustav Mahler," pp. 296–298.
6. Facsimile of the Budapest concert program in Grange, *Mahler,* fig. 32.
7. Facsimile of the critique in Mitchell, *Gustav Mahler,* p. 151.
8. Herta Blaukopf, ed., *Gustav Mahler—Richard Strauss.* p. 36f.
9. Printed in Pfohl, *Gustav Mahler,* pp. 64–67.
10. Richard Strauss worked in Weimar from 1 October 1889 until June 1894. See Max Steinitzer, *Richard Strauss* (Berlin/Leipzig, 1927), pp. 104–137. Mahler already became acquainted with Strauss in 1887. See Thomas, *Richard Strauss,* p. 156.
11. Nodnagel, *Jenseits von Wagner und Liszt,* pp. 4–10.
12. Facsimile of the Hamburg concert program in HLG 1, Ill. 47.
13. Specht, *Gustav Mahler* (1913 ed.), p. 173.
14. Stefan, *Gustav Mahler: eine Studie,* p. 113.
15. See FL 2, pp. 247–259.
16. Walter, *Gustav Mahler* (1957 ed.), p. 102.
17. Foerster, *Der Pilger,* p. 409f.
18. Jean Paul, "Herbst-Blumine, oder gesammelte Werkchen aus Zeitschriften, Erstes Bändchen," in *Jean Paul's sämmtliche Werke,* vol. 44 (Berlin, 1827).
19. Hermand, "Der vertonte 'Titan,' " pp. 1–5.
20. Pfohl, *Gustav Mahler,* p. 17.
21. Tibbe, *Über die Verwendung,* p. 43.
22. See FL 1, p. 203f.
23. Bekker, *Gustav Mahlers Sinfonien,* p. 45.
24. Adorno, *Physiognomik,* p. 11.
25. Walter, *Gustav Mahler* (1957 ed.), p. 85.
26. See, especially, Mitchell, *Gustav Mahler,* pp. 217–224.
27. Letter to Fritz Löhr on 1 January 1885 (GMB[2] 35).
28. *Musikblätter des Anbruch II* (1920), p. 296. See also the communications of Steinitzer in Stefan, ed., *Gustav Mahler: ein Bild,* p. 13f.
29. A phrase from the *Valse* in Tchaikovsky's *Symphony No. 5* crept in. See FL 2, pp. 172–178.
30. See HLG 1 (1973), pp. 728f., 754.
31. Robert Schumann, critique of Berlioz's *Symphonie fantastique* (qtd. in Robert Schumann, *Gesammelte Schriften über Musik und Musiker,* vol. I, 5th ed., Martin Kreisig, ed., Leipzig, 1914, p. 85).
32. Reproductions in HLG 1 (1973), Ill. 34, and in Mitchell, *Gustav Mahler,* p. 237.
33. Pfohl, *Gustav Mahler,* p. 17.
34. Facsimile of the Berlin concert program in HLG 1, Ill. 50.
35. Schiedermair, "Gustav Mahler als Symphoniker," p. 509.
36. Qtd. in Specht, *Gustav Mahler* (1913 ed.), p. 24.
37. Søren Kierkegaard is the author of a basic essay on Socratic irony. Regarding the entire problem, see Hans-Egon Hass and Gustav-Adolf Mohrlüder,

eds., *Ironie als literarisches Phänomen* (Neue wissenschaftliche Bibliothek LVII. Literaturwissenschaften), Cologne, 1973.

38. Jones, *Das Leben und Werk von Sigmund Freud,* p. 103f.
39. Tibbe, *Über die Verwendung,* pp. 75–85; Osthoff, "Zu Gustav Mahlers Erster Symphonie," pp. 217–227; Roman, "Connotative Irony in Mahler's Todtenmarsch," pp. 207–222.
40. The indication *Mit Parodie* is missing in the Hamburg autograph.
41. See BL² 42, 58.
42. Famous examples of *col legno* playing in symphonic literature before Mahler occur in the Finale of Berlioz's *Symphonie fantastique* and Liszt's *Mazeppa.* In his treatise on orchestration, Berlioz noted that this style is called for in symphonic movements "where the terrible and the grotesque meet." See Berlioz, *Treatise on Instrumentation,* p. 23.
43. The violin glissando in measures 57–58 creates a decidedly banal effect.
44. Adorno, *Physiognomik,* p. 160.
45. See FL 2, pp. 84–90.
46. See FL 2, pp. 152–154.
47. Herta Blaukopf, ed., *Briefwechsel Mahler—Strauss,* p. 39f.
48. Sponheuer, *Logik des Zerfalls,* p. 76f.

The Second Symphony

1. See Reilly, "Die Skizzen zu Mahlers zweiter Symphonie," pp. 266–285.
2. See also Martner and Becqué, "Zwölf unbekannte Briefe," p. 289.
3. These dates are according to Reilly, "Die Skizzen zu Mahlers zweiter Symphonie," p. 269.
4. Letter to Hermann Behn, October 1895 (GMUB 24f.).
5. Foerster, *Der Pilger,* p. 403.
6. Foerster, "Erinnerungen an Gustav Mahler," p. 294; also *Der Pilger,* p. 405.
7. The full score of the *Todtenfeier* designates the following instrumentation: three flutes (the third also piccolo), two oboes, English horn, two B-flat clarinets, one B-flat bass clarinet, three bassoons, four horns in F, three trumpets in F, three trombones, contrabass tuba, triangle, cymbals, bass drum, timpani, harp, and strings. Toward the end (mm. 439–440 of the final version) a tam-tam beat is indicated. The final version requires three flutes, three oboes, three B-flat clarinets, two E-flat clarinets, bassoons (the third also contrabassoon), six horns, four trumpets, four trombones, countrabass tuba, triangle, tam-tam (low and high), cymbals, bass drum, two timpani, two harps, and strings.
8. Herta Blaukopf, ed., *Briefwechsel Mahler—Strauss,* p. 40.
9. See FL 1, pp. 98–100, 194, 200; Floros, "Weltanschauung, p. 32f.; and BL² 185f.
10. Pfohl, *Gustav Mahler,* p. 20f.
11. Particulars regarding the memorial service for Bülow, including the text for the three Klopstock strophes that were sung at the funeral service, in Foerster, "Aus Mahlers Werkstatt," pp. 921–924. See also Foerster, *Der Pilger,* pp. 404–406.
12. Specht, *Gustav Mahlers II. Sinfonie,* p. 4.
13. See FL 1, pp. 72–83.

14. Specht, *Gustav Mahler* (1913 ed.), p. 227.
15. See Stephan, *Gustav Mahler: II. Symphonie,* p. 20ff.
16. Our discussion is based on the printed version, which differs from the some-what longer, original version in the instrumentation and in numerous details. The full score of the *Todtenfeier* has 451 or 452 measures (Mahler later divided one measure into two) and in three different places contains passages with a total of twenty-two crossed-out measures.
17. Symptomatic of Mahler's reluctance later in life to grant insights into the semantics of his music is a correction that he made in the first edition of Symphony No. 2. The Coda of the first movement (p. 49, No. 24) bears the title *Langsam und feierlich* [Slowly and solemnly] and the subtitle *Im Tempo eines Trauermarsches* [In the tempo of a funeral march]. In his personal copy Mahler crossed out both indications and wrote above them *Tempo sostenuto,* the indication in later editions. See the facsimile in Stephan, *Gustav Mahler: Werk und Interpretation,* p. 66.
18. See Constantin Floros, "Parallelen zwischen Schubert und Bruckner," in *Festschrift Othmar Wessely zum 60. Geburtstag* (Tutzing, 1982), p. 142.
19. Nodnagel, *Jenseits von Wagner und Liszt,* p. 10.
20. In the second part of the *Todtenfeier* by Mickiewicz, the shades of the departed are bid farewell by Guslar and the chorus (Lipiner-Edition, pp. 39, 44, 47):

> *Nun geh' mit Gott, wie man dich heißt,*
> *Und folget Wer nicht gern:*
> *So bann' ihn Vater, Sohn und Geist!*
> *Siehst du das Kreuz des Herrn?*

> Now God be with you: go, as told,
> Whoever does not follow willingly,
> Let him be banned by Father, Son, and Holy Ghost!
> Do you see the Lord's cross?

  Regarding Liszt's "tonal symbol of the Cross", see FL 2, pp. 243–245, 256–259.
21. Specht, *Gustav Mahler* (1913 ed.), p. 227.
22. In the autograph of *Todtenfeier,* there is a long passage between the two parts of the development that Mahler reduced by ten measures (mm. 244–253 of the final version).
23. Regarding Mahler's variation technique, see Adorno, *Physiognomik,* pp. 116–124.
24. Foerster, *Der Pilger,* p. 408.
25. Austrian National Library, sup. mus. 4364, two fascicles.
26. See also Reilly, "Die Skizzen zu Mahlers zweiter Symphonie," p. 278f.
27. See the facsimile in Stephan, *Gustav Mahler: Werk und Interpretation,* p. 33.
28. Second fascicle, fol. 4r: "Durchführ. Rückgang u. vorher kommt Meeres-stille"; fol. 5v: "jetzt kommt Meeresstille"; and fol. 6v.
29. See FL 2, p. 149f.
30. Mahler to Fritz Löhr on 28 November 1891 (GMB[1] 97f; GMB[2] 95).
31. See FL 2, p. 375.

32. Compare, for instance, the melody of the flutes and the first oboe in Mahler's Andante moderato (mm. 68–71) with the melody of the first oboe in the second movement (Andante con moto, mm. 84–92) of Schubert's "Unfinished Symphony."

33. Regarding the relation of *Fischpredigt* to the Scherzo of the Second Symphony, see Eggebrecht, *Die Musik Gustav Mahlers,* pp. 199–226.

34. Compare this with the following statement from Richard Wagner's *Beethoven* essay of 1870: "From the most frightening of such dreams, we awaken with a *scream*. It expresses quite directly the frightened will that through the scream first enters the world of sound to express itself overtly" (qtd. in Richard Wagner, *Sämtliche Schriften,* vol. 9, p. 69).

35. The corresponding markings in the *Fischpredigt* are *with humor* or *with parody*.

36. Bekker, *Gustav Mahlers Sinfonien,* pp. 11–23. See also FL 2, pp. 14–16.

37. See FL 2, pp. 291–294.

38. The four-hand keyboard edition by Hermann Behn was published in 1895 by Friedrich Hofmeister (Universal-Edition, No. 2937).

39. According to Sponheuer (*Logik des Zerfalls,* p. 97) and Stephan (*Gustav Mahler: II. Symphonie,* p. 69), the exposition does not begin until measure 62.

40. See the passages *Sterben werd' ich, um zu leben* (No. 47) and *Mit Flügeln, die ich mir errungen, werde ich entschweben!* (No. 46).

41. Qtd. from the revised version of Martin Luther's translation, *Deutsche Bibelstiftung* (Stuttgart, 1978), p. 681.

42. See also Luke 3:4–6.

43. DKW 3, pp. 132–137.

44. The first four measures of this theme are the same as the melody of the first line of the Resurrection Chorale.

45. Redlich (*Bruckner and Mahler,* p. 163) called this crescendo a predecessor to the famous crescendo in the third act of Alban Berg's *Wozzeck.*

46. See FL 2, p. 205.

47. Sponheuer (*Logik des Zerfalls,* p. 116) and Stephan (*Gustav Mahler: II. Symphonie,* p. 73) see a part with a Coda function that begins with measure 672 or 712. The strophic form of the cantata, however, precludes such an arrangement.

The Third Symphony

1. The autograph, owned by Robert O. Lehman, is kept at the Pierpont Morgan Library, New York. Five pages of it are reproduced in FL 1 (pp. 235–236, 238–240).

2. The Stanford University Memorial Library of Music owns two manuscripts of four and seven pages each (catalogue nos. 630 and 631) with sketches of the Third Symphony.

3. See Franklin, "The Gestation of Mahler's Third Symphony," pp. 439–446; and the important essay by Williamson, "Mahler's Compositional Process," pp. 338–345.

4. Bekker, *Gustav Mahlers Sinfonien,* p. 106.

5. HLG 1, p. 327.

6. The page contains a keyboard sketch of measures 1–48.
7. In letters to Hermann Behn (GMUB 24) and Arnold Berliner (GMB² 126) dated 17 August 1895, and to Fritz Löhr (GMB² 128), dated 29 August, the Finale bears the title *Das himmlische Leben,* but in a letter to Natalie Bauer-Lechner dated 3 September, Mahler calls the movement *Was mir das Kind erzählt* (BL² 37).
8. Facsimile in Stephan, *Gustav Mahler: Werk und Interpretation,* p. 6. Stephan's assumption (p. 34) that the sketch originated before 1892—the year *Das himmlische Leben* was written—is completely erroneous.
9. See FL 1, pp. 125–132.
10. Novalis, *Die Enzyklopädie IX,* fragment no. 1802.
11. Qtd. in Gustave René Hocke, "Manierismus in der Literatur. Sprach-Alchimie und esoterische Kombinationskunst," in *Rowohlts deutsche enzyklopädie 82/83* (Hamburg, 1959), p. 55f.
12. Schopenhauer, *Die Welt als Wille und Vorstellung,* vol. 1, § 52 (as qtd. in Zurich ed., *Werke in zehn Bänden,* vol. 1, p. 325). In *Zur Metaphysik der Musik* (*Die Welt als Wille und Vorstellung II,* chapter 39; Zurich ed., vol. 4, p. 526) is the statement: "The four voices of all harmony—that is, bass, tenor, alto, and soprano, or the tonic, third, fifth, and octave—correspond to the four steps in the *Reihe der Wesen* [Series of Beings], that is, the kingdoms of minerals, plants, animals, and humans."
13. During the Hamburg years Mahler read Schopenhauer and Fechner. See Walter, *Gustav Mahler* (1957 ed.), p. 102, and Pfohl, *Gustav Mahler,* p. 20.
14. Fechner, *Zend-Avesta,* vol. 1, pp. 195–293.
15. See FL 1, p. 82f.
16. The poem "Genesis" is in Lipiner's *Buch der Freude* (1880). Complete poem in FL 1, pp. 203–206.
17. Foerster, *Der Pilger,* p. 456.
18. See FL 1, p. 70f.
19. *Also sprach Zarathustra,* part 1, "Zarathustras Vorrede" (Nietzsche, *Werke,* vol. 2, p. 553).
20. *Die fröhliche Wissenschaft,* 5th book, § 344 (Nietzsche, *Werke,* vol. 2, p. 482).
21. See the letter to Fritz Löhr dated 29 August 1895. Quoted earlier in Chapter 3 under "Mahler's Cosmology and Its Sources."
22. *Also sprach Zarathustra,* 4th and final part, "Das Eselsfest" (Nietzsche, *Werke,* vol. 2, p. 824).
23. *Die fröhliche Wissenschaft,* 1st book, § 14 (Nietzsche, *Werke,* vol. 2, p. 322).
24. Schnebel, "Über Mahlers Dritte," pp. 283–288.
25. Sponheuer, *Logik des Zerfalls,* pp. 141, 160.
26. Basic observations about Mahler's symphonic writing in FL 2, pp. 107–183.
27. In a letter to Anna von Mildenburg of 9 July 1896, Mahler writes that he had been seeking a main title for the Third "for weeks" and finally had decided on *Pan,* "who, as you know, is an ancient Greek god who later became the personification of the universe (in Greek, *Pan* means 'everything')" (GMB² 170). Nevertheless, the Stanford sketch documents that the Pan concept already had occupied Mahler during the summer of 1895.
28. This was already correctly noted by Franklin ("The Gestation of Mahler's Third Symphony," p. 444).

29. The very pronounced marchlike character of parts of the movement once suggested to Richard Strauss, as he performed it, a vision of endless "battalions of workers, who are going to the May Day festivities in the Prater [Vienna's amusement park]" (Specht, *Gustav Mahler* [1913 ed.], p. 249).

30. It is strange that in discussions of the supposed triviality of Mahler's music the intentional aspect is always ignored.

31. Facsimile in Mitchell, *Gustav Mahler*, facing p. 136.

32. Trombones are also omitted in this movement.

33. See BL² 64, and the program sketch in Mitchell, *Gustav Mahler*, facing p. 136.

34. See FL 2, p. 208f.

35. Tibbe, *Über die Verwendung*, pp. 85–97.

36. Also see the more detailed discussion by Eggebrecht, *Die Musik Gustav Mahlers*, pp. 169–197.

37. Qtd. in Nodnagel, *Jenseits von Wagner und Liszt*, p. 14.

38. Decsey, "Stunden mit Mahler," p. 356.

39. *Lenaus sämtliche Werke in vier Bänden* (Stuttgart, n.d. [1893]), vol. 1, pp. 102–104.

40. *Lenaus sämtliche Werke in vier Bänden*, vol. 1, pp. 15–17.

41. In the score sketch (Cary Collection, No. 140a of the Pierpont Morgan Library in New York), this movement bears the title *Was mir die Nacht erzählt*.

42. Also see BL² 136.

43. "Das trunkne Lied" from *Also sprach Zarathustra*: *"Lust aber will nicht Erben, nicht Kinder—Lust will sich selber, will Ewigkeit, will Wiederkunft, will Alles-sich-ewig-gleich"* ("Pleasure does not want heirs, not children—pleasure desires itself, wants eternity, reincarnation, wants everything eternally equal") (Nietzsche, *Werke*, vol. 2, p. 830).

44. Siering, "Nietzsches Mitternachtslied," pp. 90–95.

45. The "mystical" harmonies of the beginning (F—a—f-sharp—a—b₆—a—e—a—G—F—c—F) are somewhat impressionistic.

46. In the summer of 1899 Mahler mentioned to Natalie Bauer-Lechner (BL² 136): "I have always wondered from where I know that theme. Today it dawned on me, that it is from something I composed during my school years. The first few measures of that piece are as in *O Mensch*; but after that it became trivial."

47. See Eggebrecht, *Die Musik Gustav Mahlers*, pp. 136–144.

48. In this movement, which completely foregoes the use of percussion, the trumpets are brought in for only two measures (mm. 97, 99).

49. See FL 2, pp. 204–206.

50. DKW 3, pp. 55.

51. An early keyboard sketch (at the Alban Berg Foundation) seems to prove that Mahler did not have the idea to include the four bells and the boys' choir until later. Here, the "ding-dong" sounds of the first three measures were not yet notated.

52. See also Floros, "Studien zur *Parsifal*," pp. 47–53.

53. Qtd. in FL 1, p. 198. The version in BL² 172 deviates from this.

54. In Greek mythology, this is a never-resting, fiery wheel upon which the transgressor Ixion was bound.

The Fourth Symphony

1. Similarly, Hans Pfitzner (*Über musikalische Inspiration,* Berlin, 1940, p. 30) defines the unconscious as "that which composes within me."
2. *Der Schildwache Nachtlied, Verlor'ne Müh', Trost im Unglück, Das him-mlische Leben,* and *Wer hat dies Liedel erdacht?* According to an entry in the autograph (owned by the Society of the Friends of Music in Vienna), Mahler completed the clean copy of the five *Humoresques* in Hamburg on Tuesday, 26 April 1892. At the close of *Das himmlische Leben* is the date Hamburg, 12 March 1892.
3. DKW 1, 2u3f.
4. Gerhard F. Hering, ed., *Meister der deutschen Kritik* (dtv. dokumente, vols. 18, 106) (Munich, 1961, 1963), vol. 1, p. 147.
5. Bekker, *Gustav Mahlers Sinfonien,* p. 145.
6. The score draft (in the Cary Collection, No. 140a, Pierpont Morgan Library) of the fifth movement of the Third bears the title *Was mir die Morgenglocken erzählen.*
7. See Fechner, *Das Büchlein vom Leben nach dem Tode.* Also see also FL 1 (1977), pp. 110–113.
8. Lindt ed., *Bruno Walter: Briefe,* p. 50.
9. Lindt ed., *Bruno Walter: Briefe,* pp. 51f.
10. Mahler must have been much affected by tombs in churches where the dead are portrayed with folded hands, because in March 1901, regarding Johann Sebastian Bach, he told Natalie Bauer-Lechner: "Bach so often reminds me of the tombstones, where the dead rests with folded hands above his ashes. These always move me, as they hang on to life beyond the earthly existence. They express a faith in life after death that they cherish more strongly than actual life" (BL[2] 184).
11. Reeser, *Gustav Mahler und Holland,* pp. 104–107.
12. Schopenhauer, *Die Welt als Wille und Vorstellung,* vol. 1, 4th book, § 68 (Zurich ed., vol. 2, p. 482).
13. Lindt, ed., *Bruno Walter: Briefe,* p. 50.
14. In the summer of 1900, Mahler told Bauer-Lechner that the Fourth would last 45 minutes (BL[2] 162). Do the numbers 15, 10, 11, 8, and (their total) 44, notated in pencil in the autograph of the Fourth on the title page of the fourth movement (page 149), indicate the duration in minutes of the indi-vidual movements? In a recording with Rafael Kubelik (DGG 2561 081) the movements last 15'48", 9'05", 18'50", and 7'58".
15. Adorno, *Physiognomik,* p. 79.
16. Lindt, ed., *Bruno Walter: Briefe,* p. 51.
17. The heading of the first movement in the autograph is *Heiter behaglich; anmuthig bewegt* (Happily comfortable; gracefully moving). Mahler changed the heading a number of times and finally replaced it with the simple *bedächtig* (gentle).
18. Adorno, "Wiener Gedenkrede," p. 119.
19. Richard Wagner, *Sämtliche Schriften und Dichtungen,* vol. 8, pp. 261–337. See also Georg Schünemann, *Geschichte des Dirigierens* (Leipzig, 1913), pp. 333–343; Constantin Floros, "Historische Phasen der Bruckner-Interpretation," in *Bruckner Symposion,* Othmar Wessely, ed. (Linz, 1983), pp. 93–102.

20. Adorno, *Physiognomik*, p. 82.
21. Adorno, *Physiognomik*, p. 77.
22. In the forest cabins in which he composed, Mahler was often stricken with panic. Alma reports: "Sensing the terrifying eye of the great Pan often frightened him. In the middle of his work he would then come out out of his seclusion to be near the human, warm proximity of our house, to regain his composure and then go on with his work" (AME 146).
23. Reeser, *Gustav Mahler und Holland*, p. 14f.; also see AME 324.
24. Reeser, *Gustav Mahler und Holland*, p. 53.
25. During a read-through of the Fourth on 12 October 1901 (as Bauer-Lechner reports), Mahler thought that the passage of the solo violin (which "was tuned a half-step higher in order to produce a particularly shrill sound") was "still not sufficiently cutting" (BL² 198). "He therefore decided to give the solo to the viola, which the concert-master played."
26. Reeser, *Gustav Mahler und Holland*, p. 105.
27. Mitchell, *Gustav Mahler*, p. 303.
28. Lutz Tittel, ed., *Arnold Böcklin: Leben und Werk in Daten und Bildern* (insel taschenbuch 284) (Frankfurt am Main, 1977), p. 62.
29. See FL 2, pp. 172–176.
30. See Scherzo, mm. 212–220.
31. Schopenhauer, *Über den Tod und sein Verhältniss zur Unzerstörbarkeit unsers Wesens an sich* (*Die Welt als Wille und Vorstellung II*, chapter 41; Zurich ed., vol. 4, p. 550f.).
32. Reinhold Hammerstein, "Die Musik im mittelalterlichen Totentanz," in *Bericht über den Internationalen Musikwissenschaftlichen Kongress* (Bonn, 1970), pp. 417–423, especially p. 422.
33. Stefan, *Gustav Mahler: ein Studie*, p. 127.
34. Floros, "Studien zur *Parsifal*," pp. 48–50.
35. Stephan, *Gustav Mahler. IV. Symphonie*, pp. 22–24.
36. In the short score for the slow movement, owned by the Pierpont Morgan Library, Lehmann Deposit (Albrecht 1150A), this variation has the heading *Presto* (Hefling, " 'Variations in nuce,' " pp. 102–126).
37. See FL 2, pp. 259f., 408.
38. Adorno (*Physiognomik*, p. 82) spoke of "a senseless Christology." Whether, of course, the poem "unintentionally accuses Christianity of being a mythical sacrifice-religion" remains undecided.
39. In a conversation with Bauer-Lechner (summer 1899), Mahler designated Carl Loewe as the "forerunner" of his humoresques, but pointed out the difference from his process: "He still cannot free himself from the old form, repeating the individual strophes, whereas I recognize a constant progression with the content of the lied—that is, a through-composed lied—as the true principle of music" (BL² 136).
40. Adler (*Gustav Mahler*, p. 64) had this choralelike phrase in mind when he said the archaic "passages of fifths" were carried out "in organum style."
41. This *nota bene* is missing in the autograph of the Fourth, and in that of the humoresque *Das himmlische Leben*.
42. Seidl, "Gustav Mahler," p. 295.
43. *New York Daily Tribune*, 18 January 1911 (original in English). Qtd. in Kurt Blaukopf, ed., *Mahler. Sein Leben, sein Werk und seine Welt*, p. 277.

The "Completely New Style"

1. Also see Mitchell, *Gustav Mahler*, pp. 348–362.
2. Erwin Ratz, *Revisionsbericht* to the Fifth in the Critical Complete Edition (Frankfurt/London/New York, 1964).
3. Also see Walter, *Thema und Variationen* (1960 ed.), p. 219f.
4. Redlich, "Die Welt der V., VI., und VII. Sinfonie Mahlers," p. 266.
5. Matter, *Connaissance de Mahler,* p. 231.

The Fifth Symphony

1. The summer of 1901 was the last Bauer-Lechner spent with Mahler.
2. See further below.
3. It is similarly stated in Alma's diary (AMML 27f.): "He should not be aware of my struggles. Day by day I am copying the full score of his Fifth Symphony. We are having a contest, who will finish sooner—he with the orchestration or I with the copying. It is difficult for me because he always writes out only one part, while I have to write out the other parts in the various clefs. I am somewhat hindered by my advanced pregnancy, but I do overcome every weakness."
4. To conclude from a dedication (to Alma) on the autograph, Mahler may have completed the clean copy of the Fifth during October 1903. The autograph is in possession of the Robert Lehman Foundation (loaned to the Pierpont Morgan Library, New York).
5. Herta Blaukopf, ed., *Briefwechsel Mahler—Strauss,* p. 90f.
6. Wessling (*Gustav Mahler,* p. 222f.) quotes extracts of a letter from Mahler to Guido Adler regarding the Fifth Symphony without indicating his source references. The content and style of the letter leave room for doubt as to its authenticity.
7. Walter, *Gustav Mahler* (1957 ed.), p. 91.
8. Newlin (*Bruckner—Mahler—Schönberg,* 1954 ed., p. 186) characterizes the relationship of C minor in the first movement of the Fifth to the D major of the Finale as "progressive tonality." In a letter to Peters Publishing House, (23 July 1904), Mahler wrote that he was unable to indicate a key for the "entire Symphony." See Klemm, "Zur Geschichte der Fünften Symphonie," p. 35.
9. See FL 2, p. 138.
10. Strangely enough, this instruction is missing in the study score published in April 1920, publisher's no. 9015.
11. The hesitating rhythm, which is first played by the trombones in measures 27–30, sporadically returns and connects the three sections of the main parts.
12. In measure 50, Mahler instructs the cellos to play *piangendo*.
13. Bekker, *Gustav Mahlers Sinfonien,* p. 181.
14. In the autograph, Mahler explicitly designates the second movement as *Hauptsatz* (main movement).
15. Nodnagel, *Gustav Mahlers Fünfte Symphonie,* p. 18.
16. Adorno, *Physiognomik,* pp. 19f., 130.

17. Bekker, *Gustav Mahlers Sinfonien,* p. 188.
18. Adorno, *Physiognomik,* p. 20.
19. Schmidt, *Formprobleme und Entwicklungslinien,* p. 107ff.
20. Sponheuer, *Logik des Zerfalls,* pp. 224–234.
21. Finale of the First, No. 12: *Mit grosser Wildheit* [Very wild]; second movement of the Fifth—measures 435, 443–444, and 448—*wild.*
22. Measures 66–72, 141–145, 176–180, 322–325, 521–525.
23. See FL 2, pp. 249–256, 404–406.
24. Measures 18–19, 65–67, 175–181, 339–340.
25. See FL 2, pp. 237–242.
26. See the outline by Karbusicky (*Gustav Mahler und seine Umwelt,* pp. 5–21).
27. Adorno, *Physiognomik,* p. 139.
28. See FL 2, pp. 176–178.
29. Karbusicky, *Gustav Mahler und seine Umwelt,* p. 83ff.
30. Adorno, *Physiognomik,* p. 139.
31. Specht, *Gustav Mahler* (1905 ed.), p. 44f.
32. An allusion to *An Schwager Kronos* is found in the spiritual poem by Eichendorff with the title *Kurze Fahrt*:

> Posthorn, wie so keck und fröhlich
> Brachst du einst den Morgen an,
> Vor mir lag's so frühlingsselig,
> Daß ich still auf Lieder sann.
>
> Dunkel rauscht es schon im Walde,
> Wie so abendkühl wird's hier,
> Schwager, stoß ins Horn—wie balde
> Sind auch wir im Nachtquartier!

33. In 1904 Mahler played and explained the Fifth to Bruno Walter (AMML 31).
34. To many of Mahler's contemporaries (according to Otto Nodnagel) the Adagietto seemed *süsslich* (sugary), and Richard Strauss, as mentioned, did not think much of it. See also AME 118 (Diary of Mrs. Ida Dehmel). Regarding the popularity of the movement, see Tibbe, "Anmerkungen zur Mahler-Rezeption," pp. 88–90.
35. Score in possession of the Willem Mengelberg Foundation, Amsterdam. Facsimile in Stephan, *Gustav Mahler: Werk und Interpretation,* ill. 38, 39.
36. The movement shows the three-part song form according to the scheme A (mm. 1–38)—B (mm. 39–71)—A¹ (mm. 72–103). While the main parts are in F major, the middle part constantly modulates: m. 41 to C minor, mm. 46–47 to G-flat major, m. 50 to D-flat major, m. 60 to E major, m. 65 to D major, m. 72 finally back to F major.
37. The similarity of the two passages also extends to the harmony, which favors major-ninth chords.
38. Before the wedding Mahler curiously insisted that Alma give up composing (AME 33). Later scruples overcame him. In the summer of 1910, after the serious marriage crisis, he took out her "poor, forgotten" songs, played and sang them, and had them published (AME 219f.).

39. Specht, *Gustav Mahler* (1913 ed.), p. 281.
40. Bekker, *Gustav Mahlers Sinfonien,* p. 201.
41. Mengelberg, *Gustav Mahler,* p. 55.
42. Newlin, *Bruckner—Mahler—Schönberg,* 1954 ed., p. 184ff.
43. Kralik, *gustav mahler* [sic], p. 51.
44. Adorno, *Physiognomik,* p. 179f.
45. Sponheuer, *Logik des Zerfalls,* pp. 277–279.
46. Adorno, *Physiognomik,* p. 180f.
47. A parallel example for Mahler's procedure is offered by the first prelude to Richard Wagner's *Die Meistersinger von Nürnberg.* The initial, weighty Mastersinger theme later undergoes a characteristic diminution, which is meant to be a caricature of Beckmesser. The key to understanding this passage is offered in that scene in the Third Act, where the apprentices lead Beckmesser to the small, grassy mound.
48. The autograph merely indicates *Allegro,* but in numerous places one finds the instruction *lustig* (merry), not included in the published score: m. 3 (horn entrance), m. 10 (bassoon entrance), m. 13 (horn entrance), m. 389 (horn entrance), m. 518 (trumpet entrance).
49. In the sense of Hans Werner Henze, *Musik und Politik, Schriften und Gespräche 1955–1975,* Jens Brockmeier, ed. (Deutscher Taschenbuch Verlag 1162) (Munich, 1976), p. 195. Further see Constantin Floros, "Musik muss zur Sprache werden. Laudatio auf Hans Werner Henze," in *Oper in Hamburg 1982–83* (Jahrbuch 10 of the Hamburg State Opera for the 1982–1983 Season), pp. 84–89.
50. The most important passages are measures 118–119, 122–123, 166–167, 306–307, 525–526, 580–581, and 781–782. See also FL 2, p. 308.
51. While composing the closing chorale of the Fifth Symphony, Mahler must have been thinking of the chorale from the Finale of Bruckner's Fifth Symphony. See Floros, "Bruckner und Mahler," p. 26.
52. Adorno, *Physiognomik,* pp. 49, 92f.

The Sixth Symphony

1. Walter, *Gustav Mahler* (1957 ed.), p. 92.
2. See, for example, the caricature in the weekly *Die Muskete* (19 January 1907) in Kurt Blaukopf, *Gustav Mahler oder Der Zeitgenosse der Zukunft,* p. 219.
3. Further see Peter Szondi, *Versuch über das Tragische* (Frankfurt am Main, 1961); Leo Schrade, *Vom Tragischen in der Musik* (Mainz, 1967). It belongs to the tragic (as Dr. Gerd Sievers remarks) that fate has to be founded in the character of the person, and that it is not merely external—like an "accident" befalling him.
4. Bekker, *Gustav Mahlers Sinfonien,* p. 232f.
5. Bekker, *Gustav Mahlers Sinfonien,* p. 209.
6. Adorno, *Physiognomik,* p. 136.
7. See AMML 31.
8. On 9 September 1904, Mahler announced the completion of the Sixth to his friend Arnold Berliner (GMB[2] 294). He did not complete the clean copy of the full score until 1 May 1905 in Vienna (according to a note in the

autograph, which is in the custody of the Society of Friends of Music in Vienna).

9. See FL 1, p. 106f.

10. According to Specht, *Gustav Mahler* (1913 ed.), p. 25.

11. See above, pp. 62, 90, and 109.

12. Nodnagel ("Sechste Symphonie," p. 241) already recognized this relationship.

13. Werner F. Korte, *Bruckner und Brahms. Die spätromantische Lösung der autonomen Konzeption* (Tutzing, 1963), pp. 28, 44.

14. See FL 1, pp. 281f., 417.

15. Bekker, *Gustav Mahlers Sinfonien*, p. 209.

16. Specht, *Gustav Mahler* (1913 ed.), p. 292f.

17. Redlich ("Mahler's enigmatic Sixth," p. 251) interpreted the major-minor seal as the motif of the cosmic catastrophe.

18. Adorno, "Epilegomena," p. 141.

19. See FL 1, pp. 323f., 430.

20. With these remarks Mahler clarified a note that he had added after the fact in the printed edition of the Sixth, published in 1906 by C. F. Kahnt. This note is in the third version of this edition (p. 35 of the score) and states: "The cowbells must be played very discreetly, in a realistic imitation of the bells, sometimes together, sometimes sounding individually (higher and lower), like those of a herd grazing in the distance. It is explicitly stated that these indications do not imply a programmatic interpretation." Regarding the three versions of the printed edition, see Redlich, Preface to the Score of the Sixth Symphony, pp. XXIV–XXVI.

21. Franz Gräflinger, "42. Tonkünstlerfest zu Essen," *Musikalische Rundschau* 2 (Munich, 1906) (first July issue), p. 194f.

22. Bekker, *Gustav Mahlers Sinfonien*, p. 219.

23. Adorno, *Physiognomik*, p. 131.

24. Matter, *Connaissance de Mahler* (1974), p. 211.

25. The strings accompany with shadowy pizzicato-motifs based on the "head" of the main theme. A harmonic analysis of the chorale theme is offered by Erpf, *Studie zur Harmonie- und Klangtechnik*, p. 134f.

26. Adler, *Mahler* (1916), p. 74.

27. Bekker, *Gustav Mahlers Sinfonien*, p. 175.

28. Karl Weigl, "Erläuterung der Sechsten Symphonie," in Istel, ed., *Mahlers Symphonien*, p. 119.

29. See FL 1, pp. 155–157.

30. Richard Strauss, who created similar effects in *Der Rosenkavalier,* seems to have studied Mahler's Sixth carefully.

31. The Coda modulates boldly. E minor and E-flat minor or E-flat major establish themselves as tonal centers of the first section. With the aid of harmonic shifts, the second section leads from C major to A major, the final key.

32. Bruckner's music offers numerous parallel examples for this procedure.

33. For a long time, Mahler was undecided about the placement of the Scherzo and Andante. According to the original concept, the Scherzo came after the first movement and the Andante before the Finale. The movements were performed in this order at the Essen premiere. According to a report by Pringsheim ("Zur Uraufführung von Mahlers Sechster Symphonie," p. 497f.), even after the dress rehearsal Mahler was still wondering whether

he should reverse the position of the two middle movements. In the first published version of the score (1906 by C. F. Kahnt), the Scherzo is in second place; in both of the other versions it comes after the Andante. The critical complete edition restores the original order of the movements.

34. Horns, mm. 26–33; trumpets, mm. 87–91, 185–188, 214–215, 261–265; trombones with mutes, mm. 261–265.
35. Adorno, "Epilegomena," p. 143.
36. Alfred Schattmann, "Erläuterung der *Sinfonia domestica*," in *Richard Strauss. Symphonien und Tondichtungen* (Schlesingersche Musik-Bibliothek, Meisterführer No. 6), Herwarth Walden, ed. (Berlin/Vienna, n.d. [1908]), p. 171; Richard Specht, *Richard Strauss und sein Werk,* vol. 1 (Leipzig/Vienna/Zurich, 1921), p. 306f. Strauss himself wrote that the oboe d'amore in the *Sinfonia domestica* "serves as symbol for the innocent dreaming, as well as the happy playing of the child." See Berlioz, *Treatise on Instrumentation,* [1905?] p. 197.
37. Asow, *Richard Strauss,* p. 335.
38. *Jahrbuch Peters 1979* (Leipzig, 1980), p. 35.
39. Bekker, *Gustav Mahlers Sinfonien,* p. 220.
40. Schoenberg, "Prager Rede," pp. 35–38.
41. David Josef Bach, *Arbeiter Zeitung* (Vienna, 4 July 1912); qtd. in Manfred Wagner, *Geschichte,* p. 402.
42. This eighth-note motif is already prepared in measures 6, 13, and 16–17.
43. Characteristic for this are the "seam-passages" between C major and A major (mm. 128–129) and between A minor and C-sharp minor (mm. 145–146).
44. Bekker, *Gustav Mahlers Sinfonien,* p. 221.
45. Adorno, *Ästhetische Theorie,* p. 56 (German ed.), p. 48 (Eng. ed.).
46. Bekker, *Gustav Mahlers Sinfonien,* p. 225.
47. Adorno, *Physiognomik,* p. 131.
48. Ratz, "Eine Analyse des Finales der VI. Symphonie," pp. 156–171.
49. Since the relationship between subject and composition in the tone poem *Death and Transfiguration* by Richard Strauss continues to create misunderstandings, it should be emphasized that although Alexander Ritter's poem was subsequently written and added to the printed score, the basic program was already established at the conception of the work. This is evident from Strauss's sketches and from a letter to Friedrich von Hausegger. See Erich H. Mueller von Asow, *Richard Strauss,* (1959), vol. I, p. 116f.
50. Sponheuer, *Logik des Zerfalls,* pp. 305, 328f.
51. Adorno, *Physiognomik,* p. 132f.
52. Ratz, "Eine Analyse des Finales der VI. Symphonie," *Sammelband Mahler* rpt., p. 111.
53. In the first edition (first and second version), next to the first blow of the hammer (on p. 194) is the indication "A short, strong but dull-sounding blow of *non*metallic character." In the edition of the third version Mahler added: "(Like the blow of an ax)." A study of the autograph (owned by the Society of Friends of Music in Vienna) reveals that Mahler came upon the idea to include the hammer only after writing out the full score. The hammer blows were subsequently written in with indelible pencil in four (!) places: mm. 336, 479, 530, and 783. Then Mahler crossed out the blow in m. 530, so that only three remained.

54. Ratz, "Eine Analyse des Finales der VI.Symphonie," *Sammelband* rpt., p. 122.
55. Regarding Strauss's relationship to Nietzsche, see Ernst Krause, *Richard Strauss. Gestalt und Werk* (Leipzig, 1975), pp. 44–46.
56. According to a report by Pringsheim ("Zur Uraufführung von Mahlers Sechster Symphonie," p. 497), Strauss felt that the Finale of the Sixth was "overorchestrated."

The Seventh Symphony

1. Reference is to the two *Nachtmusik* movements. The first of these is not an Andante, but rather an Allegro moderato.
2. Kurt Blaukopf, *Mahler: A Documentary Study,* p. 245.
3. Reilly, *Gustav Mahler und Guido Adler,* p. 46.
4. Translated: My Seventh is complete. I believe this work was happily born and turned out well.
5. In response to this letter Mahler wrote to Schoenberg in January 1910 (GMUB 186): "What you say about your impressions—earlier and now—I understand very well. Basically I have always felt the same way."
6. Regarding Schoenberg's relationship to Mahler, see Rexroth, "Mahler und Schoenberg," pp. 68–80.
7. Stefan, *Gustav Mahler: ein Studie,* p. 134.
8. Stefan, *Gustav Mahler: ein Studie,* p. 134.
9. *Der Merker* (1909), no. 2, p. 1.
10. Reeser, *Gustav Mahler und Holland,* p. 31f.
11. Specht, "Mahlers Siebente Symphonie," p. 1.
12. Walter, *Gustav Mahler* (1957 ed.), p. 92. Also see Karl Weigl, "Erläuterung der Sechsten Symphonie," in Istel, ed., *Mahlers Symphonien,* p. 136.
13. See also the statements regarding the Fifth Symphony in BL[2] 192f.
14. Adorno, "Wiener Gedenkrede," p. 129.
15. Arnold Schoenberg, "Symphonien aus Volksliedern," *Stimmen* 1 (November 1947), p. 201f.
16. Adorno, *Physiognomik,* p. 136.
17. Bekker (*Gustav Mahlers Sinfonien,* p. 249) did not recognize the connection and spoke of a *Lockmotiv* (luring motif).
18. In the score sketch for the first movement of the Seventh there is the remark in Mahler's writing (mm. 284–287): *Steine pumpeln in's Wasser* [Stones bouncing into the water]. See J. A. Stargardt, *Auktionskatalog No. 597* (23–24 November 1971), pp. 182–184.
19. In the autograph (owned by Concertgebouw Amsterdam) Mahler designates the movement as *1. Nachtmusik* (1st Night Music) and also as *1. Nachtstück* (1st Night Piece).
20. *Also sprach Zarathustra,* part 4, "Das trunkne Lied" (Nietzsche, *Werke,* vol. 2, p. 553).
21. A similar treatment occurs in the "Scène aux champs" from Berlioz's *Symphonie fantastique.*
22. Mahler entered the dissonant notes of the C-minor triad (C—E-flat—G in m. 187) into the proofs that his wife had prepared for the engraver (Austrian National Library, sup. mus. 29134).

23. Adorno, *Physiognomik,* p. 40.
24. In the autograph the movement is simply called *Scherzo.* The designation *Schattenhaft* was personally entered by Mahler into the engraving proofs. Also informative are the more detailed markings in this movement, which in the autograph read, *In stetig fortlaufender Bewegung. In den Anfangstakten noch zögernd* (In steadily constant movement. During the opening measures still hesitating). In the engraving proofs Mahler inserted the adjective *müssiger* (leisurely) between the words *fortlaufender* and *Bewegung,* and added, *Fliessend, aber nicht schnell* (Flowing, but not fast).
25. Thus by Bekker, *Gustav Mahlers Sinfonien,* p. 251.
26. Redlich, *Bruckner and Mahler,* p. 204.
27. Matter, *Connaissance de Mahler,* p. 237.
28. Adorno, *Physiognomik,* p. 140.
29. In the sketches for the third movement (New York Public Library, Bruno Walter Collection), the *lamenting* melody in the flutes and oboes is marked *Wörth* and the major-minor waltz, *Belfast.*
30. Karl Weigl, "Erläuterung der Sechsten Symphonie," in Istel, ed., *Mahlers Symphonien,* p. 145.
31. We note only the most obvious: mm. 71–72 (horns and violins), mm. 135–136 and 137–138 (violins and violas), mm. 149–150 (first violins), mm. 151–152 (horns), mm. 292–293 (tuba and double-basses), mm. 380–381 (violins and violas).
32. Matter, *Connaissance de Mahler,* p. 237.
33. Specht (*Richard Strauss und sein Werk,* p. 224f.) interpreted this passage from *Till Eulenspiegel* as follows: "It ends softly, abruptly. . . . Strange motifs suggest moments of introspection . . . a shivering fear of ignominious death."
34. Measures 185–187, 206–209, 217, and 225. Further see measures 424–425, 441–443, 452, and 471 (*molto accel.*). The *Più mosso* measures quoted from the Trio stand in contrast to one single *Pesante* measure (m. 243), which in its whole bearing seems like a bow to Johann Strauss!
35. At first it encompasses three measures (mm. 489–491), then two measures (mm. 493–494), later one measure (m. 496) and at the end only two quarters (m. 502).
36. In the autograph the indication is Andante con Moto. See the facsimile in Mengelberg, *Mahler-Feestbook,* p. 167. The word *amoroso* (Andante amoroso) was entered by Mahler into the proofs. Here he also wrote the word *Schwärmerisch* [Impassioned], but then crossed it out.
37. Autograph and proofs indicate that Mahler added the mandolin part as an afterthought.
38. *Der Merker* 2 (1909), p. 6.
39. Measures 1–4 and 23–25 (violin solo), mm. 35–37 (violoncello), mm. 51–54 (violin solo).
40. *Also sprach Zarathustra,* part 2, "Das Nachtlied" (Nietzsche, *Werke,* vol. 2, p. 636).
41. Schoenberg, "Prager Rede," p. 41.
42. Specht, *Gustav Mahler* (1913 ed.), p. 303.
43. Bekker, *Gustav Mahlers Sinfonien,* pp. 238, 265.
44. Adorno, *Physiognomik,* pp. 164f., 180.
45. A certain relationship between the Rondo-Finale and the first Prelude from

Wagner's *Die Meistersinger* became apparent to Mahler's contemporaries. Thus, Richard Specht wrote in 1913 (*Gustav Mahler,* p. 303): "County-fair jubilation, Mastersinger merriment—even if the good masters are from Austria rather than Nuremberg."

46. Schumann, *Das kleine GUSTAV MAHLER BUCH* [sic], p. 84.
47. Ruzicka, "Befragung des Materials," p. 600f.
48. Jungheinrich, "Nach der Katastrophe," p. 196f.
49. Tischler, *Die Harmonik in den Werken Gustav Mahlers,* p. 142f.
50. Sponheuer, *Logik des Zerfalls,* p. 380.
51. Measures 189–190 to D-flat major, mm. 291–306 to A major, mm. 360–367 to B-flat major, mm. 446–454 to D major.
52. Walter, *Gustav Mahler* (1957 ed.), p. 103.
53. The indication *Maestoso* does not occur in the first edition of 1909. It is found in the list of errata, based on Mahler's communication, that the publisher printed and inserted in the music after printing the full score.
54. Adorno (*Physiognomik,* p. 180) obviously quoted from memory when he stated that Mahler ridiculed the pomp of the Rondo-Finale with the epithet *etwas prachtvoll* [somewhat pompous]. Actually, the words are *etwas feierlich* [somewhat solemnly].
55. See FL 2, pp. 319–321.
56. Nietzsche, *Ecce homo. Werke,* vol. 3, p. 574.
57. See FL 1, p. 69f.

The Eighth Symphony

1. Specht, *Gustav Mahler* (1913 ed.), p. 304.
2. Adorno (*Physiognomik,* p. 182) contemptuously called the Eighth a "symbolic, monstrous volume." Regarding his interpretation, see Gottwald, "Die Achte," pp. 199–212; and Nowak, "Mahlers Hymnus," pp. 92–96.
3. The first performance received a lively response not only in Germany and Austria but also in France. Lazare Ponnelle and Willian Ritter published long articles in the *Journal des Débats* (1 October 1910) and in the *Revue musicale S. I. M* (October 1910). See Ponnelle, "Après la VIIIe symphonie de Gustav Mahler," in *A Munich,* pp. 3–17; and the (rather critical) report by Eduard Wahl in *Die Musik* 10 (1910–11), p. 53f.
4. See the statements by Kurt Blaukopf, *Gustav Mahler oder Der Zeitgenosse der Zukunft,* p. 273.
5. Roller, *Die Bildnisse von Gustav Mahler,* p. 26.
6. Specht, *Gustav Mahlers VIII. Symphonie,* p. 6.
7. Specht in *Tagespost* (14 June 1914), no. 150 (qtd. in Karl Heinz Füssl, Preface to the new edition of the Eighth Symphony, Critical Complete Edition [Vienna, 1977]).
8. Decsey, "Stunden mit Mahler," p. 353f.
9. This letter of Mahler's has no date. The date "21 June 1906" was probably added by Fritz Löhr, the recipient of the letter and co-editor of Mahler's letters (GMB¹ 290).
10. Letters to Josef Reitler in July 1906 (GMB² 310f.).
11. The initial sketch of the first four measures of the *Chorus mysticus,* written in pencil on toilet paper turned yellow (ca. 8×11 cm^2) and once owned by

Alban Berg, is now owned by the Alban Berg Foundation in Vienna.

12. In a letter to his wife (June 1910) Mahler wrote that the *Spiritus creator* had shaken and beaten him "eight weeks long" during the summer of 1906, "until the 'Great Work' was completed" (AME 451).

13. Mayer, "Musik und Literatur," p. 148f.

14. Strohm, "Die Idee der absoluten Musik als ihr (ausgesprochenes) Programm," pp. 84, 89.

15. Johann Peter Eckermann, *Gespräche mit Goethe in den letzten Jahren seines Lebens*. Fritz Bergemann, ed., new ed. (Wiesbaden, 1955), p. 471f.

16. Commemorative book for the 1920 Mahler Festival in Amsterdam, p. 210f.

17. Friedrich Wilhelm Riemer, ed., *Briefwechsel zwischen Goethe und Zelter in den Jahren 1796 bis 1832,* vol. 3 (Berlin, 1834), p. 171f.

18. See FL 1, pp. 129–132.

19. Qtd. in Hans and Rosaleen Moldenhauer, *Anton von Webern. Chronik seines Lebens und Werkes* (Zurich/Freiburg i. B., 1980), p. 121.

20. See also Richard Wagner's remarks in his Beethoveen essay (*Sämtliche Schriften und Dichtungen,* vol. 9, p. 125).

21. Heinrich Lausberg, "Der Hymnus *Veni Creator Spiritus*," in *Jahrbuch der Akademie der Wissenschaften in Göttingen 1969* 1969, pp. 26–58; also "Minuscula philologica (2): De *Veni Creator Spiritus*," in *Nachrichten der Akademie der Wissenschaften in Göttingen* 1 (1967), pp. 381–394.

22. See the chart of the various versions in Strohm, "Die Idee der absoluten Musik als ihr (ausgesprochenes) Programm," p. 91.

23. Quoted from the English translation of the accompanying notes to the recording of the Mahler symphonies by the Concertgebouw Orchestra (Bernard Haitink, Conductor; Philips 676802). Bracketed words were omitted by Mahler in his version.

24. Measures 156–161 correspond to measures 56–61.

25. Martin Luther drastically translates the passage as *das schwach Fleisch in uns* (the weak flesh in us).

26. See FL 2, p. 207.

27. Luther translates this verse: *"Zünd uns ein Licht an im Verstand, / gib uns ins Herz der Liebe Brunst"* (Light in us a light in our understanding, / give the ardor of love into our heart).

28. See FL 2, p. 125.

29. Bekker (*Gustav Mahlers Sinfonien,* p. 288) rightly noticed that in the recapitulation the "mystic D-flat and A-flat major part, with the vocal theme" are missing, but he failed to realize that Mahler newly composed the secondary and closing sections by using older materials.

30. As already noted, the verse in Mahler's source read *Vitemus omne noxium.* Mahler replaced the word *noxium* [harmful] with the word *pessimum.*

31. Hefele (*Goethes Faust,* p. 201) rightly emphasizes the musical ordering of the voices in the final scene. They clearly are arranged in three distinct groups, each in four tone colors: "The four somber male voices of the mystical fathers; the falsetto choir of the blessed boys assisted by the choir of angels divided in three; and finally the four voices of the loving, repentant women at the feet of the Mater Gloriosa."

32. Trunz, *Goethes Faust,* p. 627.

33. Mahler shortened Goethe's text by omitting the lines of Pater seraphicus, two choruses of the blessed boys (verses 11890–11925), as well as several verses

from the singing of Doctor Marianus (verses 12013–12019 and 12030–12031). Contrary to his custom, he made few other alterations. This no doubt had to do with his respect for Goethe and the formal perfection of Goethe's poetry. In contrast to this, Mahler did not consider the poems of *Des Knaben Wunderhorn* to be "vollendet" (perfected), but thought of them as "Felsblöcke, aus denen jeder das Seine formen dürfe" [Blocks of stone from which everyone may form what he desires] (AME 120).

34. Specht, *Mahlers VIII. Symphonie,* pp. 4, 33f.
35. See also Constantin Floros, "Der 'Beziehungszauber' der Musik im 'Ring des Nibelungen' von Richard Wagner," *Neue Zeitschrift für Musik* (July/August 1983), pp. 8–14.
36. Eckermann, *Gespräche mit Goethe* (1955), p. 471.
37. This figure also occurs at the words *"Bill'ge, was des Mannes Brust"* (Approve what is in the heart of a man) (mm. 662–664) and *"Unbezwinglich unser Mut"* (Our courage is invincible) (mm. 684–687).
38. A passage in a letter to Bruno Walter from the year 1909 documents how strongly Mahler was impressed by Goethe's vision of intellectual rebirth: "I see everything in a new light. I am so much in motion; I would not be surprised to see myself having a new body. (Like Faust in the final scene.)" (GMB^2 351)
39. Trunz, *Goethes Faust,* p. 629.
40. The keyboard reduction of the Eighth (prepared by Josef V. von Wöss) was published in April 1910 by Universal Edition, Vienna. On 4 September 1910, Mahler wrote to his wife regarding the dedication (AME 465): "At home I found the keyboard reductions with the dedication and hoped that Hertzka was smart enough to send a copy to Toblach. It was strange and exciting to see the tender, beloved name on the title page for all the world to see, like a joyful confession."

Regarding the Late Style

1. Adorno, "Wiener Gedenkrede," p. 131.
2. Sponheuer, *Logik des Zerfalls,* p. 411.
3. Lindt, ed., *Bruno Walter: Briefe,* p. 113f.

Das Lied von der Erde (The Song of the Earth)

1. See Kurt Blaukopf, *Gustav Mahler oder Der Zeitgenosse der Zukunft,* p. 255.
2. Mahler was examined by Professor Kovacs on 18 July 1907 (AME 384).
3. Mahler received the collection from his friend, Court Counsellor Dr. Theobald Pollak (Stefan, *Gustav Mahler: ein Studie,* p. 147). Also see AME 156: "Years ago an old friend of my father's, a friend with lung disease, transferred all his love to Mahler and thought of nothing else than to find song texts and inspiration of every kind for his idol. He brought him the newly translated *Chinese Flute* (Hans Bethge)." Alma's wording "years ago" is surely imprecise. It seems that during 1907 Mahler had frequent contact with Pollak (AME 387).

4. The score sketch of the third movement (owned by the Society of Friends of Music in Vienna) bears the date 1 August 1908 on the title page.

5. On the title page of the score owned by the Society of Friends of Music in Vienna, the work bears the title *Das Trinklied von der Erde* and the subtitle *Symphonie für eine Tenor-und eine Altstimme und Orchester* (Symphony for tenor, alto and orchestra). In the critical complete edition by Ratz (Vol. IX, Vienna, 1964), the subtitle reads *Eine Symphonie für eine Tenor- und eine Alt- (oder Bariton-) Stimme und Orchester*. According to Bruno Walter (*Thema und Variationen* [1960 ed.], p. 247), Mahler initially was in doubt about whether he should entrust the lower voice part to an alto or to a baritone.

6. Specht, *Gustav Mahler* (1913 ed.), p. 334f.

7. Walter, *Gustav Mahler* (1957 ed.), p. 94.

8. Bethge, *Die chinesische Flöte* (1907 ed.). In the following we always quote from the Leipzig (1926) edition. There is every indication that Anton Webern (Op. 12, No. 2 and Op. 13, Nos. 2 and 3) and Arnold Schoenberg (Op. 27, Nos. 3 and 4) were directed to Bethge's *Chinese Flute* by *The Song of the Earth*. See Budde, "Bemerkungen zum Verhältnis Mahler-Webern," pp. 159–173.

9. Mahler altered the original title as an afterthought. Thus in the score sketch for the third movement (owned by the Society of Friends of Music in Vienna) the title is *Der Pavillon aus Porzellan*. The sketch of the fourth movement (Pierpont Morgan Library, Robert Owen Lehman Deposit) is entitled *Am Ufer*. The score sketch of the fifth movement (Vienna City Library) bears the title *Der Trunkene im Frühling*. It is noteworthy that a title page that includes the notice "New York, Hotel Savoy" and most probably was designed after completion of the fifth movement shows the title *Der Trinker im Frühling*.

10. Bethge, *Die chinesische Flöte* (1926 ed.), p. 22.

11. Bethge, *Die chinesische Flöte* (1926 ed.), p. 108.

12. This poem from Mahler's youth was first published in 1912 in the special Gustav Mahler issue of *Der Merkur* (p. 183) and belongs to a group of poems written for Johanna Richter. See HLG 1, pp. 826–834.

13. See Mulder, "*Das Lied von der Erde*." See also Vill, *Vermittlungsformen,* pp. 155–190.

14. Wöss, *Gustav Mahler,* pp. 5, 21, 24.

15. Schnebel, "Das Spätwerk als Neue Musik," p. 161.

16. Baur, "Pentatonische Melodiebildung," pp. 141–150.

17. According to Specht, *Gustav Mahler* (1913 ed.), p. 376.

18. Adorno, *Physiognomik,* p. 191.

19. Note the first violins and the first clarinet (mm. 214–229) and later the first trumpet (mm. 236–249).

20. The word *mild* is missing in the source; it was inserted by Mahler.

21. The instrumentation: two flutes, two oboes, two clarinets, bass-clarinet, three bassoons, four horns, two harps, and strings. Trumpets, trombones and percussion were left out in this movement.

22. Characteristic for the *traurige Weise* (sad melody) in *Tristan* (Act III, Scene 1) is the lowering of the second scale step (G).

23. Measure 21 (second violins), measure 39 (clarinets), measure 78 (voice), measure 114 (first flute), measure 136 (voice).

24. Mulder, *"Das Lied von der Erde,"* p. 43.
25. Wöss, *Gustav Mahler,* p. 27.
26. Goethe, *Wilhelm Tischbeins Idyllen* (1821). *Werke,* Prophyläen-Ausgabe, vol. 35, p. 190.
27. Bethge, *Die chinesische Flöte* (1926 ed.), p. 112.
28. Mulder, *"Das Lied von der Erde,"* p. 62.
29. Bekker (*Gustav Mahlers Sinfonien,* p. 332f.) did not recognize the sonata form but organized the movement "into three stanzas," each one of which is introduced by recitative-like narration. Thus, introduction (mm. 1–18), first stanza (mm. 19–157), second stanza (mm. 158–373), and third stanza (mm. 374–572). The outline presented in the present volume also differs basically from the scheme of Tischler ("Mahler's *Das Lied von der Erde,"* pp. 111–114, especially p. 114), which did recognize the sonata form.
30. See FL 2, p. 209f.
31. FL 2, pp. 225, 394f.
32. The key relationships in the recapitulation are: First section C minor, secondary section F major, closing section C major. The Coda closes with the chord C—E—G—A (C major chord with added sixth).
33. Wildgans, "Gustav Mahler und Anton von Webern," pp. 22–26.

The Ninth Symphony

1. See GMB[2] 358f.
2. Erwin Ratz, ed., *Gustav Mahler. IX. Symphonie. Partiturentwurf der ersten drei Sätze. Faksimile nach der Handschrift* (Universal Edition 13508), Vienna, 1971.
3. Specht, *Gustav Mahler* (1913 ed.), p. 355.
4. Schoenberg, "Prager Rede," p. 55f.
5. Manfred Wagner, *Geschichte,* pp. 387–419.
6. *Wiener Allgemeine Zeitung* (newspaper), 27 June 1912, p. 2 (qtd. in Manfred Wagner, *Geschichte,* p. 393).
7. *Illustrirtes Wiener Extrablatt* (newspaper), 27 June 1912, p. 10 (qtd. in Manfred Wagner, *Geschichte,* p. 399).
8. Also see Constantin Floros, "Zur Deutung der Symphonik Bruckners. Das Adagio der Neunten Symphonie," in *Bruckner-Jahrbuch* (1981), pp. 89–96.
9. *Fremden-Blatt* (newspaper), 27 June 1912, p. 14 (qtd. in Manfred Wagner, *Geschichte,* p. 412).
10. Adler, *Mahler,* p. 87.
11. William Ritter in *Gazette de Lausanne,* 7 July 1912 (qtd. in Matter, *Connaissance de Mahler,* p. 307f.).
12. Qtd. in Andraschke, *Gustav Mahlers IX. Symphonie,* pp. 80–84.
13. Bekker, *Gustav Mahlers Sinfonien,* p. 339f.
14. Adorno (*Physiognomik,* p. 9) remarked, without mentioning Paul Bekker by name: "The silly, pompous "What Death Tells Me" foisted upon Mahler's Ninth is a distortion of the truth that is even more painful than the flowers and animals in the Third, which the author may have had in mind."
15. Berg, *Briefe an seine Frau,* p. 238f. Initially the letter was published in *23. Eine Wiener Musikzeitschrift* 26/27 (8 June 1936), p. 12. Because Berg refers to the score sketch that he did not receive as a gift until 1923, the

undated letter could have been written only in 1923 or later.

16. Walter, *Gustav Mahler* (1957 ed.), p. 94.
17. Karl H. Wörner, *Das Zeitalter der thematischen Prozesse in der Geschichte der Musik* (Studien zur Musikgeschichte des 19. Jahrhunderts, vol. 18) (Regensburg, 1969), p. 57.
18. Sponheuer, *Logik des Zerfalls*, pp. 408–410.
19. Bekker, *Gustav Mahlers Sinfonien*, p. 337.
20. Bekker, *Gustav Mahlers Sinfonien*, p. 337.
21. See FL 2, pp. 282, 418.
22. Bekker, *Gustav Mahlers Sinfonien*, p. 352.
23. In what is probably the earliest sketch of the Adagio of the Ninth (in possession of Frau Hannah Adler) the first theme begins in F major, but moves immediately to D-flat major.
24. Bekker, *Gustav Mahlers Sinfonien*, p. 315.
25. Schmidt, *Formprobleme und Entwicklungslinien*.
26. Tischler, *Die Harmonik in den Werken Gustav Mahlers*, p. 125.
27. Storjohann, *Die formalen Eigenarten in den Sinfonien Gustav Mahlers*, pp. 251–258.
28. Dahlhaus, "Form und Motiv in Mahlers Neunter Symphonie," pp. 296–299.
29. Ratz, "Eine Analyse des ersten Satzes der IX. Symphonie," pp. 169–77.
30. The tempo markings are *Etwas frischer* (somewhat more brisk) (m. 80), *Fliessend* (flowing) (m. 86), and *Allegro* (m. 102).
31. Measures 7–26, 47–53, 64–77, 148–159, 267–274, 347–364, and 434–454 where this is only suggested.
32. Motte, "Das komplizierte Einfache," pp. 145–151.
33. Andraschke, *Gustav Mahlers IX. Symphonie*, p. 50ff.
34. See the Seventh Symphony, *Nachtmusik I*, m. 320: *Wie Vogelstimmen* (Like the voices of birds).
35. The end of the movement resembles the end of the Adagio in Bruckner's Eighth Symphony. See Floros, "Bruckner und Mahler," p. 24f.
36. Bekker, *Gustav Mahlers Sinfonien*, p. 314.
37. Adorno, "Wiener Gedenkrede," p. 117.
38. Bekker, *Gustav Mahlers Sinfonien*, p. 345.
39. See FL 2, pp. 171–178.
40. Erwin Stein was the first to point out the three different tempi in the movement ("Die Tempogestaltung in Mahlers IX. Symphonie," in *Pult und Taktstock* [October/November 1924]. Eng. trans. in Stein, *Orpheus in New Guises*, pp. 19–24). Stein wrote this, knowing Mahler's score sketch.
41. In the score sketch the slow ländler is marked *Menuett*.
42. Adorno, *Physiognomik*, p. 210.
43. How deeply the passage impressed Berg is documented in his violin concerto.
44. Also see Andraschke, *Gustav Mahlers IX. Symphonie*, pp. 59–70.
45. The writer in the *Wiener Zeitung* (newspaper) spoke of the well-known "sample book of ländler-motifs that are this time dispersed through a long, long movement and give the impression of an ethnographic museum of country dances." See Manfred Wagner, *Geschichte*, p. 392.
46. Richard Specht certainly was correct when he wrote in the *Illustrirtes Wiener Extrablatt* (newspaper): "The world now seems to him [Mahler] to be only hideous, absurd, and grotesque" (Manfred Wagner, *Geschichte*, p. 398).

47. Adorno, *Physiognomik*, p. 209.
48. Several especially informative examples of montage occur in this movement: m. 168ff.—motives from the leisurely ländler combined with waltz figures; mm. 375–382—interweaving of motifs from both ländlers. The passage at measure 540ff. also is very instructive. The main ländler group in this movement, however, is not "the first case of musical montage" by Mahler, as Adorno writes. The procedure already can be observed in the third movement of the Seventh Symphony.
49. Walter, *Gustav Mahler* (1957 ed.), p. 95.
50. Hints of the *Burlesque* by Strauss are found in the Scherzo of the Fifth and in the Rondo-Burlesque of the Ninth by Mahler.
51. The claim by Adler (*Gustav Mahler*, p. 66) and Bekker (*Gustav Mahlers Sinfonien*, p. 348) that the Rondo-Burlesque bears the addition "To my brothers in Apoll" in the autograph is incorrect.
52. Adorno, *Physiognomik*, p. 211.
53. Schnebel, "Das Spätwerk als Neue Musik," pp. 166, 183.
54. Constantin Floros, *Brahms und Bruckner. Studien zur musikalischen Exegetik* (Wiesbaden, 1980), p. 53f.
55. The Gretchen Episode in the Mephisto movement of Liszt's Faust Symphony (1854) begins similarly with a tremolo in the violins on high A-flat.
56. The performance marking espressivo occurs only in this passage.
57. *Neue Freie Presse* (newspaper), 27 June 1912, p. 10 (qtd. in Manfred Wagner, *Geschichte*, p. 390).
58. Mengelberg, *Gustav Mahler*, p. 71.
59. Fischer, "Die Doppelschlagfigur," p. 103.
60. Measure 12 (violin I), m. 44 (violin II), m. 80 (viola and violoncello), m. 83 (woodwinds), m. 88 (violin I), m. 94 (woodwinds), m. 132 (horns), and m. 148 (clarinets).
61. Julius Korngold in *Neue Freie Presse*, 27 June 1912 (qtd. in Manfred Wagner, *Geschichte*, p. 390).
62. Tibbe, *Über die Verwendung*, pp. 119–124.

The Tenth Symphony

1. *Gustav Mahlers X. Symphonie. Faksimile-Ausgabe der Handschrift* (Berlin/Vienna, 1924).
2. Ratz, ed., *Gustav Mahler. X. Symphonie.*
3. Specht, *Gustav Mahler* (1925 ed.), p. 300.
4. Cooke, *A Performing Version of the Draft for the Tenth Symphony*, p. XXXIII.
5. Krenek's two-movement version of the Tenth appeared in 1951 in New York (Copyright by Associated Music Publishers) without an indication of the editor. According to Michael Kennedy (*Mahler*, London, 1974, p. 152), Otto Jokl was the editor.
6. Carpenter, "The Tenth Symphony—A Continuing Story." Typescript, 3 p.
7. Lindt, ed., *Bruno Walter: Briefe*, p. 204
8. Ratz, Preface to *Gustav Mahler: X Symphonie.*
9. Cooke, *A Performing Version of the Draft for the Tenth Symphony*, p. XIII.

10. See the documents in Kurt Blaukopf, *Gustav Mahler oder Der Zeitgenosse der Zukunft,* p. 271.
11. Freud's letter to Theodor Reik, 4 January 1935 (qtd. in Reik, *The Haunting Melody,* p. 343). Freud spoke of a "Mary-complex" because Mahler's mother's name was Marie and Mahler also called his wife Marie (AME 219 and AMML 39). Also see Jones, *Das Leben und Werk von Sigmund Freud,* vol. 2, p. 103. In psychoanalytical literature one speaks of a "Madonna-complex" when a man cannot sexually desire the woman he loves.
12. Cooke, *A Performing Version of the Draft for the Tenth Symphony,* p. XXXV.
13. In the manuscript, on two sides of a double sheet, measures 323–400 of the Finale are notated in a B-flat major version.
14. Klemm, "Über ein Spätwerk Gustav Mahlers," pp. 19–32.
15. Tyll Rohland, "Zum Adagio aus der X. Symphonie von Gustav Mahler," *Musik und Bildung* 5 (1973), pp. 605–15.
16. Rohland ("Zum Adagio," p. 612) mistakenly states that the first six measures of the melody are in G major.
17. Especially the chord in the winds containing a perfect and an augmented fourth (D-flat—G-flat—C) in measure 68—a genuine Schoenberg sound!
18. See the table in Rohland, "Zum Adagio," p. 609.
19. Specht, *Einführende Bemerkungen* (Introductory Remarks) to the facsimile edition of 1924, p. 7.
20. Martin Zenck believed the movement could be viewed as an expanded lied form, a sonata-allegro form, as double variation, and as cyclical variation. See Zenck, "Ausdruck und Konstruktion," pp. 205–222.
21. Adorno, *Physiognomik,* p. 11.
22. FL 2, p. 288.
23. FL 2, p. 305f.
24. Schnebel ("Das Spätwerk als Neue Musik," p. 177) called the nine-tone chord the "completed entropy as an allegory of death." Zenck ("Ausdruck und Konstruktion," pp. 216–219) spoke yet more abstractly of "catastrophe."
25. In the short score, the coda is notated in two versions: a compressed first and a longer second. Details in Revers, *Die Liquidation der musikalischen Struktur,* pp. 238–241.
26. Cooke, *Gustav Mahler,* p. XVII.
27. The term *asymmetrical music* to characterize the A-Parts was used by William Malloch ("Deryck Cooke's Mahler Tenth," pp. 292–304).
28. The indication *Gemächliches Ländler-Tempo* (leisurely ländler tempo) on p. 39 of the concert version cannot be found in the manuscript, but was inserted by Cooke.
29. Stefan, *Gustav Mahler: eine Studie,* p. 153.
30. Specht, *Einführende Bemerkungen* (Introductory Remarks) to the facsimile edition of 1924, p. 11.
31. Measures 1–4, 41–44, 111–114, 170–173, 230–233, 380–383 (variant).
32. FL 2, pp. 151–154.
33. The funeral rites for the fireman that impressed Mahler so profoundly took place during the first stay in New York, 1907–1908.
34. During the following the short score is the main source quoted.

35. In Cooke's concert version—as almost always—Mahler's correct musical orthography (double-sharps) regrettably was sacrificed to readability.
36. The words *Für dich leben! Für dich sterben!* (To live for you! To die for you!) and the exclamation *Almschi!* are already found in the original B-flat major version of the closing.

Selected Bibliography

Abendroth, Walter. *Vier Meister der Musik: Bruckner, Mahler, Reger, Pfitzner*. Munich, 1952.

Adler, Guido. *Gustav Mahler*. Vienna/Leipzig, 1916.

Adorno, Theodor W. *Mahler: eine musikalische Physiognomik*. Frankfurt am Main, 1960. Eng. trans. *Mahler: A Musical Physiognomy*. Chicago, 1991.

———. "Mahler: Wiener Gedenkrede" [memorial address regarding Mahler]. In *Quasi una fantasia. Musikalische Schriften II*. Frankfurt am Main, 1963.

———. "Mahler: Epilegomena." In *Quasi una fantasia. Musikalische Schriften II*. Frankfurt am Main, 1963.

———. *Ästhetische Theorie*. Frankfurt am Main, 1970. Eng. trans. *Aesthetic Theory*. London, 1984.

Andraschke, Peter. *Gustav Mahlers IX. Symphonie: Kompositionsprozeß und Analyse* (Supplements to the *Archiv für Musikwissenschaft* 14). Wiesbaden, 1976.

Barford, P. *Mahler: Symphonies and Songs*. London, 1970.

Barsova, Inna. *Simfonii Gustava Malera*. Moscow, 1975.

Bauer-Lechner, Natalie. "Aus einem Tagebuch über Mahler," *Der Merker* 3 (1912): 184–188.

———. *Erinnerungen an Gustav Mahler*. Leipzig/Vienna/Zurich, 1923. Eng. trans. *Recollections of Gustav Mahler*. London, 1980.

———. *Gustav Mahler in den Erinnerungen von Natalie Bauer-Lechner*. Diary entries ed. by H. Killian. Hamburg, 1984.

Baur, Uwe. "Pentatonische Melodiebildung in Gustav Mahlers *Das Lied von der Erde*." In *Musicologica austriaca,* vol. 2. Munich/Salzburg, 1979. 141–150.

Bekker, Paul. *Gustav Mahlers Sinfonien*. Berlin, 1921.

Berg, Alban. *Briefe an seine Frau*. Munich/Vienna, 1965. Eng. trans. *Letters to His Wife*. New York, 1971.

Berlioz, Hector. *Instrumentationslehre ergänzt und revidiert von Richard Strauss,* two parts. Leipzig, 1905. Eng. trans. rev. and enl. by Richard Strauss, *Treatise on Instrumentation,* part 1. New York, 1948.

Bethge, Hans. *Die chinesische Flöte*. Leipzig, 1907, 1926.

Blaukopf, Herta, ed. *Gustav Mahler—Richard Strauss. Briefwechsel 1888–1911*. Munich/Zurich, 1980.

———. *Gustav Mahler: Briefe 1879–1911*. See under Alma Maria Mahler.

———. *Gustav Mahler: Unbekannte Briefe*. Publications of the International Gustav Mahler Society, Vienna/Hamburg, 1983. Eng. trans. *Mahler's Unknown Letters*. London, 1986.

Blaukopf, Kurt. *Gustav Mahler oder der Zeitgenosse der Zukunft*. Vienna/Munich/Zurich, 1969. Eng. trans. by Inge Goodwin. *Gustav Mahler*. New York, 1973.

————, ed. *Mahler: sein Leben, sein Werk und seine Welt in zeitgenössischen Bildern und Texten*. Vienna, 1976. Eng. trans. *Mahler: A Documentary Study*. London, 1976.

Budde, Elmar. "Bemerkungen zum Verhältnis Mahler-Webern," *Archiv für Musikwissenschaft* 33 (1976): 159–173.

Carpenter, Clinton A. "The Tenth Symphony—A Continuing Story." Manuscript.

Casella, Alfredo. "Gustav Mahler et sa deuxième symphonie," *S. I. M, Revue musicale mensuelle* 6 (April 1910): 240f.

————. "Festrede beim Mahlerfest in Amsterdam." In *Musikblätter des Anbruch* 2 (1919/1920): 415–419.

Cooke, Deryck. *Gustav Mahler: A Performing Version of the Draft for the Tenth Symphony*. Associated Music Publishers, Inc., New York/London, 1976.

————. *Gustav Mahler: 1860–1911*. London, 1969. Rev. ed. 1980.

Dahlhaus, Carl. "Form und Motiv in Mahlers Neunter Symphonie," *Neue Zeitschrift für Musik* 135 (1974): 296–299.

Danuser, Hermann. "Versuch über Mahlers Ton." In *Jahrbuch des Staatlichen Instituts für Musikforschung Preußischer Kulturbesitz* (1975): 46–79.

Decsey, Ernst. "Stunden mit Mahler," *Die Musik* 10 (1911): 352–356.

Del Mar, N. *Mahler's Sixth Symphony*. London, 1980.

Des Knaben Wunderhorn. Alte deutsche Lieder gesammelt von L. Achim von Arnim und Clemens Brentano. Complete ed. (according to the text in the 1st ed. of 1806/1808. 3 vols. Deutscher Taschenbuch Verlag, Munich, 1963.

Duse, Ugo. *Gustav Mahler*. Turin, 1973.

Eggebrecht, Hans Heinrich. *Die Musik Gustav Mahlers*. Munich, 1982.

Erpf, Hermann. *Studien zur Harmonie- und Klangtechnik der neueren Musik*. Leipzig, 1927.

Fechner, Gustav Theodor. *Das Büchlein vom Leben nach dem Tode*. 1st ed., 1836; 5th ed., Hamburg/Leipzig, 1903.

————. *Zend-Avesta oder über die Dinge des Himmels und des Jenseits vom Standpunkt der Naturbetrachtung*. 2nd ed., Hamburg/Leipzig, 1901.

Filler, Susan M. *Gustav and Alma Mahler: A Guide to Research*. New York, 1989.

Fischer, Kurt von. "Die Doppelschlagfigur in den zwei letzten Sätzen von Gustav Mahlers 9. Symphonie," *Archiv für Musikwissenschaft* 32 (1975): 99–105.

Floros, Constantin. *Gustav Mahler*. Vol. 1, *Die geistige Welt Gustav Mahlers in systematischer Darstellung*. Vol. 2, *Mahler und die Symphonik des 19. Jahrhunderts in neuer Deutung. Zur Grundlegung einer zeitgemässen musikalischen Exegetik*. Breitkopf and Härtel, Wiesbaden, 1977.

————. "Weltanschauung und Symphonik bei Mahler." In *Gustav Mahler Kolloquium 1979*. Ed. Rudolf Klein. Kassel/Basel/London, 1981. 29–39.

————. "Studien zur 'Parsifal'-Rezeption." In *Musik-Konzepte 25. Richard Wagner. Parsifal*. May 1982: 14–57.

————. "Verschwiegene Programmusik" (Mitteilungen der Kommission für Musikforschung No. 34). In *Anzeiger der phil.-hist. Klasse der Österreichischen Akademie der Wissenschaften* 119 (1982): 204–225.

————. "Bruckner und Mahler. Gemeinsamkeiten und Unterschiede." In *Bruckner Symposion, Linz 1981, Die österreichische Symphonie nach Anton Bruckner*, ed. Othmar Wessely. Linz, 1983. 21–29.

_____ . *Alban Berg. Musik als Autobiographie*. In press.

Foerster, Josef Bohuslav. "Aus Mahlers Werkstatt" *Der Merker* 1 (1910): 921–924.

_____ . "Erinnerungen an Gustav Mahler." In *Musikblätter des Anbruch* 2 (1920): 291–295.

_____ . *Der Pilger. Erinnerungen eines Musikers*. Prague, 1955.

Franklin, P. R. "The Gestation of Mahler's Third Symphony." *Music and Letters* 58 (1977): 439–446.

Gartenberg, E. *Mahler: The Man and His Music*. New York, 1978.

Gottwald, Clytus. "Die Achte." In *Mahler—eine Herausforderung*. Ed. Peter Ruzicka. Wiesbaden, 1977. 199–212.

Grange, Henry-Louis de la. *Mahler*, vol. 1. New York, 1973.

Hanson, Wesley Luther. *The Treatment of Brass Instruments in the Symphonies of Gustav Mahler*. D.M.A. diss., University of Rochester, Eastman School of Music, 1977.

Hefele, Herman. *Goethes Faust*. 3rd ed. Stuttgart, 1946.

Hefling, Stephen E. " 'Variations in nuce': A Study of Mahler Sketches, and a Comment on Sketch Studies." In *Gustav Mahler Kolloquium 1979*. Ed. Rudolf Klein. Kassel/Basel/London, 1981. 102–126.

Hermand, Jost. "Der vertonte 'Titan.' " In *Hesperus. Blätter der Jean-Paul-Gesellschaft* 29 (Bayreuth, December 1965): 1–5.

International Gustav Mahler Society. *Sämtliche Werke: Kritische Gesamtausgabe*. Vienna, 1960ff.

Istel, Edgar. *Mahlers Symphonien*. Berlin, 1910, 1920.

Jones, Ernest. *Das Leben und Werk von Sigmund Freud*, vol. 2. Bern and Stuttgart, 1962. Trans. from English. *The Life and Work of Sigmund Freud*. 3 vols. New York, 1953–1957.

Jungheinrich, Hans-Klaus. "Nach der Katastrophe. Anmerkungen zu einer aktuellen Rezeption der Siebten Symphonie." In *Mahler—eine Herausforderung*. Ed. Peter Ruzicka. Wiesbaden, 1977. 181–198.

Karbusicky, Vladimir. *Gustav Mahler und seine Umwelt* (Impulse der Forschung 28). Darmstadt, 1978.

Klein, Rudolf, ed. *Gustav Mahler Kolloquium 1979*. Vol. 7 of Beiträge from the Austrian Society of Music. Kassel/Basel/London, 1981.

Klemm, Eberhardt. "Notizen zu Mahler." In *Festschrift Heinrich Besseler zum sechzigsten Geburtstag*. Leipzig, 1961. 447–455.

_____ . "Über ein Spätwerk Gustav Mahlers." In *Deutsches Jahrbuch für Musikwissenschaft für 1961*. Leipzig, 1962. 19–32.

_____ . "Zur Geschichte der Fünften Symphonie von Gustav Mahler." In *Jahrbuch Peters 1979*. Leipzig, 1980. 9–116.

Koenig, Arthur William, Jr. *The Orchestral Techniques of the Mahler Symphonies with Emphasis on the Second and Ninth Symphonies*. Ph.D. diss., Michigan State University, 1971.

Kolleritsch, Otto, ed. *Gustav Mahler: Sinfonie und Wirklichkeit*. Studien zur Wertungsforschung, vol. 9. Graz, 1977.

Kralik, Heinrich. *gustav mahler* [sic]. Vienna, 1968.

Lindt, Walter Lotte, ed. *Bruno Walter: Briefe 1894–1962*. Frankfurt am Main, 1969.

Loschnigg, Franz. *The Cultural Education of Gustav Mahler*. Ph.D. diss., The University of Wisconsin-Madison, 1976.

Mahler, Alma. *Gustav Mahler: Erinnerungen und Briefe.* Amsterdam, 1940, 1949. Eng. trans. by Basil Creighton, *Gustav Mahler: Memories and Letters.* New York, 1946; rev. ed. 1975, eds. D. Mitchell and K. Martner.

Mahler, Alma Maria, ed. *Gustav Mahler: Briefe 1879–1911.* Berlin/Vienna/Leipzig, 1924. Eng. trans. *Selected Letters.* Ed. K. Martner. New York, 1979. Rev. and enl. by Herta Blaukopf. Vienna, 1982.

Mahler-Werfel, Alma. *Mein Leben.* 1st ed. Frankfurt am Main, 1960; new ed., Frankfurt am Main/Hamburg 1963 (Fischer Bücherei 545). Trans. from English. *And the Bridge is Love.* London, 1959.

Mahler, Gustav. *Nachgelassene Zehnte Symphonie.* Introductory remarks by Richard Specht. Berlin/Vienna/Leipzig, 1924.

Malloch, William. "Deryck Cooke's Mahler Tenth: An Interim Report," *The Music Review* 23 (1962): 292–304.

Martner, Knud., ed. *Selected Letters of Gustav Mahler.* See under Alma Maria Mahler.

Martner, Knud, and Robert Becqué, "Zwölf unbekannte Briefe Gustav Mahlers an Ludwig Strecker," *Archiv für Musikwissenschaft* 34 (1977): 287–297.

Matter, Jean. *Connaissance de Mahler. Documents, analyses et synthèses.* Lausanne, 1974.

Mayer, Hans. "Musik und Literatur." In *Gustav Mahler.* Rainer Wunderlich Verlag, Tübingen, 1966. 142–156.

Mengelberg, Rudolf. *Gustav Mahler.* Breitkopf and Härtels Musikbücher, Leipzig, 1923.

———, ed. *Das Mahler-Fest: Amsterdam, Mai 1920: Vorträge und Berichte* [For the Mahler Festival]. Vienna, 1920.

Der Merker 3 (5). Special Gustav Mahler issue (1912).

Mitchell, Donald. *Gustav Mahler: The Wunderhorn Years. Chronicles and Commentaries.* London, 1975.

———. *Gustav Mahler: The Early Years.* London, 1958, rev. 1980.

———. *Gustav Mahler: Songs and Symphonies of Life and Death.* Berkeley, 1985.

Motte, Diether de la. "Das komplizierte Einfache. Zum ersten Satz der 9. Symphonie von Gustav Mahler." In *Musik und Bildung* (1978): 145–151.

Mulder, Ernest W. *Das Lied von der Erde: een critisch-analytische studie.* Amsterdam, 1951.

Die Musik 10 (18). Special Gustav Mahler issue (1911).

Musikblätter des Anbruch. Special Gustav Mahler issues: 2 (1920); 12 (1930).

Newlin, Dika. *Bruckner, Mahler, Schoenberg.* Vienna, 1954; New York, 1947; rev. ed. 1978.

Nietzsche, Friedrich. *Werke.* (Ullstein Materialien), 5 vols. Ed. Karl Schlechta. Frankfurt am Main/Berlin/Vienna, 1979. Eng. trans. *The Complete Works of Frederick Nietzsche.* London, 1903–1913.

Nodnagel, Ernst Otto. *Jenseits von Wagner und Liszt. Profile und Perspektiven.* Königsberg, 1902.

———. "Zweite Symphonie in c-moll von Gustav Mahler," *Die Musik* 2 (1903): 337–353.

———. *Gustav Mahlers Fünfte Symphonie. Technische Analyse.* Leipzig, 1905.

———. "Sechste Symphonie in a-moll von Gustav Mahler," *Die Musik* 5 (1905–1906): 233–246.

Nowak, Adolf. "Mahlers Hymnus." In *Schütz-Jahrbuch* (1982/83): 92–96.
Österreichische Musikzeitschrift. Special Gustav Mahler issues: 15 (1960); 34 (1979).
Osthoff, Helmuth. "Zu Gustav Mahlers Erster Symphonie," *Archiv für Musikwissenschaft* 28 (1971): 217–227.
Pfohl, Ferdinand. *Gustav Mahler: Eindrücke und Erinnerungen aus den Hamburger Jahren*. Ed. Knud Martner. Hamburg, 1973.
Ponnelle, Lazare. *A Munich*. Paris, 1913.
Pringsheim, Klaus. "Zur Uraufführung von Mahlers Sechster Symphonie." In *Musikblätter des Anbruch* 2 (1920): 496–498.
Ratz, Erwin. *Gustav Mahler: IX Symphonie*. Facs. ed. Vienna, 1971.
_____. *Gustav Mahler: X Symphonie*. Facs. ed. Walter Ricke Verlag, Munich, 1967.
_____. "Zum Formproblem bei Gustav Mahler: eine Analyse des ersten Satzes der IX. Symphonie," *Die Musikforschung* 8 (1955): 169–177. Rpt. in collected vol. *Mahler*. Tübingen, 1966. 123–141.
_____. "Zum Formproblem bei Gustav Mahler: eine Analyse des Finales der VI. Sinfonie," *Die Musikforschung* 9 (1956): 156–171. Rpt. in collected vol. *Mahler*. Eds. T. Adorno et al. Tübingen, 1966. 90–122.
Redlich, Hans Ferdinand. "Die Welt der V., VI. und VII. Sinfonie Mahlers." In *Musikblätter des Anbruch* 2 (1920): 265–268.
_____. *Bruckner and Mahler*. London/New York, 1963.
_____. "Mahler's Enigmatic Sixth," *Festschrift Otto Erich Deutsch*. Kassel, 1963. 250–256.
_____. Preface to the score of the Sixth Symphony, Edition Eulenburg (No. 586, EE 6520). London/Zurich/Mainz/New York, 1968.
Reeser, Eduard. *Gustav Mahler und Holland. Briefe*. Vienna, 1980.
Reik, Theodor. *The Haunting Melody*. New York, 1953.
Reilly, Edward R. *Gustav Mahler und Guido Adler*. Publications of the International Gustav Mahler Society, Vienna, 1978. Eng. trans. Cambridge, 1982.
_____. "Die Skizzen zu Mahlers zweiter Symphonie," *Österreichische Musikzeitschrift* 34 (1979): 266–285.
Revers, Peter. *Die Liquidation der musikalischen Struktur in den späten Symphonien Gustav Mahlers*. Ph.D. diss., Salzburg, 1980.
Rexroth, Dieter. "Mahler und Schoenberg." In *Gustav Mahler. Sinfonie und Wirklichkeit* (Studien zur Wertungsforschung, vol. 9). Ed. Otto Kolleritsch. Graz, 1977. 68–80.
Riehn, Rainer. "Über Mahlers *Lieder eines fahrenden Gesellen* und *Das Lied von der Erde* in Arnold Schoenbergs Kammerfassungen." In *Musik-Konzepte 36. Schoenbergs Verein für musikalische Privataufführungen*. Munich, March 1984. 8–30.
Roller, Alfred. *Die Bildnisse von Gustav Mahler*. Leipzig/Vienna/Zurich, 1922.
Roman, Zoltan. "Connotative Irony in Mahler's *Todtenmarsch* in 'Callots Manier,' " *The Musical Quarterly* 59 (April 1973): 207–222.
Ruzicka, Peter. "Befragung des Materials. Gustav Mahler aus der Sicht aktueller Kompositionsästhetik," *Musik und Bildung* 5 (1973): 598–603.
_____, ed. *Mahler—eine Herausforderung. Ein Symposion*. Wiesbaden, 1977.
Schaefers, Anton. *Gustav Mahlers Instrumentation*. Düsseldorf, 1935.
Schiedermair, Ludwig. "Gustav Mahler als Symphoniker," *Die Musik* 1 (1901–1902): 506–510, 603–608, 696–699.

Schmidt, Heinrich. *Formprobleme und Entwicklungslinien in Gustav Mahlers Symphonien. Ein Beitrag zur Formenlehre der musikalischen Romantik.* Ph.D. diss., Vienna, 1929.

Schmitt, Theodor. *Der langsame Symphoniesatz Gustav Mahlers. Historisch-vergleichende Studien zu Mahlers Kompositionstechnik* (Studien zur Musik, vol. 3). Munich, 1983.

Schnebel, Dieter. "Über Mahlers Dritte," *Neue Zeitschrift für Musik* 135 (1974): 283–288.

————. "Das Spätwerk als Neue Musik." In *Gustav Mahler*. Rainer Wunderlich Verlag, Tübingen, 1966. 157–188.

Schoenberg, Arnold. *"Prager Rede* auf Mahler" (1912). In *Gustav Mahler*. Rainer Wunderlich Verlag, Tübingen, 1966. 11–58. Eng. trans. "Criteria for the Evolution of Music." In *Style and Idea*. Ed. Leonard Stein. New York, 1975. 124ff.

Schopenhauer, Arthur. *Werke in zehn Bänden* (referred to as the Zurich ed.). Diogenes Verlag, Zurich, 1977. Eng. trans. *The Complete Essays of Arthur Schopenhauer*. New York, 1942.

Schumann, Karl. *Das kleine GUSTAV MAHLER BUCH* [sic]. Salzburg, 1972.

Seidl, Arthur. "Gustav Mahler. I. Zweite und vierte Symphonie (1901)." In *Neuzeitliche Tondichter und zeitgenössische Tonkünstler* (Deutsche Musik-bücherei 18/19), vol. 1. Regensburg, 1926. 287–299.

Siering, Johann. "Nietzsches Mitternachtslied," *Neue Deutsche Hefte* 9 (1962): 90–95.

Specht, Richard. *Gustav Mahler*. Berlin, 1905; Berlin/Leipzig, 1913; Stuttgart/Berlin, 1925.

————. Mahlers Siebente Symphonie," *Der Merker* 2 (1909): 1–6.

————. *Gustav Mahlers VIII. Symphonie. Thematische Analyse*. Leipzig/Vienna, 1912.

————. *Gustav Mahlers I. Symphonie. Thematische Analyse*. Vienna/Leipzig, n.d.

————. *Gustav Mahlers II. Sinfonie*. Vienna/Leipzig, n.d. [1915].

————. *Gustav Mahler. III. Symphonie d-moll*. Leipzig/Vienna, n.d.

Sponheuer, Bernd. *Logik des Zerfalls: Untersuchungen zum Finalproblem in den Symphonien Gustav Mahlers*. Tutzing, 1978.

Stahmer, Klaus Hinrich, ed. *Form und Idee in Gustav Mahlers Instrumentalmusik*. Taschenbücher zur Musikwissenschaft, 70. Wilhelmshaven, 1980.

Stefan, Paul. *Gustav Mahler: eine Studie über Persönlichkeit und Werk*. Munich, 1920. Eng. trans. by T. E. Clark, *Gustav Mahler: A Study of His Personality and Work*. New York, 1913.

————, ed. *Gustav Mahler: ein Bild seiner Persönlichkeit in Widmungen*. R. Piper & Co. Verlag, Munich, 1910.

Stein, Erwin. *Orpheus in New Guises*. London, 1953.

Stein, Leonard, ed. *Style and Idea*. New York, 1975.

Steinitzer, Max. "Erinnerungen an Gustav Mahler." In *Musikblätter des Anbruch* 2 (1920): 296–298.

Stephan, Rudolf. *Gustav Mahler: IV. Symphonie G-dur* (Meisterwerke der Musik 5). Munich, 1966.

————. *Gustav Mahler: II. Symphonie c-moll* (Meisterwerke der Musik 21). Munich, 1979.

———. *Gustav Mahler: Werk und Interpretation*. Cologne, 1979.

———. "Zu Mahlers Komposition der Schlussszene von Goethes Faust." In *Schütz-Jahrbuch* 1982/83: 97–102.

Storjohann, Helmut. *Die formalen Eigenarten in den Sinfonien Gustav Mahlers*. Ph.D. diss., Hamburg, 1952.

Strohm, Stefan, "Die Idee der absoluten Musik als ihr (ausgesprochenes) Programm. Zum unterlegten Text der Mahlerschen Achten." In *Schütz-Jahrbuch* (1982/83): 73–91.

Swarowsky, Hans. *Wahrung der Gestalt. Schriften über Werk und Wiedergabe, Stil und Interpretation in der Musik*. Vienna, 1979.

Thomas, Walter. *Richard Strauss und seine Zeitgenossen*. Munich/Vienna, 1964.

Tibbe, Monika. *Über die Verwendung von Liedern und Liedelementen in instrumentalen Symphoniesätzen Gustav Mahlers* (Berliner musikwissenschaftliche Arbeiten, vol. 1). Munich, 1971.

———. "Anmerkungen zur Mahler-Rezeption." *Mahler—eine Herausforderung*. Ed. Peter Ruzicka. Wiesbaden, 1977. 85–100.

Tischler, Hans. *Die Harmonik in den Werken Gustav Mahlers*. Ph.D. diss., University of Vienna, 1937.

———. "Mahler's *Das Lied von der Erde*," *The Music Review* 10 (1949): 111–114.

Trunz, Erich. *Goethes Faust*. Hamburg, 1963.

Vill, Susanne. *Vermittlungsformen verbalisierter und musikalischer Inhalte in der Musik Gustav Mahlers*. Frankfurter Beiträge zur Musikwissenschaft 6. Tutzing, 1979.

Wagner, Manfred. *Geschichte der österreichischen Musikkritik in Beispielen*. Tutzing, 1979.

Wagner, Richard. *Sämtliche Schriften und Dichtungen. Volks-Ausgabe.* 16 vols. Leipzig, n.d. [1911]. Eng. trans. *The Prose Works of Richard Wagner*. 8 vols. New York, 1893. Rpt. 1988.

Walter, Bruno. *Gustav Mahler. Ein Porträt.* 1st ed. Vienna/Leipzig/Zurich, 1936; 2nd ed. Berlin/Frankfurt am Main, 1957. Eng. trans. New York, 1958. New ed. New York, 1972.

———. *Thema und Variationen: Erinnerungen und Gedanken*. Frankfurt/Main, 1960. Eng. ed. *Theme and Variations*. New York, 1946.

Wessling, Berndt W. *Gustav Mahler. Ein prophetisches Leben*. Hamburg, 1974.

Wiesmann, S., ed. *Gustav Mahler in Vienna*. New York, 1976.

Wildgans, Friedrich. "Gustav Mahler und Anton von Webern," *Österreichische Musikzeitschrift* 15 (1960): 22–26.

Williamson, John. "Mahler's Compositional Process: Reflections on an Early Sketch for the Third Symphony's First Movement," *Music and Letters* 61 (1980): 338–345.

Worbs, Hans Christoph. "Gustav Mahlers Sinfonien im Urteil der zeitgenössischen Kritik," *Neue Zeitschrift für Musik* 144 (1983): 4–8.

Wörner, Karl H. *Das Zeitalter der thematischen Prozesse in der Geschichte der Musik*. (Studien zur Musikgeschichte des 19. Jahrhunderts, 18), Regensburg, 1969.

Wöss, Josef V. von. *Gustav Mahler. Das Lied von der Erde. Thematische Analyse*. Leipzig/Vienna, 1912.

Zenck, Martin. "Ausdruck und Konstruktion im Adagio der 10. Sinfonie Gustav

Mahlers." In *Beiträge zur musikalischen Hermeneutik* (Studien zur Musikgeschichte des 19. Jahrhunderts, 43). Ed. Carl Dahlhaus. Regensburg, 1975. 205–222.

Index

M = Gustav Mahler